D0769019

The Evolution of
British Disarmament Policy in the 1920s

Dick Richardson

Pinter Publishers, London
St. Martin's Press, New York

To Marianne, Joanna, Tom, Darren, Mandy, Johir and Craig

© Dick Richardson, 1989

First published in Great Britain in 1989 by
Pinter Publishers Limited
25 Floral Street, London WC2E 9DS

ISBN 0-86187-741-1

British Library Cataloguing in Publication Data
A CIP catalogue record for this book is available from the British Library

© Dick Richardson, 1989

First published in the United States of America in 1989

ISBN 0-312-03177-7

Library of Congress Cataloging-in-Publication Data
Richardson, Dick.
   The evolution of British disarmament policy in the 1920s / Dick
Richardson.
      p.   cm.
   Bibliography: p.
   Includes index.
   ISBN 0-312-03177-7
   1. Disarmament—History. 2. Great Britain—Foreign
relations—1910–1936.   I. Title.
JX1974.R47   1989
327.41—dc19

Filmset by Mayhew Typesetting, Bristol, England
Printed and bound in Great Britain by
Biddles Ltd, Guildford and King's Lynn

Contents

Preface

Disarmament — the limitation and control of armaments by international agreement — is probably the least researched question of importance in international history between the two world wars. It is the objective of the author to remedy this deficiency, at least in part.

This study is concerned with three issues of major importance to historians and political scientists. The first is the problem of disarmament arising out of the Treaty of Versailles and the Covenant of the League of Nations in 1919. The problem was to occupy the statesmen of the world for some fifteen years until the breakdown of the Geneva Disarmament Conference in 1934. The consequence of this failure, it has been claimed, was the outbreak of the Second World War in 1939. The second issue concerns the attitude of the British policy-making élite towards the problem of disarmament, at both theoretical and practical levels. The context for this is the Conservative government of 1924-9 — the second Baldwin administration — but the analysis has far wider application. Certainly it applies to the National government of 1931-5, which bears a heavy responsibility for the failure of the Geneva conference in 1934 since the composition of both Cabinet and élite had changed little since 1929. But there are also many parallels to be drawn with successive Conservative administrations in the 1980s. The third major issue, around which the other two are structured, is the formulation and implementation of disarmament policy under the Baldwin government.

Most historians still view the 1920s as a period when British governments actively promoted international disarmament in the interests of peace. Perhaps this is inevitable given the public utterances of contemporary politicians and the lack of in-depth research to date. But public utterances should not always be taken at face value, especially on topics as controversial as disarmament. There can be considerable discrepancies between political rhetoric and private thoughts and actions. It is perhaps not surprising, therefore, that the present study — the first to be based on the extensive material in the public records and the private papers of leading members of the foreign policy-making élite — should reach startlingly different conclusions. As far as the second Baldwin administration is concerned, the government and its chief advisers failed to grasp either the intricacies or importance of disarmament, were less than wholehearted in their commitment to resolving the problem and adopted policies that offered little or no hope of achieving either a general arms limitation convention through the League or, in the case of the Geneva Naval Conference of 1927, a major three-power agreement. In essence, Britain's policy was one of procrastination verging on duplicity.

Dick Richardson
Danby, North Yorkshire
3 October 1988

Acknowledgements

The author gratefully acknowledges the assistance of individuals and institutions who facilitated his research and helped in the production of this study. In particular, he is indebted to the following who gave permission to read or quote from the unpublished private papers listed in the bibliography: the University of Birmingham Library; the Bodleian Library, Oxford; the Viscount Bridgeman; the British Museum; Cambridge University Library; the Archives Centre, Churchill College, Cambridge; the Trustees of the National Maritime Museum; the Public Record Office; and Salop County Record Office. He is further indebted to Baron Noel-Baker for granting an interview and permission to quote therefrom; to the late Captain S.W. Roskill, CBE, DSC, RN for access to documents in his personal collection; to the Controller of HM Stationery Office for permission to quote from Crown copyright papers in the public records; and to Eileen McGrady for typing the final manuscript.

The author reserves his most profound thanks for his wife, Marianne, for her continued support over many years and for her assistance at various stages in the production of the manuscript; and for Mr G.A. Grün, formerly Senior Lecturer in International History at the London School of Economics, for his diligence and constant encouragement during the book's first incarnation as a doctoral dissertation at the University of London.

Part I Problem

1 The disarmament problem

In post-war Europe and America, it became widely accepted that the arms race between the great powers had played a major role in the outbreak of the First World War. Important statesmen and influential politicians, including Sir Edward Grey, British Foreign Secretary in 1914, came to believe that the incessant, insidious and seemingly uncontrolled growth of armaments and military influence in the years before 1914 had bred acute international suspicion and produced an inflammable situation which led directly to the First World War.[1] Numerous methods were canvassed for preventing a recurrence of that catastrophe, and there was general agreement that one of the most suitable and equitable would be the organization of a controlled system of international disarmament. It was an attractive concept which even gained support from the occasional military figure.[2]

Armaments, claimed the protagonists of disarmament, not only made war possible but made it more probable. Once one nation possessed arms, so must others as no nation would tempt aggression against itself by remaining defenceless. Measures taken by one nation to increase security produced counter-measures by others, giving rise to feelings of fear and insecurity. Further measures caused further counter-measures and the consequent increase in suspicion and distrust led governments to believe that any and every precaution should be taken to deter possible opponents while similar precautions by other countries were evidence of hostile intent. An arms race would develop and eventually, by accident or design, break down into war. The final spark might occur when one party utilized a temporary ascendancy in armaments to strike at an opponent; it might come through over-reaction to a minor incident; or it might just 'happen'. It did not matter which.[3]

Supporters of disarmament further suggested that the accumulation of national armaments necessarily led to the establishment of a professional military class and a sizeable armaments industry, both of which, in their own interests, continually pressed for an expansion of war potential, exacerbating feelings of fear and insecurity. Such embryo 'military-industrial complexes', it was claimed, tended to gain an inordinate amount of power within each state and encourage governments to follow unnecessarily intransigent and bellicose policies. Thus, if a state had military superiority over an opponent and relations between the two were uneasy, the military establishment of the first would advise its government to take the military path while that of the second would demand increased expenditure on armaments.[4]

General disarmament, it was claimed, would eliminate these 'scourges' of international society. In the event of disputes, states would be provided with an automatic cooling-off period during which they would be unable to go to war or mount a successful offensive because the arms they retained would be insufficient for the purpose. National resources used in the manufacture of armaments could be channelled into more productive and socially acceptable projects and states induced to follow more conciliatory policies. The influence of military-industrial complexes would be reduced and the power factor in international relations controlled more effectively.[5]

Opponents disputed both the desirability and practicability of disarmament, contending that armaments were the product rather than the cause of international tension. Peace, it was suggested, was a political problem requiring a political solution, and though security might lead to disarmament it could not result from disarmament. The influence brought to bear by military establishments would, if anything, breed a rising consciousness of the total destructiveness of modern warfare, and statesmen would always be careful to keep decisions of peace and war in their own hands.[6]

Sceptics further argued that, even if the political objections were overcome, technical objections would nullify attempts to reach a disarmament convention. A general reduction of armaments to a level necessary for police and legitimate defence purposes only was inconceivable because some countries had a far greater productive capacity and war potential than others. Moreover, national ambitions and developments in military technology would make it impracticable to freeze the distribution of power within international society. The power factor could not be removed from international relations. It was impossible, in fact, to measure the power factor, and thus it was also impossible to compare the different armaments of different states let alone take account of geographical, industrial and demographic factors. Similarly, it was inconceivable that a convention would be adequately supervised since, even with the strictest agreements regarding control, states would be able to train men and accumulate stocks of *matériel* in secret. Thus there could be no satisfactory guarantees that a convention was being observed; and the consequences of trying to impose unverifiable restrictions would be a rapid growth of international tension as states would inevitably suspect that their neighbours were not adhering to their agreements.[7]

The more appealing of these arguments are those of the disarmament protagonists. Certainly the competitive accumulation of national military power is likely to exacerbate rather than diminish international friction, while numerous instances can be cited where 'military–industrial complexes' have encouraged intransigent courses of policy and stimulated the development of arms races. For example, W.B. Shearer, a creature in the pay of the Bethlehem Shipbuilding Corporation and other large private shipyards in America, deliberately fomented dissension at the Geneva Naval Conference of 1927 with a view to preventing the negotiation of a disarmament agreement between Britain, America and Japan.[8]

Doubtless the negotiation of an international disarmament agreement would tend to ease relations between states and reduce the influence of the military within society. It would also reduce wastage in public expenditure, increase the objective elements in analyses of force capabilities and perhaps provide states with a cooling-off period in which to resolve their disputes. The difficulty lies in putting theory into practice. Technical difficulties can act as obstacles to agreement, and behind each technical objection to a certain course of action there is normally a political objection.[9]

Military establishments are related in the first instance to the problem of the status quo. The function of national power is to uphold or challenge the existing pattern of international relationships, and the urge to avoid a worsening of the national power position is the chief passion of most participants in disarmament negotiations rather than enthusiasm for disarmament itself. A scheme which freezes the status quo by stabilizing the power situation is frustrating to ambitious states; one which promises to undermine the status quo is alarming to the beneficiaries of the established order — unless they are convinced that equivalent changes in power distribution will occur even without an agreement. Thus governments of 'satiated', non-revisionist states will accept a scheme of limitation if it does not interfere with the adequacy of their power position, while revisionist states will accept if they are convinced that the agreed distribution of national power will be irrelevant in the future organization of international relations. A practical scheme, therefore, is one which takes political motivation, power and power potential into account. Total disarmament, advocated by some, is impractical because it ignores these factors.

A degree of armament is inevitable, since no country will willingly remain disarmed if its neighbours are not. And it follows that a vicious circle of 'armaments and tension' is inherent in the structure of international society. The problem is how to control the distribution and use of the power that exists. Disarmament offers a possible means for adjustment through the limitation, control and possibly reduction of national armaments within an adequate system of international security. An acceptable formula, however, can only be realized through the granting of compensatory security guarantees to states that reduce their armaments relative to other powers.

Such additional guarantees would be provided automatically under a system of collective security, since the basis of a collective system is a recognition of the indivisibility of peace and the maintenance of the territorial status quo. Disarmament and machinery for pacific settlement would form the first line of defence against an outbreak of conflict, and in the event of a failure of the procedure, aggressors would be brought to heel by an application of sanctions, military if necessary, by the international community.[10] In the absence of a collective system, compensation for disadvantaged states would be more difficult; but it would still be possible and might take one of two forms: regional security pacts based on collective principles within specified areas, or alliances or similar agreements of a bilateral or multilateral nature. Alliances might seem inconsistent with the spirit of general disarmament, since they tend to divide international society into opposing groups; but even opposing groups can find it in their interest to limit their respective armaments, especially when the development cost of new military technology is high. If no method of compensation is available, it is unlikely that disarmament can be realized.

The peace settlement of 1919 was not conducive to general disarmament since it failed to provide a security system that was acceptable or adequate for all nations. The major problem was the reconciliation of French and German claims. Successive German governments refused to acknowledge that they were committed indefinitely to the second-class role demanded of them, while French governments were alarmed that the long-term security of their country was by no means assured. The Germans demanded 'equality of rights' with other nations; the French demanded further security guarantees before agreeing to a general system of arms limitation.

The military terms of the Treaty of Versailles imposed severe restrictions on German military strength. The old Imperial army was reduced to 'the lowest limit consistent with the maintenance of order and the control of frontiers': 100,000 men in the colours, including a maximum of 4,000 officers, compared with a peacetime level of some 850,000 men in 1914. Conscription was abolished and long-term service made compulsory, twelve years for servicemen and twenty-five years for officers. The German navy was restricted to six battleships, six light cruisers, twelve destroyers and twelve torpedo boats, with a maximum personnel of 15,000, compared with seventeen modern battleships, seven battlecruisers and concomitant smaller craft and personnel in 1914. The possession of 'aggressive' weapons — tanks, heavy guns over 105 mm calibre, armoured cars, military aircraft, submarines, battleships over 10,000 tons and poisonous and asphyxiating gases — was forbidden, and quantitative restrictions placed on permitted armaments. Reserve stocks of arms and ammunition were limited and strict regulations applied to all military establishments. The general staff was abolished and the military training of civil personnel prohibited. The Rhineland was demilitarized from the western frontier to a distance fifty kilometres east of the river, and the demilitarized zone subjected to a fifteen-year occupation by Allied troops, to be withdrawn in stages at five-year intervals provided the German government fulfilled its obligations under the peace treaty. Inter-Allied control commissions with extensive powers of inspection were established to supervise the execution of the disarmament clauses and report on contraventions during the occupation period.

The peace treaty of 1919 further reduced German power by establishing an international security organization based on nominally collective principles — the League of Nations. Germany was also required to forfeit important industrial territories. Lorraine, with its extensive iron ore deposits, was ceded to France. The greater part of industrial Upper Silesia, with its important coalfield, was lost to Poland. The Saarland, with its abundant coal reserves, was assigned to the League for a period of fifteen years, after which a plebiscite would be held to ascertain the wishes of the population regarding territorial status. A heavy, though not excessive, reparations burden was also imposed, Germany's total liability being assessed at some £6,600 m by the Allied Reparations Committee in April 1921.

At no time did Germany comply willingly with the peace treaty. On the contrary, successive German governments actively hindered the execution of the treaty by defaulting on reparations payments and evading the disarmament stipulations. They tended, however, to minimize the proportions of individual defaults, as by this expedient they could place the Allies in a considerable quandary. In each case of omission, however minor, the Allies were faced with two basic policy options, both of which were unsatisfactory: applying the peace treaty to the letter, by threatening some kind of sanctions; or negotiating a compromise with the German government. The first alternative involved inconvenience, expense and the exacerbation of German ill-will, while offering no guarantee that Germany would terminate her policy of resistance; the second involved undermining the peace treaty, by placing reliance on German intentions and by muting the credibility of an application of sanctions.

If, on paper, the terms of the Treaty of Versailles were very stiff and seemed to remove the threat of German hegemony in Europe, in practice the peace treaty constituted a precarious barrier against a future German resurgence. In the circumstances of 1919 Germany posed no threat to international security, but intrinsically she remained the greatest of the continental powers. Her population numbered some sixty-five million against the forty million of the

next greatest power, France. Her economic and industrial preponder-
ance was very marked. And her one potential rival, the Soviet Union,
was in a state of chaos after five years of civil and international
conflict. Left to her own devices, and without interference from other
powers, Germany would eventually overshadow Europe as she had
done in 1914. The problem facing the former Allies was whether this
'natural' predominance could be controlled through the effective
management of international power.

Before the First World War, Germany had been held in check by
the Franco-Russian alliance. But in 1919 a resuscitation of the
alliance was inconceivable because of the internal chaos in Russia
and French hostility to the Soviet regime. Moreover, the alliance
would not necessarily have been of value against Germany since the
Treaty of Versailles had isolated the Soviet Union from central
Europe by erecting a glacis of small states on her western frontier.
France did gain allies in eastern Europe, notably Poland and Czechoslovakia, but the links with these powers did not afford the same
degree of security as the old Franco-Russian alliance. International
security was further weakened in March 1920, when the American
Senate rejected the Treaty of Versailles and a projected Anglo-
American guarantee of the French frontier; for not only did the most
powerful nation in the world decline to enter the League of Nations,
it became extremely doubtful whether the United States would even
co-operate with the European powers in frustrating a renewed
German aggression.

In theory, the League of Nations in itself should have provided
adequate guarantees against Germany since it was supposed to
establish an effective system of collective security. Members of the
new organization recognized that peace was 'indivisible' (Article 11
of the Covenant of the League) and undertook to respect and preserve
each other's political independence and territorial integrity against
external aggression (Article 10). They also agreed to submit their
differences to arbitration, judicial settlement at the Permanent Court
of International Justice, or inquiry by the League Council (Articles
12, 13 and 15), though in the event of a decision not being unanimous
the parties concerned reserved the right to go to war after a period
of three months — the so-called 'gap in the Covenant'. And if a
member resorted to war in violation of its obligations, the other
members agreed to impose an absolute and immediate economic and
diplomatic boycott on the Covenant-breaking state and respect the
decisions of the Council if it was found necessary to apply military
sanctions (Article 16).

In reality, however, the security provisions of the League were very
deficient and afforded no guarantee that the combined resources of
the international community would be available to thwart aggression. The Covenant imposed inadequate legal restrictions on potential aggressors, and its provisions for sanctions were weak even
before the Second Assembly passed a series of resolutions diluting
Article 16. There was no positive obligation for members to

participate in military measures; there was no provision for an international army or general staff; and a unanimity rule within the Council gave states who were unwilling to honour their theoretical obligations the perfect opportunity of vetoing concerted action. Besides, three of the most important members of international society remained outside the League — the Soviet Union, the United States and Germany.

There was considerable justification, therefore, for the French claim that the Treaty of Versailles did not afford security against a revived Germany. In fact, in the long term, the peace treaty provided only two means for its own enforcement: the fifteen-year occupation of the Rhineland and, more remotely, the threat of sanctions under Article 16 of the Covenant of the League. This was especially important in relation to the disarmament clauses, since the continued discharge of Germany's obligations rested with the German government, not the Allies. When the control commissions and occupying troops were withdrawn there would be no direct method of verifying whether the Germans were observing their commitments. The way would be open to German rearmament.

The likelihood of German rearmament becoming a major international issue in the medium term was increased by a clause in the preamble to Part V of the Treaty of Versailles which stipulated that the arms reductions required of Germany were 'to render possible the initiation of a general limitation of armaments of all nations'.[11] The passage was inserted on the instigation of Woodrow Wilson, President of the United States, apparently on the grounds that Germany would accept the military clauses of the peace treaty more readily.[12] It aroused only a modicum of comment at the time; but it was of tremendous significance, for it gave the Germans a near-perfect lever for asserting that, once they had fulfilled their own disarmament obligations, the Allies would be committed to disarming themselves.

The significance of the preamble to Part V of the Treaty of Versailles was quickly appreciated by the Germans, who strove to make political capital out of it at every opportunity. Most important, during the peace conference itself, they indicated that they were prepared to accept the disarmament clauses of the peace treaty only as a precursor to a general limitation. They also elicited from the Allies a clarification of disarmament intentions, which was incorporated in an official Note handed to Count Brockdorff-Rantzau, the German Foreign Minister, by the French *Président du Conseil*, Georges Clemenceau, on 16 June 1919:

I The Allied and Associated Powers wish to make it clear that their requirements in regard to German armaments were not made solely with the object of rendering it impossible for Germany to resume her policy of military aggression. They are also the first steps towards that general reduction and limitation of armaments which they seek to bring about as one of the most fruitful preventives of war, and which it will be one of the first duties of the League of Nations to promote.

II They must point out, however, that the colossal growth in armaments of the last few decades was forced upon the nations of Europe by Germany. As Germany increased her power, her neighbours had to follow suit unless they were to become impotent to resist German dictation or the German sword. It is therefore right, as it is necessary, that the process of limitation of armaments should begin with the nation which has been responsible for their expansion. It is not until the aggressor has led the way that the attacked can safely afford to follow suit.

III The Allied and Associated Powers cannot agree to any alteration in principle of the conditions laid down . . . . Germany must consent unconditionally to disarm in advance of the Allied and Associated Powers . . ..

IV . . . No deviation from the organization in armament laid down in the present treaty can be permitted until Germany is admitted to the League of Nations, which may then agree to such modifications as seem desirable . . ..

V With the amendments and modifications enumerated in paragraph IV above, the Military Clauses . . . and those affecting the carrying out of the terms therein laid down . . . are to be maintained.[13]

The Germans were to use this Note (the so-called 'Clemenceau Letter') to justify their contention that the Allies had incurred a legal obligation to disarm under the Versailles Treaty.

The Germans argued that the undertakings given by themselves and the Allies were mutually dependent and that failure by one side to observe its pledges would free the other side from its pledges. They also asserted that the phrase 'Germany must consent unconditionally to disarm in advance of the Allied and Associated Powers' implied that *all* they were required to do unconditionally was to disarm before the Allies — the obligation to remain disarmed would be conditioned by the Allied promise to accomplish general disarmament. It was a clear, forthright and superficially overwhelming case which enjoyed considerable international success. Statesmen throughout the world admitted the justice of the German contentions. Even Joseph Paul-Boncour, leader of the French disarmament negotiators throughout most of the 1920s and early 1930s and steadfast upholder of the sanctity of the peace treaty and Covenant, conceded the argument: on 8 April 1927, during the third session of the Preparatory Commission for the Disarmament Conference, convened under the auspices of the League of Nations, he declared that the preamble to Part V of the peace treaty imposed 'a duty, a moral and legal obligation . . . to proceed to a general limitation'.[14]

In strictly legal terms, the German case was far from watertight. Indeed, international lawyers disputed the nature of the Allied commitment in the preamble to Part V of the Versailles Treaty for many years without reaching agreement. In Britain especially it was argued that a preamble could only interpret an obligation already existing in the body of a treaty and not constitute a new obligation in itself — a proposition which, if accepted, destroyed the whole German position on the issue.[15] Moreover, the preamble to Part V of the peace treaty did not directly relate German disarmament to Allied disarmament, it merely indicated that German disarmament was intended 'to *render possible* the initiation of a general limitation of armaments'; and similarly, in the 'Clemenceau Letter', the Allies did not specifically pledge themselves to disarm, they merely indicated they would *'seek to bring about'* general disarmament [author's emphasis].

In any case, the Germans could not justifiably claim that their own disarmament was conditional on Allied disarmament in the light of the Allied insistence that German disarmament was 'unconditional', especially as the Allies had also declared that no deviation in the organization of the German forces could be permitted until Germany joined the League and the League agreed to modify the Versailles provisions. If the Allies had an obligation to disarm under the preamble to Part V of the Versailles treaty, it was a moral obligation — if moral obligations exist in international politics.

The statutory obligations of the Allies to reach a general disarmament agreement were limited in 1919 to the Covenant of the League of Nations, and these were unspecific, allowing the maximum opportunity for procrastination and international controversy. Under Article 8 of the Covenant, members recognized that the maintenance of peace required 'the reduction of national armaments to the lowest point consistent with national safety and the enforcement by common action of international obligations'; and the Council was charged with formulating 'plans for such reduction for the consideration and action of the several Governments ... taking account of the geographical situation and circumstances of each State'.[16]

But if, ostensibly, it was from Article 8 that the international discussions for a general disarmament convention in the 1920s and 1930s devolved, in reality the impulsion behind the negotiations was the potential threat of Germany to the security system established by the Treaty of Versailles. As the years progressed, it became increasingly clear that, if the Allies did not disarm, Germany would consider herself free to rearm unilaterally — in breadth and depth — and unless preventive action was taken, through the negotiation of a general disarmament agreement or, more remotely, through the application of sanctions on Germany, the likely consequence was an international arms race and a renewed danger of war. In essence, the disarmament problem was the problem of European security, and the problem of European security was the problem of German power.

2 Britain and the disarmament problem
1919–November 1924

Britain emerged from the First World War with her security against Germany considerably enhanced. The German naval threat had been removed by the scuttling of the High Seas fleet at Scapa Flow and by the Versailles disarmament clauses, and the immediate threat of a German-dominated Europe had been surmounted. Moreover, a resuscitation of Anglo–German rivalry appeared unlikely, even in the medium term, since Germany seemed certain to concentrate her revisionist ambitions on her continental neighbours. Imperial and naval rivalry with Germany had caused great concern to British policymakers in the decade before 1914; in the decade after 1919 such rivalry barely existed. The conditions existed for a *détente* in Anglo–German relations.

In these circumstances it was not surprising that the British reaction to the problem of German power in post-war Europe was very different to that of France. Whereas the French felt that the Treaty of Versailles provided insufficient security against a resurgent Germany and sought compensations elsewhere, in alliances with friendly powers and in the strengthening of the League of Nations as an instrument of collectivism, the British tended to emphasize the reality of German grievances against the peace treaty and suggest that it was necessary to redress the more legitimate of them to attain security. The French wanted to solve the German problem by treating Germany as a second-class power; the British came to believe that the problem could only be resolved by conciliation.

Many British statesmen in the immediate post-war years felt that French security was adequately guaranteed by the Treaty of Versailles. Indeed, some thought that France was a greater danger to European and even British security than Germany. The stabilization and maintenance of Britain's international position, economic recovery and the pacification of the European continent became the goals of British foreign policy, and the chief obstacle to achieving these goals appeared to be German grievances against the peace treaty. So successive British governments came to favour a gradual and peaceful revision of some of the more controversial items of the 1919 settlement. At the same time, no British government anticipated restoring Germany to the preponderant position she had held in 1914, as this might prove dangerous to British security. Because of developments in military technology, particularly in aviation, Britain was now more vulnerable to attack than previously; her strategic frontier was no longer the strait of Dover, it was the river Rhine. This implied that France be treated as a friendly power and, in theory therefore, Britain was faced with the problem of reconciling the 'Rhine dogma' with that of appeasing Germany. But in practice, basing their military policy on the assumption that no major war was to be expected for at least ten years (the so-called 'ten-year rule', formulated in 1919, abandoned in 1932) governments tended to emphasize conciliation of Germany rather than support for France.

The years 1919–23 saw a continuing struggle between the conflicting British and French strategies for a pacific continent. The French endeavoured to apply the provisions of the peace treaty rigidly; the British tended to seek solutions to problems that were acceptable to Germany as well as to the former Allies. The upshot was almost perpetual dissension between the two victor powers and continuing resistance to the full implementation of the Versailles treaty by successive German governments, who recognized that capital could be made out of Anglo-French dissension. Mainly, the disagreements were played out over the vexed question of reparations; but basically they concerned the position of Germany within the European security system.

The incipient crisis came to a head in December 1922, when the Reparations Commission, on French initiative, declared that Germany was in default on deliveries of timber (72,000 cubic yards of sawn timber and 200,000 telegraph poles). A conference was held in Paris on 2–4 January 1924 to resolve the problem; but it failed. The French would not agree to the British government's plan for a four-year reparations' moratorium and a reduction of Germany's total liability to £2,500 m. Instead, in conjunction with the Belgians, the French occupied the most important industrial area in Germany — the Ruhr — to obtain 'productive pledges' for the delivery of reparations. The British took no part in the operation, having cast a negative vote in the Reparations Commission; but they took no steps to hinder it, since it precipitated a rapid, if temporary, improvement in the British economy. Besides, Britain needed German reparations to help repay war debts to the United States.

The attempt to coerce Germany was only partially successful. The Germans organized a 'passive resistance' to the occupation, and in continuing their campaign the French found they were hurting their own economy as well as the German. The Germans abandoned 'passive resistance' in September 1923, but the financial burden of the occupation had overtaxed French resources. Between January and March 1924 alone, the value of the franc fell by one-third. Inflation did not approach the hyperinflation of the German mark; but it was enough to cause a profound change in French domestic politics. On 11 May 1924, French voters rejected the policy of international intransigence and returned a liberal government under Edouard Herriot. Significantly, no subsequent French government returned to the 'policy of January 1923'. The cost of following such a policy was found to be highly disproportionate to the results achieved.

Outwardly, the outcome of the occupation of the Ruhr represented a considerable victory for France because the Germans were forced to call off their campaign of passive resistance unconditionally. But the reality of the situation was otherwise; for the effect of the occupation was to display the impracticability of the policy of coercion as a solution to the German problem. Consciously or unconsciously, French leaders came to accept that the underlying weaknesses of the French economy, with its small industrial base, presaged an inability to dominate Germany indefinitely in the absence of British support and American beneficence. Thus, at the London Conference of July–August 1924, the French were driven into approving a settlement of the reparations' problem based on a British and American initiative — and British and American terms — the so-called 'Dawes Plan'.

The Dawes Plan marked a great step towards the pacification of Europe. For not only did it divert the French from the coercion of Germany, it provided the economic basis for European recovery. In the late 1920s, large American loans became freely available in the 'Old World' and in Germany in particular. Germany prospered, and her leaders reverted from the idea that only a revision of the peace treaty would stimulate a resurgence of German power; instead they concluded that a resurgence of power would lead to a revision of the peace treaty. At the same time, the Dawes Plan did not resolve the problem of European security. Indeed, it made the problem more pressing in that it marked a definite shift in the distribution of European power, from France to Germany. A further consequence of the Dawes Plan, therefore, was the acceleration of reconciliation between France and Britain. France, under Herriot, reduced her demands on Germany; Britain began to reconsider giving some kind of additional security guarantees to France, if only because the new British premier, James Ramsay MacDonald, believed they would not need to be implemented.[1] The ground was prepared for the negotiation of a mutually acceptable security settlement by the two powers.

The search for such a settlement had been carried on in rather desultory fashion since the failure of the Anglo–American guarantee of French security in March 1920, but without success. In 1922, Lloyd George had had talks with successive French *Présidents du Conseil*, Aristide Briand and Raymond Poincaré, concerning a possible Anglo–French alliance; but the negotiations foundered because the French leaders wanted the *casus foederis* to include the remilitarization of the Rhineland or a German attack on France's east European partners as well as the French homeland. The British Prime Minister offered assistance only against a direct attack on France. Briand and Poincaré wanted Britain to underwrite the new French role of great power in eastern Europe; Lloyd George intended to limit Britain's commitments to areas of vital interest — and he regarded eastern

Europe as of marginal interest. The division between the two powers over security thus paralleled the existing division over Germany. France desired to increase security by creating barriers to German expansion in eastern Europe; Britain believed that a recrudescence of German power in the area was not necessarily incompatible with security, indeed in the long run might make for increased stability.

The failure of the Anglo–French alliance discussions hastened the search for a general security settlement through the League of Nations. The powers began to explore the possibility of a more collective approach to international problems, and inevitably the security issue became linked with that of disarmament. At the Third Assembly, in September 1922, the adherents of collectivism gained theoretical acceptance for their (justified) assertion that security and disarmament essentially concerned the same problem — the effective management of power within international society. The realization was expressed in Resolution XIV of 27 September:

1. No scheme for the reduction of armaments, within the meaning of Article 8 of the Covenant, can be fully successful unless it is general.
2. In the present state of the world many Governments would be unable to accept the responsibility for a serious reduction of armaments unless they received in exchange a satisfactory guarantee of the safety of their country.[2]

Six months previously, Britain, America, Japan, France and Italy had demonstrated the link between security and disarmament in practical terms. Under the Washington Naval Treaty of 6 February 1922, the five great naval powers agreed to limit their capital ships and aircraft-carriers in the ration of five units for Britain and America, three units for Japan and 1.66 units for France and Italy. They drew up common schedules for the scrapping and construction of vessels and also accepted qualitative restrictions covering the gun calibre and displacement of individual cruisers, aircraft-carriers and capital ships.[3] A necessary condition for the agreement, however, was the simultaneous adjustment of security relations in the Far East. Britain, in deference to American pressure, agreed not to renew her alliance with Japan; and the Japanese counterclaim for increased security was met by an agreement to maintain the status quo in naval bases in the insular possessions of the three powers in the Pacific. The British base at Singapore and American base at Pearl Harbour were excepted, on grounds of their distance from the Japanese mainland. In addition, by a four-power treaty, Britain, America, Japan and France agreed to respect their mutual rights and territories in the Far East and to consult together in the event of disputes which could not be settled through normal diplomatic channels.

The negotiation of the Washington treaties connoted a substantial willingness and ability on the part of Britain, America and Japan to reorganize their security and armament relations in accordance with the changes that had occurred in the underlying distribution of power in the Pacific. Britain and America recognized that Japan was the effective master of the western Pacific, while Britain and Japan implicitly accepted that they could not compete with the United States in the major classes of warship, at least with any ultimate chance of success. At the same time, the accomplishment was offset to some extent by a failure to agree upon quantitative limitations for auxiliary craft, notably cruisers, destroyers and submarines. The governments concerned considered that the political and technical conditions that made it possible to place such restrictions on capital ships and aircraft-carriers without jeopardizing national security did not extend at that time to the smaller categories of vessel.

The lesson of the Washington treaties was that although disarmament was practicable, it was practicable only within a restricted milieu and in conjunction with a redefinition by the powers of their respective security requirements. Each party to an agreement had to be satisfied that the arrangements for both security and armaments did not adversely affect the organization of national defence. Thus, the obstacles in the way even of an extension of the naval agreement of 1922 were formidable. Not only had the 'Washington powers' found it impossible to arrive at satisfactory quantitative arrangements for auxiliary craft, at a conference held in Rome in February 1924 the lesser naval powers found it impossible to agree upon mutual quotas for capital ships and aircraft-carriers. The obstacles to a broader convention covering land, sea and air forces were prodigious.

The conclusion drawn by the powers in Resolution XIV stemmed not so much from the example of the Washington treaties but from a failure to advance disarmament as a separate entity, distinct from security. In November 1920, the First Assembly of the League had established a Temporary Mixed Commission for the Reduction of Armaments, but its attempts to conclude a general convention based on quantitative reduction and the ratio principle — notably the 'Esher Plan' — had proved unsuccessful because no provision was made for compensating disadvantaged states. The need for an alternative strategy was thus pressed home. In 1923, therefore, in accordance with the wishes of the Third Assembly, the Temporary Mixed Commission prepared a draft Treaty of Mutual Assistance which aimed at providing a general security settlement on which a disarmament agreement could be based. The scheme, which was approved by the Fourth Assembly in September 1923 and transmitted to the various governments for their further consideration, would have obliged each signatory to give military support to any other signatory in the same continent that had been the victim of aggression. The League Council was to designate an aggressor within four days of an outbreak of international hostilities, decide on the application of economic sanctions, determine and organize the military forces required to frustrate the aggressor and furnish financial help to the victim. Local alliances would be permitted if 'approved' by the Council and could be implemented without necessarily waiting for an

aggressor to be defined, but the security guarantees would not apply
to a signatory that had not reduced its armaments according to plans
prepared by the Council.[4]

The major defect of the draft treaty was that, in effect, it
endeavoured to impose regional security pacts on quasi-collective
principles on regions where the objective conditions for the
implementation of such pacts did not exist. The treaty presumed that
conditions on each continent would enable the same security system
to be applied to each. Clearly this was not the case. Security in the
Americas and the Far East, for example, depended to a large extent
on the role of the United States, a non-member of the League; and
it was inconceivable that the treaty could be executed in these areas
in the absence of American goodwill. Consequently, a number of
countries opposed the draft treaty for fear that it would bring them
into conflict with the American colossus.

The merit of the draft treaty was that it was acceptable to France
and her allies. This went to the heart of the disarmament problem.
France and her east European satellites would agree to disarm only
if they were granted additional security guarantees; and in practice
these guarantees could be provided only by Britain, since Russia had
been excluded from the ranks of the great powers and the United
States refused to become involved in European disputes. The question was thus posed whether Britain would aspire to facilitate disarmament through undertaking additional foreign commitments.

After due consideration, the Labour government of Ramsay
MacDonald decided not to accept the draft treaty. The minority
administration opposed the proposal on the grounds that the apportionment of liability on continental lines would place a disproportionate share of the burden of resisting aggression on the British
Empire and that the multiplication of commitments would
necessitate an increase rather than a decrease in armaments. The
League Council, it was contended, would become an executive body
with undesirably large powers, a most inappropriate body to be
entrusted with the control of military forces. The effectiveness of the
scheme depended to a considerable extent on the ability of the Council unanimously to name an aggressor, and in the absence of a definition of aggression an element of uncertainty would be introduced.
Moreover, there would be a long delay before the forces at the
disposal of the League could be brought into effective operation
against an aggressor. In such circumstances, the guarantees afforded
by the treaty would be insufficient to justify a state in reducing its
armaments.[5]

Ramsay MacDonald's action in repudiating the draft treaty was to
typify British policy under Conservative and National governments
in the next ten years. It was generally agreed that concessions should
be made to Germany in the matter of armaments; but a persistent
refusal to give France specific guarantees of support made French
governments less willing to make concessions to Germany, thus
frustrating the aim of conciliating Germany. Unfortunately, few

British statesmen really understood the implications of Resolution XIV, that the security and disarmament problems were indivisible, and that British power was an essential element in the solution of the problems. Consciously or unconsciously, successive British governments based their policy on the nineteenth-century liberal theory of an international 'harmony of interests'. They assumed that each nation had a common interest in peace, that the common interest was compatible with the pursuit of individual national interests and that wars arose primarily from misunderstandings. They assumed that the experiences of 1914-8 had demonstrated the futility of war and believed that acceptance of this axiom by international politicians would inevitably lead states to the path of peace. This was a misconception. Some states believed that war brought advantages. Germany attributed her sufferings to defeat in the First World War rather than the war itself; the east European successor states owed their very existence to the First World War. Some states wanted to maintain the status quo; others wanted to change it. Thus, the premise on which British governments based their policy regarding the disarmament problem was untenable. They postulated that an international harmony of interests existed; in reality, it was necessary to create that harmony.

In national politics, it is the function of the government to create harmony. But in international politics there is no similar body to carry out the task. Yet just as governments must adjust to change within society, so must states adjust to changes within international society. British governments understood this, but they did not understand that the exertion of British power through direct participation in the European security system was an essential element in the process of 'peaceful change' within international society. In trying to induce France to make concessions to Germany without offering equivalent compensation, they adopted a strategy that was not conducive to a settlement of the disarmament problem.

'Harmony of interests' was a self-serving doctrine. It permitted Britain to exert an amount of interest on the continent out of all proportion to British involvement in the European security system and allowed the government to concentrate on the protection of Britain's more immediate interests: the defence of the trade routes and the maintenance of a reasonable degree of preparedness on the part of the RAF. Ministers might look on the concept of disarmament with benevolence, but few were willing to accept that the effective pursuit of disarmament entailed commitments and responsibilities as well as the exhortation of other powers to reduce their forces.

In the immediate post-war years all the major powers had reduced their armaments from the extraordinary levels built up during wartime. And Britain, with the German menace overcome, was able to accommodate greater reductions than most since there was no longer any apparent threat to British or Imperial security. Japan, despite the abrogation of the Anglo–Japanese alliance, remained a friendly power. The United States, despite the pretensions of a vociferous minority of extreme Anglophobes, had no aggressive intentions against the Empire. The Soviet Union, notwithstanding the assertions of hardened anti-communists, was far too weak a power to pose a tangible threat. And France, in spite of occasional scare stories about a pre-emptive air strike on London, harboured no designs on the British homeland. The circumstances later proved to be transitory, but there was little point in maintaining a higher level of forces than was justified by the conditions of the time. Indeed, an intensification of the British military effort might well have stimulated opposition to Britain that was otherwise avoided.

Certainly, at no time in the early 1920s — or for that matter during the later 1920s — did the government effect reductions in armaments that were below the margin of safety. In fact, after reaching a low point of £106m in 1923, the defence estimates were to rise to a steady £113-18m in the years 1924-9, which represented some 14 per cent of government expenditure and some 3.2 per cent of national income, figures which were broadly in line with the other major powers and which compared favourably with pre-war expenditure.[6] Moreover, in their annual review of defence policy for 1926, the Chiefs of Staff asserted that although British military strength had been reduced to a 'minimum', the forces available were sufficient to deal with the problems that were liable to arise, either singly or simultaneously.[7] The difficulty was that there was no agreed enemy against which to prepare. The Admiralty, which was responsible for the naval defence of the Empire based on the one-power standard, prepared for a war in the Far East against Japan. The RAF, whose major duty was the protection of the British mainland against attack by the strongest air force within striking distance on the basis of an expanded Home Defence Force of fifty-two squadrons, prepared for war against France. And the Army, whose role was to provide fixed defences and garrisons on land and deal with such raiding forces as eluded the fleet, envisaged a Soviet adversary, probably in Afghanistan. Thus although the government expended reasonable sums on defence, lack of co-ordination between the services, together with a misdirection of resources within the services and a lack of co-ordination between defence and foreign policy ensured that the country as a whole did not receive the best return for its money.

The scope for further reducing British armaments was strictly limited. The expansion of the RAF towards its establishment level took place at a slow rate, mainly because the threat from the only nation capable of launching a direct air attack on Britain, France, was unreal. The Army held only token forces at readiness for activities beyond immediate defence and Imperial commitment. And although the Navy possessed a greater capacity for absorbing cutbacks, the margin for error was substantially reduced after the formulation of the 1925 naval programme. If further reductions were to be endorsed, the most assured and least risky method was that of international disarmament.

Acceptance of international disarmament, however, implied international commitment. And it was to this problem that Ramsay Mac-Donald, a sincere if naïve supporter of disarmament, was to apply himself after rejecting the draft Treaty of Mutual Assistance. During the summer of 1924, he had talks with Herriot concerning a general security settlement linked to future disarmament, and he came to the conclusion that the best method of procedure was to close the 'gap' in the Covenant which left war legitimate in the event of a failure of the League to provide for the peaceful settlement of disputes. A definition of aggression would be provided by means of compulsory arbitration. He outlined his ideas at the Fifth Assembly, in September 1924, and the upshot was the formulation of the Geneva Protocol.

Supporters of the Protocol claimed that it provided a means for resolving all international disputes without recourse to force. The 'gap' in the Covenant whereby states were free to go to war three months after an arbitral award or judicial decision was to be closed and signatories obliged to resolve their differences through the mediation or conciliation of the Council (non-justiciable disputes) or through arbitration or judicial settlement at the Permanent Court of International Justice or an *ad hoc* tribunal (justiciable disputes together with non-justiciable disputes not resolved by the Council). States refusing to submit their disputes or accept an award would be presumed aggressors and made liable to international sanctions in accordance with Article 16 of the Covenant if they resorted to war. In the absence of agreement in the Council as to the determination of an aggressor the Council, by a two-thirds' majority if necessary, would enjoin an armistice on the belligerents. A belligerent which refused an armistice or violated its terms would then be considered the aggressive party. There was to be no modification of Article 16 itself and states would participate in military sanctions only to the extent that their geographical situation and position as regards armaments allowed, but signatories were also pledged to co-operating 'loyally and effectively' against aggressors, to helping safeguard the communications of an attacked or threatened state and to providing 'facilities and reciprocal exchanges' such as the supply of raw materials and opening of credits. The Protocol would not, however, become operative until the conclusion of a general disarmament convention, and a conference to this end was to convene in Geneva on 15 June 1925.[8]

The drafting of the Protocol renewed the hope that a lasting solution of the disarmament problem might be imminent. The document was unanimously approved by the Fifth Assembly and its acceptance recommended to all member-governments of the League. France and nine other nations signed the instrument while the Assembly was still in progress, and the British delegates, Arthur Henderson and Baron Parmoor, would almost certainly have done so too if they had been given the requisite authority.[9] But Ramsay MacDonald, confronted by departmental objections, decided that a governmental examination of the document must precede signature, and on 2

October the Protocol was remitted to the Committee of Imperial Defence for further analysis. Within days, the government had fallen — on a trivial and irrelevant issue — and at the ensuing election the Conservatives were returned with an overall majority of more than 200 seats over the combined strength of the other parties.

3 The second Baldwin government and the disarmament problem
November 1924–May 1929

It is an open question whether the Labour government would have signed and ratified the Protocol, at least in the form that it emerged from Geneva. Not only was the administration dependent on Liberal support within the House of Commons, which might not have been forthcoming, important members of the cabinet including the First Lord of the Admiralty, Viscount Chelmsford, the Chancellor of the Exchequer, Philip Snowden, and the Lord Chancellor, Viscount Haldane, had serious objections.[1] Moreover, the Prime Minister himself occupied an equivocal position. The Protocol might have been based on the principles he espoused, but he was reluctant to translate his principles into a definite commitment to the Geneva scheme as it emerged from the Assembly.[2]

Whatever the ultimate intentions of the Labour government, the return to power of the Conservatives in November 1924 represented a severe setback for both the Protocol and disarmament. The majority of the Cabinet were sceptical of pursuing disarmament as a policy and doubted the effectiveness of the League, preferring a cautious policy based on the organization of adequate defence forces. Some were out-and-out Imperialists who cared little for internationalism; and there was a residual die-hard element which generally favoured a quasi-isolationist foreign policy.

The new Prime Minister, Stanley Baldwin, had little interest in foreign affairs, and disarmament in particular.[3] In general, he left the direction of policy to his Foreign Secretary, Austen Chamberlain, although if the integrity of the government demanded it he was not averse to over-riding his colleague's proposals. He never wholeheartedly believed in the League as an effective force in world politics and held that disarmament was visionary.[4] He sojourned regularly at Aix-les-Bains, only a few miles from Geneva, during meetings of the League Assembly, but he refused to undertake the short journey required to see the international institution at work.[5] Even less did he consider playing a part in its proceedings. He thus epitomized the attitude of a government which was doubtful of the value of the League. Viscount Cecil, Chancellor of the Duchy of Lancaster from 1924 to 1927, once asserted that Chamberlain's treatment of the League was reminiscent of a mother saying to her daughter, 'Go and see what Tommy is doing and tell him to stop at once'.[6] The suggestion applied more aptly to Baldwin.

Chamberlain owed his appointment as Foreign Secretary to his position as head of the former Coalition Conservatives in Lloyd George's National government and to the Marquess Curzon's lack of success at 'the office' in the first Baldwin government rather than to his qualifications for the post. In fact, his knowledge of foreign affairs, or rather lack of knowledge, would probably have excluded him from consideration had it not been for the absence of a more suitable candidate.[7] He had made few previous excursions into the field of foreign policy, and his speeches on the subject in the Commons were infrequent. The most important occurred on 14 July 1924, when he outlined a number of general principles for 'the consideration and attention of the Prime Minister for the future':

> What is the policy which we would follow? In the first place, we would frankly accept and uphold the Versailles Treaty and its subsidiary or collateral Treaties as the basis, and the only possible basis, for the public law of Europe. In the second place, we would make the maintenance of the Entente with France the cardinal object of our policy. We would do that both to give confidence in the stability and the execution of the Treaties and to prevent fresh causes of difference arising between ourselves and our Allies . . . we should feel . . . that there was a similar obligation on the part of our Allies to make the maintenance of that Entente the cardinal article of their policy and to meet us in the spirit in which we were prepared to meet them. Thirdly, we should make the observance by Germany of her obligations a not less cardinal feature of our policy in foreign affairs, and, in return, if Germany frankly accepted and loyally fulfilled the obligations as now presented, we should be prepared to respect the integrity of Germany and to welcome her back into the comity of nations; and always, like His Majesty's Government and like every party in this House, we should seek to secure, wherever it be possible, associations with the United States of America in such ways and under such conditions as may at any moment alone be possible to the American people.[8]

Disarmament barely entered into the foreign secretary's calculations at this time, and, although in future years he was to become more sympathetic to the concept, he always distrusted 'grandiose schemes which were to be applied everywhere logically and simultaneously', believing that the idea of an initial world disarmament conference was not the most practicable form of approach to the problem.[9] He did take office with a relatively open mind regarding specific questions, insisting that he needed time to study the Geneva Protocol so that he could discuss it intelligently;[10] but this advantage was largely offset by his innate caution, which tended to make him susceptible, at least initially, to the advice of the more conservative, anti-internationalist officials at the Foreign Office, in particular, the Permanent Under-Secretary, Sir Eyre Crowe, a vigorous opponent of disarmament.[11]

Of the service ministers, the most influential was W.C. Bridgeman, the First Lord of the Admiralty. In fact he was to be the Prime Minister's chief confidant in the new government.[12] On the die-hard wing of the Conservative Party, Bridgeman had a complete belief in the Royal Navy and consistently supported the idea of fortifying national security through the demarcation of an extensive naval programme.[13] He had no truck for general disarmament, especially if it involved reductions in British armaments or increased commitments to the League of Nations, the 'fussiness' of which he considered to be the only threat to universal peace; and he even believed — quite unjustifiably — that Viscount Cecil, a strong advocate of disarmament through the League, was desirous of leaving the settlement of international disputes 'to the tender mercies of a number of international cranks at Geneva who may have a Chinaman, or Guatemalan as Chairman'.[14]

The new Secretary for War, Sir Laming Worthington-Evans, was more at home with problems of economic policy than with disarmament and foreign affairs, and carried only a modicum of weight with his colleagues. A former Coalitionist, he was more open-minded than Bridgeman, even accepting that industrial and financial interests could stir up 'provocative competition' in armaments; but he suffered from a tendency to attach himself to whoever he thought it most important to agree with.[15] He could accept that disarmament was desirable, but thought mainly in terms of reductions by other powers. He had little sympathy for general schemes — he was an early opponent of the draft Treaty of Mutual Assistance and later reached the paradoxical conclusion that the movement for general disarmament was in itself the greatest menace to international goodwill.[16]

Sir Samuel Hoare, Secretary of State for Air, was the most junior of the service ministers, but he exercised a deal of influence over his colleagues. Chamberlain especially approved of his judgement.[17] He worked hard, was a stout defender of his department's interests and was quick and skilful in discussion; he had successfully resisted the division of the RAF between the Army and Navy during his first period as Air Minister from 1922 to 1923 and was to fight off a renewed challenge during 1925.[18] He was regarded by many as an air fanatic, having been 'bitten by a mad aeroplane', but looked on disarmament less unsympathetically than Bridgeman and Worthington-Evans.[19] At the same time, his prime concern was to use disarmament as a means of reducing Britain's inferiority to France in the air.[20]

The all-important post of Chancellor of the Exchequer was occupied by an ardent anti-internationalist, Winston Churchill. He did not consider that the League was in a position to preserve the peace of the world, and opined that both the Protocol and disarmament seemed very unreal.[21] He was willing to accept reductions in arms expenditure in line with the Treasury policy of reducing government spending as a whole, but not to the extent of endangering British security as he saw it.[22] He was much impressed by Admiral Sir John Fisher's dictum that it was best to 'Build late, build fast, each one better than the last' since advantage could then be taken of technological advances in the future; and accordingly he accepted that Britain required 'liberty' in the matter of armaments and not the 'handcuffs' of a disarmament convention.[23] The Chancellor deprecated 'these premature attempts to force agreement on disarmament' and did not accept that the Allies had undertaken even a moral commitment to disarm in 1919.[24]

Churchill's most remembered comment on disarmament, his so-called 'Zoo Allegory' of 25 October 1928 summed up his own and many of his colleague's views admirably:

> Once upon a time all the animals in the Zoo decided that they would disarm, and they arranged to have a conference to arrange the matter. So the Rhinoceros said when he opened the proceedings that the use of teeth was barbarous and horrible and ought to be strictly prohibited by general consent. Horns, which were mainly defensive weapons, would, of course, have to be allowed. The Buffalo, the Stag, the Porcupine, and even the Little Hedgehog all said they would vote with the Rhino, but the Lion and the Tiger took a different view. They defended the teeth and even claws, which they described as honourable weapons of immemorial antiquity. The Panther, the Leopard, the Puma and the whole tribe of small cats all supported the Lion and the Tiger. Then the Bear spoke. He proposed that both teeth and horns should be banned and never used again for fighting by any animal. It would be quite enough if animals were allowed to give each other a good hug when they quarrelled. No one could object to that. It was so fraternal, and that would be a great step towards peace. However, all the other animals were very offended with the Bear . . ..
>
> The discussion got so hot and angry, and all those animals began thinking so much about horns and teeth and hugging when they argued about the peaceful intentions that had brought them together that they began to look at one another in a very nasty way . . ..[25]

Baldwin was so taken by the fable that he wrote a letter of concurrence to his Cabinet colleague on 27 October 1928.[26]

Intellectually, possibly the most well-endowed member of the government was the Earl of Birkenhead, Secretary for India. He is said to have acted as a restraining influence on Churchill,[27] but nevertheless he expressed extremely strong views on foreign affairs and the role of armaments in British overseas policy. His basic philosophy was outlined in his inaugural address on installation as Rector of Glasgow University in November 1923:

> The world continues to offer glittering prizes to those who have stout hearts and sharp swords . . ..
>
> It is for us, therefore . . . to maintain in our own hand the adequate means for our own protection; and, so equipped, march with heads erect and bright eyes along the road of our Imperial destiny.[28]

His Rectorial Address represented a strong attack on internationalism and the League of Nations; and, in general, the inclusion of such a personality in the Cabinet did not improve the outlook for disarmament.

The Colonial Secretary, Leopold Amery, espoused similar views to his colleague at the India Office. He ridiculed the idea that wars arose out of competition in armaments and firmly believed that peace depended on force. He could agree that there was a case for qualitative disarmament on the twin grounds of economy and discouragement of recourse to war, but was of the opinion that any restrictions would be circumvented in practice. To him, the problem of disarmament was 'completely insoluble' as it implied the imposition of a rigid mechanical system on a constantly changing international society. Disarmament conferences were 'fundamentally wrong'.[29]

Four other members of the Cabinet gravitated to the Birkenhead-Amery conception of disarmament and foreign policy; Sir William Joynson-Hicks, the Home Secretary; the Marquess Curzon, Lord President until his death in 1925; Viscount Cave, Lord Chancellor until his death in 1928; and Walter Guinness, who succeeded Baron Irwin as Minister of Agriculture in November 1925; but their impact on disarmament policy seems to have been marginal because the nature of their offices set them aside from all but the general questions which reached Cabinet level. The same, however, could be said for three members of the government who looked on disarmament and the League more benevolently, if still sceptically: Edward Wood, Minister of Agriculture until appointed Viceroy of India as Baron Irwin; Neville Chamberlain, Minister of Health; and Lord Eustace Percy, President of the Board of Education. The Earl of Balfour, who took over from Curzon as Lord President, might also be included in this group, but as the 'elder statesman' of the Conservative Party he could on occasion wield a measure of influence out of all proportion to his nominal rank.

Of the remaining members of the Cabinet, the majority seem to have taken the line of least resistance regarding disarmament, notably Sir John Gilmour, Viscount Peel, Sir Philip Lloyd-Greame (later Cunliffe-Lister) and Sir Arthur Steel-Maitland, all of whom stayed in office for the full term. Two others, however, exercised considerable influence at times: the Marquess of Salisbury, the Lord Privy Seal; and Sir Douglas Hogg, Attorney-General until he succeeded Cave in 1928. The latter became a member of the government's Disarmament Policy Committee on its formation in October 1927 and showed an above-average perception of political realities regarding disarmament, whilst still retaining his orthodox Conservative scepticism. And the former, as chairman of the Disarmament Policy Committee and with an elevated position in the Conservative hierarchy, was a personage of importance in his own right. He had an open mind towards the League and despite his intrinsic doubts was willing to go a long way in furthering the cause of disarmament.

The one member of the Cabinet to believe wholeheartedly in disarmament was Viscount Cecil. A member of the Salisbury 'dynasty', brother of the Lord Privy Seal, his experience of the First World War — at the end of which he was Assistant Foreign Secretary —

convinced him that the only worthwhile political objective was the effort to abolish war. War, he satisfied himself, posed the major threat to the Christian civilization in which he believed, and, if the 'reign of Peace' was to be achieved, it was necessary to inculcate the habit of co-operation rather than competition at international level.[30] The means to this end was to be an international organization which would harness the 'great formless sentiment' of public opinion, and accordingly Cecil became one of the major driving forces in the creation of the League of Nations. President of the League of Nations Union from 1923 to 1945, he was the embodiment of internationalism, a staunch supporter of collective security who accepted fully the intrinsic link between disarmament and security.[31] He had been the chief architect of the draft Treaty of Mutual Assistance and preached his gospel at home and abroad with almost messianic fervour. From an early date he perceived that Germany would regard herself as free to rearm if the Allied powers reneged on their disarmament 'obligations' of 1919, and he believed that the consequences for world peace would be disastrous. The safety of European civilization, even the existence of the British Empire, depended on an international agreement for the reduction and limitation of armaments.[32]

The Prime Minister appointed Cecil very reluctantly, and according to the Chancellor of the Duchy of Lancaster, only after consultation with Wood and Salisbury.[33] The Foreign Office was especially anxious at the appointment, alleging that Cecil had departed from instructions when British representative at the League under previous administrations, and there was some fear that the assumption by the Chancellor of a special responsibility for League matters would give rise to discordant British voices in London and Geneva.[34] But Austen Chamberlain made it clear that Cecil would not be considered a kind of 'League Minister' and refused his colleague a room in the Foreign Office — and there the matter rested.[35]

Cecil was to remain in office until August 1927, when he resigned his position over the government's policy at the Geneva Naval Conference, to be succeeded by a die-hard Ulster Unionist, Baron Cushendun, who would 'fight for anything' if convinced the Pope was on the other side![36] He was not entirely new to foreign affairs, for, as Ronald McNeill, he had been Parliamentary Under-Secretary at the Foreign Office from November 1924 to November 1925; but as this was his first Cabinet appointment it seemed unlikely that he would make any great impact on disarmament policy or undertake any major initiatives. Experience at Geneva was to mellow him, however, perhaps under the inspiration of the French naval representative at the Preparatory Commission, Captain Deleuze, who referred to him, almost entirely humorously, as 'Lord Cochon d'Ane'.[37] Certainly, in the final months of the Conservative government, he was to become one of the more discerning members of the Cabinet on the disarmament issue.

The Foreign Secretary's departmental advisers, like the Conservative Party in general, tended to distrust both the League and disarmament. Sir Eyre Crowe was the chief detractor, but his subordinates and successors adopted a similar stance. As early as October 1916 Crowe had dismissed, in the most forcible terms, a tentative suggestion by Cecil that disarmament might be discussed at the peace conference, urging that Britain should refrain from bringing the question forward. He disputed both the practicability and desirability of disarmament and was to maintain his opposition to his death in 1925.[38]

The great majority of the government's official advisers took a similar line to Crowe, and none was more insidious in propagating his views than Sir Maurice Hankey, secretary to the Cabinet and Committee of Imperial Defence, an extremely astute manipulator who used his knowledge and control of the workings of the government machine to great advantage. He spent considerable time and effort endeavouring to prove that history demonstrated the futility of disarmament, despite the negotiation of the Washington Naval Treaty, and looked forward to a renewed arms race which would fill the order books of industry and provide a remedy for unemployment. He was a great believer in the supposed military virtues and was a consistent champion of increased British armaments.[39]

Not unnaturally, the Chiefs of Staff shared the Hankey–Crowe conception of disarmament. They were worried about the effects of arms reductions and regarded a general disarmament agreement with considerable apprehension — when not dismissing the possibility as utopian. At the same time, their role in policy formulation was largely passive, being confined mainly to instructing subordinates to provide plausible reasons for a strategy based on British security requirements. Of the five men to head the services during the Baldwin government, only Earl Beatty, First Sea Lord until his retirement in July 1927, took an active interest in disarmament, and then in a negative direction. His views on possible naval cuts were admirably expressed in a letter of 16 February 1926 to his wife: 'All precautions are to be thrown to the winds to completely trust the goodwill of every Nation and give up everything which will take years to reproduce for the sake of saving a few millions to spend on making roads and pay out in doles to people who don't want to work.'[40] Beatty also espoused the delusion that sea power, as opposed to military power, was essentially a power for peace, unaggressive itself and a shield against aggression.[41] He carried great weight in political circles because of his intellectual domination of Bridgeman.

Within the service departments, a large amount of responsibility for disarmament lay with the representatives on the Permanent Advisory Commission of the League of Nations, a body of service 'experts' from member countries established to advise the Council on military, naval and air questions. Probably the most open-minded and certainly the most influential (if only because of the inertia of his superiors) was Colonel A.C. Temperley, the military delegate from 1925 onwards. He first went to Geneva suspicious of the League and cynical of its workings; but over the years he became a firm supporter of the institution, convinced that some form of arms limitation was essential to a settlement of international problems.[42] He was a rare breed within the War Office. Britain's naval delegates were less flexible in their attitudes. Admiral Aubrey Smith was to maintain consistently that the search for a general agreement through the League was 'eyewash', and his successor, Admiral Howard Kelly, reflected that a formula for mutual reductions of armaments by all states was 'impossible'.[43] The latter was also quoted as saying that he was not going to Geneva to work for the League, but to fight it.[44] The air delegate, Group-Captain W.F. MacNeece, occupied a central position between the military and naval representatives. He was fully in agreement with Smith and Kelly that disarmament was impossible, if only for political reasons, but was astute enough to realise that from the service point of view a *non possumus* attitude was undesirable. He thought it better to admit that disarmament was practicable but infer that technical feasibility connoted political inconvenience.[45]

Of the principle personalities involved in the discussion of the disarmament problem, therefore, only one — Viscount Cecil — favoured a forward policy and held an intrinsic belief in the necessity of disarmament. It is often asserted that successive British governments in the years 1919-34 identified themselves with the cause of disarmament in both words and actions and that the second Baldwin government was no exception.[46] But this is not the case. The philosophical propensities of the Cabinet and the foreign policy-making élite of the country were sceptical of, if not outrightly opposed to, the whole movement for arms limitation.[47]

4 The Geneva Protocol and the Locarno treaties
November 1924–October 1925

One of the first acts of the incoming government was to reaffirm the decision to refer the Protocol to the Committee of Imperial Defence.[1] By 4 December, however, when the CID met to discuss the question for the first time, it had become apparent that the reference was little more than academic, for both ministers and departments had prepared a formidable list of objections. They claimed that acceptance of the Protocol would impose heavy new commitments on Britain, lead to difficulties with the United States, threaten the unity and security of the Empire and involve a serious loss of national independence.

The chiefs of staff suggested that the Protocol involved an encroachment on governmental control of the armed forces because it committed Britain to military action against an aggressor determined by a two-thirds majority of the League Council and to continuing sanctions until the Council decided that they should cease. The chiefs of staff also objected that the Protocol would infringe national sovereignty by increasing the danger of purely domestic affairs being brought before the Council, in particular the immigration policy of the Dominions. The Admiralty and Foreign Office made similar allegations.[2]

Many departments criticized the additional commitments that Britain would be forced to undertake if she accepted the Protocol as it stood. The Admiralty took great exception to Article 7, by which signatories agreed to 'take all measures in their power to preserve the safety of communications by land and sea of the attacked or threatened state', and all three service departments criticized the commitments arising from the enforcement of armistice conditions and the protection of demilitarized zones. Britain might find herself compelled to take part in any and every war, would have no certainty as to the number and nature of such conflicts and would be forced to increase her armaments. The Treasury and Board of Trade objected that the proposed economic sanctions would impose formidable burdens on the British economy and involve serious and immediate losses to trade. Moreover, such sanctions were unlikely to be efficacious without the co-operation of the United States and might even lead Britain into conflict with that power.[3]

The criticism that the Protocol threatened the unity and security of the Empire was put forward primarily by the chiefs of staff, who argued that Article 7 prevented signatories from increasing their armaments or effectives and from taking any measures of military, naval, air, industrial or economic mobilization either before or during the submission of a dispute to the procedure for pacific settlement. The chiefs of staff believed that, in drawing up this article, the authors of the Protocol had intended to prevent the concentration of troops on land frontiers, but that in doing so they had paid insufficient attention to the problems of the British Empire, which depended for its defence on sea power and the freedom of movement of its forces. The Empire would be forced to maintain larger forces — and on a war footing — and if the Dominions found difficulty in accepting the Protocol, the principle of Dominion co-operation in matters of defence would be at stake.[4]

Perhaps the most fundamental objection to the Protocol was that advanced by Crowe and the Foreign Office — that acceptance would involve the submission of 'grave political issues' to compulsory arbitration. Britain might be asked, for example, to submit her authority in the Sudan or presence in Egypt to such jurisdiction, and where such issues were at stake it would be merely provocative to demand blind submission to 'a body of foreign lawyers by no means all of high reputation, or to some other unknown and unspecified persons'.[5] Crowe also questioned whether it was desirable or necessary to eliminate the element of vagueness in the Covenant and substitute rigid precision and definition, especially regarding sanctions and the definition of aggression. The absence of precision had hitherto offered a loophole by which Britain could either delay or avoid taking action under her general commitments.[6]

The outcome of the government's analysis of the Protocol was never in doubt. The one minister basically in favour of the scheme was Viscount Cecil, who believed that the 'difficulties' it presented were not vital and could largely be eliminated either by amendments or by declarations at the time of signature. But he had long realized that the Protocol was incompatible with orthodox Conservative conceptions of the national interest and was concerned only with salvaging what he could from the proposal.[7]

From an early date, Chamberlain had gravitated towards acceptance of the anti-Protocol case, and on 19 November he wrote to Cecil suggesting that the French would not accept a League guarantee as sufficient for their security. He was strongly influenced by Crowe's critique of compulsory arbitration and thought that Cecil underrated the prospective changes in British obligations. He felt it undesirable to take a step that might incline the United States against the League at a time when they were beginning to co-operate with some of its organs, and was impressed by Colonial Office fears that some of the Dominions might reject the Protocol even if Britain accepted it.[8]

On 4 and 16 December, the political implications of the Protocol were discussed, or rather the numerous objections to the scheme were accepted, at two meetings of the CID. Only Cecil spoke in any sense in favour of the Protocol, proposing that the attitude of the departments be subjected to 'minute examination' and that 'certain distinguished gentlemen' of the other parties, such as MacDonald, Grey, Asquith and Lloyd George, be invited to take part in the deliberations. Amery proposed an Imperial Conference and the amendment of the Covenant to meet the objections of the Dominions and the United States. Churchill suggested that the proper method 'was to work in stages by means of regional agreements under the League of Nations to protect special points of danger, and by making definite tracts of country demilitarized zones', the sanctity of which could be guaranteed by various powers. Chamberlain opposed the Protocol but declared it would be an 'unmitigated disaster' to turn it down and put nothing in its place. Europe was dominated by feelings of fear and unless Britain could give the continent security, sooner or later there would be another European war. The Foreign Secretary's advice was adopted, and it was decided to set up a subcommittee to consider whether the Protocol could be amended to meet the criticisms made against it, also the principles that should be adopted if it was desired to substitute another instrument.[9]

Baldwin summarized the government's position on the Protocol in two telegrams to Dominion Prime Ministers on 19 December. In the first, he stated that:

> We have now been able to give preliminary examination to terms of Geneva Protocol . . .. Not only does instrument itself raise issues of highest importance involving as they do such matters as the submission to compulsory arbitration even of vital interests and the imposition of sanctions of the most drastic character, but its consideration necessarily brings to the forefront far-reaching problems affecting the security of the Empire, and its future relations to the countries of Europe and the United States of America.[10]

In the second the Prime Minister added that rejection of the Protocol without 'at least some attempt' to formulate an alternative policy to govern relations with the United States and Europe would be 'a mistaken policy and even a disastrous one'. The government therefore hoped to arrange a special meeting of the Dominion Prime Ministers in London in the first week of March 1925 so that a common Empire policy could be worked out for the presentation to the League Council in the middle of that month.

Actually, the government's anxieties regarding the Protocol were greatly exaggerated. There were no real grounds for the fear that acceptance would involve the submission of vital interests to compulsory arbitration, for the League Assembly report on the instrument stated specifically that the procedure for pacific settlement did not apply to political disputes, 'disputes which aim at revising treaties and international acts in force, or which seek to jeopardize the existing territorial integrity of existing states'.[12] Although purporting to provide for the settlement of *all* disputes, the Protocol in reality provided only for the settlement of *legal* (justiciable) disputes through acceptance of the obligatory jurisdiction of the Permanent Court. Moreover, while acceptance of compulsory jurisdiction without reservation might have required Britain to submit disputes involving vital interests to the Court for judicial settlement, Sir Cecil Hurst, the government's Chief Legal Adviser, believed that reservations could be framed to overcome this difficulty.[13]

Consequently, despite the extravagant claims of its 'authors', the Protocol could not have provided an adequate basis for a disarmament agreement. Apart from the provision for obligatory jurisdiction, its contribution to international security would have been limited to a removal of the option in the Covenant of going to war three months after an arbitral award or judicial decision and to a more precise definition of the sanctions to be imposed by the League in cases where they would still operate.

Certainly acceptance of the Protocol would have added to Britain's obligations with regard to sanctions, but there was no truth in the suggestion that Britain could be committed to military action against an aggressor determined by a two-thirds majority of Council. The Council had no powers of coercion, remaining an advisory rather than executive body. Each power retained the right to decide for itself whether it was in a position to carry out the Council's recommendations regarding sanctions;[14] and the unanimity rule within the Council made it possible for Britain to use her permanent seat to veto any suggested action. Nor was there any substance to the criticism that the Protocol would increase the danger of purely domestic affairs being brought before the Council, as Article 5 had been inserted so that paragraph 8 of Article 15 of the Covenant (which safeguarded the rights of League members in matters of domestic jurisdiction) would be unaffected.[15] The fears of the service chiefs regarding the prohibition of mobilization during the procedure for pacific settlement and the need for a unanimous Council decision before sanctions could be ended were more pertinent — though probably more so in theory than in practice, as Article 2 of the

Protocol reaffirmed the right of each state to resist acts of aggression by any means.[16] In any case, the objections to the sanctions articles — and even the objection that the United States was opposed to the whole Protocol — applied with equal validity to the Covenant.

Crowe and the Foreign Office seem to have been afraid that the government might accept the Protocol on the basis of the 'Assembly Report' interpretation of the compulsory arbitration clauses, even though the phrasing of the telegrams of 19 December to the Dominions and the terms of reference of the CID sub-committee denoted implicit acceptance of the 'Foreign Office' interpretation. Their fears, however, were dispelled when it was learnt that the sub-committee was to be composed entirely of civil servants opposed to the Protocol: Crowe himself, Hankey (the chairman), Sir Henry Lambert, (acting Permanent Secretary at the Colonial Office) and Sir Arthur Hirtzel (Under Secretary for India).[17]

At its first meeting, on 18 December, the sub-committee accepted as authoritative a statement by Chamberlain that the questions of compulsory arbitration and the application of sanctions were of such an 'impossible' nature as to be ruled out, and effectively assumed that the government had taken a decision in principle against the Protocol.[18] Crowe and Hankey effectively directed the committee in accordance with their own wishes and the suggestions of Sir Cecil Hurst (a supporter of the Protocol[19]), who had been 'associated' with the committee to give legal advice, were in most cases ignored.

After ten meetings between 18 December and 20 January, the Protocol sub-committee adopted a report recommending the rejection of nine out of the sixteen operative articles and the drastic amendment of the remainder. The committee even suggested that the government consider withdrawal from the League, and in any case seek the amendment of the Covenant, more especially Article 16, so as to limit British commitments. The League was at 'a parting of the ways' where it could develop gradually, 'forming the habit among nations of bringing their differences and apprehensions to the Council for settlement with moral force as the principal weapon and with material force in the background as a last resort', or it could be given a new orientation 'by superimposing on the Covenant a system of compulsory arbitration closely supported by coercion'; and the committee had proceeded on the assumption that the government preferred the former.[20]

Not surprisingly, the sub-committee upheld all the various criticisms of the Protocol and accepted the Foreign Office interpretation of the compulsory arbitration clauses. The report recommended a drastically amended Protocol and it was suggested that the revised articles be approved as amendments to the Covenant and come into operation only when accepted as such. Articles 2–8 providing for compulsory arbitration and obligatory jurisdiction, the suspension of defensive measures before and during proceedings for pacific settlement and the undertaking 'to abstain from any act which might constitute a threat of aggression' were rejected out of hand, as was

Article 15 which postulated that aggressors be made to pay reparations to the full limit of their capacity but in no case lose their
territorial integrity or political independence. The committee also
advised the elimination of Article 16, governing relations with non-
signatory states. The various 'sanctions' articles of the Protocol were
considerably weakened, including the article requiring a unanimous
decision of the Council for the cessation of sanctions, and it was
suggested that Article 16 of the Covenant be modified to make
aggressors *liable* to rather than *subject to* the severance of trade and
financial relations.[21]

As regards the proposed Disarmament Conference, the committee
was 'not convinced that so complicated an instrument as the Geneva
Protocol [was] required in order to pave the way to some further
limitation of armaments if otherwise feasible'. Acceptance of the
Protocol would be too high a price to pay for any possible arms reductions, though rejection would result in Britain being accused of delaying the Disarmament Conference and so tactically it would be better
to propose the suggested amendments to the Protocol and Covenant.
At the same time, the committee held out little hope for a successful
conference and felt that no one had succeeded in devising an alternative technical basis for disarmament than that advocated by the
British at the time of the Paris Peace Conference — voluntary
military service.[22]

The committee declared that its recommendations made such
fundamental changes in the character of the Protocol that it was 'no
longer likely to be regarded as of any value from the point of view
of French and Belgian security' and that if the proposed Disarmament Conference was to take place without delay an alternative
basis had to be found. In any case, France had made it clear that,
even if Britain accepted the Protocol, she would require some kind of
defensive pact in addition. The question as to whether a pact was
desirable was a political one, but the committee pointed out the
possibility of such an instrument being acceptable to France and
Belgium as compensation for the loss of the Protocol. It might take
the form of a joint declaration that any unprovoked aggression
threatening their independence would be regarded as 'one of the
contingencies in which they are determined to make their maximum
effort by sea, by land, and by air, to oppose and defeat the aggressor',
and it would have the advantage of limiting Britain's obligations
more definitely and more clearly than the Protocol. There was a
danger in extending such a pact to Germany, as Britain might be
involved in problems on Germany's eastern frontier, but the declaration would provide a model for similar declarations and justify the
proposed amendments to the Covenant.[23]

The report of the sub-committee was more a reflection of the
political beliefs of Hankey and Crowe than an objective analysis of
the Protocol under the terms of reference laid down by the CID. Both
Crowe and Hankey disapproved of the Covenant, and it was on the
former's initiative that the committee began to discuss amending the

Covenant as well as the Protocol, even though such discussion was outside the terms of reference. Crowe also put forward the project for a joint declaration with France and Belgium.[24] The 'proposal' to base British disarmament policy on the universal abolition of conscription (another question outside the terms of reference of the committee) was Hankey's, and many of the articles of the Protocol were either revised or eliminated to meet the Secretary of the Cabinet's objections.[25] The committee only rarely accepted the advice given by Sir Cecil Hurst, who had been in Geneva during the drafting of the Protocol, and even more rarely referred to the report of the British delegates to the Fifth Assembly and the Assembly Report itself.

The suggestions for the amendment of the Covenant reflected a considerable lack of realism on the part of the committee because the possibility of continental nations accepting the amendments was remote. If the government had ever decided to broach such suggestions, British relations with France and her allies would have been adversely affected, and the future of the League jeopardized. The committee also displayed considerable *naïveté* in suggesting tacitly that Britain might base her disarmament policy on the universal abolition of conscription, as neither France nor her allies were willing to adopt a policy of voluntary enlistment in the face of a possible revival by Germany, even if such a revival lay in the distant future.

During the proceedings of the sub-committee, Chamberlain had been formulating the principles on which he hoped to conduct British diplomacy. He had long been in favour of good relations with France,[26] and quickly realized the need for an alternative to the Protocol to remove her security fears. He believed that, as long as security was absent, Germany would be tempted to prepare for the *révanche*, and that the Germans would not 'settle down' unless convinced they could not divide the Allies or challenge them with any chance of success. Europe needed security, and the situation had to be stabilized 'for long enough to allow of new generations growing up who [*could*] accept the *fait accompli* and [*would*] accept it rather than face again the horrors of war with no certain prospects of success'. Britain could not afford to see France crushed and a Russo-German combination supreme on the continent; she must solve the European security problem or be drawn in the wake of France towards a new Armageddon.[27]

Despite his perceptive analysis of the European situation, Chamberlain admitted to being 'frankly at a loss' as to how to solve the security problem. He saw only two possible solutions — an Anglo-Franco–Belgian pact followed by a quadruple pact embracing Germany, or a unilateral declaration of what Britain would regard as a *casus belli*. He was determined to prevent Britain being dragged into east European problems and wanted to limit British guarantees to the west, where he thought the decisive question was whether or not Germany accepted her treaty obligations. Evidently, disarmament did not enter into his calculations.[28]

The upshot of Chamberlain's study of the security problem was a conference with Crowe, the heads of the various Foreign Office departments and Ronald McNeill, the Parliamentary Under-Secretary, on 22 January, and the conclusions of this symposium were to form the basis of the Foreign Secretary's policy. It was assumed that, given existing conditions, Germany would try to reverse the Treaty of Versailles, preferably by agreement but if necessary by force, and 'her diplomatic tendency would be in the direction of an agreement with Russia', a country that was 'the most menacing of all our uncertainties'. It was in spite of, if not because of, the Soviet Union that a policy of giving Europe security had to be framed. Germany was at that time incapable of taking aggressive action, but it was certain that eventually she would again become a powerful military and economic entity and move towards 'righting' the more objectionable clauses of the peace treaty, notably the Polish Corridor and the partition of Silesia. British policy therefore had to prevent a desire for revenge growing up in Germany and establish a nucleus of security which might provide for a possible reconstruction of the Concert of Europe and even peaceful revision; and this could best be done by means of a guarantee of French and Belgian integrity. Such a guarantee would lessen French security fears and lead the French government to place less reliance on the 'policy of the Little Entente', which made it difficult to localize disturbances and tempted Germany to look to Russia for fear of 'encirclement'. A pact would let Europe know where Britain stood, make it unlikely that Germany would attempt to reverse the peace treaty by force and deter the smaller ex-enemies from fomenting the causes of insecurity. Moreover, the development of military technology had left Britain open to invasion from the air and it was necessary to ensure a friendly France and Belgium.[29]

On 20 January, two days before the Foreign Office symposium, the British Ambassador at Berlin, Lord D'Abernon, had forwarded a German proposal for the solution of the security problem. 'The Powers interested in the Rhine', above all England, France, Germany and Italy, would conclude a non-aggression pact 'for a lengthy period', with the United States as trustee; and as part of the pact Germany would be willing to accept the territorial *status quo* on the Rhine and fulfil her obligations in the demilitarized Rhineland. The German Foreign Minister, Gustav Stresemann, further indicated that his country was willing to enter into arbitration treaties with the signatories of the pact, providing for the peaceful settlement of juridical and political conflicts. The signatories would regard a violation of the pact 'as affecting them jointly and individually'.[30]

Although believing that the German proposal was 'a move in a good direction' that ought not to be discouraged, both Chamberlain and the Foreign Office suspected, with good reason, that it had been put forward with a view to opening a breach between Britain and France. They were irritated by a German request that the proposal be kept confidential and not passed on to the French and, although officially welcoming the German overtures as evidence of good intent, Chamberlain suggested to the German Ambassador on 30 January that the proposal could not usefully be discussed until Britain had defined her attitude towards the Protocol and French security. At the same time, the Foreign Secretary did not exclude an agreement based on the German proposals in the future.[31]

The fighting services, like the Foreign Office, favoured a pact with France, and they prepared their case well in advance of the crucial meetings of the CID on the Protocol and security, which were scheduled for 13 and 19 February. The War Office argued that renewed German aggression was the greatest danger facing Britain and that alliance with France and Belgium against Germany was an essential condition of British security, more especially as Britain's strategic frontier had receded from the cliffs of Dover to the River Rhine. Moreover, the development of a peaceful atmosphere in western Europe necessitated the alleviation of French security fears, and this could only be secured by a pact. The naval staff favoured a general defensive alliance rather than a pact directed solely against Germany, as it would enable Britain to send a large fleet to the Far East in case of trouble and remove a potential danger to the British lines of communication through the Mediterranean. The air staff claimed that a pact would only bind Britain to what she almost certainly would do in any case – protect the French frontier and Channel ports from German aggression – though it had the added advantage of reducing or eliminating the air menace to the shipping lines through the Mediterranean and Suez Canal.[32]

Perhaps the most surprising argument utilized by the services in favour of a pact was that it would facilitate disarmament. The general staff suggested that there was no possibility of France reducing her armaments as long as she was forced to rely on her own resources for security, and the air staff believed a pact would reduce the justification for France maintaining her large air forces; the navy trusted that an alliance would induce France to support the British view with regard to the limitation of submarines. Considering that the staffs had submitted, correctly, that the disadvantage of a pact was the possibility that it might lead France to adopt a more provocative policy towards Germany, the argument that an alliance would facilitate disarmament was based on insecure foundations. It is also revealing that the services assumed that concessions with regard to disarmament would be made by France and not Britain.[33]

Support for an alliance with France was therefore considerable when the CID met to discuss the report of the Geneva Protocol Committee and the problem of security on 13 February. Chamberlain made 'an impassioned appeal' in favour of some kind of pact and drew on the additional argument that unless something substantial was done to provide for French security, France would be unwilling to evacuate the occupied Rhineland. The evacuation of the first (Cologne) zone had already been delayed because Germany had not fulfilled her disarmament obligations and Herriot had begun to insist that while there was no *rapport juridique* between the evacuation of the Cologne zone and security there was certainly a *rapport de causalité*. The Foreign Secretary admitted that there was no logic to the French security fears — the enforced disarmament of Germany made France secure for a considerable time — but if Germany was to be prevented from seeking revenge it was necessary to start a policy of pacification immediately and this required the alleviation of French fears.[34]

The majority of the CID were unconvinced by Chamberlain's arguments and opposed such a binding commitment as an alliance. Lord Balfour suggested a kind of consultative pact, Birkenhead an Anglo–Franco–German guarantee of the inviolability of Belgium and possibly the French frontier. Amery claimed that the Dominions were against a pact and proposed a declaration that Britain would not tolerate interference with the territorial integrity of Belgium and Luxemburg. Churchill repeated his arguments in favour of regional agreements and opposed a pact with France on the grounds that, with Britain behind them, the French would feel strong enough to keep Franco–German antagonism alive — though Britain might act as a guarantor of a 'real peace' between the two continental powers. Chamberlain introduced the idea of a quadruple pact including Germany and revealed the German proposals of 20 January, taking good care to explain that they were not dependent on the evacuation of occupied territory or revision of the peace treaty. His initial doubts regarding the German government's intentions had to some extent been dispelled, and it seems that he regarded a quadruple pact as being an adequate substitute for an alliance with France if a bilateral arrangement was rejected by the Cabinet.[35]

Only rarely was the problem of disarmament brought into the discussion of security, though Hoare believed that 'so dangerous a commitment of foreign and military policy' as an Anglo–French pact should only be embarked on if France were willing to reduce her armaments. With considerable justification, the Air Minister suggested that France was militarily secure for the next ten or fifteen years and that after the Versailles' restrictions on Germany were eased Britain would find herself in danger of being bound to a country that was growing weaker and weaker relative to her neighbour on the Rhine. Hoare also believed that the amended Protocol proposed by Hankey would not induce the French to disarm and this point was taken up in earnest by Cecil, who suggested that the original Protocol offered far more hope. Chamberlain, however, whilst clinging to the Foreign Office interpretation of the document, considered it would only advance the cause of European disarmament in conjunction with further security guarantees.[36]

On two points only did the CID reach even tacit agreement: that a despatch should be sent to the League explaining the government's objections to the Protocol; and that it would be futile to put forward as an alternative the amended Protocol suggested by the Hankey Committee since there was no chance of the continental powers

accepting it. A further meeting of the CID, on 19 February, failed to
heal the divisions on the security issue, and the problem was left for
the Cabinet to resolve.[37]

On 2 March, the Cabinet officially accepted the view of the CID
that the Protocol was 'open to grave objections' but that a straight
rejection was likely to prolong the state of insecurity in Europe. Cecil
argued in favour of an innocuous Protocol together with a mutual
assistance arrangement between Britain, France and Germany; but
he received no support.[38]

The main discussion within the Cabinet centred round Chamberlain's proposal for a pact with France and Belgium, and the outcome
was never really in doubt as it seems that the Foreign Secretary was
supported only by Sir Laming Worthington-Evans, W.C. Bridgeman
and possibly Lord Eustace Percy. Churchill led the opposition, refusing to accept as an axiom that the fate of Britain was involved in
that of France. He pointed out that if Britain held air and sea
supremacy there was no reason why she could not stand alone even
if the Channel ports were in the hands of 'a vast hostile military
power' and suggested that Britain and France were no effective
counterpoise to Germany — such a grouping required the adhesion of
the United States or the Soviet Union. A British guarantee would
not induce a decisive modification of French policy — at best it would
lead to the evacuation of Cologne — and in any case it was doubtful
whether the British people would be willing to accept definite obligations to France. Britain should content herself with promoting
improved Franco–German relations and creating an atmosphere in
which Germany had the least possible incentive to 'renew the war'.
Once the two continental powers had composed their differences,
Britain might step in and negotiate a triple accord, but in the meantime the government should risk a breach with France. It seems that
Curzon, Hoare, Amery, Birkenhead, Cecil and Joynson-Hicks also
opposed a pact, using much the same arguments as Churchill.[39]

The outcome of the Cabinet discussion of 2 March was a realistic
compromise between the opposing views, based on Stresemann's
proposals of 20 January. Chamberlain drafted a rough formula to act
as a basis for further consideration:

> His Majesty's Government do not feel able to enter into a dual pact with
> France with or without Belgium. The question of a quadrilateral agree-
> ment between France, Germany, Great Britain, Belgium and, if possible
> with the accord of Italy, for mutual security (and for guaranteeing each
> other's frontiers in the West of Europe), stands on a different footing and
> might become a great assurance to the peace of Europe and lead to a rapid
> reduction of armaments . . ..[40]

Balfour, who had drafted a despatch to the League stating the
government's reasons for rejecting the Protocol, was asked to concert
with Chamberlain to revise the draft in order to attune it with the
policy outlined.[41]

A further Cabinet meeting was held on 4 March to clarify the situation. Chamberlain took the chair — the Prime Minister was visiting his mother who was seriously ill — and in the changed circumstances the more isolationist members of the government gained the upper hand in the debate. Accordingly, a weakened formula was adopted to serve as the basis of Chamberlain's instructions in his forthcoming discussions with Herriot; the Foreign Secretary's colleagues authorized him to say that they would 'use their best endeavours to secure that such a project [as the German proposal of 20 January] should not fail for want of British concurrence'. It was also decided to withdraw the sections dealing in detail with the difficulties of economic sanctions from the draft despatch to the League, Cecil having convinced his Cabinet colleagues that the inclusion of these sections would throw doubt on British intentions to enforce the Covenant. The draft was to be communicated to the Dominions, with whom the government had been in constant touch by telegram during the discussion on the Protocol, an Imperial Conference on this issue having proved impractical because of the prior commitments of Dominion Prime Ministers.[42]

The compromise formula on security, agreed upon to heal a dangerous split within the Cabinet, was actually more appropriate to European circumstances and more likely to facilitate disarmament than the alternative proposals of semi-isolation or alliance with France and Belgium. Chamberlain was quite correct in asserting that European stabilization depended on the removal of French security fears and the appeasement of Germany; but Churchill and Hoare were equally correct in suggesting that an alliance would reduce British bargaining power in European politics unless accompanied by a decisive modification of French policy on such issues as the enforcement of the peace treaty and disarmament. Stresemann's proposals offered a reasonable compromise — a hope that Germany would pursue a peaceful policy even in eastern Europe, and the prospect that France might accept a multilateral guarantee as a substitute for alliance with Britain. Such an agreement would have the added attraction for an intensely anti-Bolshevik British government of possibly weakening the ties between Germany and the Soviet Union; and it would, in any case, provide a foundation for a disarmament agreement in that it provided for mutual acceptance of the existing distribution of power within Europe.

Chamberlain saw Herriot in Paris on 6–7 March while *en route* to Rome for a meeting of the League Council, and after informing the French premier of the decision to reject the Protocol and a bilateral pact he made it clear that the German overtures offered the only hope of a solution of the security problem in which Britain could co-operate. At the same time, the inelasticity of the Foreign Secretary's instructions of 4 March encouraged the belief that the British contribution would be limited, and Herriot's immediate reactions were 'ominous of future trouble', half-threatening to prolong the occupation of Cologne. However, after Chamberlain had made a statement of British policy (on the lines of the Balfour despatch) at the League Council on 12 March and cleared up the Cabinet's intentions with regard to the extent of the British contribution in the proposed quadrilateral pact, the *Président du Conseil* seems to have accepted that an agreement on the basis of the German proposals was the best France could achieve in the circumstances.[43]

Effectively, Herriot's acceptance in principle of the German proposals was conditional on some form of British guarantee of the Franco-German frontier. And it was this condition that posed the greatest difficulty for the British Government. A substantial section of the Cabinet hoped that Chamberlain's instructions of 4 March might be interpreted so as to preclude an automatic commitment to France, and at an informal meeting of nine Cabinet members, called at short notice for the evening of 11 March it seemed that they had carried the day. Churchill, Birkenhead and Amery opposed any kind of pact, while Hoare and Salisbury suggested that a unilateral 'declaration of intent' was as far as Britain could go. Cecil and Bridgeman supported the concept of mutual guarantee as espoused by Chamberlain, but Baldwin and Crowe, in transmitting the conclusions of the meeting to Chamberlain, now in Geneva, made it clear that a firm and final decision in favour of a quadrilateral pact had not been taken.[44]

Chamberlain's reaction to events in London was trenchant. Complaining that he had been placed in 'a wholly false and absolutely untenable position', he threatened resignation unless his own personal position in favour of a mutual guarantee including Britain was adopted. Faced with this threat, Baldwin put his full weight behind the Foreign Secretary, and on 20 March the Cabinet fell into line.[45]

By this time, the main points of the prospective agreement had been settled between Chamberlain and Herriot. The Allies were to come to an understanding among themselves before entering into formal negotiations with the Germans, and Germany was to enter the League on the same conditions as the other powers. Britain would undertake no new obligations in respect of frontiers other than those of the Rhine — though existing treaties with regard to other frontiers would not be affected — and though the shortening of the occupation of the Rhineland could not be part of an agreement, it was essential to reach an amicable arrangement over the evacuation of Cologne.[46]

Seven months of hard bargaining and negotiations were to elapse before the principles of settlement agreed by Chamberlain and Herriot were consummated in the Locarno treaties of 16 October 1925. At various times during this period, the whole edifice of negotiation seemed likely to crumble; but under the guidance of Chamberlain, who acted as 'honest broker' between the French and the Germans, a settlement was finally reached — to the great relief of all concerned.

The most important of the Locarno treaties was the so-called 'Rhineland Pact', by which France and Belgium on the one hand and

Germany on the other recognized the inviolability of their common frontiers and agreed in no case to resort to war except in resistance to attack or invasion or in agreement with the League. Germany recognized the demilitarization of the Rhineland, and the whole Rhenish settlement was placed under the guarantee of Britain and Italy. If any of the parties alleged a violation of the agreement, the question was to be brought before the League Council, and if that body was satisfied that an infraction had taken place, the other parties would come immediately to the assistance of the violated power. In a case of 'flagrant aggression', however, the signatories would act against the indicted party without prior reference to the Council. Any disputes between Germany and France or Germany and Belgium that could not be settled by negotiation would be settled by arbitration, for which purpose the three powers signed detailed arbitration treaties. Germany signed similar conventions with Poland and Czechoslovakia, but refused to recognize her frontiers with those countries as definitive, a breach in the security system that was filled by a reaffirmation of the Franco–Czech and Franco–Polish alliances of 1924 and 1921 respectively and by an understanding among the Locarno signatories that action by France under these alliances would not constitute aggression against Germany. Germany was to join the League with a permanent seat on the Council, but her obligations under Article 16 of the Covenant would be conditioned by her geographical situation and position with regard to armaments.

The problem of disarmament was barely considered during the security negotiations of March–October 1925. However, in the final protocol of the Locarno Conference, the representatives of the governments concerned in the negotiations expressed their 'firm conviction' that the agreements would not only provide peace and security but would hasten the move towards an international convention under Article 8 of the Covenant.[47] The insertion stemmed originally from a suggestion made by Cecil on 28 May 1925, and so far as many of the delegates at Locarno were concerned it was probably an academic reference only; but it did have value for Cecil and the other advocates of disarmament within Britain in that it provided a further governmental commitment to the concept of disarmament.[48]

In general, the conclusion of the Locarno agreements was a triumph for British diplomacy, and for Chamberlain in particular. The Foreign Secretary had been the driving force in the negotiations and had upheld the Cabinet's conception of British interests to the point of almost rewriting the original French reply to the German memorandum of 20 January.[49] He had restricted British commitments to western Europe, ensured that the government retained complete freedom as to how it would fulfil its pledges, yet brought about a reconciliation between France and Germany. He had satisfied the French demand for security (or so it seemed) whilst taking a considerable step towards the appeasement of Germany. He had reconciled the Labour Party to a regional agreement, since the Rhineland Pact was not directed against any one power, and removed the threat of an intimate Russo–German alliance. He had healed the threatened breach in the Cabinet on the security issue.

France, too, had gained much from the Locarno treaties, for Germany had recognized the loss of Alsace–Lorraine and even accepted the demilitarization of the Rhineland. Britain and Italy had guaranteed the *status quo* on the Rhine, and Germany, whilst not renouncing her claims for revision of her eastern frontiers, had given assurances that she would pursue her objectives through peaceful channels. Moreover, France had retained the right to take action under her alliances with Poland and Czechoslovakia without risk of being determined an aggressor.

Germany also made substantial gains. The Anglo–Italian guarantee of her western frontiers gave some assurance against another occupation of the Ruhr, and the way had been left open for a future revision of the eastern frontiers. Yet whilst signing this agreement with the western powers, the Germans were able to maintain their link with Russia by pointing to an assurance made by the western powers at the time of signature that Germany would only be expected to take action under Article 16 of the Covenant to an extent that was compatible with her military situation and geographical position. This reassured the Soviets as to German goodwill; they had feared that the western powers were intending to build an anti-Soviet coalition with Germany in the vanguard.[50]

The Locarno treaties reflected a shift in the distribution of power within Europe in favour of Germany. Though the French still feared a German revival, the outcome of the Ruhr invasion had taught them that there was little profit in trying to enforce the peace treaty by coercion. In December 1922, the Poincaré government had felt strong enough to turn down a German proposal for a non-aggression pact; in 1925, Herriot and his successor at the Quai d'Orsay, Aristide Briand, were willing to accept such a pact, fortified by assurances of mutual assistance. French fears of a rejuvenated Germany now balanced German fears of the existing military superiority of France. The change in the distribution of power might have been minor — Germany was still an occupied country and in no position to renounce her obligations under the peace treaty — but it had a significant effect on the direction of French policy; the French government now tacitly accepted that a policy of coercion could not resolve the German problem.

At first sight, the conclusion of the Rhineland Pact seemed to offer great hopes for the future settlement of the German problem as it reflected an apparent willingness of the British, French and German leaders to adjust their policies in line with the configuration of power existing in 1925. The pact itself could not solve the problem, for Germany would grow stronger in the future, and as she did so she would step up her demands for a revision of the peace treaty; but if Britain and France continued to adjust to changes in the distribution of power, by consolidating their relationship on the one hand and by appeasing German grievances on the other, a peaceful long-term solution might be possible.

In practice, the twin problems of French security and the position of Germany within the international political system were to come together in the discussion of the disarmament problem for, in essence, the three issues were concerned with differing facets of the same question — the distribution of power on the European continent.

The great majority of continental powers, including France and Germany, recognized the importance of the disarmament problem and began to consider the means by which Article 8 of the Covenant might be implemented. Accordingly, in the calmer atmosphere of international relations following the signature of the Locarno treaties, disarmament discussions were to occupy a pre-eminent position on the international stage. During the period October 1925–May 1929 there were few crises or problems which diverted the attention of national policymakers from the arms limitation negotiations at Geneva; the time and environment seemed ripe for disarmament.[51]

5 The evolution of a policy
July 1925–April 1926

It was not until July 1925, eight months after taking office, that the Cabinet began to outline a disarmament policy. On 30 June, Cecil informed Baldwin that he could not justify his position in a government that had 'struck disarmament out of its international policy', and on the following day the Cabinet invited the Chancellor of the Duchy of Lancaster to explain his position in detail and make suggestions for positive action.[1]

Cecil adduced two main arguments in support of his case. He pointed out that Britain was under a treaty obligation to promote a general scheme of arms limitation — by the preamble to Part V of the Treaty of Versailles, the Allied note of 16 June 1919 and Article 8 of the Covenant — and that the German government was embarking on a campaign against the 'one-sided disarmament' of the treaty. And, more interestingly, he suggested that disarmament would increase British strength in relation to the other European powers since there was no danger of Britain being asked to reduce her 'already meagre' forces. He knew there were difficulties in the way of an agreement, but thought they were probably more apparent than real. He held that the main difficulty would be the attitude of the Soviet Union, believing that as long as the Soviets retained their existing level of armaments, Poland, Rumania, Czechoslovakia and the Baltic States would be forced to do the same; but even so, he thought a freezing of arms levels in eastern Europe would be preferable to nothing. As a first step, therefore, he suggested that the British delegates to the Sixth Assembly should be instructed to propose a 'searching international enquiry' into the whole question of disarmament.[2]

The Foreign Office was not impressed by Cecil's arguments and put heavy pressure on Chamberlain to oppose an international enquiry, at least until the 'Western Pact' had been concluded and its effect on Europe examined. G.H. Villiers, head of the Western Department, outlined the case in a minute of 13 July, and his arguments were taken up in detail by G.A. Mounsey, head of the Northern Department, and Sir William Tyrrell, who had become Permanent Secretary after Sir Eyre Crowe had died suddenly on 28 April 1925. They recalled that two earlier initiatives by Britain — the Treaty of Mutual Assistance and the Geneva Protocol — had failed, and insisted that it was unwise to make another while negotiations for a security agreement were still in progress. They agreed that reductions by France would help Britain, but thought there was no reason to think the French contemplated such reductions; and if Britain merely proposed that other states disarm, she would expose herself to charges of hypocrisy and bad faith.[3]

Chamberlain, as usual, adhered to the Foreign Office line. Declaring himself 'very much opposed' to the proposed instructions to the British delegates at Geneva, he asserted that an initiative such as suggested might lead to a revival of the Protocol by France. On 16 July, he drafted a cabinet paper which repeated, often verbatim, the arguments of the permanent officials, and he added that so long as the Soviet Union maintained large military forces, it might not be in Britain's interest for the continental powers to reduce their arms to the British level.[4]

Despite the efforts of Chamberlain and the Foreign Office, Cecil still hoped his proposals would gain acceptance in the Cabinet, and he counted on support from Churchill, who for financial reasons was urging a severe restriction of Britain's cruiser-building programme.[5] But on 22 July, when the Cabinet met to discuss the question, support was not forthcoming, and the Chancellor of the Duchy of Lancaster had to be content with the establishment of a government enquiry into the 'principles as to the best method to be adopted' when the time was ripe for another step. Hankey was asked to consult with the chiefs of staff and make recommendations on the scope and nature of the enquiry, and the Cabinet accepted his proposals on 29 July. It was agreed that an exploration of the technical side of disarmament was a necessary preliminary to an examination from the political side, and the services were invited to submit memoranda on technical possibilities which could be analysed by the Chiefs of Staff Committee or an *ad hoc* committee prior to discussion in the CID and Cabinet.[6]

The decisions taken on 29 July were crucial and were to have lasting effects on British policy. Most important, responsibility for the formulation of policy was effectively transferred from the elected representatives of the people to the service departments; by subordinating the political evaluation of disarmament to the technical, the government gave the services a *de facto* veto over any policy to which they took exception. Ministers missed perhaps the best opportunity they were to have of analysing the essential concepts of disarmament and preparing an overall plan and long-term strategy covering both foreign and military policy. They failed to work out the ultimate objectives of a disarmament policy, made no real evaluation of the possibility of using such a policy as a catalyst towards solving the German problem and barely even discussed the fundamental question of why Britain needed a disarmament policy.

Basically, ministers were sceptical of the very idea of disarmament.

They had grown up during the high noon of the Empire, when British power was unrivalled, and found it difficult to adjust to the changed circumstances of the 1920s. They might declare themselves in favour of disarmament in public, but in the confines of the Cabinet room they were reluctant to take decisions that would translate their words into action. Chamberlain remained under the influence of the Foreign Office and always doubted the practicability of a general disarmament conference, despite his willingness to 'contribute to its success'; he attached far more importance to other factors in preserving world peace. Churchill, Birkenhead and Amery remained Imperialists at heart and did their best to forestall any new initiatives towards arms limitation. Bridgeman and Worthington-Evans seem to have used all their influence to back the demands of their departments, with little thought to the possible consequences on the international scene. Hoare, apparently, was more concerned with building up the RAF or inducing France to reduce her air armaments than with promoting a scheme of general limitation. The only minister to believe implicitly in disarmament, and to equate the disarmament problem with the German problem, was Cecil — and even he admitted to Professor Gilbert Murray, a colleague in the League of Nations Union, in November 1925 that the practical implications of the policies he advocated required further detailed study.[7]

Nevile Butler, private secretary to Ronald McNeill, summed up the official British position in a note of August 1925. The government was in favour of reducing armaments to the lowest point consistent with safety and fulfilment of international obligations and had taken the greatest interest in the 'sustained examination' of the disarmament problem by the League; but further progress was impossible without security and as 'universal' security pacts had proved unacceptable, new attempts at arms reductions should be deferred until the negotiations for the Rhineland Pact had been completed. Britain herself had already reduced her arms to the lowest possible limit.[8]

Other powers did not appreciate this policy of exclaiming in favour of disarmament whilst being unwilling to take steps to secure its realization and, at the Sixth Assembly, the Netherlands and Hungary demanded that preparatory work for a disarmament conference be undertaken immediately. France and most of the minor powers backed the demand and Britain was forced to reconsider her *non possumus* attitude. Chamberlain was aghast and minuted: 'This is folly .... Busybodies want to do "something" and don't know what.'[9] He doubted the sincerity of the French, and was convinced that their support of the Dutch-Hungarian proposals was little more than a sop for public and international opinion and an attempt to forestall a possible American initiative. Although he tried to shelve the proposals, he soon realized he could do nothing to resist them, for resistance would have brought accusations of hypocrisy and bad faith.[10] On 19 September, the Assembly adopted an amended version of the Dutch-Hungarian proposals, and six days later it decided to entrust the preparatory study to the Co-ordination

Commission, the successor to the Temporary Mixed Commission. The Committee of the Council was asked to look into the organization, composition and agenda of the proposed 'Preparatory Committee', and it was hoped that work could begin on the study itself as soon as the Council Committee had reported to the December meeting of the Council.

The Assembly's decisions prompted the government to hasten its disarmament discussions and formulate a skeleton policy before the convening of the Council Committee. Despite the doubts of some members of the government, the establishment of the Preparatory Committee more or less obliged this action. Cecil was well aware of this, and took the opportunity to press for a forward policy. Reiterating his belief that Britain had nothing to lose and 'almost everything' to gain by disarmament, he condemned his colleagues for the 'almost entirely negative' attitude of the British delegation at the Sixth Assembly and urged them to be in the vanguard of the disarmament movement in the future.[11] Chamberlain was more cautious, but he realized that Britain had been defeated at the Assembly and wanted to ensure that it did not happen again. He continued to doubt the advisability of setting up the Preparatory Committee — it was 'not really the best way of attacking the [disarmament] problem' — but thought it could do no great harm provided it did not lose touch with realities. The Foreign Secretary was convinced that British advice would carry weight at an international conference and thought it imperative that Britain know clearly what she wanted and exactly what she was prepared to do. So he asked the Cabinet to instruct the service departments to continue their analysis of disarmament in order that the British representatives on the Council and the Committee of the Council could be given a definite policy.[12]

The main question at hand was not so much what measure of disarmament was practicable, but what subjects should be referred to the Preparatory Committee. The Cabinet decided to submit the problem to the CID, and on 17 November the latter body set up a subcommittee to investigate the matter. Cecil was placed in charge of the enquiry and all departments even remotely connected with disarmament were asked to send delegates: the Foreign Office, the service departments, the Treasury and the Dominions and India Offices.[13]

The establishment of the new sub-committee had a mixed reception. The Treasury — as distinct from Churchill — was enthusiastic and declared that arms limitation was so vital for the future that, provided the vital requirements of Imperial security were met, Britain should be prepared to take 'some risks' to secure 'proportionate reductions in the armaments of other nations'. But the service departments and Foreign Office were openly sceptical, if not critical. The general staff even tried to prove that there was no peaceful means of regulating the expansion and contraction of competing states, asserting that nations had to 'rise and fall by their strength and weakness'.[14]

In a long paper on the subject, the generals declared that all schemes of disarmament had the fundamental defect of perpetuating the *status quo*. They pointed out that Britain had barely sufficient forces for maintaining internal order and garrisoning overseas territories and suggested that her correct role at the Preparatory Committee would be to avoid playing a prominent part in discussions on land disarmament and to make no positive suggestions. They thought the chief practicable expression Britain could give to the 'ideal of disarmament' was the development of regional pacts, which might lead to regional disarmament; they believed that, if the Western Pact was ratified, France, Belgium and Italy might disarm to a certain degree, followed by the 'Central European Powers' — presumably the Little Entente and Poland, considering that the other powers in central Europe had been disarmed compulsorily after the First World War. It was an interesting argument, more so as earlier in the same paper the staff had concluded that for disarmament to be practicable it had to be universal![15]

The generals were more concerned with possible difficulties than with practical suggestions. They put forward only one definite proposal — the abolition of conscription — otherwise they restricted themselves almost entirely to criticizing the various methods of disarmament that had been put forward by others. They could see no criteria by which the armed forces of various countries could be related to each other, except possibly 'risk', which nations would not allow outsiders to assess, and thought that other methods of disarmament posed similar problems. They argued that limitation of national defence expenditure was difficult because of differences in exchange rates and prices, the need for comparable budgets and the possibility of 'camouflaging' military spending; and they asserted that no closer supervision over armaments than the supervision normally exercised by military attachés would be acceptable.[16]

The evidence appears to suggest that the staff's proposals were designed deliberately for the advantage of Britain, with little regard to the consequences for disarmament. The generals offered no real hope of arms limitation and put forward their one definite suggestion — the abolition of conscription — in the knowledge that, in the past, it had been rejected consistently by France, Italy and many other powers. The introduction of volunteer armies in all countries would have benefitted Britain considerably — at the expense of her continental neighbours.

The air staff were almost as pessimistic about disarmament as the military. In a detailed analysis of what they considered to be the technical possibilities, they declared that a general limitation of air power could be made effective only as regards dirigibles, unless all aviation was abolished. They thought there would be great problems in assessing an initial ratio for each country and believed that the mere existence of civil aviation made any limitation of military aviation extremely difficult. If arbitrary rules were applied to military aviation, the powers would merely subsidize and increase civil aviation, which it was impracticable to limit because of the possibilities for evasion. The staff thought bilateral and multilateral agreements were the most hopeful means of securing air disarmament and suggested that the basis of the agreements should be the limitation of first-line, home-based aircraft as this would restrict a nation's striking power at the beginning of the war.[17]

Sir Hugh Trenchard and his colleagues held that other methods of limitation would pose considerable difficulties. They believed that a restriction of aircraft factories would compromise the development of civil aviation and that a limitation of the number of pilots or technical personnel could be countered by an increase in the number of civil pilots or personnel. They did admit that a limitation of aircraft by horse-power or lift tonnage might be imposed, but they argued that in time of war more powerful engines could be substituted for the original, and that, in any case, the difficulties of inspection and control would be prohibitive. They were opposed to carrier-based and overseas machines being included in an agreement, since it would prevent Britain from following a policy of 'substitution', of keeping the peace in outlying parts of the Empire by relying on air power rather than the more expensive ground forces; and, for similar reasons, they were opposed to schemes for budgetary limitation.[18]

It appears that the proposals of the air staff, like those of the general staff, were framed to benefit Britain rather than facilitate general disarmament. The suggested exclusion of carrier-based and overseas machines seems to have been designed to enable Britain to build up her air power overseas, leaving continental powers at a disadvantage, while it had always been inconceivable that powers such as France would agree to a limitation of military aviation if civil aviation remained unrestricted. Moreover, the air staff were adamant that the size of the British Home Defence Force should be the approved limit of fifty-two squadrons; they were not opposed to considering a limitation of the rate of expansion of the force, but only on condition that France would reduce her existing air armaments: at that time the French had 1,275 first-line aircraft as against Britain's 643.[19]

Hankey, as Secretary to the CID, used his not inconsiderable influence to reinforce the anti-disarmament case. On 6 August, he sent a private paper to Balfour, Cecil and the chiefs of staff suggesting that a prolonged period of peace might lead to moral degeneracy, and in the following month he drafted a CID paper that was critical of the very concept of disarmament.[20] He was convinced that war was an intrinsic part of human existence, and saw a direct relationship between a decline in 'military spirit' and a decline in civilization; he deplored the loss of military spirit in Britain, and regretted 'No longer does the flower of our youth flock, as it did before the War, to become officers of Services which are exposed to the full brunt of the League of Nations' axe.'[21] He believed an allegation by Lord Riddell that, in some parts of the country, history texts in primary schools taught 'nothing but internationalism' and were 'contemptuous of patriotism as we understand it'.[22] His accusations were absurd, but they were typical of a mentality that was prevalent in both government and the Civil Service at the time.

It was with few illusions that Cecil accepted the chairmanship of the Disarmament Committee. He commented to a Geneva correspondent 'We are in for a very difficult and troublesome job in trying to secure disarmament ... The forces against us are very strong. They comprise all the bureaucracies, military and civil, all the old feudal feeling ... and perhaps most important of all certain very big and powerful financial interests.'[23] It was an accusation the Chancellor of the Duchy of Lancaster was to repeat many times in the next two years. But in the meantime he sought to conciliate his opponents and convince them he was a realist rather than an incautious radical. On 24 August, he wrote to Hankey suggesting there was no danger of Britain disarming too quickly under a general scheme, and he pointed out that, far from being asked to reduce her army, it was more likely that she would be asked to increase it. His aims and hopes were far from revolutionary; indeed, he asserted that he would be delighted if Britain's efforts over the next few years resulted in a slight reduction of the French and Russian armies, and possibly those of the other Slav powers, together with Britain's general agreement not to expand for a period. He believed that, unless a general scheme was negotiated, there was a danger that public opinion might force western European governments into making reckless reductions.[24]

The first meetings of the Disarmament Committee, which convened on 19 November to draft instructions for the British representatives on the Committee of the Council, were characterized by the narrow and negative attitude of the service delegates. The main task was to draw up a questionnaire for consideration at Geneva, and the service delegates consistently opposed the inclusion of questions on types of disarmament they did not favour. They were especially adamant that there should be no questions on supervision or control, and were vehemently opposed to a study of war potential. Consequently, the draft questionnaire that finally emerged was as notable for its omissions as its contents — in particular, there was no reference to war potential, supervision or the limitation or regulation of methods of warfare.[25]

The main questions recommended by the committee were: was it practicable to limit the ultimate war strength of a country, or had any measures of disarmament to be confined to peace strength? By what methods was it possible to measure the armaments of one country against those of others, based on such factors as numbers, period of service, equipment and expenditure? On what principle would it be possible to draw up a scale of armaments permissible to the various states, taking into account particularly population, resources and geographical position? Admitting that disarmament depended on security, to what extent was regional disarmament possible in return for regional security? Was there any, and if so, what, device by which civil and military aircraft or their components could be distinguished? If not, how could the value of civil aircraft be computed in estimating the air strength of a country? And would the universal abandonment of conscription operate as an effectual limitation on armaments without other measures?

Despite the omissions in the questionnaire, the Cabinet and CID received the committee's report with a marked lack of enthusiasm. Balfour, apparently influenced by Hankey's August memorandum, even suggested that the great majority of the questions were 'quite insoluble'. But the majority of the Cabinet, although sceptical of disarmament, agreed with Chamberlain that Cecil should be allowed to go to Geneva and do his best to 'reduce abstract discussions into practical results'.[26]

It was stressed in the CID that the discussions of the Preparatory Committee should be limited to peacetime armaments, with no probes into war capacity. But at the Committee of the Council, which held six meetings between 3 and 7 December, the French pressed strongly for a wider study; they wanted to ensure that the industrial, economic and demographic potential of Germany was taken into account in any agreement. Joseph Paul-Boncour, the French representative, put forward an alternative questionnaire to the British, and after some discussion a number of his points were accepted. He agreed to drop the French questionnaire, but only on condition that a number of additional questions were added to the British. These were: what was to be understood by the term 'armaments'? What was to be understood by the expression 'reduction and limitation of armaments'? Could the reduction of armaments be promoted by ensuring that Article 16 would be brought quickly into operation as soon as an act of aggression had been committed? Could there be said to be 'offensive' and 'defensive' armaments? And was it possible to attach military value to commercial fleets?[27]

On 12 December, the Council approved the final questionnaire and agreed to call the body charged with the preparatory study 'The Preparatory Commission for the Disarmament Conference'. The composition of the commission was limited to members of the Council and certain states that were considered to have a special position as regards the disarmament problem — Germany, the Soviet Union, America, Bulgaria, Finland, the Netherlands, Poland, Rumania and Yugoslavia — and a definite, though flexible, mode of procedure was drawn up for the new body. A scheme was worked out for co-operation with the Permanent Advisory Commission of the League of Nations on questions relating to the military aspects of disarmament and with a Joint Commission composed of members of the technical organizations of the League and International Labour Office on the economic aspects. The Commission was also empowered to call in outside 'experts' if it saw fit.

The first session of the Preparatory Commission was scheduled for

15 February 1926, but it was postponed until 18 May mainly because of a Russo–Swiss dispute. The Soviets refused to come to Geneva until the Swiss had paid reparation for the assassination of the Soviet observer to the Lausanne Conference of 1923.

During the postponement, the Disarmament Committee reassembled to carry out its examination of disarmament in greater detail, and between 6 January and 26 April 1926 it held seven meetings concerning policy at Geneva.[28] But the obstructive attitude of the services made initial progress slow, and Cecil complained to Baldwin that: 'The Admiralty and the War Office almost frankly regard the whole thing as nonsense, and dangerous nonsense at that'.[29] He thought that if the War Office was taking the question seriously, it would have a regular section considering what plans were possible. He wanted at least one officer in the section to be constantly available for service at Geneva — at the Committee of the Council he had had to put up with 'a charming individual, Colonel Wavell, who is unfortunately totally ignorant of even the elements of the subject'.[30] Cecil emphasized that cogent arguments were needed to support British views, otherwise events at Geneva might pass out of control, and he asked the Prime Minister to galvanize the service departments into action. He enquired whether it was impossible to convince 'people like Bridgeman and Worthington-Evans' that the Germans were merely looking for an excuse to rearm, and looked forward to the disarmament discussions proceeding more rapidly in future.[31]

Consideration of the League questionnaire took up most of the committee's time, though the answers to some of the questions were thought to be almost self-evident. There was quick agreement on the definition of 'reduction and limitation of armaments', and it was accepted almost without discussion that war potential could not be limited and that measures of disarmament should be confined to peace strength. Armaments themselves were defined as the forces immediately available on the outbreak of war and the *matériel* maintained for their use. The question of 'offensive' and 'defensive' armaments was passed over quickly, as it was clear that, except for certain fixed defences, all armaments could be either offensive or defensive, according to circumstances.[32]

Perhaps the most important discussion concerned the standards by which the armaments of one nation could be measured against those of another. The general staff originally suggested that it was impossible to define any standards, on the grounds that a country with a large war potential could start a war with forces merely capable of defending the national territory but the Director of Military Operations and Intelligence, General Sir J.T. Burnett-Stuart, admitted to the committee that this view was wrong — land armaments could be measured by the number of effectives, together with the amount of equipment appropriate to their use. The staff even conceded it was possible to assess a 'reasonable equipment' for any army of a defined size, and they drew up a scale of armament appropriate to a force of

100,000 men — though as the scale was far in excess of the armament of the German army, and even, in some respects, the French, it was decided to make no reference to the figures outside the committee.[33]

The Disarmament Committee soon agreed that it was impossible to devise a coefficient for calculating the armaments of a power on the basis of population, resources, geographical situation or the other factors mentioned in the questionnaire. Burnett-Stuart argued that the factors would settle themselves if agreement was reached on other points, and Cecil acquiesced. The War Office believed the only way to arrive at a ratio was to ask each country to formulate its own requirements, taking the compulsory disarmament of Germany and the other defeated powers of the First World War as a datum level, and to submit these 'requirements' to international examination. Cecil liked the idea and agreed to incorporate it in the committee's report. It was agreed that a suggestion made in December 1925 by Sir Arthur Salter, that a ratio should be based on the armaments of 1913, should be rejected, as the military and political situation had undergone an almost complete transformation since the First World War.[34]

The examination of the air section of the questionnaire took very little time, as the committee adopted most of the air staff's proposals with little or no amendment. It was quickly agreed that air armaments should be considered as a separate entity at Geneva because units earmarked for army and navy co-operation could always be used as part of an independent air arm; and it was accepted with very little discussion that the most practical standard by which forces could be compared was that of personnel and aircraft in first-line units of metropolitan (home-based) forces. The committee thought there was no device by which civil and military aircraft or their components could be distinguished and that there was no practical means of computing the military value of civil aircraft — though it was suggested that it might be possible to make an arbitrary distinction between military and civil units solely to facilitate disarmament.[35]

The question of the efficacy of Article 16 caused many problems as there was some divergence of view between Cecil and his colleagues. The Treasury and Board of Trade believed that application of Article 16 in the absence of the United States would be impossible, and that difficulties would still arise unless the Americans were benevolently neutral, whilst Cecil thought a 'universal' application of the blockade by the League would have positive results. The Chancellor of the Duchy of Lancaster agreed that it would be intolerable for one country to be required to take action alone and suggested that a blockade would only be imposed on the understanding that no country would continue unless assured that the other states were going to co-operate. He proposed, therefore, that the Board of Trade and Treasury examine the resolutions of the Second Assembly concerning the application of Article 16 to see whether a scheme on these lines would remove the objections to the sanctions clauses.[36]

After considering the matter carefully, the two economic departments agreed that the 1921 proposals clarified issues and offered lines of advance. But they still believed that the proposals did not solve the practical difficulties of applying Article 16 without the co-operation of the United States. The departments argued that economic pressure had to be enforced simultaneously and uniformly by all members of the League, otherwise countries applying sanctions would hurt themselves more than the aggressor, and that, if greater precision of Article 16 was required, it would be necessary to draw up a list of measures that all members would undertake to apply. This might include severance of diplomatic (and subsequently consular) relations and the prohibition of exports of *matériel*, leading up to a suspension of direct postal, telegraphic and telephonic communications. Financial sanctions were more difficult to control, but might be enforced indirectly through the stoppage of communications or through financial aid to states which were victims of aggression. The League should consider a general declaration of war only if this series of measures failed to coerce an aggressor into accepting conciliation.[37]

Cecil thought the Board of Trade and Treasury underrated the effects of united action by the League, but had no real objection to their proposals, which were adopted by the Disarmament Committee with few amendments. The committee also accepted the view of the departments that the proposals should be considered only in exchange for disarmament, and it was agreed that every effort should be made at Geneva to avoid taking on new commitments. It was further agreed that it was desirable to secure a stipulation by which states would agree not to claim damages from League members or other signatories of the disarmament convention in respect of any action in conformity with a decision or recommendation by the Council to apply Article 16.[38]

In addition to answering the questionnaire, the committee investigated a number of other disarmament proposals. Chief of these was the question of supervision, which had been raised by the Spanish delegate at the Committee of the Council. Cecil knew the French were likely to demand more effective supervision than that of attachés, and he thought Britain must face the question as to whether there should be some means of investigation if well-supported charges were laid against a country. He agreed with the services that the objections to permanent and compulsory supervision were overwhelming, but he believed there were cases when an impartial enquiry was necessary and that there could be no objection to an enquiry if it was carried out with the consent of the 'accused'. But, despite Cecil's promptings, the services remained adamant that any form of arms limitation had to be dependent on good faith alone. The general staff thought commissions of investigation would be 'gravely detrimental' to the national interest and that, in any case, other countries were unlikely to accept them of their own free will. The

Admiralty thought investigation might reveal plans for defence and information concerning secret devices, patents, apparatus and ingredients. The Air Staff believed a system of control would merely cause friction; they had visions of an international inspectorate descending on Paddington goods yard, causing 'the gravest effect on the civil community'. The committee could only agree that in cases where a breach of agreements was alleged, the Council should enquire into the matter and appoint a committee of investigation if the indicted party invited it.[39]

The other main question examined by the Disarmament Committee was the problem of budgetary limitation. The service departments were sceptical of its practicality, but, in two convincing and authoritative memoranda, the Treasury argued that, although actual limitation would be 'very difficult' because of the different practices of different countries, a comparison of annual expenditures was both possible and desirable although it would be necessary to define the categories of arms to be covered so that statements of estimates and expenditure could be sent to the League in a prescribed form. It would be useless to limit expenditure on such items as provisions, fuel and mechanical transport as these could be requisitioned in time of war, and on clothing, stationery, medical and dental supplies and miscellaneous small stores and equipment because of the difficulty of checking; but it would be useful to have information on guns and gun-carriages, small arms, ammunition, tanks, anti-gas stores and miscellaneous ordnance stores. The operation of the scheme would depend on the good faith of governments, but it would be difficult for any nation to send deliberately erroneous statements to the League continuously and on any large scale. The committee agreed, and adopted the Treasury's proposals.[40]

Considered as a whole, the Disarmament Committee's recommendations were neither numerous nor particularly radical, though certainly they were an improvement on the suggestions of the previous November. The air proposals had been framed by the air staff in October 1925 with the apparent intention of promoting British interests rather than facilitating general disarmament; and the supervision proposals were so weak as to be unacceptable to many continental powers. The most constructive proposals were those of the Treasury and Board of Trade, who to some extent admitted that Britain might have to undertake new commitments in order to facilitate disarmament; and the most radical was the suggestion by the general staff that an arms agreement should be based on the 'datum level' of existing German disarmament.

Despite the omissions and weaknesses of the Disarmament Committee's report — for example on the regulation of methods of warfare — the CID thought many of the suggestions were too dangerous for presentation at Geneva. At a meeting on 19 April, Chamberlain secured the deletion of the clause taking German disarmament as a datum level for other powers by asserting that there was never any intention of France disarming in proportion to her continental neighbour; and he also compelled the reconsideration of the proposal for financial assistance to states who were victims of aggression on the grounds that more research into its implications was needed. Worthington-Evans and Philip Lloyd-Greame managed to eliminate the plan for 'extending' sanctions to the suspension of postal, telegraphic and telephonic communications - they thought such measures would stifle trade relations — and Hoare secured the rejection of a limitation of air personnel, even though this put Britain in the rather hypocritical position of advocating a limitation of military effectives but not air effectives. On 28 April, the Cabinet gave general approval to the report as amended by the CID.[41]

The emasculation of the original draft report epitomized the attitude of a government that had little interest in disarmament. The programme adopted for presentation at the Preparatory Commission was one of offering a few diluted proposals and opposing or avoiding others, though, intrinsically, this had been almost inevitable since the decision of 29 July 1925 to subordinate the political evaluation of disarmament to the military. The CID and Cabinet took decisions on each limitation proposal individually, with little regard to the effect on other proposals, and gave no real consideration to a plan encompassing both foreign and military policy that might help solve the German problem. The government relied on the old logic of making special arrangements to meet special needs — the rationale behind the rejection of the Protocol and the negotiation of the Locarno Treaty — without discussing whether a policy based on this principle offered any hope of solving the problems involved in disarmament. This approach to disarmament might be satisfactory in the short term, when Germany was in no position to make extravagant claims, but it was almost certain to prove inadequate in the long run, when German power had been restored. Sooner or later, Germany would claim 'equality of rights' and threaten to rearm if the other powers refused to move in the direction of greater equality; and if an arms race was to be prevented and European peace maintained, the other powers, Britain included, would have to adjust to the new configuration of power by making concessions.

General disarmament demanded a comprehensive agreement, not a piecemeal attack on a few specific issues; and in adopting a piecemeal approach to the subject, the government conveniently evaded the real issue involved — the German problem. The government preferred to concentrate on defending Britain's more immediate interests — the security of the Empire and the protection of trade routes — and made no attempt to prepare schemes whose objective was the reconciliation of French and German interests, the main problem that would face the eventual Disarmament Conference. Only Cecil equated the disarmament problem with the German problem.

6 International technical discussions
January 1926–March 1927

Cecil was in one of his despondent moods at the beginning of 1926. He recognized that he was in no real position to influence general policy towards the League and was not very hopeful about the possibility of disarmament, lamenting to Gilbert Murray that the Labour Party was insufficiently keen in its support of the concept.[1] However, his feelings seem to have been assuaged to some extent when Chamberlain officially put him in charge of the disarmament question with very wide powers. The Foreign Secretary believed that the handling of the question required the closest correlation with foreign policy and, to ensure that Cecil was kept in the fullest possession of the political as well as the military aspects of the problem, instructed the Foreign Office to pass all papers dealing with disarmament to his Cabinet colleague as a matter of routine.[2] It was a notable reversal of his previous attitude towards Cecil's involvement in the formulation and direction of policy, and a move which suggested an increasing confidence in Cecil's abilities — possibly as a result of the Chancellor of the Duchy of Lancaster's support during the negotiations leading to the Locarno treaties, and more especially during the 'informal Cabinet' of 11 March 1925.

Certainly Chamberlain agreed with Cecil on two fundamental points concerning disarmament policy: that a 'real effort' should be made towards securing a general limitation, and that, if the effort failed, there was nothing Britain could do to prevent Germany rearming. Although stressing that Germany's disarmament under Part

V of the Treaty of Versailles was *sans conditions*, the Foreign Secretary observed that, law or no law, treaty or no treaty, no power on earth could keep Germany at her existing level of armaments indefinitely unless a measure of general disarmament was effected.[3]

There were some questions on which Chamberlain and Cecil found they disagreed. The Foreign Secretary was opposed to the contention that the German standard of disarmament should be applied proportionately to all countries, whereas Cecil believed that, ultimately, it would be difficult to maintain that the armaments allowable to one member of the League should not be allowable to another. Further, Chamberlain was adamant that the disarmament clauses of the peace treaty would remain binding even if the powers failed to agree on a general limitation, while Cecil doubted the validity of the Foreign Secretary's interpretation and pointed out that the former Allies were under at least a very strong moral obligation to disarm.[4]

The question of Germany's obligations under Part V of the Treaty of Versailles was of more than academic interest, for it was certain that the German delegation at the Preparatory Commission would endeavour to use the preamble to Part V to claim a revision of the military clauses if general disarmament was not carried out. Indeed, the strength and apparent reasonableness of the contention was such that the French government put pressure on the British not only to reject the probable German claim, but to insist that Germany's role on the Preparatory Commission should be limited essentially to one of providing information concerning her own disarmament experiences. The demand provoked no response from London.[5]

The inaugural session of the Preparatory Commission, held at Geneva between 18 and 26 May 1926, was mainly formal in character and focused on the appointment of two sub-commissions, 'A' and 'B', which were charged with undertaking a detailed technical analysis of military and non-military questions respectively. Originally, it has been anticipated that technical questions would be referred to the Permanent Advisory Commission and a Joint Commission, in line with the Council's recommendations, but the scheme was dropped because the United States' government thought the bodies in question were too closely acquainted with the League and therefore 'untouchable' in the eyes of American opinion.[6] Thereafter, Sub-Commission 'A' held three long sessions, which lasted until 5 November 1926, and Sub-Commission 'B', which preferred to delegate its work, met at somewhat infrequent intervals, culminating in a final session on 17 March 1927.[7] Twenty states took part in the substantive discussions — the states originally invited, with the exception of the Soviet Union (still in dispute with the Swiss government) and two states invited later, Argentina and Chile.

The first tasks of the Preparatory Commission concerned administrative problems such as the election of officers, compilation of agenda and apportionment of work, and most points at issue were easily settled. It was quickly agreed, for example, that the Council questionnaire should be augmented by a series of questions covering chemical warfare, exchange of information and supervision, and it was also accepted that the two sub-commissions should investigate only the technical aspect of problems, reserving the political aspect for discussion in the full commission. However, on 22 May, at a meeting of the commission's drafting committee, the chief French representative, Paul-Boncour, introduced concrete proposals which effectively would have given precedence to issues of security. He thereby precipitated a major clash with the British delegation.

Paul-Boncour's instructions, in keeping with the advice of the *Conseil Supérieur de la Défense Nationale*, were to maintain the link between security and disarmament. Accordingly, he tabled a number of suggestions for the improvement of international security under the auspices of the League. The Council, Paul-Boncour insisted, should be asked to investigate 'methods and regulations' which would facilitate its meeting in the shortest possible time in the case of war or threat of war and expedite any decisions concerned with enforcing the obligations of the Covenant. Sub-Commission 'A' would be instructed to investigate procedures allowing the rapid drafting of recommendations regarding the implementation of military assistance under Article 16, also measures that might be taken to prevent the development or preparation of hostilities in the case of previously notified conflicts. Sub-Commission 'B' would be instructed to investigate a number of questions concerned with the improvement of telegraphic and telephonic communications to the League, measures of financial and economic aid to states who were victims of aggression, the composition and procedure of committees for the supply and allocation of resources and the means by which such committees could keep up-to-date information regarding the economic deficiencies and possible needs of states that were attacked.[8]

In support of his proposals, Paul-Boncour argued that it was essential for states to be in a position to form an estimate of available security guarantees in order to calculate acceptable measures of disarmament, and that there was a need to render the potential war strengths of nations sufficiently comparable to take into account the admitted deficiencies of the less well-endowed members of international society.[9] But the chief authors of British policy suspected that the real reason for the sudden advancement of the French memorandum was a desire on the part of Paul-Boncour to deflect the Geneva discussions onto the principles, if not the essence, of the Geneva Protocol. Cecil felt that the production of the document had imperilled the whole proceedings at Geneva — at one point he even believed that the French were trying to break up the Preparatory Commission — and he sought assurances that a revival of the Protocol was not intended.[10] Chamberlain, in obvious exasperation at the apparent French ingratitude over his efforts to help them in previous months, felt compelled to minute:

The French are sawing at the branch on which they sit. Do they want our assistance under the Locarno Treaty to be defined by the least common denominator of our effort in every conceivable international dispute? If they press these questions, we can only answer with the minimum obligatory on us (whatever that is) in some conceivable dispute in which we have no interest or next to none.[11]

The Foreign Secretary agreed with Cecil that a major portion of the French proposals was inadmissible and thought that their discussion within the Preparatory Commission would entail the postponement of measures that might be immediately practicable.[12]

The possibility of adjourning the Geneva proceedings was mooted, but it soon became clear that the French memorandum was little more than a *ballon d'essai* aimed at gauging the reaction of the other powers. As early as 23 May, Paul-Boncour rejected a suggestion that the proposals envisaged a return to the Protocol or that they amounted to a directive to Sub-Commission 'A' to draw up a kind of military convention for applying Article 16; and he assured Cecil that the purpose of the proposals was to secure rapid and effective action on the part of the League only after the Council had previously decided to implement the sanctions article. The principal French delegate also apparently realized that there were serious inconveniences in asking the Preparatory Commission to consider new means of making the security guarantees of the Covenant more effective, as some members of the commission — and by no means the least important — were non-members of the League, and so he readily fell in with a suggestion made by Cecil that an amended version of the proposals be forwarded to the Council for referral to appropriate organs of the League, notably the Permanent Advisory Commission and the Joint Commission. Proposals by the Polish and Finnish delegations regarding regional and financial assistance were dealt with in a similar manner, and the Preparatory Commission had overcome its first major crisis; but it had done so merely by transferring issues to other bodies.[13]

In elaborating the Council questionnaire, the Preparatory Commission took a number of major preliminary decisions. Of crucial importance, it resolved that it would not be practicable at that time to limit the ultimate war strength of a country and that the armaments to be maintained in each state could not be determined solely on the basis of mathematical considerations; and, implicitly, it was accepted that it was impossible to draw up a scale of armaments for each country based on factors such as population, resources and geographical situation. Nevertheless, the importance of resources in the assessment of national arms levels was conceded, and the two sub-commissions were asked to undertake a thorough examination of the whole question of war potential and its constituent elements.[14]

On 28 May, Sub-Commission 'A', which comprised the service experts of the various delegations, commenced discussion of the numerous questions on its agenda. Progress was slow, however, and Cecil, although impressed by the seriousness with which the discussions were being approached by the delegates, began to investigate means by which the labours of the commission might be hastened. Only five days after the commencement of deliberations, he asked the Cabinet to consider attaching more senior officers to the British delegation on the grounds that they would be in a position to take decisions on technical matters without reference to home authorities. Chamberlain 'warmly supported' the move; but it came to nothing when the service ministers explained the difficulties in sparing senior general staff officers for the comparatively long periods of time involved and the dangers of authorizing even senior officers to take decisions without consulting London. A week later, however, the government took the positive step of agreeing to send a junior War Office minister, Lord Onslow, to Geneva to take control of the proceedings in the technical committees in an attempt to co-ordinate the activities of the British delegation and generally speed matters.[15]

Certainly the delegates on Sub-Commission 'A' evinced a military temperament. The powers quickly aligned themselves into two major groupings — one led by Britain, the other by France — and the two blocs began to treat questions at issue like successive lines of trenches in a dialectical battle, first at the level of definition and then at the levels of comparability and limitation.[16] The United States, Germany and Sweden, together with Spain and the Netherlands, gave Britain general support on most questions, while France received the backing of her east European allies together with Belgium and Italy. Three major divergences of opinion arose at the theoretical level, concerning the definition of armaments, the delineation of limitable armaments and the interdependence of the three main branches of the services (land, sea and air); and four arose at the practical, regarding land *matériel*, air armaments, supervision and trained reserves.

On each of the main issues, the representatives of Britain and France developed technical arguments which reflected the underlying political and strategic differences between the two states. The French government's conception of disarmament, like the British, was based firmly on security requirements, and the evident objective of the French service 'experts' was to prevent, as far as possible, the erosion of France's existing military superiority over Germany.[17] While Britain, an island state, remained relatively immune from the threat of an attack by a major power, France was potentially vulnerable to a military upsurge on the part of her eastern neighbour. There was no immediate threat to French security, but French ministers were well aware that their country had been invaded from the east twice within living memory.

The first major divergence of opinion between the British and French delegations concerned the definition of armaments. This was an exceedingly important question as the specification of 'limitable' armaments was dependent on the overall definition, and each power wished to manoeuvre for position when the sub-commission considered the seemingly more awkward problems of comparability, reduction and limitation. The British government had framed its definition with a view to excluding a limitation of war potential whilst making it feasible to limit immediately mobilizable armaments such as trained reserves; similarly, the French, in an apparent attempt to exclude a limitation of trained reserves and other immediately mobilizable resources, insisted that a distinction should be made between peacetime armaments (defined as those which could be used *without* measures of mobilization) and ultimate war strength, the former category being limitable and the second not. A deadlock on the issue seemed inevitable until, on 11 June, a compromise was arrived at by designating three categories of armament and leaving governments to decide the categories that were limitable. The classification was: forces in service in peacetime; forces prepared for war in time of peace, such as reserves of *matériel* and trained personnel; and ultimate war strength.[18]

Officials at the Foreign Office deplored the fact that ultimate war forces had been included in the definition, and tried to convince Chamberlain that the Geneva delegation would find it difficult to carry out instructions on the question of 'limitable' armaments.[19] On this occasion, however, the Foreign Secretary rejected the advice of his departmental colleagues, having been persuaded by Cecil that the delegation had not been manoeuvred into an untenable position.[20] Indeed, Chamberlain seems to have satisfied himself that, hitherto, the Foreign Office had been too cautious in its approach to the disarmament problem. In the coming months he was to exercise a less stringent supervision over the activities of the British representatives. Implicitly, he placed a greater trust in the judgement and abilities of the Chancellor of the Duchy of Lancaster.

Despite the nominal resolution of the problem on 11 June, the question of armaments' definition was to erupt again towards the end of the sub-commission's labours. In a somewhat surprising move, nine delegations — the French, Czech, Argentine, Belgian, Italian, Polish, Rumanian, Yugoslavian and Japanese — supported a new formula based solely on the distinction between wartime armaments and peacetime armaments originally advocated by the French. Reverting to former arguments, these powers declared that designations based on preparations for mobilization would not be generally applicable since the preparations could only come into operation in time of war and would not include machinery set in motion in time of peace; they also asserted that the notion of easily mobilizable armaments was an extremely vague one and that the necessity for mobilization preparations depended essentially on the special circumstances of each state. The delegations of Britain, Germany, America, Bulgaria, Finland, The Netherlands, Sweden and Spain could not accept the new formula and adhered to that of 11 June, with the result that the report of the sub-commission merely laid out the alternative definitions in parallel columns together with declarations on the problem from the United States on the one hand and the supporters of the

French definition on the other. The procedure was to become standard practice on all contentious questions.[21]

The powers divided along almost identical lines on the question of 'limitable' armaments. The two major groupings agreed that peacetime forces could be limited and that ultimate war strength could not, but they disagreed as to the limitability of forces prepared in peacetime for use in hostilities. The French delegation and its supporters substantially identified themselves with the view that any forces not included within their definition of peacetime armaments should be classified as war armaments and therefore not subject to limitation; the British delegation and its adherents held that wider restrictions were possible. The French argued that, even if it were possible to adduce 'more or less effective and practical methods' of limiting trained reserves and reserves of *matériel*, their limitation was inadmissible in principle since it discriminated against states with a low war potential; the British countered that it was technically possible to limit reserves of both *matériel* and personnel and that, in theory, all land armaments prepared for wartime in time of peace should be subject to limitation. A compromise on the issue was found to be impossible.[22]

A further division between the two major groupings concerned the interdependence of armaments. The British grouping favoured separate consideration of the three main categories (land, sea and air) in the hope of isolating specific areas where disarmament might be immediately practicable; the French supported an integrated study, on the grounds that measures taken in one category by one country might have consequences on different categories in other states. The French representatives argued that the experience of the First World War had shown that independent action by one arm alone was an unlikely eventuality in future hostilities; the British contended that the French were looking at the problem from a purely continental point of view and that factors which applied to continental countries did not apply equally to insular nations. Maritime empires, suggested the British, maintained armies primarily to supply the needs of overseas commitments and could fix their establishment almost independently of the size of armies in neighbouring states, whereas continental countries had to relate their needs to the forces kept by adjacent powers to protect themselves against aggression. Eventually, a kind of *de facto* compromise emerged. The French secured the passage of a resolution affirming the concept of interdependence, while the British secured the establishment of military, naval and air sub-committees for the discussion of limitation and comparability questions.[23]

The divergence of views over interdependence was not caused solely by strategic factors; political factors were also important. The French apparently wanted to warn the British and Americans against trying to safeguard the supremacy of their navies whilst advocating drastic cuts in the French army; and the British hoped to forestall a possible French initiative aimed at formulating index figures to govern the ratios of armaments between powers in all three services.[24] An arrangement based on a numerical coefficient would not only have precluded the isolation of areas where disarmament was immediately practicable but would have been so complex and arbitrary as to be unrealistic. In practice, however, the fears of both delegations were exaggerated. Colonel Réquin, the chief French military representative, stated categorically that his government was opposed to a mathematical index figure governing ratios between powers; and Chamberlain acknowledged that it was not in Britain's interest to see France defenceless, rather France should be strong enough on land to prevent her weakness from inviting attack.[25]

Perhaps the most important Anglo-French controversies concerned standards of comparison and methods of limitation. The strategic position and military requirements of the two powers were so radically different that their respective representatives found it impossible to agree on many fundamental issues. The French needed to compensate for their inferiority in manpower and resources relative to Germany by maintaining a large military establishment with 'first strike' capability and by ensuring that the whole nation could be mobilized for war in the shortest possible time; the British wished to retain the smallest establishment compatible with foreign and military commitments and the rapid mobilization of resources. The French desired restrictions which would further impede Germany's war-making capacity; the British wanted to reduce the striking power of opponents during the initial stages of hostilities.

The politico-strategic differences between Britain and France first came to a head in the military sub-commission on the question of trained reserves, when the French representatives began to argue that a limitation of numbers was 'inadmissible in principle' rather than technically impossible. Whilst accepting that reserves were an important factor in a comparison of land armaments, they declared that limitation would 'compromise absolutely' the security of numerous countries. In any struggle, the state with the highest war potential would be certain of ultimate victory, since fundamentally weaker adversaries would be prevented from inflicting a decisive blow at the commencement of hostilities. Reservists were merely one element of war potential, and it was inequitable to limit them unless restrictions were placed on other elements, such as civilian pilots, chemical factories and financial resources. Moreover, states exposed to aggression would continue to organize their defence on the basis of universal service until they were assured of equivalent guarantees under an international security system.[26]

Only conscriptionist countries supported the case against a limitation of reserves, but as they outnumbered states with voluntarist forces they were able to secure a majority on the sub-commission. For their part, the proponents of limitation argued that trained personnel constituted one of the most important elements of peacetime armaments, being immediately mobilizable on the outbreak of hostilities, and that there were five possible methods of numerical restriction. Britain's chief military representative, Colonel A.C. Temperley, was especially vigorous in supporting the limitation of annual contingents, the restriction of which he believed to be one of the simplest and most effective of all methods of disarmament. His view was that such a limitation would ease the financial burdens of conscriptionist states, relieve the personal burden on the male population and reduce the proportion of men withdrawn from productive work. The French, however, made it clear that their refusal to limit reserves was absolute; they were unwilling to decrease their war strength by a single man and were prepared to concede only that the quality of trained personnel might be restricted by means of a reduction in the period of military service.[27]

On the questions of comparability and limitation of land *matériel*, the Anglo-American grouping tended to favour direct (quantitative and qualitative) methods of restriction, whereas the French grouping inclined to indirect (budgetary) methods. However, within each bloc there were significant discrepancies in the presentation of arguments and underlying policy. The Anglo-American grouping was more cohesive in arguing against budgetary limitation than in promoting direct restrictions, and the French grouping was more united in opposing direct limitation than in advocating expenditure restrictions. Thus, although the British group agreed that direct limitation might be an effective standard of comparison, some members of the group were wary of translating the concept into practical form. Britain's policy, for example, was to avoid any firm restrictions on *matériel*, and her military representatives found it necessary to argue that, while there were theoretical merits in employing *matériel* as a primary standard of comparison, direct limitation would lead inevitably to an irksome form of supervision. They further suggested that, as a given number of effectives could handle usefully only a limited quantity of *matériel*, the primary standard should be effectives.[28]

The French and their supporters maintained that *matériel* was qualitatively too complicated a factor to be utilized as a standard of comparison, but they could hardly deny that it might be deployed as a method of limitation, since direct restrictions had been imposed on Germany under the Treaty of Versailles. Instead, they claimed that direct limitations were ineffectual and inadmissible unless accompanied by permanent and effective supervision and that, if restrictions were applied to reserve as well as service *matériel*, the mobilization powers of states would become calculable and the secrecy of measures for the organization of defence removed.[29]

As an alternative to direct limitation, the French grouping promoted the concept of indirect limitation through budgetary restriction as part of a grand scheme for the limitation of all national defence expenditure within a number of overall categories. Whilst accepting that an international comparison of armaments based on expenditure would be misleading, because of differences in recruitment methods, diverse conditions of life and difficulties in obtaining equivalent information, the representatives of these powers insisted that, for individual countries, a limitation of expenditure was both practicable and verifiable, and could be used to compensate for imperfections in other methods of restriction. Such limitations would be easily understood by public opinion and might be checked by the examination of public documents and the production of standardized extracts from budgets.[30]

A number of delegations supported the concept of budgetary restriction only at the theoretical level and refused to associate themselves with proposals for its practical application. The most prominent was the Italian delegation, whose representatives showed little enthusiasm for any kind of disarmament; and thus, of the great powers, the solitary advocate of a limitation of expenditure was France. The British delegation considered that Sub-Commission 'A' was not competent to express a technical opinion on proposals for budgetary restriction and submitted that positive suggestions should be examined in the first place by financial experts; and the German, American and Japanese delegations held that defence expenditure constituted neither an equitable nor practicable basis for limitation because of cost factor differences between states. In any case, suggested the latter powers, reductions in expenditure would follow automatically from any effective disarmament agreement.[31]

Questions of air disarmament provoked almost as much controversy as those of land disarmament, the most contentious issue being the role of civil aviation. The sub-commission accepted unanimously that it was impossible to draw a distinction between military and civil aircraft on purely technical grounds, since similar characteristics, notably horse-power and wing area, governed the performance of both categories of machine; but there was dissension among delegations as to the implications of this premise. The French grouping drew the conclusion that any limitation of air armaments must either include civil aviation within its scope or at least take into fullest account the existing importance and possibilities of development of the civil arm, while the British grouping opposed a limitation of civil aeronautics on political grounds and maintained that Sub-Commission 'A' was not competent to discuss the question.[32]

In support of their contentions, the French air representatives argued that all civil aircraft had a military value, calculable on the basis of horse-power, and that civil machines could play a number of important roles in wartime service. For example, sporting aircraft might be used for communications purposes and postal and high-speed passenger machines for reconnaissance and observation; heavy commercial craft might be utilized as night bombers and racing machines as fighters. If there was no limitation of civil aeronautics, states in which civil aviation was of small importance and unlikely to develop would be compromised in the face of neighbouring countries with an advanced civil sector, and thus it was necessary to establish a computable relationship between civil and military machines which would enable any expansion of civil aviation to be followed automatically by a corresponding restriction of military aviation.[33]

Not unnaturally, the French were concerned about the rapid and massive development of the civil aviation industry in Germany since 1919, and they were anxious to forestall any incipient threat from that direction by the application of international restrictions. Group-Captain MacNeece, the chief British air representative, soon discerned that the French government would refuse to accept a limitation that did not take into consideration the potentialities of civil aircraft, even civil personnel, and he recommended to the Air Ministry that Britain should recognize that civil aviation was a considerable resource and should be taken into account when allocating military quotas to the various nations. The government agreed, although Hoare in his personal capacity could not believe that German civil aviation was a threat either to Britain or France.[34]

The Air Minister, whilst evidently not opposing the theoretical concession on civil aviation, was more concerned at the expansion of the French military air arm and was convinced that it would be impossible to keep marking time with the British air programme. He was eager to put pressure on France to limit her air armaments, and openly scoffed at what he considered to be exaggerated fears of German aerial capacity. In December 1926, he believed that Germany possessed only one machine that could be used in an air attack on Britain with a full bomb load, and asserted that Britain and France could cripple German air bases at the outset of a conflict, making retaliatory attacks impossible. He had examined many German commercial aircraft and concluded that they were ill-adapted for conversion to war use — unlike British and French machines, which were designed for service purposes — and inspection had shown that German factories were geared to commercial production. He agreed that Germans could be trained in military aviation in Russia, but thought the danger was overstated as they could not go undetected unless their numbers were negligible.[35]

Hoare could see no practical way of limiting civil aviation, and the British government in any case stood firm against limitation on political grounds. But at Geneva the main opposition to limitation came from Germany and America. Both powers severely criticized the French proposal for a combined restriction of military and civil aviation, and the Germans even suggested that the proposed method would be tantamount to subordinating the legitimate economic interests of a country to military and political aims. The two delegations maintained that implementation of the proposals would involve international control of both civil and military aeronautics, and they believed that any such surveillance would hinder the growth of the aviation industry and retard the development of aeronautical science. Besides, added the Americans, civil aviation constituted a part of a country's resources and should not therefore be subject to limitation;

restrictions should be applied only to visible and tangible air armaments: *matériel* and military personnel.[36]

When the sub-commission and its air sub-committee examined standards of comparison and methods of limitation, the divisions between the powers were rather different. There was no polarization between the two major groupings, rather a broad consensus on questions of theoretical applicability together with a fragmentation of attitudes regarding practical acceptability. It was unanimously agreed that comparisons between countries should in theory cover the quantity and quality of both *matériel* and personnel, but it was recognized that any estimate of quality would necessarily be inaccurate and that technical progress in the science of aeronautics might produce important alterations in the value of any given class of *matériel*. There was universal agreement therefore that any limitation could be accepted for only a short duration of time.[37]

Four main methods of comparing and limiting air armaments were suggested. The British representatives submitted that limitation should be confined to the number of aircraft maintained in commission in the first-line units of metropolitan forces; the French and Italians advocated the standard of total horse-power; the Americans proposed a limitation of 'lift tonnage' (the difference between the weight of an aeroplane loaded to capacity and its tare weight); and the Japanese supported restrictions on personnel. Each method had its advantages and disadvantages, and they were analysed separately with a remarkable absence of bad feeling between the delegations. It was agreed, for example, that the British proposals had the virtues of simplicity and freedom from complication and would not interfere with commercial activities or require improved measures of control. At the same time, it was pointed out that the scheme was far from comprehensive, making no reference to reserve aircraft and engines, air personnel or the quality and characteristics of different types of machines; and thus it was felt that states with aggressive intentions would be able to maintain an unjustified number of units overseas, or transfer combatant aircraft to civil undertakings for storage.[38]

Similarly, the sub-commission agreed that the Franco–Italian proposal for limiting the total horse-power of peacetime military aircraft had the advantage of effecting a simultaneous limitation of both number and characteristics of machines whilst allowing states to distribute their allocated horse-power as best suited their needs. But it was objected that even this scheme was not all-embracing since it ignored reserve *matériel* and engines and failed to take into consideration the possibility of preparing aircraft in advance for the installation of more powerful engines. A Spanish proposal for including reserve *matériel* within the limitation partially overcame the first of the objections, but suffered from the disadvantage of requiring more detailed supervision.[39]

The method of limitation least favoured by the sub-commission was that of lift tonnage. Whilst admitting that its application would restrict the number of large-capacity aircraft and thereby control the expansion of bombing forces, the delegates considered that it lacked comprehension and made no allowances for dismantled engines and spare parts. Besides, the technical complexity of the method required the exchange of detailed information between governments, and the lift tonnage of individual aircraft could be varied by the rapid substitution of engine and wings.[40]

In contrast, there was widespread support for the limitation of air effectives. It was anticipated that a number of specialist categories would be delineated, including pilots, and it was agreed that personnel required a lengthy period of training and could not be concealed or stored like *matériel*. Nevertheless, it was pointed out that the Japanese proposal made no provision for trained reserves, and a number of delegations, the most prominent being the French, indicated that they would find it inadmissible unless accompanied by a limitation of *matériel* and the restriction of civil air personnel.[41]

Arguably the most important question faced by the delegates at Geneva was that of supervision, since throughout 1926 negotiations were taking place for the withdrawal from Germany of the Allied Control Commission. A final general inspection of German armaments by the commission had revealed a number of violations of the disarmament clauses of the peace treaty, and discussions were held between the powers concerned to establish which infractions should be rectified before withdrawal could be effected. There was much bickering over terms, and it was not until 11 December 1926 that agreement was reached and the date of withdrawal set for 31 January 1927.

It cannot be said that the Allied Control Commission was totally successful in carrying out its allotted duties. Particular items of *matériel*, such as rifles and machine-guns, were so small that their manufacture and storage was easy to conceal, and the control commission found it difficult to secure compliance with some of the detailed provisions concerning these articles. In fact, the commission did not even succeed in finding 'Big Bertha', the long-range gun that had been used to shell Paris during the First World War, although the Germans had been known to extricate it.[42] Nevertheless, the experience of the commission showed that the imposition of a system of control was a practical possibility and might prove a valuable safeguard against violations of a disarmament convention. The Chief of the Imperial General Staff, Sir George Milne, thought it unlikely that the Germans had succeeded in invading the investigations of the commission to any large extent, despite the fact that its members had been faced with 'every possible form of obstruction and evasion', and was of the opinion that a lack of armaments and equipment made it impossible for Germany to wage an aggressive war in existing circumstances.[43]

Possibly the most convincing argument suggesting the efficacy of international supervision is that, during the discussions concerning the withdrawal of the Allied Control Commission, Stresemann made it clear that he would not agree to any further provision for on-site inspection by the former Allied powers. Chamberlain and Briand had hoped to establish a permanent civilian control organ in the Rhineland as compensation for withdrawal, and even contemplated a reduction in the period of occupation in return; Stresemann maintained (quite justifiably) that there was no provision in the peace treaty for such a commission, and the British and French leaders eventually conceded the point. After 31 January 1927, the former Allies could check German disarmament only by asserting their right under Article 213 of the Treaty of Versailles to go to the Council of the League and demand a special commission of investigation in cases of suspected violation.[44]

The negotiations over the withdrawal of the control commission revealed a certain discrepancy in British policy regarding supervision. Chamberlain's support of a permanent resident commission in the demilitarized Rhineland was scarcely compatible with his instructions to the delegation at the Preparatory Commission which were to oppose the institution of a general system of compulsory supervision by direct enquiry. A way of overcoming the discrepancy might have been for Britain to have taken the lead in offering to open her garrisons and seaports to international inspection once a scheme of general disarmament had been set on foot, a course put forward by the Marquess of Crewe, Ambassador at Paris, in a letter to Chamberlain's private secretary, Walford Selby; but the Foreign Secretary remained unmoved, despite the attraction of having an additional lever for demanding a somewhat tighter system of inspection in the Rhineland than might otherwise prove politically feasible.[45]

The French delegation at the Preparatory Commission was under no illusions as to the inter-relationship of control in Germany and general control under a disarmament convention and wanted the methods of investigation in both cases to be identical. The French wanted to prevent the commission from doing anything to prejudice the Council scheme for investigation in Germany, and, being willing to accept international control of their own armaments in return for a similar degree of control over Germany's, supported the concept of detailed investigations and the collation and processing of data by an international commission.[46]

In support of their proposals, the French asserted that the organization of a permanent service for the collection and comparison of public documents would make it possible to conduct a continuous enquiry into the evolution of the military, naval and air organizations of a state and identify variations in evolution that might transform defensive systems into aggressive ones. The investigations might be carried out without affecting the secrecy of military preparations and would enable commissions of enquiry to be limited to points not elucidated in the examination of public documents. In cases where violation of a disarmament convention was alleged, an enquiry commission might be necessary, and could be constituted along the lines of the Council scheme for investigating German armaments.[47]

France was the only great power to support strict control measures. Britain admitted the technical possibility of supervision by enquiry commission, but joined with Italy, Japan and the United States in opposing on-site inspections and itinerant inquisitions on the grounds that any form of supervision by an international body was calculated to foment ill-will rather than create a spirit of international confidence. The four powers argued that political considerations would hinder an impartial enquiry by the proposed central commission at Geneva, and claimed that, to be effective, a body such as that envisaged by the French would have to become a kind of international general staff, encroaching on the legitimate functions of national staffs. The Italians even resuscitated a report of the Permanent Advisory Commission of 7 September 1921 which affirmed that control exercised independently of the power to be controlled appeared inconsistent with the concept of national sovereignty and that retrospective enquiries would generally be illusory and ineffective since accused states would have time to conceal incriminating evidence. The Americans declared that they were unable to contemplate any kind of supervision which would interfere with the liberty of action of their government, and the Germans maintained that enquiry questions were fully covered by Article 11 of the Covenant. The most stringent form of supervision acceptable to these powers was the compilation of an improved and amplified Armaments Year Book and the publication of statistical returns according to a uniform type.[48]

On other points, substantial agreement was reached. Four acceptable methods of limiting land effectives were outlined — the restriction of total numbers; the separate limitation of defined elements, such as home and overseas forces; the limitation of duration of service; and the restriction of the number of man-days per annum — and it was conceded that the limitation or suppression of chemical armaments would be either impossible or ineffective because of the speed with which commercial plants could be converted for military preparation and aircraft modified for effective distribution. It was also agreed that, in general, armaments were neither intrinsically offensive nor defensive in character, although component elements which were incapable of mobility by means of self-contained power or which could only be transported after a long delay could normally only be used for territorial protection.[49]

Originally, it was anticipated that the sub-commission's report would be confined to a statement of majority opinions. But the procedure had a number of drawbacks and at the second session of the Preparatory Commission, held between 22 and 27 September 1926, the chief American representative, Hugh Gibson, secured the passage of a resolution directing the sub-commission to report on all divergent views, the arguments brought forward in support of them and the relative advantages and disadvantages of individual proposals. Consequently, the document that finally emerged from the sub-commission's proceedings was extremely comprehensive and represented an outstanding analysis of the technical possibilities of disarmament. If parts of the report were characterized by a delineation of opposing arguments and theories, there was compensation in the detail with which individual problems were dissected.

In contrast to Sub-Commission 'A', Sub-Commission 'B' registered considerable agreement. This was not however an altogether surprising phenomenon since the economic and social consequences of disarmament were potentially less dangerous than the military. The work of the sub-commission was actually delegated to the Joint Commission (on which there was no American representative), a Committee of Experts on Civil Aviation and a Committee of Experts on Budgetary Questions, and the reports of these three bodies were passed to the Preparatory Commission with Sub-Commission 'B' offering no authoritative opinions of its own.

The Joint Commission, which comprised experts chosen by the Council rather than government representatives, studied the questions on its agenda with comparative immunity from national prejudice and reached unanimous conclusions on all points. On the delicate question of supervision it was agreed that there were no serious economic difficulties preventing the application of control measures, and the commission outlined a possible procedure regarding complaints and enquiries along the lines of a similar scheme already in operation under the auspices of the International Labour Office; it further suggested the establishment of a permanent organization for the collection and study of statistical information. The commission also agreed that it would be impossible to determine the relative importance of elements of war potential such as population, raw materials and industrial production, although it recommended that the relevant factors should be 'broadly and empirically' taken into account when concrete disarmament proposals were made.[50]

In examining the financial aspects of disarmament, the Joint Commission concluded that it was impracticable in existing circumstances for states to adopt a standard system of budget accounting, but that it was possible to eliminate many of the difficulties arising from divergences in budgetary systems by the preparation of uniform statements of defence expenditure on a standard model. The commission was reluctant to go into details — this was left to the Committee of Budgetary Experts — but it contemplated a limitation of defence expenditure as a whole combined with separate restrictions on key items and categories.[51]

The main objectives of the Committee of Budgetary Experts were to confirm the practicability of uniform statements of expenditure and to formulate a 'trial model statement' as a basis for future study. Many difficulties were encountered, but it soon became clear that none were insuperable. The committee drew up a catalogue of items for inclusion in a statement, and it was found that there were no appreciable differences as to the composition of the list. It was generally admitted that the schedules submitted required considerable condensation before eventual adoption, but in forwarding its report to Sub-Commission 'B' the committee stressed that its first draft statement should not prejudge a final model. The committee further took the view that any such statement should be used as an indicator of trends within individual countries rather than as a method of international comparison, and it was suggested that, in its final form, the model might serve as 'a means of watching over the effective observance' of a convention.[52]

The Italian member of the Budgetary Committee, whilst not disagreeing with his colleagues on individual technical points, could not approve the procedure adopted in the course of discussions, and so presented a minority report. Notwithstanding the reservations of the full committee, he suggested that it was wrong to submit an elaborate first draft, lest the efficacy of certain measures still be in doubt; and he dissented entirely from the suggestion that any model statement might be used as an instrument of supervision.[53]

The Committee of Experts on Civil Aviation reached unanimous conclusions. Acting on the principle that any limitation of air armaments must not hamper the development of civil aviation, the committee warned that 'serious economic consequences' would follow the application of qualitative restrictions to civil aircraft and devoted most of its time to the formulation of guidelines aimed at differentiating between civil and military aviation in the hope that civil machines would become less and less useful for military purposes. Eight points were outlined, but they represented platitudes rather than serious proposals and were of little intrinsic importance.[54]

Taken together, the proceedings of the two sub-commissions substantially vindicate the dictum, vigorously espoused by Temperley, that technical arguments are merely political arguments 'dressed up in uniform'.[55] In Sub-Commission 'A' especially, each of the major delegations introduced political contentions into the nominally technical discussions. The French and the Italians were the most open offenders, their posture on the question of trained reserves being flagrantly non-technical, but the British were hardly less culpable, their attitude towards the direct limitation of land *matériel* being governed to a large extent by opposition to supervision. Political considerations also dominated the British attitude towards regional disarmament. The delegation at Geneva refused to debate the issue on the grounds that it was not predominantly a technical matter, but it seems more likely that Chamberlain was worried about the possible exposure of the government's counterfeit position regarding regional agreements. In public, the Foreign Secretary had been urging other governments to conclude Locarno-type agreements for increased security; in private, he admitted that it was useless to frame imaginary pacts for countries that would not adopt them or suggest guarantees by countries that either would not give them or would not be allowed to give them.[56]

Political considerations may have taken precedence over the technical on many of the problems discussed by the sub-commissions, but the importance of technical factors in evaluating methods of disarmament must not therefore be overlooked. There were many instances where there were genuine differences of opinion between the various delegations, possibly the best example being the division in the Committee of Budgetary Experts between the Italian member and the rest of his colleagues. Cecil had always maintained that progress towards disarmament would necessarily be slow; the technical enquiries of May 1926 to March 1927 justified his caution.

Salvador de Madariaga, head of the League Secretariat's disarmament section and chief bureaucrat of the Preparatory Commission, asserted that the work of Sub-Commission 'A' was 'a signal failure' since its report was 'so crowded with minority views, reservations, counter-reservations and explanations as to be almost unintelligible without the help of a specialist'.[57] His judgement, however, is hypercritical. Certainly, parts of the report (published in December 1926) may have been little more than a compendium of opposing arguments, and others of little intrinsic value;[58] but on a majority of points there was a 'least common denominator' of agreement and, within its compass, the 176-page document presented an intricate study of the problems and possibilities of disarmament. Almost every conceivable method of limitation was investigated and the putative advantages and disadvantages of each set down in considerable, even minute, detail. It could hardly be claimed that the technical preparation for disarmament had been skimped.

Sub-Commission 'A' has also been criticized for the slowness of its proceedings — and with some justification since in certain respects the time at its disposal might have been utilized more efficiently. At one point, the French delegation suggested the compilation of a list of essentially defensive armaments — apparently because the French general staff hoped to prove that the construction of a strong fortification system on France's eastern frontier would be entirely legitimate in character — and the sub-commission thereupon spent a number of days reaching full agreement on a matter which, in practical terms, was of little importance.[59] In general, however, the length of the proceedings should be attributed to the nature and extent of the problems examined and the seriousness with which the delegates discussed them. The questions set by the Council were so extremely intricate and so closely associated with the functions of national power that lengthy debate could scarcely be avoided. Moreover, the agenda of the commission was so comprehensive that Madariaga, in attempting to elicit questions that had been overlooked, found it necessary to resort to problems such as the influence of monotheism and polytheism on armaments and the beauty of princesses as causes of war![60]

The course of events on Sub-Commission 'A' was also influenced by the temperament of the delegates. At a personal level, there was a remarkable absence of bad feeling and even a genuine camaraderie among the land and air experts but in official discussions they tended to adhere to instructions rigidly, precipitating frequent deadlocks.[61]

It was only to be expected that they would frame their answers to questions in accordance with the requirements of national security, and in any given situation sought to extract the greatest possible advantage for their own national position. They were especially concerned lest inconsistencies in argumentation might be exploited by opponents and became adept at identifying significant discrepancies. MacNeece, for example, continually pointed to the divergence in the British air and army directives, whereby Temperley was expected to press strongly for a restriction of effectives and reserves whereas he (MacNeece) was required to oppose any restrictions.[62]

One important outcome of the sub-commission's proceedings was that the service delegates gained a further understanding of the strengths and weaknesses of their own rationalizations and the policies and methods of opponents. They also became attuned to the possibility that their respective governments might be contemplating disarmament seriously. Many fighting departments began to suspect that their political masters were willing to offer important concessions in the interest of international agreement, and in the particular case of Britain, the Admiralty apprehended a change in policy on the question of supervision.[63] The fears might well have been exaggerated, but undoubtedly they would have been worse if the services had not been allowed such an integral role in the negotiations.

There is little doubt that the opinions expressed by the various delegations were held in perfect good faith, as Madariaga and the more open-minded service representatives appreciated.[64] At the same time, arguments that sound reasonable in the formulation of national policy often sound hypocritical in international discussion, and in private it was common practice for delegates to impugn the motives of opposing states. The raising of fundamental issues produced a deal of mistrust, and the prevailing impression at Geneva — according to Admiral Aubrey Smith, Britain's chief naval representative — was that the French delegation desired a breakdown of the Preparatory Commission on British or American responsibility.[65] The imputation was actually quite erroneous, for the French had studied disarmament far more carefully than any other nation and had engaged some of the best brains of their general and naval staffs and the Quai d'Orsay in months of research on the subject,[66] but their methods of procedure and clear perception of objectives evoked natural hostility. In contrast to the British, the French government had successfully integrated its disarmament and foreign policies.

By March 1927, the technical phase of the Preparatory Commission's enquiries was over. Each nation had aired its maximum demands, based on requirements for security, and a breakdown of discussions had not occurred. The question now was whether statesmen could take over the negotiations and bring them to a successful conclusion.

7 International political discussions
September 1926–May 1927

At the Seventh Assembly of the League, in September 1926, the Preparatory Commission came under heavy criticism for the slowness of its proceedings. The great majority of powers expressed disappointment that progress towards disarmament had not been more substantial; and the French, in an apparent attempt to guide the course of future discussions, introduced a resolution urging the Council to convene the Disarmament Conference before the Eighth Assembly. It was an astute move, which placed the British delegation in something of a quandary for whilst the British government viewed the summoning of the Disarmament Conference with considerable scepticism, even apprehension, it was impolitic to voice such feelings too strongly at Geneva.

Cecil and Lord Onslow, the most prominent British delegates at the Assembly, resolved to dilute the French resolution rather than oppose it outright, and with help from the Italian, Polish and Swedish delegations, who deprecated the apparent haste of the French, they secured important amendments to the original draft.[1] The final resolution, adopted on 24 September, called for the rapid completion of the Preparatory Commission's technical enquiries, the drafting by the commission of a programme for a disarmament conference consistent with existing conditions of regional and general security and the convening of a conference before the Eighth Assembly unless material conditions rendered it impossible.

The events at the Seventh Assembly evidently convinced Cecil that the government's attitude towards disarmament had become far too casual, for in the ensuing weeks he began to plan a major British initiative at Geneva. His first objective was to gain acceptance in principle for the need for a forward policy, and in an important memorandum, dated 3 November, he set out the case for such a policy in substantial detail. On grounds of obligations, he considered the arguments for disarmament to be overwhelming — in support of his views he cited the Allied letter of June 1919, the preamble to Part V of the Treaty of Versailles, Article 8 of the Covenant, League resolutions and the final protocol of the Locarno conference — and he believed the case on merits to be no less strong. In general terms, he stressed the economic advantages of arms limitation and the need to avoid an arms race; and he emphasized the psychological argument that the maintenance of large armaments did more than perhaps anything else to keep alive international hatred and suspicion and divert the ablest scientific talent on the continent to the discovery of new and more deadly weapons. More specifically, he claimed that it was in Britain's interest to see that disputes were settled by peaceful means rather than by force, since Britain was a satisfied rather than a revisionist power. He further asserted that there was a need for economy and lower taxation at home, that there was no real opportunity for cuts in expenditure except on armaments and that any such cuts could be attempted safely only through international agreement. Rather sanguinely, he declared that the work of the League had shown that there did not seem to be any insoluble technical difficulties in the way of arms reductions and that, given goodwill, the differences between the powers could be adjusted; but he pointed out that discussions had shown the great delicacy of the problems involved and that there were 'moral vested interests of great strength' that would try to bar the way to any international convention. It was not improbable that the first step towards disarmament would be a small one, and the chief responsibility for success or failure would rest with the British Empire.[2]

Cecil's memorandum was discussed by the CID on 11 November at a special session attended by the prime ministers of Canada, Australia, New Zealand and South Africa, who were in London for the Imperial Conference. No radical decisions were taken, indeed the discussion was not very full, but the Dominion premiers expressed general agreement with Cecil and a resolution was adopted for presentation at the conference stating that it was their common desire to do the utmost in pursuit of disarmament consistent with the safety and integrity of all parts of the Empire and its communications.[3]

The Chancellor of the Duchy of Lancaster seems to have accepted the resolution as a kind of *carte blanche* for pursuing his own ends, although at the time he apparently had no clear conception of the exact course he would follow. Possibly he had come round to the view that the best mode of procedure would be to present a draft skeleton convention (a convention with figures omitted) at the next session of the Preparatory Commission, as the Labour opposition, after months of relative silence on the disarmament issue, were now suggesting that Britain might profitably bring forward concrete suggestions at Geneva.[4] But he moved with caution and it was not until the following month that he definitely became committed to this course.

Cecil's principal objective was the conclusion of an understanding with the French, and whilst accompanying Chamberlain to the December meeting of the Council, he had a long conversation with Briand and Paul-Boncour in an attempt to iron out the differences that had arisen in Sub-Commission 'A' and settle future procedure. The dialogue was successful and the French ministers proved very amenable to the suggestion that a skeleton convention be formulated, even conceding that it was important for Britain and France to agree on its terms before the Preparatory Commission reconvened.[5]

Elated at the response to his proposal, Cecil asked Chamberlain if the Foreign Office could spare one of its legal advisers to help draft a skeleton convention. The Foreign Secretary quickly agreed to make an official available and Sir Cecil Hurst duly accepted the responsibility.[6] Cecil produced preliminary sketch proposals which he forwarded to Trenchard and Philip Noel-Baker (a Labour colleague in the League of Nations Union and a keen supporter of disarmament) for private comment, and Sir Cecil Hurst endeavoured to give practical shape to the ideas by framing a draft which would incur as little opposition as possible at Geneva. By February 1927 a detailed draft was ready for discussion by the Disarmament Committee and the way was open for Britain's first real initiative on the disarmament question since MacDonald sponsored the Geneva Protocol.[7]

Chamberlain by this time had such confidence in Cecil's judgement that he gave his colleague the go-ahead for producing a draft convention before the Foreign Office had considered the political advisability of presenting it at Geneva. On this occasion, however, the Foreign Secretary's advisers accepted that Britain was committed to supporting the concept of general disarmament and agreed that, in the circumstances, there were advantages in being the first power to lay a definite plan before the Preparatory Commission. Not only would Britain gain credit for taking the lead, benefits would accrue from using a British draft as a basis for negotiation.[8]

In reaching this conclusion, Alexander Cadogan, Foreign Office assistant to the British delegate at the League of Nations and putative expert on arms limitation, pointed out a number of inadequacies in the government's approach to disarmament. He appreciated the reluctance with which the fighting departments had been co-operating on the question, and in a perceptive minute of 7 February he recorded that the services had not provided answers to a number of fundamental questions relating to the discussions at Geneva, in particular whether Britain had anything to fear — or gain — from disarmament and whether there were any concessions that the country might offer. In other words, the British government had hitherto followed an *ad hoc*, confusing and even confused policy towards disarmament instead of analysing first principles and proceeding accordingly.[9]

Cecil's draft treaty envisaged a limitation on the number of troops available for despatch to the fighting line within a week of an outbreak of hostilities. Effectives were classified as those serving with the colours together with those who had served within the past eight years and undergone twelve or more months' training in addition, and the number of officers and NCOs per number of men was to be restricted to 5 per cent and 10 per cent respectively. All aircraft of service types commissioned in first-line combatant units in both home and overseas forces were to be limited, and expenditure on armaments restricted to agreed amounts for each service. The provisions for armament reductions were to be effected within two years, and the Secretary-General of the League was to be given annual notification, in specified form, of expenditure during the previous year and of estimates for the current year. Increases in the size of forces and budgets would be permitted only in the event of war or rebellion or with the concurrence of the Council, and any party that suspected another of violating its commitments was to bring the matter to the notice of the other signatories. Each state was to co-operate in measures for investigation and join in any action deemed wise and effectual for ensuring the future observance of the convention and the safeguarding of peace. Accused states would afford 'every facility' for investigation provided that a majority of parties considered the action necessary and that four out of seven specified powers concurred in the decision. These powers were Germany, the United States, Britain, France, Italy, Japan and the Soviet Union, and the disarmament treaty itself would become effective only when ratified by them.[10]

In general, Cecil's draft treaty accorded with the policy espoused by the British representatives on Sub-Commission 'A', although the Chancellor of the Duchy of Lancaster did incorporate a number of personal proposals in an attempt to ensure a greater measure of agreement with the other powers. Hoare's proposal for limiting air armaments was reinforced by the provision covering overseas forces, and the articles concerning supervision and budgetary limitation, particularly the latter, were far more stringent than hitherto had been considered acceptable by the Cabinet. Even so, there were no provisions in the draft that were likely to affect the British interest adversely; many other powers would be committed to accepting proportionately greater sacrifices.

The services viewed the situation rather differently. The military claimed that the only way to stop aggression was to limit the number of trained reserves and that under Cecil's plan reductions would take eight years to become effective; and the general staff suggested that Britain should continue to press for a limitation of annual contingents, despite the opposition of the French, to restrict the supply of reserves at source. The generals also maintained their opposition to investigation by international commission, asserting that the proposals for supervision entailed a grave risk of friction between states and the possibility of unjustifiable requests for investigation. If Britain were subjected to an international enquiry, mobilization plans might be revealed and war intentions and military secrets disclosed. The Admiralty, through Admiral Field, Deputy Chief of the Naval Staff, contended that a disarmament treaty must depend solely on goodwill and that there should be no sanctions or investigations; and the senior service held that any limitation of defence expenditure was impracticable and inequitable, misleading, undesirable and of no value. The Admiralty was against comparing armaments by means of expenditure since it opened the

door to 'every sort of camouflage and concealment', and even opposed
the idea of model statements on the grounds that they would involve
more work for departmental officials with no commensurate results.
The Air Ministry opposed the application of restrictions to non-
metropolitan aircraft.[11]

The servicemen's fears were certainly exaggerated, indeed their
analysis of a number of Cecil's proposals was remarkably unobjec-
tive. The view that only a limitation of trained reserves would
prevent aggression was excessive, and, considering that the French
had made it clear during the proceedings of Sub-Commission 'A' that
there was no possibility of their agreeing to a limitation of reserves,
it was unrealistic of the general staff to propose a restriction of
annual contingents, except as a bargaining counter. The attitude of
the services towards supervision and expenditure restrictions was
prejudiced in the extreme since there was no greater danger in
Britain accepting the form of limitation proposed by Cecil than any
other power; and the Chancellor of the Duchy's proposals for
budgetary publicity through model statements of expenditure could
have been advantageous to Britain in that other powers might have
been committed to increased revelations whereas the British government, which gave extensive information to Parliament, would not.

On 8 February, ostensibly as Secretary to the CID, but more
probably because of his own fundamental antipathy towards disarmament, Hankey produced a critique of Cecil's draft treaty from the
general standpoint of imperial defence. Broadly speaking, he considered Cecil's scheme much too rigid, and he asserted that Britain
must be absolutely free to deal with any emergencies that might
arise, unhampered by international rules. He suggested that the
existing situation in China, which had necessitated sending a division of troops to protect British interests and property in Shanghai,
would not have been covered by the reservations regarding belliger-
ency or a rebellion; and he even claimed that the government would
have to ask the League for permission to spend money on projects
such as the Singapore base or to meet Russian encroachments on
Persia or Afghanistan. He also contended that the draft treaty
apparently made insufficient provision for the development of new
methods of warfare, in particular the 'substitution' of aircraft for the
older branches of the service and what he termed the 'mechanicalisa-
tion' of armies.[12]

Hankey's document represented a considerable attack on the
underlying philosophy of Cecil's proposals, and his feelings were
shared by many members of the government. But his criticisms were
wide of the mark. The idea that Britain would have to gain permission from the League to spend money was little more than fantasy,
and his belief that the situation in China would not be covered by the
reservations of the draft treaty was, at best, debatable. Moreover, his
underlying philosophy assumed that international restrictions on the
use of national power would militate against the British interest,
whereas in practice the lack of restrictions tended to favour

revisionist states. It was to Britain's advantage as a 'satiated' power to control — or at least attempt to control — redistribution of power on a world or European scale, and a redistribution achieved through the negotiation of a disarmament convention offered greater hope of a long-term settlement of security problems than one which resulted from an overt threat of force and the operation of an 'international anarchy'.

At the meetings of the Disarmament Committee, the service representatives managed to water down Cecil's draft treaty considerably. The definition of effectives was altered to include all troops serving with the colours, discharged or passed to the reserve within the previous seven years, and those that could be despatched to the fighting line within four weeks of the outbreak of hostilities. The provisions for budgetary limitation were omitted (except as regards land armaments) and replaced by a clause whereby states had to provide explanatory memoranda if their estimated or actual expenditure in any one year exceeded the previous year's figure by more than 10 per cent. The supervision article was recast so that no investigations would be permitted on the territory of an accused power without the consent of that power. Non-metropolitan aircraft were excluded from the formula for aerial limitation. The time limit of two years for effecting limitations was dropped; and the duration of the proposed treaty, which Cecil had set at ten years, was reduced to five years only in the case of land armaments and air *matériel*.[13]

Despite its dilution in the Disarmament Committee, the draft convention came under heavy fire in the CID, where the more important ministers had an opportunity to make detailed criticisms on 4 March. Worthington-Evans resisted the budgetary limitation of land armaments, claiming that states would inflate their monetary requirements. Baldwin, Hoare and Bridgeman opposed the concept of explanatory memoranda in cases of excessively increased expenditure, arguing that flexibility of budgetary provision was necessary and that Britain might be subjected to interrogation at Geneva on fundamental questions of defence policy. Hoare insinuated that the clauses covering information might lead to attempts to create a permanent commission of examination which could form the nucleus of an international general staff. Chamberlain gave Cecil effective support, but, as Amery stated in his diary, the draft was sanctioned 'with some hope that nothing would come of it all'.[14]

In reality, the fears and claims of the various ministers were almost entirely groundless. Many powers favoured the establishment of a permanent disarmament commission at Geneva, but the possibility of such a body being directed to undertake staff functions was extremely remote and Britain could have vetoed any concrete proposal at conception. Moreover, the argument that it would be against the British interest to provide interpretive documentation when expenditure exceeded an agreed margin was little more than polemic, since Britain already published relevant information as a matter of course. In fact, as Cecil pointed out to the CID — and the

Treasury representative on the Disarmament Committee agreed —
the provision envisaged would have been advantageous in that
Britain would have been in a position to gain additional information
about the armaments of other powers.[15] Although it was probably
true that budgetary limitation would lead powers into inflating their
defence estimates, it might be argued that any universal limitation,
at whatever level, was better than no limitation at all.

Cecil was extremely frustrated at the further weakening of the
draft convention, and in readiness for placing the amended version
before the Cabinet composed an important memorandum outlining
his major differences with his service colleagues:

> The Draft Convention ... is a compromise between the views of the
> fighting Services and those who believe that an international agreement
> for the Reduction and Limitation of Armaments is essential for the safety
> of European civilisation and the existence of the British Empire. It follows
> that the Draft is not satisfactory to those who like myself hold the latter
> view. In particular I think it regrettable that it contains no provision
> limiting the material of land armies, that the limitation of aircraft is
> confined to shore-based metropolitan forces, that naval and air personnel
> are not dealt with at all, and that the provisions for international supervi-
> sion are so insufficient. However, it does represent a step in advance —
> albeit a very small one.[16]

The Chancellor of the Duchy of Lancaster also seems to have been
concerned that the Cabinet had not accepted his view that failure to
negotiate an international disarmament agreement would lead to
German rearmament, an arms race and European war.[17] So at the
end of his memorandum he set out his own views in no uncertain
terms:

> In conclusion I desire to place on record my conviction that at no time in
> the last three or four centuries has the British Empire been in such peril
> as it is at the present time. It is true that the peril is not immediate. There
> is no prospect of any serious war at the moment. But if it comes, and we
> are engaged in it, the fabric of credit and confidence by which we live can
> scarcely be expected to survive it. Further, we are for the first time
> exposed to direct attack against which our Fleet gives us no protection. An
> air bombardment of London by explosives, incendiary substance and poison
> gas is admittedly a fearful menace for which there is no defence other than
> the threat of similar bombardment abroad. In those circumstances the
> recrudescence of competition in armaments of which there are many signs
> is a grave danger. Unless arrested it is bound to lead to war. To avert that
> result is worth many sacrifices and even, as a lesser evil, the acceptance
> of some risk.[18]

It was a powerful statement of a plausible argument — and one
which showed considerable insight into the working of international
society.

If Cecil expected his colleagues to reform their views and accept his
philosophy of disarmament, he was soon disappointed. On 9 March
1927, the Cabinet approved his draft convention, but only in accordance with the amendments adopted by the CID.[19] Evidently, the

majority of ministers continued to regard general disarmament as visionary and remained unmoved by the possible efficacy of a convention for stimulating international conciliation.[20] Certainly many ministers inclined to the Hankey conception of disarmament, and there is little doubt that a number of them would not have objected if the talks at Geneva had broken down, or at least been postponed. Bridgeman, for instance, actually suggested delaying consideration of the draft convention until new proposals for naval limitation, specifically designed to improve Britain's security position, had been examined.[21] Ministers did, however, accept that Britain had been committed to the path of disarmament by various international agreements and that the price of reneging on these obligations was too high; so they were willing to pay lip-service to the concept of general limitation and give Cecil a degree of latitude in pursuing his ideals, provided always that the proposals he took to Geneva were adjusted in line with the services' criteria for security requirements.

The government's duality of approach was reflected in the revised draft convention. Ostensibly, the draft was framed as the basis of a general convention, but in practice it was so dovetailed to Britain's security needs that it stood little chance of international acceptance. The majority of the proposals had been broached on Sub-Commission 'A', and many had been accorded a decidedly cool reception by the other powers. The provision for a limitation of trained reserves was likely to prove unacceptable to France and conscriptionist states in general; the articles covering supervision, air *matériel* and budgetary restriction could be expected to arouse considerable opposition because they were not comprehensive; and there was no provision at all for the limitation of air effectives and land *matériel*. As a bargaining counter, the draft had its uses, although the government did not conceive it as such and made no attempt to estimate possible concessions or grade individual questions in terms of vital interest; as a foundation for general disarmament, it was wholly inadequate.

At the same time, the course of international relations had run smoothly since the inaugural session of the Preparatory Commission, and on the surface the portents for agreement at the third session, which was scheduled to convene on 21 March, were not entirely inauspicious. Germany had been admitted to the League with a permanent seat at the Council of the Seventh Assembly and had begun to play an important role in the international body. The 'Locarno triumvirate' of Briand, Chamberlain and Stresemann had guided their respective countries further along the road of appeasement. The March meeting of the Council seemed to mark a highpoint of co-operation between the European powers, with agreements being reached on issues such as the Saar railways and the use of German in the schools of Polish Silesia. Anglo–French relations had become intimate, and the Americans had steadily increased their interest and collaboration in the activities of the League

Below the surface, however, without even considering the British stand on disarmament, the prospects for agreement were not so good.

The Soviets had still not settled their dispute with the Swiss government, although the ground between the two parties had been narrowed considerably, and a number of powers, notably Japan, Poland, Rumania and Finland, had indicated that it would be doubtful whether they could participate in a disarmament conference at which there was no Russian representation.[22] Anglo–Soviet relations were at a very low ebb and were to be severed by the British government at the end of May 1927, it being alleged that the offices of Arcos Limited and the Russian trade delegation in London had been used as a centre for espionage and subversion. The latent hostility between France and Italy over Mediterranean and Balkan questions had begun to manifest itself once again; and the relationships of the Locarno triumvirate had started to come under increasing strain as Stresemann pressed for more concessions, in particular the withdrawal of the occupying forces from the Rhineland.

At Geneva, Cecil found the atmosphere towards disarmament 'not unfavourable but . . . slightly sceptical'. He detected very little direct opposition to the concept, and in a series of private conversations between 13 and 15 March began to probe his fellow delegates as to their attitude towards a draft convention. Most were sympathetic. Edouard Benes, Czechoslovakian Foreign Minister, proclaimed himself strongly in favour of a draft and believed there would be no great impossibility in formulating one; the chief Belgian representative on the Preparatory Commission, Louis de Brouckère, conveyed that he would accept 'practically anything' that was a real convention; and Paul-Boncour proved 'very amenable', making a strong stand only on the question of supervision. Of the representatives consulted by Cecil, the Italian General de Marinis alone cast doubts on the desirability of a convention, explaining that disarmament could not solve his country's practical problems.[23]

Certainly one of the chief obstacles to a far-reaching convention was the fundamental antipathy of the Italians towards the control and limitation of armaments. The Fascist government might not have been alone in looking suspiciously at measures that bound its hands, but no other government represented at Geneva tried so assiduously to exalt military virtues and inculcate its population with martial ideals. The army had recently been re-organized as a step towards greater efficiency; the air force was being expanded to achieve parity with France; an anti-disarmament campaign had been running in the press almost continuously for three years; and the Italian nation as a whole was constantly being urged to steel itself against the 'insidious and treacherous' proposals of other powers. It was only fortunate, as Cecil perceived, that the Italians were more capable of militarism than of war and that they would not voluntarily accept the odium of being the refractory party at Geneva.[24]

In his interview with Paul-Boncour on 13 March, Cecil raised the important question of future procedure at the Preparatory Commission, and found himself at odds with the French representative. Paul-Boncour preferred a general discussion of disarmament lasting some two or three days — a course that was geared to the logical French approach to disarmament; Cecil thought it better to canalize discussion by tabling a draft skeleton convention immediately on the resumption of negotiations — a course that was more attuned to the *ad hoc* approach of the British. No agreement was reached at the time, but on 17 March, when Cecil communicated the British draft convention confidentially to the French and invited their observations preparatory to laying it before the full commission, the British representative indicated a willingness to delay formal presentation until after a general discussion. Two days later, however, Cecil reverted to his original plan, after the substance of the British draft had been leaked to the Paris press and became the subject of adverse, even abusive, comment. On the afternoon of 21 March, at the opening meeting of the third session of the commission, he formally submitted his draft.[25]

Having been pre-empted by Cecil on the question of procedure, Paul-Boncour laid a French draft convention before the Preparatory Commission on the afternoon of 23 March. It was more comprehensive than the British draft and envisaged a general distinction between home and overseas forces (the latter including designated reinforcements) for each separate category of limitation. Within this overall formula there was to be a limitation of all effectives employable without mobilization in the military, naval and air services and in 'units organized on a military basis' such as police forces, gendarmerie, customs officials and forest guards; and a maximum period of service was to be prescribed for each of the four subdivisions. There was, however, to be no restriction on the percentage of officers. Aircraft and dirigibles in commission, including those in reserve, were to be limited by total horse-power (and in the case of dirigibles by volume also), with a distinction between regular and non-regular forces. There was to be a fixed annual budgetary allotment covering the upkeep, purchase and manufacture of *matériel* for each of the three services, also a global allocation for the duration of the convention. Each party was to forward annually to the Secretary-General of the League, in prescribed form, a statement of budgetary expenditure in the preceding year, estimated expenditure in the coming year, the average daily effectives in service with the regular forces and actual effectives in 'units organized on a military basis'. A Permanent Disarmament Commission, effectively controlled by the great powers, would be established at Geneva for the centralization of information and the study of progress towards reduction and limitation; and any party that considered its security requirements to be materially affected by fresh circumstances, such as the development of civil aviation in a signatory state or of civil or military aviation in a non-signatory, could appeal to the commission for a revision of its limitations. In such circumstances, the commission might decide by two-thirds majority on an enquiry for the verification of facts, and by a similar majority it might authorize an on-the-spot investigation, members of the enquiry committee being selected from a list of experts duly qualified in the different areas of limitation. The treaty would remain in force for whatever period was specified by the Disarmament Conference.[26]

Paul-Boncour's draft was as perfectly adapted to French security requirements as Cecil's draft was to Britain's. It gave the French the liberty they desired in the matter of reservists whilst affording maximum security against Germany through the provisions for control and supervision, budgetary limitation and civil aviation. The discussions of Sub-Commission 'A' might have shown that it stood little chance of universal acceptance; but, together with Cecil's draft, it represented a positive contribution to the cause of disarmament in that it provided a documentary framework for the evolution of practical steps towards effective political action.

There were five main differences between the two draft conventions. Britain anticipated a limitation of military reservists but not air effectives; France wanted air effectives to be limited but not military reservists. Britain wanted the limitation of air *matériel* to be confined to first-line metropolitan units; France advocated a more comprehensive limitation covering overseas forces and reserve *matériel*. Britain favoured budgetary publicity but not budgetary limitation; France favoured both. Britain desired only a modicum of supervision, with no compulsory investigations by an international body; France preferred strict measures of international control. The task of the Preparatory Commission was to synthesize the documents into a common formula acceptable to all powers.

Such a proposition was daunting in the extreme. Each power had its own conception of disarmament — and many were exceedingly diverse, as the general discussion of disarmament held between 21 and 25 March was to demonstrate. The British aimed at limiting the power of aggression and made no distinction between peacetime and wartime armaments; the French sought to limit permanent peacetime armaments that were susceptible to supervision. The Italians aspired to equality of armaments with the most heavily armed power in continental Europe; and the Germans demanded that the other powers fulfil their obligations under the peace treaty and bring about a situation where no state was powerful enough to prevail against the armed might of the League yet where the combination of forces available to the League would be sufficient to enforce the 'common will'. The Japanese asserted that the spirit of Article 8 required that, in the last instance, each power should fix its own degree of disarmament and that practical limitations could be best achieved through methods that were easy of application and execution. A number of powers, notably Poland, Greece and the Little Entente, placed considerable emphasis on the necessity to base any form of limitation on the strengthening of the League as an organ of collective security. The Americans maintained a discreet silence, on the grounds that they were awaiting instructions.[27]

The first major problem to come to a head was that of trained reserves. Even before the public discussion of the issue in the

Preparatory Commission, Paul-Boncour made it clear that the French government still maintained the view, vigorously propounded in Sub-Commission 'A', that a limitation of annual contingents such as that foreshadowed in the British proposals was politically unacceptable, primarily because individual Frenchmen regarded the methods of effecting such limitation as undemocratic, unfair and open to abuse. The French representative remained singularly unimpressed by the argument that the military provisions of the Treaty of Versailles might not remain in force *ad infinitum* and that France would be at a serious disadvantage *vis-à-vis* Germany if armies were maintained in direct proportion to population; the most he would concede to the British view was that the efficiency of effectives might be restricted through a reduction in the period of service. He did hint that his government might be prepared to count as effectives the two annual classes most recently passed into reserve, but the value of this 'concession' was practically nil as it was also proposed that the two classes in question might be recalled to the colours without resort to mobilization.[28]

In public discussion, the representatives of Japan, Italy and Belgium made effective speeches in support of the French point of view; and it became more and more obvious that the British proposal concerning effectives and reservists stood no chance of acceptance. Nevertheless, one member of the British delegation, Temperley, believed that Britain should make a stand on the issue and press strongly for a limitation of annual contingents, possibly through the raising of fitness qualifications. He was especially concerned at the effect on Germany if reservists were excluded from the scope of a convention, and pointed out that, at that very moment, the French government was endeavouring to enact comprehensive legislation that aimed at strengthening the army and increasing its overall efficiency whilst reducing the period of service for conscripts from eighteen months to a year. Cecil, however, perceived the futility of arguing at length against the resolute opposition of three great powers, and after formally presenting the British case made a declaration to the effect that he had not succeeded in shaking the convictions of his opponents and would accept the French article on land effectives at first reading (subject to a minor drafting amendment) since it represented the views of the countries most concerned with land armaments. At the same time, he emphasized that he still considered his own views to be right.[29]

Cecil was severely criticized in the Foreign Office for making what appeared to be a major concession.[30] And certainly Britain would have been far from isolated at Geneva if he had continued to press the British proposals on effectives, for other opponents of the French standpoint, notably Germany and Sweden, adhered to the view that no disarmament convention would be complete without a limitation of reserves.[31] The German delegate, Count Bernstorff, made a specific reservation on the issue. But there were solid reasons behind Cecil's action, not the least of which was the impracticability of opposing the wishes of three great powers. Chamberlain's foreign policy and Cecil's disarmament policy were directed towards securing intimate co-operation with France, and an Anglo–French breach at the outset of discussions would not only have reduced the possibility of a successful issue to the negotiations but would have run counter to their general desires regarding overall strategy. Indeed, it might be argued that if Chamberlain wanted France to remain sufficiently strong to avoid her weakness inviting attack, it might have been politic to give outright support to the French contention of reserves — assuming, of course, that the French knew best how to defend themselves. Moreover, the lack of a limitation on reservists could scarcely have been detrimental to British security, in the sense that the existing organization of military forces would not have been affected. A further reason for not pressing the British case on effectives was the imprecision of the government's own proposals. Effectives were defined in two different ways in the draft convention accepted by the Cabinet on 9 March: troops who within an agreed number of weeks of the outbreak of hostilities could be made available for despatch to the fighting line; and those who were serving with the colours or had been discharged or passed to reserve within the previous seven years. There were difficulties in defining both 'the fighting line' and the men that could be sent to it, and for presentation at Geneva the second of the two definitions was dropped. Even Temperley agreed that the British draft needed refining; he also accepted that the French scheme for basing limitation on 'average daily effectives' appeared to be the most scientific way of calculating the number and value of men trained annually.[32]

On the other points regarding effectives, there was considerable agreement in the commission. The British accepted that limitation should apply to 'units organized on a military basis' as well as the national army, and that there should be separate maximum allotments within each category for metropolitan forces, overseas forces, 'overseas forces stationed at home' and 'total forces stationed at home', provided that latitude was given for modification between home and abroad if security requirements demanded it. The French accepted the proposal for a restriction of the number of officers, although not to the same fixed percentage for each country. The concept of 'average daily effectives' was taken as the basis for limitation, and it was agreed that countries with conscript armies should impose a limit on the total period which the annual contingent was compelled to serve.[33]

The War Office willingly made concessions on the lesser points at issue during the debate on effectives. But the Air Ministry, because of its exaggerated insistence on simple proposals and evident conviction that concessions would be interpreted as a sign of weakness, was decidedly unhelpful and pedantic in its dealings and incurred the Chancellor of the Duchy of Lancaster's wrath on a number of occasions. Cecil had nothing personal against MacNeece, but found that the representative's superiors compelled him to take positions that were impossible to state effectively at an international gathering.[34]

The friction between Cecil and the Air Ministry came to a head on the question of air effectives. The Chancellor believed that, given some degree of honesty and fair dealing on the part of the signatories to a convention, direct limitation of personnel was fundamentally unnecessary since a restriction of aircraft automatically imposed an indirect limitation; but by the same criterion it could hardly be asserted that direct limitation entailed any intrinsic inconveniences or dangers and he thought Britain would be placed in an invidious position at Geneva if the government stood out against such limitation. Consequently, even before the subject was discussed in public session, he enquired whether there was a possibility of a change of heart by the Air Ministry. The immediate reply was negative.[35]

The Air Ministry's principal objection to limitation of personnel was its difficulty of application since air services were organized along very different lines in the various countries. Britain and Italy had independent air forces with their own, necessarily larger, establishments, while most other powers preferred to integrate their air services with the army and navy. Some nations employed service personnel for repairs and maintenance, others utilized private contractors. Categories of officers and men varied widely between states, there being no adequate standards of comparison, and in general the whole question of limitation was confused by the existence of civil aviation and its specialist personnel.[36]

On 1 April, the Chancellor of the Duchy of Lancaster presented the British case at the Preparatory Commission, and found he had no support. It had been anticipated that the Americans would offer assistance, but none was forthcoming; indeed the chief American delegate, Hugh Gibson, read out a statement accepting a limitation both of air effectives and trained reserves and expressing a willingness to consider a separate restriction of pilots.[37] Cecil was indignant at being placed in such a humiliating position and vented his wrath in two strongly worded telegrams to the Prime Minister. In the first, he asked how a limitation of air personnel could possibly hurt Britain, more especially as Britain already made an annual return of such personnel to the House of Commons, and added: '. . . you will not forget the intolerable position of a British delegate who has to resist reasonable measures of air disarmament which to me at any rate appear to contribute to our national security.'[38] In the second he drew attention to the possible consequences of a refusal to make a concession:

Those at home who follow matter will be simply bewildered to find British government resisting limitation of air armaments. It has produced extremely bad effect on committee where we have lost position and authority which has passed very largely into the hands of the French and that may hamper us a great deal when we come to discuss really important questions such as naval limitation. I really cannot undertake to go through such an experience as I went through this afternoon again and I must formally ask for liberty to make concessions when I feel it is in the interests of the country that I should do so. Otherwise perhaps it would be better for someone else to take my place here.[39]

Earlier that same day, 1 April, the Disarmament Committee had met under Salisbury's chairmanship to consider Cecil's original enquiry about the possible change of instructions, but had found itself in deadlock. The Lord Privy Seal had suggested that a compromise was acceptable, but the air representative, Air-Commodore Newall, had obstinately refused to make substantive concessions, making it clear that his service was afraid of committing itself to a limitation of personnel because of the rapid development of the RAF and the potential needs of expansion. And so, pending a full enquiry by the CID and individual conversations between Salisbury and the service ministers, the matter was held in abeyance.[40]

At this point, another violent controversy arose between Cecil and the Air Ministry, over the question of air *matériel*. The Chancellor of the Duchy of Lancaster had long been convinced that the proposal for limiting only first-line combatant units in metropolitan forces was much too narrow to be acceptable to the other major powers and when he laid the formula before the Preparatory Commission, he again found he had no support from his fellow delegates. The other representatives favoured the more comprehensive French scheme for air disarmament, holding that limitation must apply to all aircraft, home or overseas, and include machines in reserve.[41]

Three main grounds were adduced by the Air Ministry for opposing the inclusion of aircraft in reserve: simplicity, economy and operational convenience. It was argued that the British air formula represented the most practicable first step towards disarmament because of its ease of application and that, as it gave virtually no information which did not already appear in the Armaments Year Book, it called for the minimum of 'irksome supervision'. It was also apprehended that, if a definite ratio of reserve machines was allotted, many countries would raise their demands considerably, claiming a ratio of around 2.5 to 1 reserve machines rather than their existing norm of around 1 to 2 and so increase rather than reduce both armaments and expenditure. From the operational point of view, the air staff was reluctant to disclose reserves, asserting that to do so would be to divulge a secret of mobilization that had always been jealously guarded in the past.[42]

The air staff's opposition to a limitation of overseas aircraft stemmed from a fear that the policy of 'substitution' might be jeopardized if restrictions were placed on Dominion and colonial machines; but by the evening of 1 April it had become clear that Trenchard would concede the point provided that the Fleet Air Arm was excluded and that a statement was made to the effect that Britain would ask for a substantial allotment for her colonies and mandated territories because of their distance from the British mainland. By the time the relevant debate took place at Geneva, however, Cecil had not been authorized by the government to change his stance, so he reserved the British position on the question until the second reading of the draft convention.[43]

At this time, there was still no indication that either the government or the air staff were willing to make concessions on reserve aircraft and so Cecil followed his own devices and offered to recommend acceptance of an Italian compromise proposal whereby limitation would be restricted to the 'immediate reserve' for making good normal wastage.[44] Then, on the following day, 2 April, he sent a further telegram to Baldwin, stating that the rigidity of his instructions and the attitude of the Air Ministry had caused a serious deterioration in the situation at Geneva:

> I cannot conceal from you that the effect of the last two days has been to seriously hamper the whole of our negotiations out here. I found it impossible in London to [? bring] home to representatives of fighting services that it was not enough merely to consider what was administratively convenient to British departments but that in an international convention you had to provide what was effective for the purpose of the convention as applied to all the different nations. That is why I am so very anxious to be given greater liberty of action than I am at present afforded by my instructions. Nothing could be more disastrous than that disarmament conference should fail by reason of contentions put forward by British government which no one outside Great Britain will regard as reasonable.[45]

In effect, Cecil was issuing an ultimatum to the government to accept his views or face the possible consequences — his personal resignation and the breakdown of the Preparatory Commission on British responsibility.

On 4 April, a special meeting of the CID was held to review the more serious of the two questions dividing Cecil and his air colleagues — effectives. A long debate took place and Hoare and Trenchard remained firm against concessions, arguing that the proper unit of air disarmament was aircraft and that the different methods of air force organization presented formidable complications. Hoare asserted further that a limitation of effectives might hinder the expansion of the RAF and make it difficult to continue the policy of 'substitution'; and Trenchard, who thought a breakdown of negotiations almost inevitable once numbers were discussed, suggested it would be preferable for a rupture to occur on a question of principle. Although the air leaders obtained a degree of support, notably from Bridgeman and Amery, they were unable to convince the committee that a British concession occasioned serious dangers. Baldwin and Chamberlain strongly supported the Cecil line and, in the circumstances, it was agreed that the principle of a limitation of personnel might be conceded provided the restrictions applied to total numbers only and that an explanation was given at the time of acceptance that, owing to the 'special manner' in which the RAF was organized, the number of British personnel would appear to be larger than the number maintained by other powers.[46]

The debate of 4 April was especially important in that it revealed some of the inner thoughts of important members of the government. Baldwin, for example, was shown to be extremely unwilling to adopt a positive approach at Geneva, taking the attitude that it was doubtful whether the negotiations would be brought to a successful conclusion; he insisted merely that 'every endeavour' should be made to avoid the failure of discussion being charged against Britain. Together with Salisbury and Worthington-Evans, he apparently felt it impolitic to risk breaking up the Preparatory Commission on an issue which the British public took to be comparatively unimportant.[47]

Certainly it would have been difficult for the government to defend a breakdown of negotiations on such a relatively obscure point if the British public sincerely and consciously sought an alleviation of the arms burden through international agreement. But the nature of public opinion itself was at issue in the committee. Amery, for example, stressed his own belief that the general public viewed the Geneva discussions with such misapprehension and distrust that there would be no difficulty in defending a breakdown in the Commons. His argument is not entirely convincing — although it is certainly true that the government had such a massive majority in the House that there was little if any danger of a parliamentary defeat — but at the same time Salisbury's contention that the public genuinely and emphatically desired disarmament might also be considered exaggerated. Apart from the fact that no one apparently defined what he meant by 'public opinion', there is no indication that ministers would have agreed on the nature of 'opinion' even if they had agreed on a definition. It seems likely, therefore, that the ministers who raised the issue merely adduced 'opinion' as an argument in favour of pre-conceived ideas.[48]

At first sight, the greatest division between the British and French draft conventions over air disarmament remained the method of applying restrictions to limitable categories. But it soon became clear at Geneva that a compromise was possible between the British proposal for a quantitative limitation of aircraft and the French proposal for a limitation of total horse-power. The Swedish representative, Einar Hennings, suggested that a combination of both methods might facilitate an agreement, and his suggestion was accepted in principle by the great majority of delegations, including those of all the great powers, subject to governmental confirmation.[49]

Budgetary questions also produced a surprising degree of unity among the assembled delegations. The Preparatory Commission was unanimous in supporting the principle of annual standardized returns to the Secretary-General of the League concerning proposed and actual expenditure on armaments; and the proponents of budgetary limitation were unwilling to press their case against the entrenched objections of Britain, Japan and the United States. Brouckère admitted that it was useless to prolong discussions on the point; and Paul-Boncour, while not formally abandoning the French position, stated that his government did not consider the inclusion of a provision for budgetary limitation as a *sine qua non* for accepting the convention as a whole. It was agreed, therefore, on Cecil's suggestion, that a preamble to the expenditure clauses be adopted, expressing the hope that budgetary publicity (accepted in principle by all powers) might merely be a precursor to full budgetary limitation.[50]

In effect, the 'agreement to disagree' over budgetary limitation — whether applied to armaments as a whole or to land, sea and air armaments separately — left both British and French delegations without proposals for the limitation of land *matériel*, a situation which did not appeal to the German representatives, whose country remained under the wide restrictions imposed by the Treaty of Versailles. Count Bernstorff, therefore, endeavoured to rectify the situation by inserting a provision for the direct limitation of seven major categories of *matériel* both in service and reserve: rifles or carbines; machine-guns and rifles; guns and howitzers under 15 cm calibre; guns and howitzers over 15 cm calibre; motors; tanks; and armoured cars. Although his proposal gained support from the Swedish, Finnish, Dutch and American delegations, the negative reaction of others — notably the Belgian and Japanese — caused him to withdraw the suggestion on the understanding that he would return to the subject on the second reading of the convention. The result of the debate was not surprising — the discussions of Sub-Commission 'A' had already revealed the divisions of the powers — but it gave the German case for 'real disarmament' increased publicity. It also elicited an intimation from the Dutch representative that he would submit a proposal obliging states to issue annual statements of *matériel* along similar lines to the agreed budgetary statements.[51]

The Dutch proposal for publicity of *matériel* came up for discussion on 21-2 April. A number of delegates criticized the details of the scheme, despite the fact that the categories of weapons designated for publication were in accordance with the Convention for the Supervision of the International Trade in Arms, signed on 17 June 1925, but in general it received a favourable reception. The Belgian delegation accepted it, subject to minor reservations, and so did the French, subject to emendation and a degree of supervision. However, the Japanese delegate, M.N. Sato, rejected it on the rather specious grounds that it was inconsistent with Article 8 of the Covenant since it would reveal information concerning preparations for defence. There being a lack of complete unanimity, therefore, the proposal was 'noted' rather than adopted on first reading. The British delegate maintained a discreet silence throughout the debate.[52]

Probably the most serious point of issue between the British and French delegations concerned the problem of supervision. The British service representatives fulminated against the proposal for a Permanent Disarmament Commission on the grounds that it would become virtually an international general staff, duplicate functions of the League Council and Permanent Advisory Commission and cause friction and distrust; and even Cecil, who regarded the British position on supervision as 'largely unreasonable', thought the French proposal 'very objectionable'. At an early date, however, he perceived that Paul-Boncour felt more deeply on this issue than any other. In mid-April, when deadlock had been reached between the British and French governments on naval questions and the French appeared to be fomenting a breakdown of the conference on the issue, the Chancellor of the Duchy of Lancaster surmised that control questions concerned Paul-Boncour as much as naval issues, and Lord Salisbury, who had taken over Cecil's responsibilities for disarmament in London while the Chancellor of the Duchy was in Geneva, agreed — even suggesting that the chief French representative considered the control provisions the more vital.[53]

As events turned out, the protracted discussion of the naval problem left little time for discussion of the control problem. With Easter approaching, the close of the third session of the Preparatory Commission was scheduled for 26 April, and it was considered very unlikely that a new session would be convened before the autumn since the intervening period would be utilized for the preparation and convention of a naval disarmament conference at Geneva. Invitations to this conference had been issued by the American President, Calvin Coolidge, on 10 February, and although only the three great naval powers — Britain, America and Japan — were expected to participate, it would have been difficult for the Preparatory Commission to hold parallel discussions. As a result, therefore, the control problem was effectively shelved by the commission pending further consideration by governments, private negotiations between the powers and the reconvening of the commission.

The short debate on supervision did give some indication of possible lines of advance towards an agreement. In particular, Hugh Gibson, the chief American delegate, suggested the possibility of a two-part convention, one for members of the League which might include agreed measures of control, and one for powers outside the League who would be under no obligations whatsoever as regards control. Even Paul-Boncour, who suggested that Gibson's approach would 'mutilate' the convention, could see no realistic alternative; and Cecil gave the American initiative his personal approval. At the same time, the League powers remained as intrinsically disunited on the control problem as they had been in Sub-Commission 'A', the French grouping desiring a comprehensive system of supervision through a permanent body of experts with extensive powers of investigation, a concept to which Britain, Japan and Italy were resolutely opposed. The Japanese delegate expressed a willingness to accept a supervisory commission under the auspices of the League to facilitate the publication and exchange of information, but no more.[54]

The differences between Britain and France over many facets of disarmament may have been spectacular, and certainly vociferous, but at times they served to obscure the more fundamental differences between France and Germany. The Germans contented themselves with playing a quiet, even minor, role on the commission, but the strength of feeling of the German government on the issue of disarmament was made perfectly clear by Count Bernstorff on 22 April, four days before the adjournment. Making a general reservation on the draft convention as a whole, he `declared:

> The draft Convention does not yet enable us to foresee whether certain fundamental conditions [of acceptance] will be fulfilled . . . . Unless they are fulfilled, Germany will be unable to regard the Convention as a first step towards general disarmament. Furthermore, guarantees must be given that this first step will be followed within a reasonable time by other steps entailing more marked progress towards reduction of armaments.[55]

Bernstorff did not suggest that Germany would endeavour to rearm if the 'fundamental conditions' — notably the direct limitation of *matériel*, the limitation of trained reserves and the abolition of methods of warfare already prohibited to Germany under the Treaty of Versailles — remained unfulfilled. But the implication of his remarks was all too clear. The French, Belgian, Rumanian and Polish representatives endeavoured to counter his arguments by maintaining that Germany too had obligations, under the Covenant of the League of Nations and Part V of the Treaty of Versailles, but they failed to make any impact and the other delegations remained silent.[56]

The inherent dangers of further substantive negotiations increased the pessimism of one member of the British delegation, Alexander Cadogan. He openly regretted the decision to frame a draft convention and urged very strongly that the Preparatory Commission should not meet again unless agreement had been reached on the important points that were still outstanding. In a Foreign Office memorandum of 17 May, giving his personal impressions of the proceedings at Geneva, he declared that the overall results were of doubtful value and that, while some progress towards disarmament had been achieved, the effect on the relations of the powers had not been good. The problems considered by the Preparatory Commission were of a delicate nature, touching the powers 'on the raw', and consequently the tone of discussions had become 'somewhat unusually acrimonious'. It was not surprising, therefore, that he considered that, even if agreement was reached on outstanding questions, it would be well to proceed as slowly as possible, for once the commission produced an agreed draft Britain would be committed to an international conference at which 'the real difficulties — and dangers' of disarmament would begin, filling in the skeleton tables and trying to resolve the German problem.[57]

In support of what he admitted to be 'a purely dilatory and obstructive attitude', Cadogan suggested that a sizeable delay and even postponement of the next meeting of the Preparatory Commission might give time for reflection and the opportunity of finding an alternative course. He believed that general disarmament should follow general security and regretted the decision to embark on a discussion of disarmament in the absence of a prior security settlement, but he was at a loss to explain how a general security agreement might be brought about. Successive British governments had been largely responsible for frustrating the two great attempts to settle the problem — the Treaty of Mutual Assistance and the Geneva Protocol — and he had agreed with his political masters on both occasions. Britain had done her 'utmost' towards further international security at Locarno. He was driven to hope that a general settlement might be realized in the sum of regional security pacts covering the globe.[58]

Intrinsically, Cadogan was suggesting that the governments's policy offered little chance of a satisfactory outcome to the security and disarmament problems, indeed that negotiated settlements would be almost impossible without additional British commitments. It was an authoritative, if pessimistic, evaluation of the situation at Geneva, and one which, surprisingly enough, had much in common with Cecil's evaluation. But whilst Cadogan thought the greatest danger facing Britain was the possibility of being drawn into further commitments, whether on the continent of Europe or with regard to her own defence forces, Cecil felt that a greater threat was the potential denunciation by Germany of the disarmament clauses of the Treaty of Versailles. Cecil was loath, therefore, to dismiss the proceedings at Geneva as of little consequence, and in a critique of Cadogan's memorandum emphasized the measure of agreement that had already been reached. He admitted that very little armaments' reduction might occur when the principles of the draft convention were translated into practice, but pointed out that arms limitation would in itself represent a considerable step forward and be an immense advance on the pre-1914 situation. Nations would have accepted formally that the armaments of individual countries were of concern to the international community and machinery would have been established which might facilitate arms reductions after the expiry of the first convention.[59]

In support of his thesis, Cecil reiterated the 'very specific obligation' made by Britain and others to promote a scheme of general disarmament — in Article 8 of the Covenant of the League, the preamble to Part V of the Treaty of Versailles, the 'Clemenceau letter' and the documents signed at Locarno. The Germans, he claimed, might fairly say that it was in return for a promise to promote such a scheme that they agreed to the disarmament clauses of the Versailles treaty, and if the League negotiations were indefinitely postponed they would have 'every ground' for saying that the ex-Allies were not keeping faith with them. Thus Cadogan's suggestion that Britain either propose or agree to an 'indefinite postponement' of the Preparatory Commission unless an agreement had been arranged with France beforehand was 'impracticable'.[60]

The Foreign Office, as a whole, remained antipathetic to the idea of general disarmament, although elements within it, for example J.D. Gregory, recently promoted to Assistant Under-Secretary of

State, did admit that Cecil's arguments with regard to the German problem were 'very difficult to answer'. Even Cadogan saw Cecil's point and, in a private communication to the Chancellor of the Duchy, he agreed that his own views were based on cowardice and that the policy he advocated was one of 'procrastination verging on duplicity'. No one within the ministry seemed willing to advocate a change of policy aimed at actively promoting the cause of disarmament, and the consensus of opinion was that the best way of preventing, or at least postponing, an international controversy over Germany's position *vis-à-vis* the Versailles disarmament clauses was for Britain to continue her existing policy.[61]

One of the reasons behind Cadogan's preparation of the memorandum of 17 May may have been a desire to clarify the ultimate objectives of British disarmament policy. The questions he had formulated in this respect, in his minute of 7 February, had still not been answered. But his position within the Foreign Office hierarchy at this time was not sufficiently high to prompt a new analysis either among his superiors or at governmental level. Indeed, discussion was cut short by Chamberlain, who, in a minute of 27 May, laid down his own views on the disarmament problem.

I am not attracted by schemes so vast as that of general (i.e. universal) disarmament for they are never realised & to my mind divert attention from more modest but more practicable proposals. But the decision has been taken to proceed on the larger lines & we must continue to do our best to get the best possible result from it.[62]

The Foreign Secretary seemed bent on continuing a policy which his critics agreed offered little chance of success.

Chamberlain's reluctance to change course on the disarmament issue stemmed partly from his natural conservatism. He was unwilling to choose between the suggested alternatives of outright procrastination, which would have brought the potential threat of Germany much nearer, and of an active pursuit of a general convention, which to be successful would have involved many concessions by Britain, even commitments to other powers. He preferred to meet each situation as it arose and hope that a satisfactory outcome might somehow be obtained. At the same time, more practical considerations might well have affected his judgement. Within the Cabinet he had to steer a judicious course between the detractors of disarmament such as Amery, Birkenhead and Churchill; the 'patron' of disarmament, Cecil, and the doubtful well-wishers such as Salisbury. The existing course of policy seemed likely to cause less dissension than the alternatives. Above all, however, Chamberlain was fundamentally disinterested in disarmament, regarding it as a peripheral problem outside the mainstream of international politics. He admitted he was not well informed on the question and was content to leave matters in the hands of Cecil. Further, in April 1927, he decided to relieve himself of the greater part of his remaining disarmament duties — the monitoring of events while Cecil was absent

in Geneva. He felt his time could be utilized more profitably considering other matters. Baldwin approved the move, and the duties were
allocated to Salisbury.[63]

The Foreign Secretary was actually closer to Cecil's position than
the great majority of his cabinet colleagues. In fact, the relationship
between the two men had become very warm, as the Chancellor of
the Duchy of Lancaster recounted in a letter to Lord Irwin of 7 June:

> From a personal point of view the brightest spot is that I get on so much
> better with Austen than I used to. I nearly always agree with him on ques-
> tions of foreign policy, and do my best to prevent him giving way to F.E.
> and Winston who seem to me really insans [sic — insane?] on all such ques-
> tions, especially the latter.[64]

Chamberlain for his part indicated the value he attached to the
relationship in a number of ways. He chose Salisbury as Cecil's
understudy in London considering him the minister most likely to
give sympathetic attention to the Chancellor of the Duchy of Lancaster's views, and gave the Lord Privy Seal full authority to approve
telegrams to Cecil without further reference to the Foreign Office. He
strongly supported the Chancellor of the Duchy of Lancaster on the
question of air effectives; and he acted swiftly when Cecil complained
about the uncompromising attitude of the French delegation. He
asked the British Ambassador at Paris, the Marquess of Crewe, to
draw Briand's attention to the matter, so that the French Prime
Minister might keep a closer watch on the French delegation at
Geneva; and he approached the French Ambassador at London, Aimé
de Fleuriau, in similar vein. He was especially concerned since Cecil
had continually urged concessions to the French point of view. He
was also aggrieved that Briand had not responded officially to a
suggestion that Britain be given a substantially free hand on naval
issues in return for France being allowed a similar initiative on land
disarmament questions.[65]

Cecil did not receive the same degree of support from the majority
of the Cabinet. In his letter of 7 June to Irwin he complained:

> Much against their will the majority of my Colleagues have accepted a
> policy of international disarmament but they don't like it and the result
> is that they drag back at every moment, giving the impression that they
> are not really in earnest, and thereby ... making the policy itself
> exceedingly difficult to carry to a successful issue.[66]

It was an apt assessment. The concessions urged by Cecil during the
third session of the Preparatory Commission, at least as far as land
and air disarmament were concerned, could hardly be construed as
affecting vital British interests, military or political, but they were
granted only after a strenuous fight and on a number of conditions.
The CID debate of 4 April showed that Baldwin's support of disarmament was insubstantial; the Prime Minister had serious doubts as
to the utility of the proceedings at Geneva and endorsed the Cecil position on air effectives to avoid being blamed for a breakdown of the

Preparatory Commission rather than to promote the cause of arms limitation. Hoare was concerned with furthering the Air Ministry's conception of disarmament rather than seeking a formula that had a chance of international acceptance — though he admitted to Cecil privately that he was willing to make a number of concessions in the general interest. Bridgeman took a stiff departmental line, incurring the Chancellor of the Duchy of Lancaster's wrath on a number of occasions. Amery displayed his almost total lack of sympathy for disarmament, a feeling shared by Birkenhead, Churchill, Joynson-Hicks and Walter Guinness. And Worthington-Evans, despite a realization that concessions would have to be made if Britain was to avoid the responsibility for a failure at Geneva, gave no indication that he was willing to make concessions on behalf of his own department. Indeed, it had been on his instigation that the provision for a limitation of aggregate expenditure on land armaments had been excluded from the British draft convention, even though it had been included originally on the suggestion of the War Office representative, Colonel Temperley.[67]

At the same time, the Chancellor of the Duchy of Lancaster was not the easiest of colleagues to work with. He tended to over-react to criticism and opposition, at times talking vaguely of resignation, and at Geneva he became positively impatient if events did not follow the course he desired. Mostly, he vented his wrath in private letters to the two ministers he trusted implicitly, Chamberlain and Salisbury; for example, in a letter to Chamberlain of 6 April, he disparaged, in turn, the French delegation at the Preparatory Commission, the British Admiralty, the RAF and the Japanese and Italian delegations. But on occasion his heat-of-the-moment opinions came to the attention of other colleagues through official communications with the result that he did not endear himself to the Cabinet. Hoare, for example, was upset by a report from Geneva on the question of air effectives in which Cecil seemed to imply that the Air Ministry was not in earnest about disarmament.[68]

The Chancellor of the Duchy of Lancaster's considered assessments of the situation at Geneva showed greater insight than his impulsive comments and revealed a sound understanding of the problems and possibilities of disarmament. He appreciated that a first disarmament convention would not be far-reaching and would concern limitation rather than reduction of armaments; and he was fully convinced that the best method of facilitating future progress was an Anglo–French agreement whereby France would have the leading say on land armaments and Britain a paramount voice on naval armaments. He comprehended that, if Britain wanted France to make concessions on naval questions and the control problem, the government would be forced to back down on trained reserves.[69]

Cecil also displayed considerable astuteness at recognizing the genuine fears of other powers — whether they were justified or not — and in appreciating how these fears might be reconciled without sacrificing British interests. For example, the Chancellor of the

Duchy of Lancaster quickly discerned that the concessions asked of Britain on the question of air limitation would not affect the national interest adversely, indeed would further the cause of disarmament. He realized that any system backed by France and Britain and not opposed in principle by the other powers could be expected to achieve positive results, and the French air proposals, which encountered no serious opposition, were more far-reaching than the British. Even Hoare admitted that, in the final analysis, the concessions urged from Geneva were impossible to resist on grounds of principle; instead, he claimed that the cumulative effects of the concessions would endanger a vital — though unspecified and probably unspecifiable — interest. Cecil was justified, therefore, in commenting to Salisbury that the propositions advanced by the Air Ministry were far too simple to be maintained successfully at an international gathering. They were founded purely on British interests — or rather the government's conception of British interests. They took virtually no account of the feelings or desires of any other nation. He was also justified in complaining that the CID concessions of 4 April did not include a limitation of aircraft in the Fleet Air Arm. At the time, Britain based about 100 combatant aircraft on ships, and it was hypocritical for a maritime nation to contend that shore-based aircraft should be limited but that sea-based should not. The argument that a limitation of aircraft-carriers would automatically limit the number of sea-borne machines carried little weight at Geneva, where it was countered by a suggestion that there was nothing to prevent ships being converted into carriers that were outside the agreed definition, whether it be the Washington Naval Treaty definition or a new one. The possibility of a nation basing a considerable portion of its air force on ships to avoid limitation might have seemed absurd to the British, but it did not seem absurd to certain continental countries.[70]

Certainly, if there was an advance towards agreement at Geneva in the period from December 1926 to April 1927, the credit on the British side must devolve mainly on Cecil. It was he who formulated the idea of a skeleton draft convention; it was he who pressed the cause of disarmament within the government; it was he who shaped the British draft convention; it was he who bore the brunt of international negotiations; and it was he who mobilized the support of Chamberlain, Salisbury and Baldwin, the latter rather unwillingly, to force concessions on a hesitant CID when the breakdown of the Preparatory Commission seemed possible over the British attitude to air effectives.

On 26 April, when the Preparatory Commission adjourned until November, a large number of problems remained unresolved. A measure of agreement had been reached on a number of questions, such as air limitation, defence expenditure and the restriction of personnel in the colours, but on other points the divergence of views between the powers was considerable. Some problems had been shelved until the second reading of the draft convention; reservations on both general and specific points were numerous; and many articles in the convention had to be laid out with alternative texts in parallel columns because of the inability of the powers to agree on a single united text. Even with goodwill on all sides it was questionable whether the powers could reach full agreement in private negotiations over the six months' adjournment. But at least, as Paul-Boncour pointed out and Jonkheer Loudon, President of the Preparatory Commission, reiterated, the disarmament problem was no longer wrapped in mystery; it was a real and concrete question.[71]

8 Naval disarmament
November 1924–May 1927

Within weeks of taking office, the government was faced with an American initiative for extending the Washington agreement of 1922. Charles Evans Hughes, the outgoing Secretary of State, told Sir Esme Howard, the British Ambassador at Washington, that the American President, Calvin Coolidge, was determined, as far as he could, to put an end to competition in armaments; and Curtis D. Wilbur, Secretary of the Navy, confirmed that Coolidge was 'most anxious and eager' to cut down expenditure on naval armaments and that it was necessary to extend the Washington ratios to all other branches of the service. Wilbur also spoke of the great expense that would be incurred if the United States was to build twenty-two modern scout cruisers, the number required to raise the American fleet to the standard of the British, and Howard concluded that everything pointed to the President wanting to call a naval conference in the near future. There was little surprise in British government circles, therefore, when Frank B. Kellogg, the American Ambassador at London and prospective Secretary of State, approached Chamberlain in February 1925 with the idea of holding a further naval disarmament conference in Washington. Chamberlain's reply, however, was very cautious. While welcoming in principle the plan for a conference, he was careful to make a *caveat* regarding the rationing of cruisers on the same lines as capital ships, since it had been British policy at the Washington conference to seek superiority over other powers in this class of vessel. He further suggested that the United States' government might put out feelers to other governments to ascertain their views.[1]

The Cabinet approved the Foreign Secretary's actions on 12 February,[2] and on the following day the Plans Division of the Admiralty produced outline disarmament proposals which marked a turning point in British policy regarding cruiser limitation. At the Washington conference, Britain had advocated limits of 10,000 tons displacement and eight-inch gun calibre — dimensions that had been readily accepted by the other powers — but now the Admiralty recommended a discussion of reduced limits and the possibility of establishing two classes of cruiser, the 'Washington standard' type and a smaller, less powerful type armed with six-inch guns. Further elaborated, this suggestion became one of the cornerstones of British naval disarmament policy in the later 1920s and one of the crucial factors in the deterioration of Anglo–American relations between 1927 and 1929. On other points, the Plans Division recommended no great change in British policy. A quantitative limitation of cruisers, it was declared, would be welcomed only if two conditions were fulfilled: that the total number allowed to the British Empire was 'not less than the minimum required for the scouting line of the main fleet plus the minimum number required for the protection of trade'; and that the other naval powers recognized 'the special needs of the British Empire' and consented to Britain possessing 'the necessary superiority in this class of vessel'. It was further suggested that the Washington agreement should not be modified as regards capital ships, though eventually it might be possible to agree to a reduction in the individual and total tonnage of aircraft carriers; and that as there was no chance of securing the complete abolition of submarines — the chief threat to British shipping in the First World War — Britain should welcome a limitation of total tonnage of these craft and of the dimensions and armament of individual submersibles, destroyers and flotilla leaders. At the same time, any considerable development of naval power by the Soviet Union or Germany might make it necessary to denounce an agreement, and all parties to the Washington Naval Treaty had to accept the agreement if Britain was to give her consent.[3]

Admiral Beatty, the First Sea Lord, composed a memorandum for Chamberlain on the basis of the Plans Division's recommendations, and on 18 February the Cabinet broadly endorsed his proposals with a view to putting them before the Americans. Significantly, it was declared that there were geographical and other reasons why the ratio already agreed for capital ships could not be applied to cruisers and that the terms of reference of a naval conference should be restricted to four main areas: dimensions and armament of cruisers; armament of aircraft-carriers; total number, dimensions and armament of submarines; and dimensions and armament of destroyers. It was agreed, however, that Britain should take no initiative in Washington until the French Prime Minister had been informed of the proposed action.[4]

In conversations with Chamberlain during March 1925, Herriot made it clear that a disarmament conference in Washington would be very unwelcome to the French government in the international situation resulting from the rejection of the Geneva Protocol; and on 1 April Chamberlain informed his Cabinet colleagues that he had received information which led him to believe that a British initiative would not be welcome in Washington. In the circumstances, therefore, the government decided that Sir Esme Howard, if approached by the American government, should limit his action to informing the Americans officially that Britain would be prepared to enter a conference only if the other great naval powers agreed. A suggestion that a three-power conference of Britain, America and Japan might produce results was discounted by the Admiralty on the grounds that any naval conference excluding France and Italy 'would jeopardise the safety of the Empire's sea communications'.[5]

At the same time, the government was setting out the bases of its naval policy. On 2 April 1925, the Committee of Imperial Defence accepted Chamberlain's view that aggressive action on the part of Japan against the British Empire in the next ten years was 'not a contingency seriously to be apprehended'. This had the effect of undermining the Admiralty argument that an extensive cruiser programme was required because of possible Japanese aggression and it recommended the continuance of the 'one-Power standard' of naval construction on a purely numerical basis; the geographical situation of world powers was no longer to be taken into consideration in assessing the particular requirements of the British fleet. No reference was made to any standard by which British *cruiser* strength should be measured.[6]

The genesis of the naval policy discussions lay in a controversy between the Treasury and Admiralty over the naval estimates. Churchill had initiated the debate in November 1924 in an attempt to secure drastic reductions in naval expenditure, and Bridgeman had taken up the challenge on behalf of the Sea Lords. The Admiralty asserted that Britain needed seventy cruisers in wartime, to provide a scouting line for the main fleet and to protect British trade, and claimed that, to reach this figure by 1936 whilst compensating for the scrapping of older craft, it would be necessary to build fifty-one new vessels over a ten-year period. If Britain reduced her programme, she would be placed in a relatively weak position at any naval conference. Churchill disputed the need for such extensive construction and claimed that the Admiralty case was based on a non-existent danger from Japan. On 12 February 1925, the Cabinet set up a Naval Programme Committee to examine the matter.[7]

The Admiralty reduced their demands considerably during the discussions of this committee, on the grounds that the CID recommendations of 2 April (which were approved by the Cabinet on 6 May) created a new situation. Whilst still maintaining that Britain needed a minimum of seventy cruisers, they agreed to cut the number of vessels laid down in the ensuing six years from thirty-one to twenty and to construct half of them to new standard dimensions of 8,000 tons rather than the Washington 'standard' of 10,000 tons. They also agreed to extend the life of cruisers from fifteen to twenty years and destroyers from twelve to sixteen years and to make substantial cuts in the destroyer, submarine and aircraft-carrier programmes.[8] But still Churchill remained unsatisfied. The discussions became acrid and, eventually, when the committee agreed to adopt the Chancellor's programme of a one-year delay in the entire Admiralty programme, Bridgeman and the whole Board of Admiralty threatened resignation. The crisis was settled only when Baldwin intervened personally in the dispute on 22 July and made compromise recommendations that were acceptable to all. The number of cruisers to be laid down during the next six years was to be twenty — the quota the Admiralty demanded — while the submarine, destroyer and aircraft-carrier programmes were to be set back a year.[9]

By November 1925 there was no immediate prospect of a naval conference, and as far as the British government was concerned the problem of naval disarmament became merged with that of general disarmament. At this juncture, the Disarmament Committee took up the question and the naval staff produced a long and important memorandum which reflected the decisions reached by the Cabinet on the cruiser question. Based on a Plans Division draft of August 1925, the memorandum argued that there was a great need for caution in approaching naval limitation because British supplies of food and raw materials depended on the adequate protection of sea communications and the security of the Empire on the maintenance of sea power. The effect of the Washington agreement had been to level up the minor in relation to the major naval powers, and seaborne trade was under a greater threat since the development of air power. It appeared essential, therefore, that any further reductions of naval armaments should take into consideration the actual and potential forces of powers other than those represented at the Washington conference, in particular the Soviet Union. Moreover, it was impossible for Britain to attend a naval conference at which the United States was not represented. As for actual proposals, the naval staff declared that the time was not ripe to discuss modifications of the Washington agreement, at least regarding capital ships. If a general reduction was agreed, Britain would have to undertake greater numerical reductions than any other power except the United States and, if individual ships were reduced below 35,000 tons, smaller powers would find them easier to acquire, being less prohibitively expensive. Besides, a smaller ship could not combine the necessary offensive power with adequate defence against torpedo and air attack. At the same time, the displacement of aircraft-carriers might be reduced from a maximum of 27,000 tons to 23,000 tons and the maximum gun calibre of these vessels from eight inches to six inches. Submarines and destroyers might be limited along the lines suggested in February.[10]

The most interesting section of the memorandum concerned cruisers. In the original Plans Division draft, it was declared that:

> The prospects of effecting any considerable reductions in naval forces depends chiefly on the recognition . . . by the other Powers [of the fact that the need for Cruisers by the British Empire is proportionately greater than that of any other Power]; *refusal to recognise this at Washington* was the principal reason why no agreement was found possible for limiting the number of cruisers to be retained by the Powers.

Beatty, however, objected to the wording, and on his instructions the cardinal clause was reversed so that it read: [The need for Cruisers by the British Empire is proportionately greater than that of any other Power.] *This was generally recognised at Washington* ....[11] Apparently, the First Sea Lord did not want the Disarmament Committee - and therefore the Cabinet — to know the truth. The naval staff also decided to alter the section on the qualitative limitation of cruisers. The Plans Division had suggested the application of the Washington Treaty ratios to the 'Washington standard' type, Britain and America being allowed eleven vessels each. This, of course, would have benefited Britain greatly, as she had just laid down her eleventh 10,000 ton eight-inch gun vessel and would have been able to build all future cruisers to a smaller and considerably cheaper standard. The naval staff, however, for unknown reasons, made a less specific suggestion that Britain could accept a further limitation of the size of individual cruisers if such restriction was accompanied by a further reduction in gun calibre.[12]

As the League's preparatory committee was authorized to discuss merely principles of arms limitation and the Disarmament Committee was concerned mainly with drafting the questionnaire for Geneva, the naval staff memorandum was not considered in detail at this time. But within the Disarmament Committee there was an immediate confrontation between Cecil and the Admiralty representative, Admiral Sir Frederick Field. The latter declared that, although it would not be right to abstain from discussing means by which disarmament could best be approached, Britain could not discuss proposals affecting British naval strength in the absence of the Soviet Union and the United States, two non-League powers. Cecil, on the other hand, argued that the government was already committed to discussing the principles of arms limitation and that, if Britain acted merely as an observer, she would lose the initiative to other powers and be accused of holding up disarmament. Eventually a compromise was reached, and on 3 December it was accepted by the Cabinet. It was agreed that a naval conference could best be held in Washington and that it was useless to discuss naval disarmament outside a conference in which the United States participated, but that Britain should co-operate with the League enquiry and avoid giving the impression of passive obstruction.[13]

In January 1926, in preparation for the meeting of the Preparatory Commission, the Admiralty composed a long memorandum on the principles of naval disarmament for discussion within the Disarmament Committee. Eight possible methods of limitation were outlined, of which four were rejected as either impracticable or against the British interest. The only really practical method, it was declared, was limitation of numbers of ships by classes, which was better than the possible alternative of total tonnage by classes since the latter method would lead to difficulties of comparison between the fleets of the various powers. For example, it was impossible to compare two 15,000-ton battleships with one of 30,000 tons. Two other methods of limitation were acceptable: the restriction of the size of individual ships within classes, which was essential if comparison was to be made by numbers (otherwise increased displacement in one type of vessel might make that type indistinguishable from another); and the restriction of gun calibre and torpedo size. Two methods were unacceptable because they were inequitable unless combined with a limitation by classes — limitation by total tonnage and limitation by total number of warships. The limitation of naval estimates was considered neither practical nor satisfactory on the grounds that there were too many indefinable factors such as the rate of exchange and cost of living. The limitation of personnel was considered undesirable since it involved factors that were difficult to determine, such as the quality of personnel.[14]

Whilst indicating these possibilities, the Admiralty was able to convince the Disarmament Committee that the only directions in which Britain could carry out a further reduction or limitation of her naval armaments concerned the number, size and gun armament of submarines; the size and gun calibre of cruisers, and the restriction of torpedo size. The reason, it was declared, was that the strength of the Royal Navy was not dependent solely on the strengths of the naval forces of other countries, but was governed by the length and vulnerability of British trade routes. It was further suggested that, as the Washington Conference had imposed no restrictions on the defensive armament of submarines or aircraft, it might even be advisable to ask for an increase in the tonnages allowed under the Washington Treaty. Otherwise the larger types of surface vessel might become more vulnerable to submarine or aircraft attack.[15]

Thus the Disarmament Committee's recommendations of April 1926 regarding naval disarmament, like those on land and air disarmament, were framed primarily to meet British security requirements rather than the needs of an international convention; and, in accepting these recommendations on 28 April, the government cannot be accused of adopting a policy that could jeopardize the national interest. Indeed, if anything, the government might be criticized for over-caution, as the British representative on the Preparatory Commission was instructed to maintain a rather stricter attitude towards definitive limitation proposals than was envisaged in February 1925 when the Americans had proposed a naval conference. Now, it was asserted that before any further limitation of British naval forces could be considered, an international agreement should be obtained as to the number, size and gun calibre of submarines.[16]

At the Preparatory Commission, the main discussions of naval disarmament took place within the naval committee of Sub-Commission 'A'. The corresponding discussions in the military and air committees had shown that there was often only a modicum of common ground between the proposals of the various delegations, and in some cases no common ground at all, and it was no surprise that discussions within the naval committee followed almost exactly the same course. If there was a difference, it was one of degree — the proceedings of the naval committee tended to be more acrimonious than those of the other bodies.

On the two major problems — the standards by which naval armaments could be compared and the methods by which limitation could be effected — two broad groupings of powers emerged. One, led by France and Italy, favoured limitation by total tonnage; the other, led by Britain, the United States and Japan, favoured limitation by classes. The former group adduced six main arguments in support of its case. Total tonnage, it was declared, was equitable for all powers since it could be applied to all fleets whatever their composition, and ought to be universally acceptable as each country was given the maximum latitude in the distribution of the permitted tonnage. Financial burdens would be reduced because powers were not forced to build vessels of specified and possibly unsuitable standard types, and competition would be avoided as countries could distribute their allotted tonnage according to its maximum fighting value. Total tonnage could be applied permanently since it allowed renewals at a rate governed by the age limit of vessels, and was suited to the security of all nations since it allowed replacement of obsolete units by units which corresponded to contemporary security requirements. Britain, the United States and Japan, however, objected that the total tonnage would permit rather than prevent competitive building because it did not necessarily give an indication of the fighting value of a fleet, while the fixing of one maximum limit for the individual tonnage and armament of warships would permit increases in the size of cruisers, aircraft-carriers, destroyers and submarines. Further, limitation by total tonnage would cause international mistrust because it disguised the composition of fleets and allowed changes of relative strength during the lifetime of a convention. The maintenance of equilibrium would be impossible and powers whose existence depended on overseas communication would be especially disadvantaged.[17]

If Britain, the United States and Japan were united in their opposition to limitation by total tonnage, they were divided as to the best method of limitation by classes. Britain favoured limitation by the number of ships in each of at least six classes — capital ships, aircraft-carriers, cruisers, destroyers and flotilla leaders, submarines and minelayers — and Japan the total tonnage within each of four defined classes: capital ships, aircraft-carriers, auxiliary surface vessels and submarines. All three proposals, however, anticipated a maximum permitted displacement and gun calibre for units of each class, also the restriction of torpedo size or torpedo tube diameter.[18]

In support of their general case, the three great naval powers pointed out that limitation by classes had been practically and satisfactorily applied under the terms of the Washington Treaty. Such limitation would allow a fairly accurate comparison to be made between the fighting strength of each country, and all countries would be informed as to the maximum strength of other countries during the lifetime of a convention, thus eliminating international mistrust. No sudden alterations could be made to fleet strength and it would be more difficult to evade the spirit of the treaty than under total tonnage limitation.[19]

In reply, the Franco–Italian group contended that it was impossible to formulate adequate definitions covering all types of vessel and that any limitation by classes would fail to give powers the freedom to arrange their permitted tonnage to its best advantage. Further, the standardization of types of vessel would compel small- and medium-sized powers either to demand tonnage in excess of their requirements or build types of ship that were ill-adapted to their security and economic needs. The Rome Conference of February 1924 had shown the extreme difficulty in 'generalizing' the Washington Treaty, and the restriction of torpedo size would be disadvantageous to powers that could not afford capital ships.[20]

The responsibility for the impasse in the naval committee lay with all states, as each delegation introduced political as well as technical arguments into the debate, but a special responsibility must devolve on France and Italy, who spared no pains to exclude all standards of comparison except that of total tonnage and resolutely prevented the free discussion of other standards. The two Latin powers even manoeuvred the committee into declaring that limitation by classes was impossible, in spite of the fact that the Washington Treaty had been negotiated on that basis! At one point, in a bizarre situation, Britain, the United States and Japan found themselves outvoted by a combination that included the landlocked state of Czechoslovakia and powers such as Yugoslavia that had insignificant naval forces.[21]

The question remains as to why the French and Italians adopted such a dogmatic attitude. Admiral Aubrey Smith, the chief British naval representative, asserted that an 'insidious attempt' was being made to undermine and discredit the Washington Treaty and that the prevailing impression at Geneva was that France would have liked the whole proceedings of the Preparatory Commission to have broken down on British or American responsibility.[22] But it seems more likely that the objective of the French was to put extreme pressure on Britain and the United States on naval matters to counterbalance the Anglo–American proposals on trained reserves in the military committee which, if implemented, might have entailed drastic reductions in French military power.[23] At the same time, much bad feeling might have been avoided if the language and manner of some members of the French delegation had been less provocative. It was not unusual for the French to prepare declarations for the Polish delegation and hand them across the table in full view of the other delegations, and on one occasion Captain Deleuze, the second French naval delegate, caused an uproar by stigmatizing a British proposal as 'iniquitous', an almost unprecedented remark at a League gathering.[24]

At one point, the Foreign Office considered making an official protest about the behaviour of the French delegation. But Chamberlain, whose overall foreign policy was based on a close relationship with France, rejected the idea on the grounds that it would not be good tactics at a time when French policy in general was uncertain.[25] Soon afterwards, however, British policy at the Preparatory Commission itself became more openly political, causing the French, Spanish and Italian delegates on the naval committee to reserve the right to vote on political rather than technical lines when discussing methods of limitation other than total tonnage.[26]

A further difference between the two broad groups of powers concerned naval personnel. Britain, the United States and Japan contended that the number of trained personnel was controlled by the number of ships and that the quality of personnel was too difficult to quantify. The French group maintained that a specific limitation of personnel was necessary to reduce the possibility of rapidly using merchant ships as auxiliary cruisers and to prevent the training of land and air effectives under the guise of naval personnel.[27]

The powers did manage to reach general agreement on two points — that age limits should be applied to all vessels, and that it was impossible to quantify the military value of commercial fleets. But these problems were of little practical importance and, in general, the naval portion of Sub-Commission 'A''s report of December 1926 was a catalogue of opposing arguments. Nevertheless, as Admiral Aubrey Smith admitted, the work of the sub-commisison had not been entirely fruitless in that it had allowed the opinions of the various delegations to emerge and be placed on record, to the general benefit.[28]

In January 1927 the government turned its attention to the draft disarmament convention produced by Cecil. The chief feature of the naval proposals was a division of ships into specified classes, together with a limitation of the number and tonnage of ships within each class but a number of other provisions were also important. In particular, the provision for a limitation of defence expenditure had its naval aspect, and the Chancellor of the Duchy of Lancaster also inserted a clause whereby all parties not bound by Articles 13-18 of the Washington Treaty (which prohibited *inter alia* the peacetime preparation of merchant vessels for the installation of guns over six-inch calibre) would accede to those articles. In addition specific rules were to be laid down for the replacement of warships.[29]

Although the fighting services objected to many of the military and air provisions of Cecil's draft treaty, they disagreed with very few of the naval proposals, which consequently received a very easy passage in the Disarmament Committee, CID and Cabinet. Except for the addition of definitions of classes of vessel, nine in all, and the deletion of the section on budgetary limitation, the naval chapter of the draft underwent little fundamental revision.[30]

In accepting the naval draft, the Cabinet was not moved by dreams of a disarmed world in which there would be everlasting peace. The various proposals were based firmly on Britain's requirements for security and were hardly likely to prove acceptable to the other powers at Geneva. In particular, the other powers were extremely unlikely to accept the suggested classification of ships: battleships and battle-cruisers; coast defence battleships; cruisers; aircraft-carriers; destroyers and flotilla leaders; torpedo-boats; submarines; sloops and minesweepers; and river gunboats. The discussions of Sub-Commission 'A' had shown that the great majority of powers, including the other great naval powers, favoured a more restricted classification.

Perhaps the most interesting aspect of the British naval proposals concerned the sub-divisions of the various classes. Two sub-classes of submarines were projected and three sub-classes of destroyer, but no sub-division of the cruiser class was anticipated, despite the previous insistence of the Admiralty that any future limitation of cruisers should provide for reductions in displacement and gun calibre. The reason, it seems, was that the Admiralty were already preparing for the naval conference proposed by President Coolidge in February and wanted to conceal their intentions of securing a division of the cruiser class at that conference. The conference would concern only the three great naval powers, Britain, the United States and Japan.[31]

The possibility of Britain and France coming to a compromise on naval questions at the Preparatory Commission had been discussed by Cecil and Paul-Boncour in December 1926, when the Frenchman had suggested a limitation by total tonnage combined with a communication of building programmes.[32] But the French draft convention of 23 March 1927 revealed little change in the position adopted by the French in Sub-Commission 'A'. The main method of limitation was to be total tonnage, but in addition no individual vessel of war was to exceed a defined tonnage or carry a gun exceeding a defined calibre, and in assessing total tonnage only a fraction of the real tonnage was to be counted in the case of vessels exceeding the age limit. Naval effectives were to be limited and annual expenditure on naval forces restricted. There were thus three main differences between the British and French proposals. Britain advocated limitation by classes and no restrictions on personnel and expenditure; France advocated limitation by total tonnage and restrictions on personnel and expenditure. The task of the Preparatory Commission was to facilitate a compromise.[33]

The first of the three problems to come to a head was that of naval effectives. Cecil had long been in favour of making a concession on this point, and he wrote to Chamberlain soon after the Preparatory Commission had reconvened suggesting a change of instructions. He felt it would be difficult to contend strongly that a limitation of personnel was undesirable, and thought it would be asserted in Geneva that Britain was trying to limit the military personnel of other powers while refusing to limit her own naval personnel. In London, however, the Admiralty stood firm against any concession, on the grounds that it was impracticable to draw up a scheme that could deal with all types of recruitment and that the Navy had to be treated as an Imperial rather than British unit. Admiral Field even asserted that the development of 'naval mechanical devices' made elasticity of effectives essential, and that a change in Cecil's instructions might compromise discussions at the 'Coolidge conference', now scheduled to convene in June. Although at one stage it seemed as if the Admiralty would be successful in opposing a change in British policy, the government finally accepted Cecil's principal demands. The turning point came when Cecil asserted that the Preparatory Commission might break down if the government adhered to its original line and that, if this happened, not only would Europe blame Britain for the breakdown, he himself would resign. Faced with this threat, the government gave way, and the Chancellor of the Duchy of Lancaster announced the concession at Geneva.[34]

A further difference between delegations concerned the preparation of merchant ships for the installation of guns up to six inches in calibre. The British proposals on this point were generally acceptable to the other powers, but the Netherlands' delegation wanted to include a provision requiring parties to inform the League Secretariat of the name and tonnage of vessels whose decks had been strengthened for the mounting of six-inch guns. Only Britain resisted the Dutch amendment, Cecil claiming that he had no direct instructions on the point. Apart from technical objections, the Admiralty feared that communication of the details suggested would be 'liable to misunderstanding' and argued that merchant ships did not come within the scope of the draft convention as they were not *matériel* available at the outbreak of war without mobilization. Cecil later pointed out a more serious objection: vessels specified in a communication to the League would become a target for enemy attack on a declaration of war.[35]

On the question of budgetary limitation, the French were forced to make concessions as Britain and the other great powers were opposed to a restriction of defence expenditure. While not formally withdrawing the French proposal on this point, Paul-Boncour declared that his country would not necessarily decline to accept a convention if budgetary limitation was excluded.[36] It was clear, therefore, that there would be no restriction of naval budgets except as part of the general provisions regarding budgetary publicity.

If a modicum of agreement was reached on the questions of effectives and expenditure, the same could not be said for the method of limiting vessels of war. There was still a wide gulf between the two main groups of powers when the Preparatory Commission adjourned on 26 April. Attempts were made by Paul-Boncour to facilitate a compromise, but they came to nothing. His first suggestion was that limitation should be by total tonnage and the submission of a five-year building programme, each power retaining the right to modify the programme on notification to the League, but this was so similar to the original French proposal that Cecil turned it down summarily.[37]

In private, Paul-Boncour expressed himself ready to accept limitation by classes. His difficulty, apparently, was that the Minister of

Marine, Georges Leygues, would agree only to limitation by total tonnage and the submission of a five-year construction programme.[38] On 6 April, however, ostensibly without seeking prior approval from Paris, the chief French delegate made a second, improved offer: limitation would be by total tonnage within each of four categories — capital ships; aircraft-carriers; vessels under 10,000 tons; and submarines — and a re-allocation between categories would be permitted only in conditions deemed indispensible for national security and on notification being given to the League Secretariat. There would be a separate limitation of 'home' and 'overseas' tonnage and powers would state for each of these divisions the amount of tonnage considered essential for security and the defence of the national interest — a theoretical undertaking — and the tonnage to be completed before the expiry of the convention.[39]

Paul-Boncour's second compromise offer represented a considerable concession to the British point of view, and Cecil told the chief French delegate within a few hours of receiving the proposal that he would be prepared to recommend its acceptance if certain conditions were fulfilled: that at least a year's notice was given to the Secretary-General of the League before ships not included in the convention were laid down; that all parties to the convention were at liberty to make changes in their construction programmes if one party decided to do so; that any powers that wished to were free to accept the 'Washington Treaty method' of limitation; that categories of vessel were more closely defined by the ultimate Disarmament Conference; and that states with fleets of under 100,000 tons total tonnage were under no obligation to accept the conditions regarding construction programmes.[40]

In telegraphing the new French proposals to London, Cecil put his projected amendments in more definite form. Fleets of over 500,000 tons would be governed by the 'Washington Treaty system' of limitation; medium-sized navies of between 100,000 tons and 500,000 tons would be regulated by a combination of total tonnage, notification of programme (changeable on twelve month's notice) and a classification of ships drawn up at the Disarmament Conference; and small fleets of under 100,000 tons would be limited by a notification of programme only, without restrictions governing types of vessel. It was an arrangement which, according to Cecil, was acceptable to Japan and also, probably, the United States.[41]

Not unexpectedly, Bridgeman opposed both the Paul-Boncour 'compromise' and the Cecil 'amendments', arguing that an agreement must be dependent on France and Italy not building types of vessel that would prejudice British security, and that, unless additional qualitative restrictions were imposed, competitive building could not be stopped. The First Lord demanded a limitation by numbers within categories, with each nation being allocated the number of vessels considered necessary for security. Cecil, however, retorted that Britain was the only power at Geneva to favour such limitation.[42]

Members of the French delegation were apparently hopeful that their government would accept the condition of twelve month's notice before vessels not in accordance with stated programmes were laid down and, in an important telegram to London despatched on 8 April, Cecil suggested that if this hope materialized 'it would surely be very unfortunate if the chance of getting French to agree to a limitation of naval armaments should be missed'.[43] The Chancellor of the Duchy of Lancaster therefore enquired as to the minimum demands consistent with British naval security, in particular the classes of vessel on which it was really essential to impose a tonnage limit and the extent to which restrictions on gun calibre should be applied. Making his own position clear, he asked if a limit of the total tonnage of each class together with a limit on the maximum tonnage of an individual ship did not in reality give Britain all the security required against powers such as France and Italy, even if 'Washington-type' terms applied to Britain, the United States and Japan.[44]

On 11 April, a reply was telegraphed to Cecil stating that the Admiralty was prepared to accept the principle of a total tonnage limitation for France, Italy and the smaller naval powers only if the total tonnage in each of five defined categories — battleships, aircraft-carriers, cruisers, destroyers, and submarines — was limited strictly and could not be transferred from one category to another.[45] Meanwhile, Cecil had incorporated his own suggestions in the naval chapter of the British draft convention and transmitted the modification to the Admiralty for comment. This redraft showed that his position had hardened slightly in the previous twenty-four hours — possibly because of the influence of Admiral Aubrey Smith as the telegram from London defining the Admiralty's minimum demands had not then arrived — but it still portrayed a willingness to make considerable concessions to the French point of view. The new suggestion was similar to that of 6 April, but differed in two important respects. In deference to the French, who apparently insisted that all nations receive similar treatment regardless of the size of their navies, the special provision for fleets of 100,000 to 500,000 tons was dropped; and in deference to the Admiralty, surface vessels under 10,000 tons were divided into two classes, cruisers and destroyers.[46]

A crisis within the British government now seemed inevitable since the Admiralty refused to accept the 'amended Cecil proposals', stigmatizing the provision for a transfer of tonnage as 'dangerous and unacceptable'.[47] Cecil, for his part, was furious with the naval authorities over what he considered an extreme lack of co-operation; and in a letter to Chamberlain of 12 April asserted that Bridgeman had adopted an attitude of 'malevolent neutrality' throughout the Geneva proceedings, on two occasions expressing the opinion that it would not be displeasing if the negotiations came to an end.[48] The Foreign Secretary thought his correspondent in 'something of a dangerous mood', possibly contemplating resignation.[49]

Fortunately for the government, the French forestalled the

incipient crisis by rejecting the 'Cecil amendments', except for the provision concerning notification of programmes. The Chancellor of the Duchy of Lancaster quickly cooled down and began to blame the French for the impasse that developed at Geneva. On 26 April, the Preparatory Commission adjourned with no immediate prospect of agreement on naval *matériel*.[50]

In essence, the impasse at Geneva on the naval question again reflected the political and strategic differences between the powers. Each government was afraid of being forced into making concessions that were incompatible with national security. The Britain believed that if no qualitative restrictions were placed on the various types of vessel, states such as France, Italy and Japan might be able to build ships that were more powerful than their British counterparts, thus jeopardizing the security of the trade routes on which British depended for her existence.[51] The Italians, who had only three maritime channels of communication to the rest of the world — Suez, Gibraltar and the Dardanelles — wanted freedom to build ships that would threaten the powers that menaced those communications, notably France.[52] And the French, who needed secure communications with North Africa to transport colonial troops to Europe in case of emergency, wanted freedom to build vessels that would safeguard these communications, especially against the threat imposed by the Italian navy.[53]

At the same time, the two Latin powers seem to have been eager for a political agreement which might have enabled them to make concessions. The Italians, through Marinis, and the French, through Paul-Boncour, sounded Cecil as to the possibility of an agreement by which Britain would guarantee their respective fleets against attack in the Mediterranean. But the Chancellor of the Duchy of Lancaster gave his fellow delegates no encouragement and described their overtures as 'foolish policy . . . which is bound to be unsuccessful'.[54]

Briand made a more substantial suggestion during conversations with Chamberlain in London on 18 May. The French Foreign Minister pointed out that his country had not built the quota of ships permissible under the Washington Treaty and indicated that his government could easily reach an agreement with the British if it were not for the difficulties with the Italians in the Mediterranean. He wondered, therefore, whether it might not be possible to make 'a Mediterranean agreement including Great Britain, Italy and France which would solve the problem'. Chamberlain, aware of the soundings made previously by Paul-Boncour, had no doubt that Briand anticipated 'a kind of territorial guarantee of the Mediterranean position'. Such an undertaking would have increased Britain's security commitments, but the Foreign Secretary thought the question well worth pursuing and asked his French colleague to study the matter with a view to formulating the outlines of an agreement. He was anxious that the initiative remain with France, but intimated that he would consider any proposal 'extremely interesting' and study it 'most carefully'. He even suggested the possibility of Briand making an unofficial approach, on the understanding that it would be treated as not having been made if a basis of discussion or agreement was not found. Briand was evidently satisfied with his British counterpart's reaction and expressed the hope that diplomatic conversations would take place between the two powers in an attempt to reach an agreement before the Preparatory Commission reconvened. The proposal offered a most promising line of advance towards a solution of naval disarmament problems.[55]

If the third session of the Preparatory Commission had fallen short of its primary objective — the formulation of a draft outline for a disarmament convention — it did throw light on the policies of the powers taking part in the naval conference of June. In particular, it demonstrated the extremely rigid attitude of the British Admiralty. Cecil complained consistently about the Admiralty and its representatives, and in a series of letters to Cabinet colleagues, culminating in the one to Chamberlain of 12 April, he suggested that the naval authorities were doing their best to wreck the Geneva proceedings.[56]

There was much truth in Cecil's accusations. Even Lord Salisbury, who doubted whether the Preparatory Commission would lead to any practical result, maintained that the British admirals were 'as stiff as a poker' and, as far as explaining their reasons was concerned, 'almost as unintelligent'. He considered them 'splendid people', but thought their notion of an argument closely resembled 'an order from the quarter deck' and that it put them off if everybody did not fall in with it!'[57] The Lord Privy Seal agreed that the Admiralty did not want the Preparatory Commission to succeed — or at any rate did not care if it failed — although he was unwilling to say that the naval authorities were against disarmament altogether as they were 'evidently keen' about the success of the impending three-power conference.[58]

In contrast to the British, the American and Japanese delegations on the Preparatory Commission had shown themselves rather more willing to compromise on naval questions. The chief Japanese delegate thought the Paul-Boncour 'compromise' offered a basis for discussion and the Americans maintained a conciliatory spirit, according to Cecil being genuinely anxious that the commission should succeed.[59] More important, the discussions of March and April made it clear that neither the Americans nor the Japanese favoured the British proposal for limiting the number of ships in each defined class or the scheme to designate nine classes of vessel; the two Pacific powers preferred a reduced number of classes and limitation by total tonnage within the agreed categories.[60] It was a divergence of view that was to become extremely important when the three powers came to discuss definitive proposals.

Part IV Failure

9 The Geneva Naval Conference
December 1926–August 1927

The Geneva Naval Conference of 20 June to 4 August 1927, which originated in President Coolidge's invitation to the five great naval powers of 10 February 1927, was eventually to concern only three powers directly — Britain, the United States and Japan. Nevertheless it is of intrinsic importance to an evaluation of the disarmament problem and the British attitude to the problem. Not only were there numerous links between the three-power negotiations and the discussions at the Preparatory Commission, but the conference was to throw revealing light on British policy towards individual elements of the overall problem.

The British Admiralty had never been keen on disarmament discussions through the League and prior to Coolidge's initiative had even been considering the utility of Britain convening a naval conference in London.[1] Altogether, the possibility of putting forward practicable proposals had been under discussion for some two years, and on 21 December 1926 Admirals Field, Chatfield and Dreyer (Deputy Chief of Naval Staff, Controller and Assistant Chief of Naval Staff respectively) had advanced a new scheme of limitation for discussion at international level. Their reason for doing so, however, was not an intrinsic belief in disarmament, rather a perceptive evaluation of the government's future attitude towards naval construction. The three admirals realized that with new battleships costing over £7m each and cruisers over £2m each, the naval estimates would soon approach £80m a year, an increase of about 30 per cent on existing expenditure; and they feared that it would become increasingly difficult to persuade the government to meet naval requirements.[2] It was also feared that, if the Admiralty did not take the lead in broaching the disarmament question at international level, it might be forced 'either to accept a policy incompatible with the security of the Empire, or to bear the odium of refusing to accept proposals made by other Countries'.[3] On 27 January 1927 the Admiralty Board adopted a series of proposals based on the Field–Chatfield–Dreyer suggestions.[4]

In formulating their proposals, the Sea Lords assessed the minimum number of vessels needed to meet the initial requirements of the British Empire in a war with a first-class naval power — in effect Japan — as from 1924 onwards naval preparations had been made on the basis of a war in the Far East specifically against that power. The figures envisaged, however, were so considerable — fifteen battleships and battlecruisers (in accordance with the Washington Treaty), seventy cruisers, five large aircraft-carriers, 144 destroyers and seventy-two submarines - that it was necessary to propose severe qualitative restrictions for future construction if economies on the desired scale were to be achieved. It was suggested, therefore, that the maximum displacement of capital ships be reduced from the Washington 'standard' of 35,000 tons to 28,000 tons and limits placed on flotilla leaders and destroyers of 1,750 tons and 1,400 tons respectively; also that the maximum displacement of aircraft-carriers be reduced from 27,000 tons (again a Washington 'standard') to 25,000 tons, and submarines divided into two classes, with maximum surface displacements of 600 tons and 1,600 tons. It was further suggested that the age of older battleships made it possible for future capital ships to be rather less powerful than existing vessels, carrying thirteen-and-a-half inch instead of sixteen-inch guns, and that the armament of aircraft-carriers might be reduced from the Washington Treaty maximum of eight-inch calibre to six-inch calibre, though the latter would probably depend on a corresponding reduction in the armament of cruisers.[5]

Cruisers presented the most difficult problem for the Sea Lords. It was necessary to ensure comparability of vessels with other fleets and under existing circumstances this could only be assured if the whole British building programme consisted of vessels armed with eight-inch guns, the Washington Treaty maximum. The cost of maintaining seventy such vessels appeared prohibitive, yet if their number was limited by a ratio and a secondary type of vessel agreed upon a strategical risk had to be taken. Such a risk had always existed, and under the Washington agreements it would have continued for many years; but now the Sea Lords decided to try to terminate it by limiting eight-inch gun cruisers in the 'Washington ratio' and restricting the size and power of ships built in replacement to a new secondary standard. The suggested maximum dimensions of the new cruisers were 7,500 tons displacement and six-inch gun calibre, and the Sea Lords insisted that 'special consideration' should be given to the needs of the British Empire in regard to the numbers of this type of vessel — in other words, the other powers should recognize British superiority.[6]

Because of the advantages it offered to Britain, the Admiralty scheme of limitation was always unlikely to commend itself to other powers; and even at this early date the Sea Lords were under no illusion that their cruiser proposals would prove acceptable to Britain's naval rivals.[7] Any lingering doubts on the issue were removed in President Coolidge's communication of 10 February; for whilst 'hesitating' to put forward rigid proposals, he declared that the American government was disposed to accept 'an extension of the 5-5-3 ratio as regards the United States, Great Britain and Japan, and to leave to discussion at Geneva the ratios of France and Italy, taking into full account their special conditions and requirements'.[8] In essence, Britain should accept parity in cruisers with the United States.

The American approach placed Britain's policy-makers in something of a quandary. Although an extension of the Washington ratios to all the smaller types of vessel was clearly unacceptable to the Admiralty, the government had an interest in limitation, if only for financial reasons. Chamberlain realized the dilemma but hoped that Britain might be able to overcome the problem by offering an alternative line of advance to the American proposal.[9] A possible means of escape from the difficulty was offered when France and Italy rejected the Coolidge invitation, claiming that all armaments — land, sea and air — were interdependent and that a solution of the problems should be sought through the Preparatory Commission;[10] but the government, despite the fact that the Admiralty, as recently as 28 July 1926, had reiterated its opposition to a conference in which France and Italy were not represented, decided to accept the American invitation because of the political and diplomatic consequences of a refusal.[11] At the same time, in an official note handed to the American Ambassador at London, Alanson Houghton on 25 February 1927, the government made it clear that a straight extension of the Washington ratios to the smaller classes of vessel was considered undesirable and that the invitation was accepted only on the proviso that Britain 'would not be prevented from putting forward alternative methods of limitation'. Ominously, the Americans were forewarned that:

> The views of His Majesty's Government upon the special geographical position of the British Empire, the length of inter-imperial communications, and the necessity for the protection of its food supplies are well known . . . and must be taken into account.[12]

In an important memorandum of 14 April, the naval staff set out the case for the Admiralty's new proposals in terms more suitable for political consumption. In particular, a theme was developed, originally worked out in the Plans Division on Beatty's instructions, which put the claim for superiority in cruisers on a rational basis.

Such vessels, it was argued, had two primary functions — fleet work and control of sea communications — and only for the first function was the 5–5–3 ratio acceptable. The number of cruisers required for the control of sea communications was declared to be dependent on the length of the sea routes and the density of trade normally using those routes, and on this basis Britain would require a total of seventy cruisers (twenty-five for fleet work and forty-five for trade defence), the United States forty-seven (twenty-five for fleet work and twenty-two for trade defence) and Japan a mere twenty-one (fifteen for fleet work and six for trade defence). The Admiralty did not believe that the United States and Japan would accept these claims in full, but evidently hoped to secure a certain superiority in small cruisers.[13]

Prompted by the possibility of the naval conference holding public sessions, the Admiralty decided to keep its new disarmament proposals a very close secret. Beatty wanted to gain tactical advantages for Britain by presenting the proposals in open session as evidence of 'an earnest endeavour to limit Naval Armaments and Expenditure', and as late as 20 May, a month to the day before the conference opened, Bridgeman was allowed to present the scheme to the CID only by word of mouth.[14] This procedure also had the advantage — as far as the Admiralty was concerned — of making it impossible for the CID to undertake a detailed study of the scheme and its possible ramifications. Consequently, the scheme received only a cursory examination before being approved. The one question to be considered at all fully by the CID was the likely American claim to parity, more especially in cruisers; but this did not seem to be a contentious issue as Bridgeman asserted that the Admiralty 'would not take a grave view' if the United States built up to the British limit. The CID's recommendation that the Admiralty's proposals be accepted as the basis of the British position at Geneva was approved by the Cabinet on 25 May.[15]

On the surface, it seemed there would be little difficulty in obtaining an agreement at Geneva, for relations between the three great naval powers had been improving steadily over the previous five years and their delegations at the Preparatory Commission had maintained a harmonious relationship. Even the expected American claim for parity with Britain in all classes of vessel appeared to have been settled in advance. On 24 September 1926, eight months before Bridgeman's remark to the same effect in the CID, Cecil had told Gibson that he understood the Admiralty did not object to parity provided Britain's minimum requirements for defence were met.[16] And either Beatty or Bridgeman, according to Kellogg, expressed an exactly similar view to Admiral Jones, America's second delegate at the forthcoming conference, during conversations in London in March 1927.[17]

In reality, there were wide divergences between the British and American points of view, a fact that quickly became apparent when the powers presented their proposals at the first plenary session of the conference on 20 June. At this meeting, the Americans suggested that the 5–5–3 ratio be applied rigidly to three defined classes of vessel — cruisers, destroyers and submarines. Britain and the United States would be allocated a total cruiser tonnage of between 250,000 and 300,000 tons, a destroyer tonnage of between 200,000 and 250,000 tons and a submarine tonnage within the limits of 60,000 and 90,000 tons; Japan would be allowed 60 per cent of the figure agreed for Britain and the United States. Cruisers would be limited qualitatively on the same basis as the Washington Treaty and include all surface combatant vessels between 3,000 tons and 10,000 tons; destroyers were defined as surface combatant vessels of between 600 tons and 3,000 tons with a designed speed of over thirty knots; and age limits would be imposed for each class of vessel: twenty years for cruisers, fifteen to seventeen for destroyers and twelve or thirteen for submarines.[18]

The Japanese proposed that the three powers limit the total tonnage of their surface auxiliary craft and submarines separately, to the levels reached at the end of existing construction programmes and in conformity with certain qualitative restrictions. Age limits would be imposed of sixteen years for surface craft over 3,000 tons (in effect, cruisers) and twelve years for surface vessels under 3,000 tons (destroyers) and submarines.[19]

The British proposals differed in only a few minor respects from those envisaged by the Sea Lords in January. Addressing the plenary session, Bridgeman, as Britain's first delegate, suggested that cruisers be divided into two classes, the 'Washington standard' type of 10,000 tons armed with eight-inch guns (to be limited in the 5–5–3 ratio) and a smaller, less powerful type of 7,500 tons armed with six-inch guns (which was to be unlimited); also that, as the larger type reached the age for replacement, it would be superseded by the smaller. Submarines would be divided into two classes, with maximum displacements of 600 tons and 1,600 tons, while destroyers would be limited to 1,400 tons and leaders to 1,750 tons. Gun calibre limits would be five inches for destroyers and submarines and six inches for aircraft-carriers, while the maximum displacement of carriers would be reduced from the Washington Treaty figure of 27,000 tons to 25,000 tons. Age limits would be imposed of twenty-four years for eight-inch cruisers, twenty years for destroyers and fifteen years for submarines. The replacement age for capital ships would be extended from twenty years up to twenty-six years, and new qualitative limits would be set for all new capital ships of thirteen-and-a-half-inch gun calibre and under 30,000 tons displacement. Britain also demanded a 'safe guarding clause' whereby it would be possible to reopen the question of auxiliary craft if a non-signatory power increased its naval strength so as to imperil British safety.[20]

The presentation of the British proposals produced an immediate storm in the American press since it was believed, correctly, that the British government was claiming superiority in auxiliary vessels, notably cruisers.[21] The reaction was so intense that, as early as 22 June, Howard thought it necessary to suggest that the British press be encouraged to reply to allegations that Britain wanted to 'cheat' the United States.[22] Even at Geneva, the reaction of the American delegation was far more hostile than anticipated. Diplomatically, however, the Americans played their cards well. Hugh Gibson, their first delegate, having discerned Bridgeman's intention of forcing both Japan and the United States to state their requirements in open conference in order to claim superiority for Britain, played for time and put pressure on the British through all possible channels to make a formal concession of parity. The pressure became so intense that by 28 June Howard was convinced that the Americans would continue the conference only on the basis of parity for all units.[23]

Faced with this situation, the British government was forced to reconsider its strategy, and a crucial Cabinet meeting was held on 29 June. The meeting was asked (possibly by Admiral Pound, the new Assistant Chief of Naval Staff, though it is not clear from the Cabinet conclusions) 'not to adopt the principle of parity of naval strength in so many words, as this was contrary to previous policy and was believed to be strongly opposed by the Admiralty'; but it was decided that the concession should be made and that Tyrrell should send a telegram to the British representatives at Geneva, Bridgeman and Cecil, based on a formula drawn up by Balfour:

> For diplomatic reasons we think it most desirable to say publicly and at once what we believe to be your view, namely, that, while we mean to build cruisers up to our own needs, we lay down no conditions limiting [America's] cruisers to a smaller number. Do you see any objections?[24]

The telegram was transmitted later that day.[25]

In Geneva, Bridgeman pre-empted the situation by making a statement along these lines to the Associated Press of America on the evening of 29 June, shortly before he received the government's telegram:

> Great Britain has no intention of contesting the principle of parity between the naval strength of the United States and Great Britain . . .. It is true that we think our special needs demand higher number in certain types of vessels but we do not deny the right of the United States to build up to an equal figure in any type of warship if she thought it necessary.[26]

The First Lord did not, apparently, think it necessary to transmit the text of his statement to the Foreign Office in view of the telegram he had received from London, but in a telegraphic communication of 30 June he reaffirmed the view that Britain had 'no intention or desire to question American claim to parity' and suggested that it would be desirable for Howard to repeat this formally to the State Department in Washington.[27]

In response to Bridgeman's suggestion, a telegram was drafted instructing Howard to

... confirm to the United States Government statement made by Mr. Bridgeman and Lord Cecil to Mr. Gibson at Geneva that His Majesty's Government do not dispute or contest in any way claim of the United States to absolute parity and that they fully agree that Geneva negotiations should be conducted on that basis.[28]

Baldwin authorized the despatch of the telegram,[29] and it seemed that the whole issue of parity had been settled. However, on the afternoon of 1 July, Beatty objected to the wording of the telegram, and, although it had already been sent to Washington, action on it was suspended on the Prime Minister's instructions pending further discussion.[30]

The suspension of the telegram allowed Beatty and his supporters to confuse the issue of parity, and on 4 July a further Cabinet was held to clarify the situation. The First Sea Lord attended the meeting and apparently argued that Bridgeman had not in fact conceded parity in auxiliary vessels and that the government should therefore adhere to the original plan of forcing the Americans to justify their demands in open conference. It was pointed out, however, that Bridgeman's language on the parity issue had been 'most precise', and so Beatty was forced to argue against a concession on strategical grounds, emphasizing that if America was allowed to build up to the British figure of seventy cruisers, the Japanese would demand 'something in the neighbourhood of 50' and that the Admiralty would be unable in these circumstances to guarantee the protection of trade routes.[31] The British war plan against Japan, from which the figure of seventy cruisers had been derived, apparently envisaged the Japanese possessing only about thirty cruisers.[32]

The First Sea Lord received a degree of support from within the Cabinet, and Churchill argued that there could be no real parity between a power whose navy was 'its life' and another whose navy was only 'for prestige'. However, notwithstanding these arguments, the view of the Cabinet was that Howard should use the 'same language' in Washington as had been used in Geneva. Even Amery conceded that to press the Churchill-Beatty line would break up the conference and provoke a general competition in armaments.[33] So it was decided to instruct Howard to

... confirm to the United States government statement made by Mr. Bridgeman and Lord Cecil to Mr. Gibson at Geneva that while we must build cruisers up to our needs, we lay down no conditions limiting American cruisers to a smaller number.[34]

No one, apparently, pointed out that the language used was not that of the Geneva delegates but that of the telegram to Geneva of 29 June. But at the time, it hardly seemed to matter. The government had reiterated in no uncertain terms that Britain had conceded the principle of parity — in terms of numerical equality — with regard to the one class of vessel in which it had been seriously contested, cruisers.

Whilst these discussions were taking place in London, the primary objective of the delegation in Geneva was to open negotiations on the further limitation of capital ships. The British proposals on this question had been designed to secure substantial reductions in future expenditure on battleship construction, some £33m in the period 1931–40, and the Sea Lords had reckoned that the amount saved would either permit an increase or prevent a decrease in the amount spent on cruiser construction.[35] The Americans, who firmly believed that the proposals were merely another attempt to further British interests at the expense of the United States, took the not unreasonable line that it was impossible to open discussions concerned with the Washington Treaty in the absence of France and Italy, and that there was no real point in entering into negotiations at that time since the Washington Treaty powers were not allowed to lay down new battleships until 1931. The Americans therefore would promise no more than an exchange of views at Geneva once an agreement had been reached on auxiliary craft. The Japanese took a rather similar line, and in the circumstances all Bridgeman could do was to reserve the right to make a public statement on the subject if the conference broke down.[36]

The lack of progress on the capital ship question was offset by a number of preliminary agreements on the submarine and destroyer questions. By 8 July the Technical Committee of the conference, comprising the senior technical advisers of the three delegations, had agreed that there should be only one class of submarines, with a maximum individual displacement of 1,800 tons and gun calibre of five inches, and that there should be two types of destroyer, a 'normal' type limited to 1,500 tons and leaders of 1,850 tons, both carrying guns of no more than five-inch calibre. It was also agreed that 'discretionary' minimum age limits should be introduced for the various classes of vessel, thirteen years for submarines and fifteen years for destroyers, and that the ratio of leaders to destroyers should be fixed at a maximum of 16 per cent.[37] The Americans declared that these arrangements were provisional, pending final agreement as to total tonnage limitations in all categories of vessel, including cruisers, but there appeared to be no real difficulties preventing the negotiation of agreed allocations as far as submarines and destroyers were concerned since the British proposals for these two categories, the only firm proposals put forward at the Technical Committee, were lower than those envisaged by the Americans at the outset of the conference.[38] Admiral Field, the chief Admiralty adviser at Geneva, even told the American and Japanese advisers that the British requirements regarding destroyers 'would not be altered in order to meet the minimum requirements of other nations even if these were above their own', in other words that Britain would be prepared, if necessary, to accept inferiority in this class of vessel.[39]

On cruisers, the fundamental differences between Britain and the United States remained. The British delegation insisted that seventy cruisers were necessary to fulfil British requirements: fifteen of the 'Washington standard' type and fifty-five of the smaller type, 7,500 tons armed with six-inch guns, which was equivalent to a total tonnage claim of 562,000 tons.[40] The Americans, for their part, claimed twenty-five 'Washington standard' cruisers and liberty to arm all other cruisers with eight-inch guns, within a total tonnage limit of 400,000 tons.[41] Attempts were made to bridge the gulf between the two parties, through the submission of building programmes over a defined period, the retention of 'overage' vessels and the aggregation of cruiser and destroyer tonnage. Each attempt ended in failure because of the rigid attitude adopted by both Britain and the United States over three crucial questions — the gun calibre of the smaller type of cruiser, total tonnage allocations and the number of 'Washington standard' cruisers to be retained.

The American proposals, like the British, were based on strategical considerations. The United States' possessions and interests were concentrated in the Pacific, and the General Board of Admiralty considered that the 10,000-ton, eight-inch-gun type of cruiser was the most suitable for upholding those interests, more especially against Japan, the power most likely to threaten them. The General Board also pointed out that, so long as the 5–3 ratio with Japan was maintained, it was to the United States' advantage to keep the total number of cruisers as low as possible because each additional Japanese cruiser was a great potential threat to American lines of communication in the western Pacific. Paradoxically, if Britain had been the nation against which America was building, it would have been to the United States' interest to advocate a high total tonnage of cruisers to diminish the importance of Britain's armed merchant cruisers. Britain's proposal at Geneva, for fifteen 'Washington standard' cruisers and fifty-five 7,500-ton, six-inch-gun cruisers, would therefore have weakened the United States' strategic position.[42]

At the Geneva conference, the American delegation argued that the United States needed large cruisers because of a lack of bases in the Pacific. It may be that the American naval authorities were using this argument as a pretext rather than a reason for their demands for on one occasion Admiral Jones admitted that a 7,000-ton six-inch gun cruiser could meet the necessary cruising range requirements. To obtain this radius, however, it was argued that it would be necessary to sacrifice defensive armour, giving such cruisers an insufficient margin of superiority over Britain's large number of merchant cruisers armed with six-inch guns. This was a rather unsafe argument, as experience had shown that a converted merchant ship armed with six-inch guns stood little chance against a similarly armed naval cruiser, but there was a good deal to be said for the less emphatic argument that armed merchant cruisers as a body assumed greater importance if naval cruisers were armed with the six-inch rather than the eight-inch weapon.[43]

The British objections to the eight-inch gun were that its offensive qualities were some two-and-a-half times greater than the six-inch weapon and that an extensive American programme of eight-inch gun cruisers would have made British six-inch gun cruisers obsolescent —

though the latter argument apparently was not used at Geneva. Instead, the British delegation argued that 'Washington standard' cruisers were offensive vessels and the proposed six-inch gun type defensive, and that Britain required a large number of the latter type for trade defence and the protection of imperial communications. It was also pointed out that the proposed six-inch gun vessels were much cheaper to build and maintain than the 'Washington standard' type, though, in reality, the whole British case had devolved from the intention of the Sea Lords to control the size of cruisers in an attempt to improve Britain's maritime position.[44]

Similarly, the British case regarding the total tonnage of cruisers was derived from the need for seventy such vessels under the war plan against Japan or, as it was euphemistically suggested at the Cabinet, for trade protection. The Admiralty, therefore, was willing to go to almost any lengths in reducing the displacement of the smaller type of cruiser, provided always that the demand for numbers was met. The objection to America's proposal for a large number of 'Washington standard' cruisers within a total tonnage limit of 400,000 tons was that, unless Britain built cruisers to dimensions very much inferior to the American vessels, it would be impossible for Britain to build the number considered necessary for the defence of imperial communications.[45]

At only one point during the Geneva Conference did an agreement on cruisers seem possible. The senior delegates of the powers having failed to reach a settlement, the junior delegates were given an opportunity to do so, and on 12 July they came forward with the basis of an agreement. At a plenary session on 14 July, Gibson insisted that, if the British and Japanese could come to a suitable compromise on the outstanding points, he felt sure it would be possible 'to make agreement complete'; and on 16 July, the British and Japanese came to such an agreement.[46]

Under the 'Anglo–Japanese proposals', Britain and the United States would have been allotted a combined tonnage of cruisers and destroyers of 500,000 tons and Japan 325,000 tons, though each power would have been permitted an additional 25 per cent of the total tonnage in overage vessels. The allocation of 'Washington standard' cruisers would have been twelve for Britain and the United States and eight for Japan, and the smaller cruisers would have displaced a maximum of 6,000 tons and carried guns of no more than six-inch calibre. Within the total tonnage allotment for each power, there would have been a 'definite agreed percentage' for both cruisers and destroyers and special arrangements would have been made to overcome the difficulties created by existing 'non-standard' vessels. The agreement would have terminated on 31 December 1936.[47]

By the time the Anglo–Japanese proposals were formulated, however, a change of policy had been agreed in London. Churchill had canvassed the idea that mathematical parity with America in all classes of warship meant British inferiority because of the extent of Britain's commitments; and at a Cabinet meeting on 6 July the opponents of an agreement based on mathematical parity had gained the upper hand. The discussion focussed on two important telegrams from Geneva which reported the Americans as having presented their proposal for a total tonnage of 400,000 tons and twenty-five 'Washington standard' cruisers as a kind of ultimatum, and Beatty, who was present at the meeting, apparently converted the Cabinet to the original Admiralty proposals, that 'Washington standard' cruisers be limited in the 5-5-3 ratio but that the smaller class remain unlimited. It was agreed that Balfour, in consultation with the First Sea Lord, should draft a telegram to Geneva containing full instructions to the British delegation.[48]

Balfour and Beatty actually produced alternative drafts, which were considered by the CID on 7 July. Both argued for much the same end — acceptance of the 5-5-3 ratio in heavy cruisers but the limitation of small cruisers along qualitative lines only — but the Lord President of the Council's draft, being less technical and, incidentally, more diplomatic and less clear, was considered the more appropriate for transmission to Geneva.[49] Approved by Chamberlain and Birkenhead, it was despatched the same day in the form of a 'statement of British case' which Bridgeman was authorized to utilize whenever he considered it desirable. It was not noticed at the time, however, that the vague language resulted in the telegram containing an inherent contradiction. The first half advanced a claim for superiority in cruisers:

> We propose to divide cruisers into two classes — the heavy and the light; and to adopt for the heavy class the same principles as those adopted at Washington in the case of capital ships. We think, in other words, that their size and armament might with advantage be limited, and that the numbers permitted to each of the Treaty powers should be in the Washington ratio.
>
> . . . But when we turn from heavy cruisers to light, wholly different conditions must be taken into account.
>
> It is of course true that a fleet of a given size requires auxiliary vessels of a given number, whatever be the position of the country to which the fleet belongs or the seas in which it is required to operate . . . . But in addition to these auxiliary vessels cruisers are required by all maritime countries to perform duties quite unconnected with organised fleets, and by no country so much as by the British Empire. This special position is, of course, due to a geographical subdivision which has no parallel in history.[50]

This claim for superiority, however, was apparently refuted in the last paragraph:

> Great Britain, it has been said, refuses 'parity' to the United States. The statement has already been formally contradicted. It is wholly without foundation.[51]

As a result of this ambiguous phraseology, the change of policy in London was not appreciated in Geneva, where the British delegation continued to explore proposals conceding mathematical parity in all types of auxiliary vessel, including small cruisers.

The incipient conflict between the delegates in Geneva and the Cabinet in London was brought to a head over the bases of agreement drawn up by the junior delegates of the powers on 12 July. Beatty mounted a scathing attack on the proposals within the CID on 14 July, declaring that if Britain accepted parity with America,

> ... it was his duty to state quite definitely that the Admiralty would no longer be capable of shouldering the responsibility which was ... laid upon them, namely, the protection of the territories of the Empire from invasion and the protection of the sea communications of the Empire.[52]

Churchill, not unduly anxious at a possible breakdown of the conference, maintained he was 'absolutely opposed' to accepting the total tonnage limitations contemplated on the grounds that it might cause increased expense and that he would be sorry to sign a document entailing 'inferiority' to the Americans in cruisers; and, in deference to the demands of the Chancellor, it was decided to recall the Geneva delegates for consultation. A telegram to this effect was despatched the next day.[53]

Bridgeman and Cecil felt that an adjournment of the conference while they returned to London would seriously impair the prospect of agreement, since it would give the impression that they were doubtful of their position and no longer possessed the full confidence of the government. They therefore resisted recall, and the government deferred to their judgement.[54] The government was still anxious, however, to confirm that there was no divergence of view between London and Geneva and despatched a further telegram containing a full 'statement of views':

PART I   We are now prepared to agree by treaty to equality of large cruisers .... But we cannot admit by treaty that in regard to small cruisers the case of the British Empire resembles other Powers; or that parity of number means parity of strength. We cannot consent therefore to the insertion in a great international instrument of any provision which could be interpreted as meaning that we had bound ourselves to any arrangement which placed us in a position of permanent naval inferiority.

PART II Although therefore ready to agree to a ratio for the 10,000 ton 8" cruisers, we could not agree to fixing *by treaty* a permanent total tonnage limit for all classes of ships whether specified in classes or lumped together. But we are ready to approve an agreement fixing the actual units of the annual programmes of new cruisers for the three Powers during say the next five years or if absolutely necessary up to 1936, and of course tonnage of these units when added up could be embodied in the agreement ....

As to period of agreement we should much prefer the shorter as it better safeguards our position and affords better chance of agreement. The longer the period the nearer the Americans might come to equality of numbers in practice as distinguished from theoretical right to parity, and ... equality of numbers ... would result in actual inferiority for us.[55]

This telegram, dated 15 July, reflected the new balance of forces in London and conveyed the decisions made by the Further Limitation of Naval Armaments Committee which had been established on 14 July. This committee, which consisted of Baldwin, Chamberlain, Balfour, Salisbury, Churchill and Beatty, gave the Chancellor of the Exchequer and First Sea Lord a new and improved power base from which to develop their machinations against Bridgeman and Cecil's policy. The Prime Minister, Foreign Secretary, Lord Privy Seal and Lord President of the Council were apparently unable to stand up to their two colleagues in the committee and demurred to Churchill and Beatty's wishes. Baldwin took little part in the discussions and gave little indication of his personal preferences. Chamberlain, who had been on holiday in Zermatt during the early part of the Geneva Conference, admitted that he found it difficult to follow the proceedings. Balfour was almost certainly as confused as Chamberlain and confessed that he 'did not quite understand' Part II of the telegram (though he suggested no alternative). And Salisbury, the only member of the committee to point out that Britain had 'emphatically admitted' the United States' right to build an equal number of smaller cruisers, did not press his point.[56]

Before receiving the telegram of 15 July, the British delegation had decided to recommend acceptance of the Anglo–Japanese compromise, since it brought about a position within a measurable distance of Britain's purported requirements — twelve 'Washington standard' cruisers, fifty four smaller cruisers of 6,000 tons armed with six-inch guns, and fourteen flotillas of destroyers.[57] The delegation pointed out that, under the existing building programme, Britain would not have exceeded the contemplated number of cruisers by 1936, and there is little wonder, therefore, that the receipt of the telegram caused consternation at Geneva. Cecil complained bitterly to Chamberlain in a personal letter dated 17 July:

You will no doubt remember the telegram No. 89 from London in which we were specifically directed that we laid down no conditions limiting American cruisers to a smaller number than ours. It cannot then be intended now to suggest that all the time we did not really accept American parity, or rather only accepted it in the sense that they might have as many cruisers as we in proportion to the asserted needs of the two countries. I am perfectly certain that ... if we were to hint it at this time we should be rightly accused of vacillation amounting almost to sharp practice. When we said we accepted American parity we here certainly meant parity in ship strength and nothing else, and it is equally certain that the Americans so understood us. We tried hard to induce them to measure that parity by a yearly programme ... until 1934 or '36 ... ..

But they altogether refused that proposal. They wanted a definite number of tons fixed for the duration of the Treaty . . . .[58]

Cecil was especially concerned at the use of the phrase 'permanent naval inferiority' in the telegram from London, pointing out that there could be no permanence about a treaty scheduled to last only a limited number of years; and he also perceived that the Americans would not agree to a treaty which limited larger cruisers but not the contemplated smaller class.[59] Bridgeman, too, was alarmed at the change of policy in London, seeing no alternative to an agreement based on the Anglo–Japanese compromise except a breakdown of the Geneva Conference. He was not sure, in view of the telegram of 15 July, if the plan envisaged would present difficulties to the Cabinet, but asked for permission to proceed with negotiations.[60]

On receiving Cecil's letter of 17 July, Chamberlain apparently appreciated that the government had reversed its policy and that a divergence of view had arisen between London and Geneva. At the next meeting of the Limitation of Naval Armaments Committee, therefore, he mounted a strong counter-attack on Churchill and Beatty, suggesting that Britain had already agreed to parity with the United States. But his efforts were of little avail. Balfour, despite having drafted the telegram to Geneva of 7 July 'contradicting' the statement that parity had not been conceded, now suggested that the phrase was merely a polite way of saying that Britain did not intend to go to war with America; and the Foreign Secretary received only a modicum of support from Salisbury and Baldwin, the latter even endorsing a wildly unrealistic proposal of Beatty's that America should have the right to build as many small cruisers as Britain but should scrap them after sixteen years in services as against twenty-four for Britain. Reserving a final decision until the following day, 19 July, the committee agreed that it seemed impossible to accept the Anglo–Japanese proposals as they stood but that, with certain modifications, 'they might be made the basis of a temporary arrangement terminating in or before 1936' provided that the limits fixed for small cruisers were only a temporary expedient to secure a working arrangement for a number of years and not the acceptance of a principle that the needs of the United States and Britain for small cruisers were equal.[61]

There was no real agreement at the committee on 19 July. Beatty declared that the Anglo–Japanese proposals were unacceptable because they gave the United States the right to parity in all classes of vessel by treaty because the 5–3.25 ratio with Japan in cruisers was too high and the total tonnage of cruisers and destroyers allocated to Britain insufficient. Churchill, although unconvinced by the Admiralty's claim for seventy cruisers, suggested that the proposals provided for 'large programmes, naval inferiority and handcuffs' whereas what was needed in practice was 'liberty and a small building programme'. Chamberlain emphatically restated the delegation in Geneva's view that parity had already been conceded.

In the circumstances, all that could be agreed was that the chief British delegates should be recalled so that the 'misunderstanding' between London and Geneva could be settled.[62]

Bridgeman and Cecil secured a week's adjournment of the conference and returned to London in time for a special Cabinet meeting on 22 July which was chaired by Baldwin before his departure for Canada on a prearranged tour. By this time, the Limitation of Naval Armaments Committee had narrowed the issues to two alternative proposals. The first, in effect, was that the delegates should return to Geneva and announce that the Anglo–Japanese proposal was unacceptable but that an agreement could be considered on the basis of the Technical Committee's recommendations regarding submarines and destroyers and the Admiralty's original proposals regarding cruisers. The only modifications of the latter were that 'Washington standard' cruisers would be limited on the basis of twelve for Britain and the United States and eight for Japan (instead of fifteen, fifteen, nine) and that the displacement of the smaller class of cruiser would be 6,000 tons. The majority of the Cabinet, however, considered that this scheme would prove unacceptable to the Americans and that to propose it would cause a breakdown of the conference. So the government adopted the second alternative, which involved a continuation of discussions on the basis of the Anglo–Japanese proposals, subject to a comprehensive statement of the policy Britain would have preferred and a *caveat* which made it clear that, so far as the proposals related to small cruisers, they could be accepted only as a *modus vivendi* without committing the government to any principle of limitation. Bridgeman was asked to prepare draft instructions along these lines for consideration by the Limitation of Naval Armaments Committee on 25 July.[63]

Perhaps the most surprising aspect of the Cabinet's decisions was that Bridgeman and Cecil acceded to them without apparent difficulty, despite the implication that Britain was not committed to the principle of parity in small cruisers. Indeed, on 23 July, the two delegates composed a joint memorandum supporting a further decision of the Cabinet which was inconsistent with the spirit of their acceptance of parity — that a statement should be made to the effect that, in assenting to a limitation of total tonnage, Britain was merely trying to facilitate an agreement lasting a specific number of years, and that the rights of parties regarding principles of limitation would not be prejudiced by the termination of the agreement.[64] Balfour had drafted a statement along these lines, using most uncompromising language, and presented it to the Cabinet on 22 July.[65] But by 24 July, Cecil had appreciated the true implications of making such a statement. He wrote to Chamberlain claiming that, as it stood, Balfour's draft seemed quite certain to lead to a breakdown of negotiations, for the United States would say that the British were proposing a temporary arrangement by virtue of her older cruisers and that the British government would seek to perpetuate that position after the agreement had terminated.[66]

At the Limitation of Naval Armaments Committee on 25 July, the Admiralty put forward a number of modifications to the Anglo-Japanese proposals. An adjustment of the proposed replacement ages for cruisers and destroyers was suggested and the demand for two classes of submarine revived; otherwise the only important difference was a proposal to combine the total tonnage of permitted destroyers, cruisers and submarines within an overall limit for the three types of vessel. Figures of 590,000 tons for Britain and the United States and 385,000 tons for Japan were projected, and each power would be allowed to retain an additional 25 per cent of the total tonnage in cruisers and destroyers. The scheme would have allowed Britain to allocate additional tonnage to cruisers, but even so, Beatty warned that the proposals involved a ratio towards Japan in smaller cruisers and destroyers that was well below that which the Admiralty deemed necessary. The First Sea Lord maintained that in the event of difficulties with Japan the greater part of Britain's destroyer force would have to be sent to the Far East, leaving an insufficient margin in home waters and the Mediterranean in the event of serious trouble there.[67]

On 26 July, on the advice of the committee, the Cabinet agreed to accept responsibility for the purported risk involved in the Admiralty's new proposals, but there was considerable, almost violent, disagreement as to the form the proposals should take. The main issue was whether they should be presented as a *modus vivendi* terminating in 1931, based on the right to arm the class of small cruisers with eight-inch guns, or as an agreement extending to 1936 with the smaller cruisers restricted to six-inch guns. Cecil and Bridgeman argued that they should be given latitude at Geneva and wanted freedom, in the last resort, to base negotiations on the former plan; but the majority of the Cabinet demurred to the Admiralty's objection and would agree only to the latter. The discussions were so heated that Chamberlain, who chaired the meeting in Baldwin's absence in Canada, was forced to take a vote on the issue, the result being ten to six in favour of an agreement terminating in 1936 only. Cecil, Bridgeman and Balfour were evidently among the minority group, and Cecil asked that it be placed on record that he was free to reconsider his position as a member of the government if the conference broke down on the question of the six-inch gun.[68]

A significant element in the Cabinet's decision in favour of an agreement terminating in 1936 was the *volte-face* made by Churchill on the issue. In previous weeks the Chancellor of the Exchequer had been a fervent advocate of an agreement lasting only until 1931, on the grounds that this would enable Britain to retain maritime superiority, and as late as 25 July he had argued that to fix a programme until 1936 was dangerous since it would enable the United States to achieve parity.[69] But on 26 July he reversed his position and supported an agreement lasting until 1936.[70] Cecil believed that Churchill wanted to wreck the Geneva negotiations and, having heard that the United States attached 'essential importance' to secondary cruisers being allowed to carry eight-inch guns, thought the Americans were more likely to accept an agreement ending in 1931; Neville Chamberlain agreed.[71] Certainly it can be said that Churchill's advocacy of a policy based on British superiority in small cruisers was hardly compatible with the American position at the conference.

The Cabinet of 26 July also approved a parliamentary statement based on Balfour's draft of 22 July, the chief feature of which was an assertion that no long-term precedent would be created by Britain accepting a treaty on the basis of theoretical mathematical parity until 1936.[72] Announced in both Houses on 27 July, and couched in provocative language, it had the adverse effect that Cecil feared — it stiffened American resolve.[73] When the British delegates returned to Geneva and put forward the amended Anglo–Japanese proposals on 28 July, Gibson stated that he could hold out no hope of his government giving way on the gun calibre question.[74]

It was evident to both Bridgeman and Cecil that unless some compromise was agreed on the gun calibre question, the conference would break down, and so each put forward suggestions for consideration by the Cabinet. The former suggested the possibility of an agreement based on a gun calibre between six inches and seven-and-a-half inches; the latter reverted to the proposal for an agreement terminating in 1931 based on an eight-inch gun.[75] The Cabinet, which reconvened on 29 July, refused the delegates the authority to offer a compromise; whilst recognizing that the United States might force Britain to adopt the eight-inch gun, the government decided it should not accept by treaty that this was the necessary or proper armament for small cruisers.[76]

The Americans had produced their own proposal for a compromise on the gun calibre question, a 'political clause' whereby a contracting party could convoke a new meeting of the three powers if any of them constructed cruisers 'in a manner to call for an adjustment of the total tonnage allocation of that class'. The British delegates, however, were not empowered to accept a clause that left open the question of the eight-inch gun, and on 28 July Bridgeman told the Americans that their proposals were unacceptable. On 1 August Cecil produced a counter-suggestion for consideration by the Cabinet which required any party desirous of building cruisers over 6,000 tons or carrying a gun over six-inch calibre, except as otherwise provided for, to give prior notice to the other parties; and if such notice was given, each party would retain the right to convoke a new meeting of the three powers 'with a view to ascertaining whether any necessary adjustment of tonnage and other conditions' could be made by mutual agreement. It was an ingenious proposal, supported by Bridgeman on the grounds that it met the American claim for arming cruisers with eight-inch guns while preserving Britain's right to put an end to the agreement if the Americans exercised their freedom.[77] A further last-minute attempt to save the conference was made by the Japanese delegation. On the evening of 1 August the chief Japanese delegates, Viscount Ishii and Admiral Viscount Saito, put forward a new suggestion to the Americans. Revealed to the British on 2 August, it envisaged a quantitative limitation of 'Washington standard' cruisers — twelve for Britain and the United States and eight for Japan — together with an agreement that no new auxiliary craft would be laid down during the period of the convention other than vessels included in existing authorized programmes and those required for replacement purposes. The maximum unit tonnage in the small-cruiser class would be 8,000 tons, and the United States would undertake not to exceed the naval strength of the British Empire before the agreement terminated on 31 December 1931.[78]

On 31 July Gibson informed the British delegation officially that the amended Anglo–Japanese proposals offered no basis for agreement because of the limitations placed on eight-inch gun cruisers, although he insisted to Cecil that if the gun calibre difficulty was overcome, all other matters were negotiable.[79] This latter statement reinforced Cecil's belief that a compromise on the gun calibre question offered the only hope of saving the conference, and on the following day he telegraphed Salisbury to say that he would resign if the government refused such a compromise.[80] The scene was set for a further acrimonious debate when the Cabinet reconvened.

On 3 August a decisive Cabinet meeting was held which lasted for five hours with only a short break for lunch. Tempers were high, and Chamberlain seems to have had considerable difficulty in controlling the meeting, for at one point he was faced with four threats of resignation. Much of the discussion centred around Cecil's 'improved political clause', but though, according to Salisbury, it had a good deal in its favour, the Cabinet decided to defer to the judgement of the new First Sea Lord, Sir Charles Madden, who argued that if, at any point, the United States embarked on a programme of 8,000-ton, eight-inch gun cruisers, any British six-inch gun cruisers built in the meantime would be rendered obsolete.[81] The Japanese proposal, however, whilst requiring further definition, was thought to offer a possible basis of agreement. Neville Chamberlain, the Minister of Health, and Lord Eustace Percy, President of the Board of Education, put forward a number of amendments to this latter proposal, and the Cabinet decided to discuss them on the following day in the light of an Admiralty examination.[82]

Any chance of the government's possible new initiative meeting with success was forestalled on the evening of 3 August, when Gibson informed the British delegation that the United States could not accept the Japanese proposal unless the total British cruiser tonnage within the period of agreement did not exceed 400,000 tons.[83] It was an impossible condition, for under the building programme authorized in 1925, which had a time span of five years, Britain's cruisers would have totalled some 458,000 tons.[84] On 4 August, there being no further proposals on the table, the delegates of the three powers were forced to admit defeat. The Geneva Conference was dead.

In view of the inconsistency of British policy during the conference, the question arises as to whether the government and Admiralty were justified and sincere in their claims, more especially regarding the demand for seventy cruisers and their insistence on the six-inch gun. Many British authorities have accepted the former claim on the grounds that the widespread nature of the Empire required a large number of cruisers for defence. But there is some doubt on the matter, for when asked to give an estimate of Britain's cruiser requirements at the Washington Conference in 1921, Beatty had replied, tentatively, that fifty would be sufficient.[85] Sir Charles Madden later explained that the discrepancy arose because the Anglo–Japanese alliance was still in existence at the time the remark was made and that since the abrogation of the alliance the distribution of the fleet had had to be changed.[86] This is not a wholly convincing explanation since Balfour, who headed the British delegation at Washington, thought the Admiralty was making an error on the point and asserted that neither the British government of the time, nor the Admiralty, had had any intention of profoundly modifying their attitude towards Japan as a consequence of renouncing the alliance.[87] It should also be pointed out that, under the cruiser construction programme adopted in 1925, the total number of cruisers possessed by Britain would eventually have totalled sixty, not seventy, unless the programme had been increased in the 1930s, an unlikely event as it was at that time the government had to find money to finance the battleship construction programme scheduled under the Washington Treaty. Moreover, after the Geneva Conference had broken down, Admirals Madden and Field admitted to Churchill that they had 'never expected to realise a total of seventy cruisers, except by keeping alive a considerable proportion of vessels over the twenty years' [replacement age] limit, and that fifty good ships was probably all they were likely to get'.[88] At the time of the Geneva Conference, the British Empire had only forty-eight cruisers in commission, against Japan and America's twenty-two each.[89]

It seems that the only Cabinet minister to question seriously the claim for seventy cruisers was Churchill, and even he did not press the point, presumably because it might have influenced his colleagues in favour of the policy pursued by Bridgeman and Cecil. Certainly when Churchill did press his case, in the Naval Programme Committee during November and December 1927, his views had a marked effect in turning his fellow ministers against the Admiralty's claim.[90] Criticism of the claim at the time of the conference tended to be indirect. For example, Chamberlain wrote to Baldwin on 22 July stating that he was wholly unable to understand how a man of Field's knowledge and ability could have allowed Bridgeman to proceed on the assumption that the Anglo–Japanese proposals offered an acceptable basis for discussion if they were really open to Beatty's sweeping condemnation.[91] There was much to be said for the view of the naval advisers at Geneva that if Britain could be satisfied with seventy cruisers without an agreement, then one or two cruisers could be sacrificed on the strength of an agreement.[92] But the majority of the Cabinet deferred to Beatty and the naval advisers in London.

If the British position regarding the claim for seventy cruisers rested on shaky foundations, the insistence on the six-inch gun in the secondary class of cruisers rested on similarly unsatisfactory ground. The argument that 'Washington standard' cruisers were offensive and the proposed class of six-inch cruisers was defensive was applicable in only a relative context. The argument that an eight-inch gun small cruiser would cost some £250,000 more than a six-inch gun cruiser is open to question, since the figures for the six-inch gun vessel were apparently based on a unit tonnage of 6,000 tons whereas those for the eight-inch gun vessel were based on a displacement of 7,000 tons, despite the fact that it is feasible to mount eight-inch guns in a 6,000 ton ship.[93] Moreover, it was wishful thinking to expect the United States to forego the advantages of possessing eight-inch gun vessels, especially as Britain had both proposed and accepted the eight-inch limit at the Washington Conference; and in the absence of an agreement the United States possessed the resources to outbuild Britain in eight-inch gun cruisers at any time. Further, Britain's existing cruiser construction programme envisaged the provision of eight-inch gun vessels; and, if an agreement embodying a six-inch limit had been negotiated at Geneva, neither France nor Italy would have been bound by it and would have remained free to build cruisers carrying eight-inch guns which might have been used to threaten British trade. It is significant that, until 10 July at least, Beatty evidently was willing to concede the gun calibre issue, and that in the initial stages of the preparation of the British proposals, he had found it necessary to mislead the government by asserting that the 10,000-ton cruiser had been forced on the Admiralty at the Washington Conference.[94]

The question remains whether a British concession on the eight-inch gun would have brought about a successful conclusion to the Geneva negotiations, since Gibson claimed that the gun calibre issue was the only insuperable obstacle to an agreement.[95] It does seem unlikely, however, unless the British were willing to make concessions on unit displacement and possibly numbers. Certainly the Americans were as rigid in their views as the British, if less inconsistent. Far from accepting the Anglo–Japanese proposals, the Americans decided to insist on the smaller type of cruiser displacing at least 7,500 tons (as against 6,000 tons), while they never formally accepted the proposed 12-12-8 allocation of 'Washington standard' cruisers and considered the ratio allowed to Japan far too high.[96] Moreover, the Americans were even more disingenuous than the British in their methods of negotiation. Gibson's statement of 14 July that if the British and Japanese could arrive at a suitable compromise the Americans were sure to be able to complete an agreement was misguided if not misleading; and a remark made by

Kellogg to Howard, again on 14 July, that 'he had never heard of' Admiral Jones' proposal that the United States be allotted twenty-five 'Washington standard' cruisers was mischievously deceitful.[97] This, however, does not make the British policy any more justifiable. A concession on the eight-inch gun could not reasonably have been expected to jeopardize British security; and failure to make a concession led to Britain being blamed for the breakdown of the conference — and Cecil's resignation.

The Geneva Conference may have broken down primarily on the failure of Britain and the United States to reconcile their differing concepts of limitation; and it is evident that a large measure of responsibility for the failure must rest on British shoulders, and in particular the shoulders of Churchill and Beatty. But Anglo-American rivalry does not fully explain the rigidity of their respective governments, nor does it provide a complete explanation of the breakdown of the conference. It is certainly true that British and American strategic interests differed, but there was one common interest which outweighed the others — opposition to the ambitions of Japan — and it was on this common interest that the naval authorities of the two states formulated their policies. Britain's claim for seventy cruisers devolved from the war plan against Japan; America's need for large cruisers and demand for a low total tonnage limit stemmed from requirements in the western Pacific. Both Boards of Admiralty objected to the Anglo–Japanese proposals on the grounds that Japan was being treated too favourably, and while the Americans put parity with Britain in the forefront of their campaign at Geneva, it was not, apparently, for prestige reasons. Ronald Campbell, the secretary of the British delegation, discerned that it was to maintain the 5–3 ratio with Japan.[98] Although the British Admiralty objected to mathematical parity with the United States, it was mainly for fear that the Japanese would raise their cruiser demands to a level at which it would be impossible for the Admiralty to guarantee the protection of the trade routes.[99] There is much truth, therefore, in the suggestion that the Geneva Conference broke down, not because of a dispute between Britain and America, but because of an Anglo–American dispute with Japan which never broke the surface at the conference.

10 A reconsideration of policy
April 1927–December 1927

The failure of the Geneva Naval Conference precipitated a major crisis within the British government. Cecil, who believed the Cabinet bore a great responsibility for the breakdown of negotiations, decided to reconsider his position as Chancellor of the Duchy of Lancaster. He consulted Salisbury, who tried to dissuade him from resigning because of the possible effect on public opinion, but he was unconvinced by his brother's arguments and on 7 August 1927 he indicated to Chamberlain that he would write a formal letter of resignation to Baldwin on the following day.[1]

Chamberlain's immediate reaction was one of deep regret and some surprise. He thought no body of ministers could have done more to seek a compromise with the United States than the British Cabinet and urged Cecil to review the step he was contemplating. On 8 August he wrote asserting that his departure from the government would be welcomed only by those who had no love for him or for the things for which he stood, and, in doing so, he initiated a correspondence depicting a closeness that could hardly have been anticipated when the Conservatives took office in December 1924.[2]

Replying on 10 August, Cecil explained that he was resigning because the Geneva Conference had brought out 'latent but profound' differences between himself and Churchill and because, in effect, he had been defeated by the Chancellor of the Exchequer on a major issue of policy. The Cabinet meeting of 26 July had shown that in existing circumstances he had no chance of carrying his views against Churchill and 'so able and resourceful a controversialist' as Birkenhead, and it was 'mere futile optimism' to hope that in any future controversy the opposite would be the case. Besides, he had already intimated that he would resign if the Cabinet maintained its irreconcilable attitude on the eight-inch gun question, and by withdrawing his resignation he could hope to have very little influence in a similar crisis in the future.[3]

In a letter of 14 August, Chamberlain expressed surprise that his colleague should resign on the eight-inch gun question when the Cabinet was seeking a last-minute compromise on the issue, and suggested that he would have been equally eager to resign if the

British government had supported the large cruiser and the United States the smaller. Like Salisbury, the Foreign Secretary thought Cecil's resignation would be interpreted as a justification of American policy. He also asserted that it was not true that Churchill, Birkenhead and their supporters were against an agreement, rather that the Cabinet in general had concluded that agreement could be purchased at too high a price because the suggested terms would have failed to give Britain a reasonable measure of security or would have resulted in an increase in costs and armaments. As for disarmament in general, the Foreign Secretary suggested that it was not fair to complain that the Cabinet showed little interest in the question. Cecil had been given 'the largest authority ... and fullest support' that any member of the Cabinet could have expected in the circumstances; and, if the Cabinet had not given more time to the discussion of the disarmament issue, it was because the Cabinet was not the best place for the discussion of questions dealing with technical points.[4]

Chamberlain went to great pains to stress his own support of Cecil at various times and explained his personal position on disarmament in some detail:

> I too attach great importance to the limitation & restriction of armaments. If I differ from you at all on the broad issues it is that I attach more importance to other factors in preserving the peace of the world & that I have never thought that the idea of beginning with a great world conference was the most practical form of approach to the problem. However this was decided before my time & I have done my best to contribute to its success.[5]

In a sincere appeal for Cecil to reconsider, the Foreign Secretary declared:

> You and I, my dear Bob, have succeeded in working very well together in all League matters. I have made your share in them as large as I could & in particular have left the whole question of disarmament in your hands. Only once have we differed seriously & then not on a disarmament question. Is this to be the end of it all? Are you going to throw up the sponge & do infinite damage to the cause because Winston said this or that in the course of one Cabinet discussion where you admit that what he said did not represent the spirit or purpose of the Cabinet?
>
> Forgive me, but I think that you are making a disastrous mistake ....[6]

Chamberlain's letter evidently had an effect on Cecil, for on 16 August he replied stating that he would consider 'very anxiously' all the Foreign Secretary had said. But at the same time he pointed out the difficulties he would face if he remained in the government:

> My difficulty is not that my colleagues have behaved badly to me but that they do not agree with me. You have always shown yourself as among those most favourable to the policy of Disarmament. But you with characteristic candour say in your letter that you do not think it the most important step in the pacification of the world (as I do), & that you do not

believe in a world congress for disarmament or anything of that kind as the best way of reaching the goal. Other members of the Cabinet would not go nearly so far — Winston, F.E., Jix, Amery, Bridgeman, Worthington Evans, Walter Guinness etc are definitely hostile or sceptical of the whole idea.[7]

Cecil further asserted that the failure of the three-power conference seemed to be 'a staggering blow' at the policy of disarmament and that, in the aftermath of such a blow, it was unlikely that the government would take any other direct steps towards arms limitation.[8] Whilst disagreeing with the American contention on the eight-inch gun, he maintained that an agreement with the United States was well worth a concession on the question.[9] He made it clear, therefore, that although willing to re-examine his position, he still favoured resignation.[10] By 21 August he had concluded that he must carry out his threat.[11]

Cecil's first letter of resignation, dated 9 August 1927, was sent to Baldwin while the Prime Minister was still in Canada. He informed the Premier that on the broad policy of disarmament his views were at variance with the rest of the Cabinet, and that, in the circumstances, he saw little point in remaining within the government:

> I believe that a general reduction and limitation of armaments is essential to the peace of the World, and that on peace depends not only the existence of the British Empire but even that of European civilisation itself. It follows that I regard the limitation of armaments as by far the most important public question of the day. Further I am convinced that no considerable limitation of armaments can be obtained except by international agreement. On the attainment of such an agreement, therefore, in my judgement the chief energies of the Government ought to be concentrated. I do not say that it should be bought at any price. But I do say that it is of greater value than any other political object.
>
> ... I believe it is true that the nations must either disarm or perish . . .. In the late discussions the issue was joined between those in the Government who are devoted to that policy and those who oppose it, and the latter won. All that remains for those who were defeated is to submit or resign . . ..[12]

Cecil also made a number of specific accusations relating to policy at the Preparatory Commission and the Geneva Conference. He suggested that the Admiralty had 'scarcely concealed their opinion that the whole of the Commission's proceedings were futile, if not pernicious', and maintained that, at the naval conference, the Cabinet had succumbed to the pressure of a group led by Churchill who were determined to avoid an agreement with the Americans.[13]

Cecil's letter, evidently written in the heat of the moment, contained a number of exaggerations and inaccuracies, and on 25 August he handed Baldwin, newly returned to England a minute drawn up in more moderate language. He omitted some of the more contentious passages relating to events within the Cabinet and included a statement of his disagreements with his colleagues over the previous three years, notably concerning the Treaty of Mutual Assistance and the Geneva Protocol.[14] Even so, the new draft was a severe indictment of government policy, couched in very strong language, which did not meet with the approval of some of Cecil's colleagues, who disliked its tone and felt doubts about the accuracy of some of its statements. Hankey was therefore instructed to submit the minute to a detailed analysis in the light of government documents. The Secretary of the Cabinet consulted Balfour, and received the advice that, if Cecil refused to give 'at least a reasonably correct' version of events, more especially by omitting references to the attitude of ministers, then Baldwin in the last resort ought to advise the king not to release the Chancellor of the Duchy from his Privy Councillor's oath concerning the secrecy of Cabinet discussions.[15]

On 28 August Cecil had an interview with Baldwin to clear up the situation. The Prime Minister objected to the publication of the letter of resignation in its existing form, despite the fact that Cecil had excised the passage to which the Premier had had the strongest objection, and apparently made no real attempt to avert the resignation. Indeed, Cecil formed a distinct impression that Baldwin had scarcely read and had not appreciated either of the letters written to him and that on the whole was 'rather glad to be rid of' his colleague.[16] Eventually, it was arranged that Hankey and Cecil should consider the alterations thought necessary in the latter's minute, and Hankey was instructed to prepare a reply for simultaneous publication. At the eleventh hour, however, Cecil changed his mind and submitted a drastically shortened version of his minute, cutting out all detailed references to the three-power conference and the proceedings of the Cabinet whilst reserving the right to raise the questions in Parliament; he had convinced himself that this was necessary to avoid re-opening the Geneva controversies.[17] On 30 August Cecil's revised minute, together with a short reply by Baldwin, was issued to the press for publication.[18]

Hankey bitterly regretted Cecil's decision to publish a shortened minute for he had drafted a detailed reply to the original which he believed 'would have smashed Cecil's whole case to smithereens'.[19] Fourteen pages long and based on a judicious selection of government documents, many of which Hankey had prepared himself, this reply was as contentious, if not more so, than Cecil's first version of events.[20] But, in consequence of Cecil's decision as to the form of his letter of resignation, this reply was not published.

Baldwin's final reply, dated 29 August 1927, was calculated to smooth over differences and play down the Geneva controversy. The Prime Minister asserted that there were no real differences between Cecil and the rest of the Cabinet over disarmament policy, except perhaps over the means by which it could be most effectively pursued, and suggested that, once having decided upon resignation, Cecil had exaggerated any differences there might have been:

As regards the work of the Preparatory Committee of the League you presided over the Sub-Committee which prepared the British case and practically drafted your own instructions, and in your absence your place as Chairman of the Sub-Committee was taken by a colleague whom you certainly will not accuse of luke-warmness in the cause.

As regards the recent Conference of the Three Powers ... I can take no blame for its failure either to myself or to my colleagues who, after my departure and up to the very moment when a telegram from the delegation at Geneva informed them that the Conference was at an end, were still working for such a compromise as might yet attain the twin objects of limitation of armaments and national security ....

As to the future, I refuse to share your pessimism. It is true that no great progress has as yet been made on the lines of the great world Conference to which you refer ... [but the] Washington Conference, the Locarno Treaty, and the settlement with Turkey have all led to some measure of disarmament and indicate that progress can be made on the lines we are pursuing ....[21]

In retrospect, it can be seen that there was a good deal to be said for a number of Cecil's allegations. Certainly there were profound differences between his own concept of a disarmament policy and that of the government in general. Chamberlain's policy towards European and world problems was based on cordial co-operation and understanding between Britain and France, not on disarmament.[22] As he intimated to Cecil in his letter of 14 August, he thought disarmament was a minor factor in preserving peace, whereas Cecil considered an international arms limitation agreement should be the chief objective of government policy. It is significant that the Foreign Secretary did not attempt to refute Cecil's accusation that a large number of Cabinet ministers were hostile to or sceptical of the idea of disarmament; and, as regards the Geneva Naval Conference, even Bridgeman believed there was evidence to support Cecil's claim that a number of ministers were against an agreement with the Americans. Writing to Hankey on 21 August, the First Lord suggested that although the Cabinet as a whole were not against agreement, Churchill and Birkenhead had taken that line at the meeting chaired by Chamberlain and had met with little or no resistance from Chamberlain and Balfour.[23] Chamberlain maintained that the real difference between Cecil and the rest of the Cabinet concerned the price that Britain could pay for an agreement; but it might be asked whether some members of the Cabinet deliberately held out for a price they knew the Americans would not pay.

Cecil's withdrawal from the government had important implications at both national and international levels. Chamberlain opined that there was no subject now of greater importance for the position of the government in the country than that of disarmament and advocated a thorough review of British policy on the question. Having previously left policy almost entirely in the hands of Cecil, he was unwilling to make precise propositions, but apparently he had been convinced by Sir Cecil Hurst and Lord Onslow (a junior War Office minister and Cecil's replacement at the Eighth Assembly of the League) that the Disarmament Committee was 'far too large to be effective and that the fighting departments gave too little attention to the political aspects of the case ... indeed, treated the whole matter altogether too lightly'. The Foreign Secretary felt the constant change of service delegates on the committee caused a lack of continuity and authority, and favoured the establishment of a small but strong Cabinet committee before which the service experts would be heard and which would be headed by a person who gave due weight to the 'large political issues' involved and would not arrive at decisions purely on technical grounds.[24]

Chamberlain's arguments to a large extent vindicate Cecil in his complaints about the way disarmament policy had been treated since the government took office. The Foreign Secretary effectively admitted that the government had had no broad conception of the ultimate aims of disarmament policy and had to a large extent ignored its political aspects, dwelling far too heavily on the technical aspects. Certainly the role played hitherto by the services had been instrumental in causing obstruction at the Preparatory Commission on a number of relatively minor matters such as naval effectives; and at the Coolidge Conference the role played by Beatty and the Admiralty after the rejection of the original British proposals had successfully clouded a number of issues, particularly that of parity.[25] Indeed, Beatty's whole policy towards the recent conference had been to tie down the British delegates so that they could take no decisions on important questions without reference to himself.[26]

The failure of the Geneva Naval Conference and the breach with America severely complicated the government's position at the Preparatory Commission, which was due to reconvene in November 1927. Originally, Chamberlain had intended to take up a suggestion made by Briand in April that points at issue should be examined carefully by the British and French governments. The idea, elaborated in June, was for Cecil to go through the draft convention clause by clause with the French Ambassador, Aimé de Fleuriau, in an attempt to reach agreement on outstanding points; if it proved impossible to make progress in this way, it was anticipated that Cecil would go to Paris for direct conversations with the French government.[27] With the breakdown of the Coolidge Conference it seemed less likely than ever that Britain could convert the French (or, for that matter, the Italians) to the British viewpoint on principles of naval limitation, leaving one of the principal obstacles to an agreement at the Preparatory Commission unresolved.

The government's difficulties were compounded at the Eighth Assembly of the League where the British delegates were confronted by a number of unwelcome resolutions. The Germans had decided the moment had arrived to put increased pressure on the other powers to disarm, and Bernstorff demanded that the Preparatory Commission be urged to complete its technical work so that the Disarmament

Conference proper could be convened within a year. It had long been clear that the problem of Germany's position *vis-à-vis* the disarmament clauses of the Treaty of Versailles would have to be faced at one time or another — indeed the problem had been discussed rather anxiously in the Foreign Office as recently as May 1927 — and it appeared from the observations of the new British Ambassador at Berlin, Sir Ronald Lindsay, that the time was soon approaching.[28] Chamberlain might consider 'unreasonable and impracticable' the contention that Germany's level of disarmament be applied to France, but, as Cecil pointed out, if the League negotiations were indefinitely postponed, the Germans would have 'every ground' for saying that the ex-Allies were not keeping faith with them, a position which was only one step from saying they no longer felt bound by the obligations imposed in 1919.[29]

Equally important was a resolution moved by the Dutch delegate Jonkheer van Blokland, seeking a renewed discussion of the principles of the Geneva Protocol — disarmament, security and arbitration — though ostensibly without reopening the question of the Protocol itself. A resumption of discussions, it was claimed, would facilitate the work of the Preparatory Commission. It was a powerful argument which appealed especially to the smaller powers, who were anxious about their security, and it became clear that the resolution had extensive support. But, to the British government, a possible reopening of the Protocol controversies was anathema since Britain would be placed in the invidious position of having to oppose consistently the demands of a large number of powers, including France. Even Baldwin, who rarely made written comments on foreign affairs, least of all on disarmament, felt moved to write to Chamberlain that he would have nothing to do with the Dutch resolution if there was 'any risk' that Britain would be plunged into the 'Protocol quagmire' again.[30]

The difficulties of the British position were apparently appreciated by the French, who determined to gain every advantage for themselves. Notwithstanding the activities of the Dutch delegation, the French put forward a resolution linking a new discussion of security directly with the Preparatory Commission. Evidently, the French were opposed to a resumption of disarmament negotiations, fearing there was little chance of making progress; but they dared not propose an adjournment of the Preparatory Commission. In an attempt to avoid a breakdown, therefore, they cleverly advocated that the commission be charged with studying 'measures calculated to give to all states such guarantees of security as will enable them to fix the scale of their armaments at the lowest possible figure in an international disarmament treaty'.[31] It was suggested that the measures be sought through the multiplication and co-ordination of special security arrangements under the auspices of the League, systematic preparation for applying the articles of the Covenant, or an amended Protocol.[32]

Chamberlain's first inclination was to reject the French resolution outright.[33] But in the face of the overwhelming demand at the Assembly for a new look at the security problem he found the resolution offered a number of advantages provided it could be modified slightly to take into account the more important British susceptibilities. The resolution offered an effective means of postponing the disarmament negotiations in November, more especially since the Germans indicated a willingness to discuss security questions so long as discussions on disarmament proceeded *pari passu*. It was diplomatic for Britain to co-operate. The Foreign Secretary also concluded that if other nations chose to invent a Protocol binding on themselves, in effect the result would be 'an extension of the Locarno principle', which Britain had constantly advocated.[34] He aimed, therefore, at securing amendments to the French resolution which would not commit Britain to new obligations; and he did so by indicating to the French that any request for increased commitments would have an opposite effect.[35]

Eventually, the powers reached a compromise which was embodied in a Council resolution of 27 September 1927. The Franco–Dutch demand for a study of arbitration and security was met by instructing the Preparatory Commission to set up a committee which would undertake an immediate examination of the two questions. As a sop to Germany the commission was asked to hasten the completion of its technical work so that the Disarmament Conference could be called as soon as possible thereafter. British feelings were assuaged by framing the terms of reference of the new committee so as to eliminate all mention of the Protocol. It was understood that the Preparatory Commission would meet in November, but only for the off-shoot committee to be appointed, after which it would adjourn until either January or February 1928.[36]

The events at the Eighth Assembly, following directly on the failure of the Geneva Naval Conference and Cecil's resignation, had an important effect on the attitude of the Cabinet towards disarmament. The Labour and Liberal opposition, whose criticism of the government had been rather muted since the negotiation of the Locarno treaties, now had the ammunition to charge the government with being reactionary and obscurantist in its policy. There was a danger, as far as the government was concerned, that non-committed voters might identify the Conservative Party as being hostile to the League and the principles for which it stood. Hoare was particularly alarmed at this prospect and, like Chamberlain, advocated a major reappraisal of disarmament policy. The Air Minister, who considered the Preparatory Commission's discussions premature and likely to prove abortive, suggested that only two realistic courses of action were open to the government: to break off the discussions; or to try to recover whatever might be possible from 'the tangle' into which the question had collapsed.[37] Hoare himself favoured the latter course, believing that a continuously negative policy would leave an unfavourable impression both at home and abroad.[38] On 12 October the Cabinet discussed the situation and decided to set up a strong committee to examine the whole question of disarmament in the light of the most recent developments.[39] Known as the Disarmament Policy Committee, it consisted of Salisbury (chairman), the three service ministers, Ronald McNeill (who as Lord Cushendun took over Cecil's former post as Chancellor of the Duchy of Lancaster) and Sir Douglas Hogg, the Attorney-General.

In readiness for the next session of the Preparatory Commission, the new committee held three long meetings covering the whole spectrum of disarmament and security policy. The discussions centred on a paper produced by Salisbury which elucidated the more important questions, and it was quickly agreed that the British representative should make no proposals at the November meeting of the commission provided its activities remained purely formal. It was anticipated, however, that the Soviets would join the proceedings, having settled their dispute with the Swiss government, and that a Soviet-German combination might precipitate a discussion of disarmament on its merits. So, in case a discussion proved unavoidable, a number of general guidelines of policy were elaborated.[40]

On land disarmament, Worthington-Evans did little more than repeat the objections of his technical advisers against any change of policy on the two most crucial questions, trained reserves and the limitation of *matériel*. He showed little appreciation of Chamberlain's call for political realities to be taken into account, and asserted that Britain should adhere to the 'fundamental' principle of limiting trained reserves and press the case to the utmost so that if the Preparatory Commission broke down, it would not break down on a naval issue alone. In other words, he wanted to blame a breakdown on France. The committee agreed, but thought a more diplomatic method of presenting the British case was called for. The Germans and Russians were expected to press strongly for a limitation of reserves, and it was thought that Britain should not be ranged publicly on the side of the Soviet–German coalition against France. Similarly, regarding limitation of *matériel*, the committee recommended no change of policy. Worthington-Evans thought Britain could not afford to stabilize a defined position 'for all time', either by direct means or, indirectly, through a restriction of expenditure, since it might interfere with the policy of mechanizing the army; but even he and his advisers were forced to admit that this would leave Britain without a definite policy on *matériel* and that it would be unwise to rely on other powers disagreeing on the issue indefinitely, so they advocated a further examination of Cecil's old proposal for a limitation of military expenditure as a whole, considering it less objectionable than other proposals if applied to the British army. The other services, however, would not give even this moderate suggestion their approval, the Admiralty taking a very strong line on the issue.[41]

The Admiralty showed almost as little appreciation of the changed international environment as the War Office, and steadfastly adhered to the great majority of its previous proposals. It was suggested that the basis of British policy on naval questions should be a division of vessels into classes, but it was agreed that a limitation by total tonnage rather than numbers within classes could be conceded, at least up to the point agreed at the Coolidge Conference. The classes proposed were very similar to those envisaged in the original scheme laid before the Geneva Conference: battleships; aircraft-carriers; coast defence vessels; cruisers, in two categories; flotilla leaders and destroyers; and submarines, in two categories. The Admiralty still regarded the transfer of tonnage between classes as unacceptable, but, to facilitate an agreement with the French and Italians on the proposed classification of ships, they declared they would reconsider their objections to a limit on the percentage of officers and agree to the exclusion of trained reserves if the Army Council acquiesced.[42]

The Disarmament Policy Committee would have preferred the international discussion of naval questions to have been deferred for a few months. As this was clearly impossible, it was decided that the British representatives on the Preparatory Commission should adopt the policy proposals advocated by the Admiralty. The committee also agreed that the scheme for limiting capital ships put forward at the Coolidge Conference should be placed in the forefront of the British proposals, on the grounds that they were important both for the cause of peace and as a means of securing economy.[43]

Hoare was more imaginative in his appraisal of the situation than his other colleagues on the committee. Agreement had already been reached at the Preparatory Commission on the units by which air forces should be compared — number and total horse-power of machines — but the minister had heard that the French were considering a simpler approach to the problem and so put forward a practicable, if somewhat unrealistic scheme, for possible implementation. He had become convinced that the only effective way of restricting air armaments was by means of a tripartite agreement between the three great air powers of western Europe — Britain, France and Italy — and suggested that it might be possible to have preliminary talks between the three governments with a view to an agreement based on equality of forces. His colleagues acquiesced, and it was proposed that Chamberlain should initiate conversations as soon as he saw fit.[44]

It was at this point that Hankey made one of his periodic attempts to influence British disarmament policy directly by contributing a proposal for increasing security by the afforestation of frontiers. Drawing on the experience of the First World War, and being assured by the chairman of the Forestry Commission, Lord Clinton, that there were no insuperable technical difficulties, the Secretary to the Cabinet argued that afforested zones might inspire greater confidence among nations and incline states towards reducing their armaments. Forwarding the suggestion to the Foreign Office for discussion by the Disarmament Policy Committee, he stated that it must not be assumed that he was 'off his rocker'.[45]

As events turned out, the Foreign Office effectively killed Hankey's scheme by pointing out its more obvious defects, such as the difficulty in finding sufficient territory for afforestation and the cost of expropriating land and displacing industry. It was pointed out that, in Belgium alone, more than one-third of the land area would be required to provide a tree belt only five miles wide, while it was more than possible that foreign military opinion would have regarded such a belt as offering no inducement to disarm - even if a scheme could have been implemented in time for it to become a practical factor in resolving the disarmament problem.[46]

A more important concern of the Foreign Office was the delineation of policy towards the Preparatory Commission's Security Committee. A number of thorny problems had been raised by the terms of reference of the committee, in particular the extent to which Britain could promote or participate in arbitration agreements, and many permanent officials were alarmed by the very nature of the proposed enquiry.[47] An exception was Sir Cecil Hurst, the old advocate of the Protocol, who suggested that the government should reconsider its attitude towards the compulsory arbitration of international disputes. Claiming that progress towards security and disarmament could not be made unless disputes were settled by peaceful means, he argued that if Britain refused to enter binding engagements for peaceful settlement other nations would pay scant attention to exhortations from Britain to do so and would be entitled to assume that Britain intended to settle disputes by war when it suited her.[48] Chamberlain, however, was unmoved. In the previous year, a cabinet committee had advised strongly against a change of policy, and the Foreign Secretary decided to adhere to its recommendations. He felt that the special circumstances of the British Empire — primarily the lack of a unitary constitution and the absence of agreement as to belligerent rights at sea — precluded any acceptance of obligatory arbitration, though at the same time he was willing to recommend 'the widest extension' of obligatory arbitration amongst other powers.[49]

Rather hypocritically, Chamberlain was willing to co-operate in formulating a draft model treaty for compulsory arbitration open for all states to sign, a proposal put forward at the Eighth Assembly by Dr Fridtjof Nansen, the Norwegian internationalist. The Foreign Secretary did not anticipate Britain signing the treaty; he wanted to eliminate features that he considered undesirable such as the reference of political disputes to the Permanent Court of International Justice.[50]

Chamberlain adopted a similarly negative attitude towards the great majority of questions referred to the Security Committee, interpreting the decisions of the Eighth Assembly broadly as a call on other nations to do what had been done at Locarno. Thus, he favoured the conclusion of 'Locarno model' treaties by other powers but was against Britain entering such agreements herself; and, if invited by the Council to list the measures Britain would take in support of its decisions and recommendations in the event of international conflict, irrespective of the obligations under the Covenant, he would specify only the commitments assumed under the Rhineland Pact. Moreover, he was against developing the machinery of the League to facilitate the application of the Covenant; he wanted to follow the Security Committee's proceedings on this point carefully, but he was prepared if necessary to question the efficacy of Article 16 in the absence from the League of the United States.[51]

The most positive aspect of Chamberlain's approach to security problems was his acceptance in principle of a scheme to provide financial assistance for states who were victims of aggression. A proposal to this effect had been put forward by the Finnish delegation at the first session of the Preparatory Commission, and the Foreign Secretary thought Britain should now press strongly for its acceptance by the other powers. The Treasury favoured the scheme, as it provided a practical alternative to the application of economic pressure under Article 16 of the Covenant.[52]

Significantly, the Disarmament Policy Committee felt Britain had no reason to regret the introduction of security issues into the deliberations of the Preparatory Commission. The committee thought security questions were likely to present fewer problems at that time than disarmament questions, even though Britain could not go very far in undertaking new obligations. It was agreed, therefore, that the British representatives in the forthcoming discussions should make it clear that the government had no desire to postpone consideration of security matters, despite a belief that an arms limitation agreement was not dependent on a prior settlement of international security problems.[53]

In making its recommendations to the Cabinet, the Disarmament Policy Committee adhered generally to Chamberlain's line on security. There were some differences, but they mainly concerned procedure and strategy rather than policy. In particular, it was suggested that Britain should emphasize the possibility of concluding conciliation, as distinct from arbitration, agreements. It was also agreed that Britain should not advocate the Nansen proposal, since it would be difficult to refuse to sign it, but that a model bilateral treaty on similar lines would be welcome as it might prevent other powers from concluding treaties which incorporated undesirable provisions. The committee took care to point out that if the representatives at Geneva were not careful in their use of language, the government might be hampered in resisting political pressure at home in favour of signing the 'Optional Clause'.[54]

The Cabinet approved the Salisbury's Committee's report on 24 November, after a discussion of disarmament and security stretching over two days. The government was still apparently worried about the impact of its policy in the country at large, and the length of the debate indicated the increased importance that was attached to the problem. A severely critical resolution had been tabled in the Commons which deplored the lack of progress at the Preparatory

Commission, and the Cabinet decided to lay down guidelines for use in debate. Ministers were to assert that Britain could not be held responsible for the slowness of the Geneva deliberations, as 'great and unparalleled' measures of disarmament had been undertaken since the First World War, and it was for other powers to follow the British example. The government had 'constantly directed' its efforts towards the reduction of armaments, and at the Coolidge Conference the Admiralty had presented limitation proposals which were 'a most important contribution to the cause of peace and economy'.[55]

In recent weeks, the Cabinet had taken a number of other decisions impinging on disarmament policy. A committee had been established to review the naval construction programme, and as a gesture to the other powers it had been decided to lay down only one new cruiser in the 1927 financial year instead of the three authorized in 1925.[56] The government had then turned its attention to the question of belligerent rights at sea. Independently, Chamberlain and Cushendun had concluded that the root cause of Anglo–American differences over naval disarmament was Britain's wide conception of belligerent rights and they wanted to explore the possibility of an agreement between the two powers on disputed points of law. Chamberlain thought the American claim to parity in small cruisers stemmed from a realization that these vessels were not purely defensive in character but rather the instrument of British blockade policy. He asserted that the United States' government would never again submit to a blockade so rigorous as that enforced by Britain in the First World War. Cushendun argued that there were very few countries on which Britain could impose an effective blockade — the position of Germany in the First World War had been exceptional — and that, unless Britain abandoned her traditional policy regarding belligerent rights, there appeared to be no alternative to an Anglo–American competition in cruiser building. On 23 November, the Cabinet set up a committee of enquiry into the problem.[57]

On a number of occasions in the past, Cecil had put forward the idea of an Anglo–French agreement whereby France would be given special consideration in matters of military disarmament and Britain in matters of naval disarmament.[58] Chamberlain had been impressed by the idea and had sounded Briand on the subject,[59] but he had not followed up his initial enquiries to any great extent, possibly because the response had been inadequate or because he was expecting a French move on the question of a Mediterranean agreement. By November 1927, however, the French had evidently reconsidered the question as Fleuriau brought one of Paul-Boncour's chief assistants, Count Clauzel, the Quai d'Orsay liaison officer of the League of Nations, to London for talks with Cushendun.

The eagerness with which the French now embraced the idea of direct discussions with Britain was apparently due to the Russian decision to join the Preparatory Commission. Fleuriau expressed a personal conviction that the Soviets were coming to Geneva for 'mischief' and not disarmament, and he understood from Clauzel that the French government suspected it was Germany that had induced them into sending representatives. The French Ambassador feared Germany and Russia would press for an immediate resumption of technical discussions and provoke a breakdown of negotiations, and he was convinced that in these circumstances the Germans would argue that the preamble to Part V of the Treaty of Versailles gave them a moral right to rearm. He was alarmed at Anglo–French differences on the Preparatory Commission and, in an evident effort to precipitate substantive negotiations, suggested that it would be regrettable if the two powers were still directly opposed on the questions of trained reserves and naval tonnage when the draft convention was next considered at Geneva.[60]

There were some grounds for Fleuriau's suspicions for at the fourth session of the Preparatory Commission (30 November to 3 December 1927) both Germany and the Soviet Union pressed for the earliest possible resumption of technical negotiations. The Germans were not particularly concerned about the date provided the work of the commission was not made dependent on the work of the Security Committee and it was materially possible to call the first Disarmament Conference before the end of 1928; but the Russians outlined a programme of work towards the 'complete' abolition of armaments and suggested that discussion of the programme commence on 10 January 1928.[61]

Not surprisingly, the majority of powers opposed the Soviet–German manoeuvres and stressed the need to adhere to the decision of the Eighth Assembly. Britain and France wanted to limit the discussions as far as possible to the establishment of the Security Committee (which was accomplished on 30 November) and held that the most convenient arrangement would be to reconvene the Preparatory Commission after the off-shoot committee had undertaken its enquiries. Undue delay in reconvening the commission would have brought charges of obstruction and both powers found it expedient to come to a compromise with the Germans. It was agreed, therefore, that the Security Committee would reconvene on 20 February 1928 (it held two short meetings on 1 and 2 December to elect officers and formulate a programme of work) and the commission itself on 15 March, but on the understanding that intergovernmental discussions towards a resolution of outstanding difficulties would continue and that it was technically possible to call the Disarmament Conference by December 1928. Discussion of the Soviet Proposals was held over to the fifth session of the commission.[62]

The major importance of the fourth session of the Preparatory Commission was its illustration of the new balance of diplomatic forces on the disarmament problem. Previous sessions had been distinguished by intense Anglo–French disputes on technical questions, with the German delegation keeping well in the background; the fourth session was distinguished by the co-operation of Germany and the Soviet Union on political questions in opposition to France and Britain. The Germans were very concerned at the slowness of the Preparatory Commission's proceedings and found it very useful to secure the assistance of the Soviets in pressing the case for a renewed effort towards disarmament. The British and French, in face of their longstanding differences, found it necessary to play for time before embarking on a second reading of the draft convention.

Certainly by this time the British government had begun to realize that there were advantages to be gained from co-operation with the French and that a reconsideration of policy on the whole question of disarmament was essential. Indeed, in the previous four months the attitude of the Cabinet towards the disarmament problem had undergone a considerable change. Significantly, however, the factors that had induced this change were mainly negative: the failure of the Geneva Naval Conference and the breach with America; the impact of Cecil's resignation; political expediency; and Britain's isolation among the powers at the Preparatory Commission. Ministers in general still had no great love for or belief in international disarmament. Some were openly sceptical as to the prospects of the League Commission, and Churchill insinuated that he was against any further limitation of naval armaments, even a renewal of the Washington Treaty.[63] Nevertheless, the government had a somewhat clearer view as to the ultimate objectives of participation in the disarmament negotiations than previously. Chamberlain, for example, believed Britain's aim should be to reach an agreement for the greatest amount of arms limitation or reduction as was practicable.[64] Others, less sanguine about the prospects of success, anticipated a breakdown of negotiations and were apparently more concerned at ensuring that Britain was not held responsible for the failure.[65]

The Cabinet's attitude towards disarmament may still not have been very positive, but unquestionably the review of policy undertaken by the Salisbury Committee improved the prospects of a greater measure of agreement at Geneva. In particular, an attempt had been made to examine some of the underlying political implications of disarmament and the possibility of coming to some kind of an agreement with the French had been explored. Hoare's plan for a tripartite air agreement stood little chance of success because of the susceptibilities of the French, but the Admiralty's intimation that concessions might be made on the questions of trained reserves and naval effectives in return for French concessions on the limitation of naval *matériel* held distinct possibilities. At the same time, on the security front, the rigid attitude of the government towards increased commitments limited the prospects of advance through the Committee on Arbitration and Security.

11 Renewed security negotiations and Anglo–French compromise
November 1927–October 1928

The existing deadlock over disarmament at the Preparatory Commission and the establishment of the Committee on Arbitration and Security gave rise to a new phenomenon in international negotiations — public discussions over security running parallel and concurrently with private discussions over disarmament. The personnel who participated in the discussions were often the same; nevertheless, the questions discussed tended to be treated discretely even though they basically revolved around the same problem, the problem of power and its distribution, more especially within Europe.

The first move came on the disarmament front. On 28 November 1927, *en route* to Geneva for the fourth session of the Preparatory Commission, Britain's newly appointed naval representative at the League of Nations, Admiral Howard Kelly, visited Admiral Saläun, chief of the French naval staff, for preliminary talks on the naval problem. The two admirals discussed a range of issues in the friendliest spirit, and after a long exchange of views there seemed to be a narrowing of Anglo–French differences on a number of points. Saläun, in fact, made a number of concessions. Whilst emphasizing that a rigid classification of ships on the lines proposed by Britain would not be sanctioned, he expressed a willingness to amend the French counter-proposal of April 1927 to meet the British demand that tonnage should not be transferable from the battleship and carrier classes to other categories of vessel. He also agreed to discuss the possibility of dividing submarines into two classes and extending the age limit of all classes of vessel.[1]

Apart from the general diplomatic problems arising from Russia joining the Preparatory Commission, the major factor to have influenced the French move towards Britain seems to have been the resurgence, actual and potential, of German and Italian naval power. The Italian navy already posed a threat to French lines of communication across the Mediterranean, and its development was watched by France 'with a jealous eye'. And there was considerable alarm in the French Admiralty that Germany would replace her existing fleet, when it reached its age limit, with heavy cruisers of 10,000 tons carrying eleven-inch and possibly twelve-inch guns — a type of vessel which would cut across existing standards and entail the construction by France of new vessels of comparable or improved potential. Thus, there was every incentive for France to mend her naval fences with Britain, and Saläun hinted that the favoured method was an agreement exchanging support on the parity question against America for analogous support against Italy.[2]

An interesting facet of the Kelly–Saläun conversation was a profession by the latter that his country did not approve the concept of global tonnage limitation for small navies since the Spanish navy would remain free from restrictions of classification and a Spanish-Italian naval combination might prejudice the French position in the Mediterranean. The assertion was especially notable in that, previously, France had championed both the cause of the smaller naval powers and limitation by total tonnage. This reversal of attitude was perhaps more theoretical than real, since the French proposals of April 1927 anticipated a limited degree of categorization and the objective of the total tonnage proposal in the first instance was to counter Anglo-American proposals for the drastic limitation of land armaments, especially trained reserves. It was an additional indication that now the French had secured their bargaining position, the way was open for a compromise with Britain and the United States.

The French naval representative on the Preparatory Commission further prepared the ground for a Franco-British *rapprochement* in an interview with Kelly on 3 December. With some justification, he suggested that the great majority of governments would accept a compromise on the basis of the French proposals of April 1927, and, after enquiring whether Britain had changed her position since the failure of the 'Coolidge Conference', claimed that the 'final' British proposals at the conference were different in only one real respect from the French proposals — in limiting the number of heavy cruisers. The major stumbling block between the two powers was continued British insistence on the six-inch gun in future cruiser construction, and acceptance of the British position was inconceivable since the other powers would demand a cruiser gun of greater calibre than the six-inch gun allowed in merchant vessels under the Washington Treaty. The clear implication was that Britain should make a concession on the gun calibre issue to facilitate agreement.[3]

A further obstacle to a naval agreement was the position of Italy. The Italians desired theoretical parity with France — which France, naturally, opposed — and adhered firmly to their proposal for mitigating total tonnage limitation only by a year's notice of future construction. The reason, according to Captain Ruspoli, the Italian naval delegate at Geneva, was that limitation by classes in practice entailed the standardization of vessel types and that as Italy could not aspire to superiority in numbers of vessels she must secure the maximum freedom to build vessels which suited her individual requirements. This was especially necessary in that Italy was almost as dependent on sea communications for survival as Britain, having barely seven days' stocks of coal as a national reserve and being strategically vulnerable to blockade. At the same time, the Italians were philosophically 'most strongly opposed' to reducing armaments by 'Act of Parliament', on the grounds that an *increase* in armaments would result. The 'only way' to obtain effective reductions would be for nations to agree not to discuss reductions for ten years![4]

The British Admiralty was far from satisfied that Saläun's suggestions represented major concessions. Indeed, W.A. Egerton, Director of Plans, and Alex Flint, Principal Assistant Secretary (Staff), suggested that the French position had barely changed and that consequently there was no need for Britain to modify her own stance. French willingness to discuss a division of submarines into two categories was referred to slightingly as a step in the right direction which if put into practice would establish the British contention that there was a real difference in character between large and small ships of the same type, French endorsal of the non-transference of tonnage from the battleship and carrier classes was stigmatized as meaningless on the grounds that non-transference from these categories was already forbidden under the Washington Treaty.[5]

On 7 December 1927 Temperley noted that the French were disposed to make a modicum of concessions on land disarmament and in particular scale down their demands on supervision. In an interview with Colonel Réquin, covering the major differences between Britain and France, the British military representative discerned that although Paul-Boncour would not abandon his stated principles on supervision he might accept the British proposals as a basis for further development. Réquin also reiterated the view that France would be prepared to give up the idea of budgetary limitation in favour of budgetary publicity. The one point on which the French held firm was trained reserves.[6]

Cushendun was eager to take advantage of the narrowing of Anglo–French differences to press the policy of close Anglo–French cooperation on disarmament. He was worried that French 'intransigence' might force Britain to side with Germany and the Soviet Union at the next session of the Preparatory Commission, and so he suggested to Paul-Boncour that Britain and France should agree on 'a joint programme which could show an appreciable contribution towards a reduction of armed forces'.[7] He requested — and obtained — Chamberlain's support, and on 11 December the Foreign Secretary raised the possibility with Briand. But the French Foreign Minister was wary of entering into substantive negotiations because of the parliamentary elections scheduled for April 1928, and on 19 January 1928 Fleuriau told Cushendun specifically that on no account would the French government take an initiative which might be distorted for electoral purposes.[8]

The temporary unwillingness of the French to continue disarmament discussions, together with the imminent meeting of the Committee on Arbitration and Security, led the British government to broach the security question once again. On 8 February 1928, on the basis of the Disarmament Policy Committee's report of 23 November 1927, an official note was addressed to the Committee on Arbitration and Security regarding the programme of work delineated by the committee in December 1927. The document amounted to little more than an extended reaffirmation of existing governmental policy, but it is of considerable importance in that it forewarned the other powers against attempting to revive the Geneva Protocol in any form. The government deprecated the idea that sanctions might be imposed by the international community to secure the enforcement of arbitration treaties, reiterated the view that the time was not ripe for establishing a general system of compulsory arbitration or even obligatory jurisdiction at the Permanent Court, advocated wide reservations (vital interests, independence, honour and interests of third parties) in any treaties of arbitration agreed by the powers and scorned the idea of formulating a definition of aggression. The government further suggested that the pacific settlement of non-justiciable disputes might best be facilitated through the establishment of conciliation commissions, whose recommendations would not be binding, although it was agreed that if any states felt able to accept an *optional* treaty for compulsory arbitration — the Nansen proposal — a draft model treaty might be formulated. Britain, it was emphasized, could undertake no new obligations of a general character in the matters of security and arbitration except those arising from a scheme to provide financial assistance to states who were victims of aggression, but if other states felt the need for increased security the best method would be to 'supplement the Covenant by making special arrangements in order to meet special needs'. The nations most immediately concerned and whose differences might lead to a renewal of strife should frame treaties 'with the sole object of maintaining, as between themselves, an unbroken peace'. Britain had taken the initiative in securing one such agreement, at Locarno; it was now up to other powers to follow the British example.[9]

Chamberlain's policy of attempting to put the obligation to increase international security on other powers without involving Britain reflected his continuing adherence to the conception of an international harmony of interests, the idea that nations have a common interest in peace and that nations breaching or wishing to breach the peace are irrational if not immoral.[10] As he suggested to the Disarmament Policy Committee on 10 February 1928:

> It could be urged on the Powers in Eastern Europe and the Balkans that they had only so far made alliances between parties who had no quarrel among themselves. It was up to them now to make arrangements between groups of Powers so as to eliminate the chances of the old quarrels being brought to a head.[11]

The inapplicability of Chamberlain's reasoning was realized by Cushendun, who objected that there was no third party to facilitate an adjustment of the interests of the Balkan and east European states in the way that Britain had facilitated an adjustment between

France and Germany at Locarno, but Chamberlain, while admitting
that he did not have a complete or perfect answer to the objections,
would not be moved from his basic philosophical position, maintaining that the essence of the Locarno treaty was not that Britain had
acted as a guarantor but that it was a pact between former
enemies.[12]

Chamberlain's failure to understand the connection between international security responsibilities and the amelioration of international relations not only led him to seek influence for Britain on
the continent of Europe without concomitant security commitments,
but to envisage a reduction in the commitments Britain had already
undertaken, at least regarding the League. For example, he admitted
to Cushendun that although it could not be said publicly, Britain
accepted the Finnish proposal for financial assistance as a substitute
for rather than an addition to Article 16 of the Covenant. The
Cabinet supported him wholeheartedly on the question and, not
surprisingly, Cushendun was given instructions for the Security
Committee which were hardly conducive to the committee achieving
a breakthrough on the security question or providing a more
adequate basis for the conclusion of a disarmament convention.[13]

At Geneva, as Cushendun anticipated, the British security
proposals were received without enthusiasm, especially by the
French and their supporters, who were convinced of the utility of
general rather than bilateral or regional agreements and of the
advantages of arbitration and security agreements of the broadest
possible scope. The French in particular favoured a general arbitration treaty 'which would cover every kind of dispute and would apply
to all possible relations of the contracting states *inter se*.[14] In drawing up its procedure, therefore, the Security Committee undertook
the not inconsiderable task of drafting model arbitration and security
conventions on both a general and bilateral basis. The work of the
Security Committee proceeded smoothly and in the course of two
sessions (20 February to 7 March and 27 June to 4 July 1928)
adopted nine model conventions: a General Convention for the Pacific
Settlement of all International Disputes (Convention A); a General
Convention for Judicial Settlement, Arbitration and Conciliation
(Convention B); a General Conciliation Convention (C); a Collective
Treaty of Mutual Assistance (D); a Collective Treaty of Non-
Aggression (E); a Bilateral Treaty of Non-Aggression (F); a Bilateral
Convention for the Pacific Settlement of all International Disputes
(a); a Bilateral Convention for Judicial Settlement, Arbitration and
Conciliation (b); and a Bilateral Conciliation Convention (c). The
formulae were then recommended to the Ninth Assembly together
with a draft Model Treaty to Strengthen the Means of Preventing
War based on a suggestion made by the German delegation on 20
February.[15]

Under Convention A, justiciable disputes were to be submitted to
the Permanent Court of International Justice or a special arbitral
tribunal, although by agreement between the parties concerned such

disputes might in the first instance be submitted to a conciliation commission. Non-justiciable disputes were to be submitted to a conciliation commission and in the absence of a settlement were to be brought before the arbitral tribunal. Convention B was basically a generalized version of the arbitration and conciliation conventions concluded at Locarno; and Convention C provided for the submission of disputes to a conciliation commission only. Convention D, which incorporated the three elements of non-aggression, peaceful settlement of disputes and mutual assistance, was modelled on the Locarno treaty. Convention E was very similar except that there was no provision for mutual assistance; and Convention F was no more than a bilateral version of E. Equally, Conventions (a), (b) and (c) were bilateral versions of A, B and C.

As far as possible, the British representatives at Geneva played a low-key role in the negotiation of the model conventions. Sir Cecil Hurst, a member of the all-important Committee of Three, which finalized the drafting of the various conventions, was able to utilize his position to remove features from the conventions which were objectionable to the government. And Cushendun, at periodic intervals, reaffirmed British objections to increased commitments and made it clear that approval of the model texts carried no obligation to negotiate substantive treaties.

The proposal to which the government took the greatest exception at the Security Committee was the German proposal for reinforcing the methods of preventing war, Article I of which anticipated, in cases of dispute submitted to the Council, that states would undertake in advance 'to accept and execute provisional recommendations of the Council for the purpose of preventing an aggravation or extension of the dispute'. Article II provided for an analogous undertaking in cases where war was threatened, whereby states would accept Council recommendations for maintaining or re-establishing the military *status quo* normally existing in peacetime. Article III, which was to operate if hostilities had broken out without, in the Council's opinion, all chances of a peaceful settlement being exhausted, foreshadowed an advance undertaking to accept Council proposals for an armistice, including the obligation to withdraw forces that had penetrated into foreign territory. Article IV anticipated a relaxation of the unanimity rule in Council if the scenarios envisaged by Articles I-III eventuated. Article V suggested the possibility of the agreed obligations being the subject of a protocol open for all states to sign, in a similar manner to the Optional Clause, and of the protocol coming into force separately in the several continents, along the lines of the draft Treaty of Mutual Assistance of 1923. Not surprisingly, the spectre of the Geneva Protocol arose in the minds of ministers.[16]

Cushendun adumbrated a number of specific objections to the German proposals at the Security Committee on 29 February and during the summer of 1928 these objections were refined by the Disarmament Policy Committee, Chiefs of Staff Committee and

Cabinet. The chiefs of staff were particularly severe in their criticisms, claiming that Article I would give the Council unlimited — and therefore unacceptable — discretionary powers and that Article II would prevent states such as Britain from taking precautionary defensive measures during times of crisis and give an undue advantage to aggressors. They further argued that Article III attempted the 'almost impossible' task of imposing an armistice on aggressors. However, as in the case of the Geneva Protocol, the criticisms were largely unfair. Regarding Article I, the Security Committee rapporteur, Baron Rolin Jacquemyns, pointed out that there was no question of giving the Council unlimited discretionary powers, and Chamberlain himself agreed that the situations envisaged by the article were already covered by the Covenant or by the Council resolution of 7 June 1928 on the so-called 'St. Gothard incident'. There seemed less risk of the Council preventing precautionary defensive measures being carried out under Article II than of failing to prevent the precipitation of a conflict. While it might theoretically be difficult to impose an armistice once hostilities had broken out, the example of the Greco–Bulgar crisis of October 1925 indicated otherwise. Nevertheless, on 23 June 1928 the Disarmament Policy Committee suggested that the wisest course for the government to follow would be to reject the German proposals in their entirety.[17]

The Disarmament Policy Committee did not, in fact, intend its suggestion to be carried out. Instead, for tactical reasons, it recommended that Britain should adopt a low profile on the German proposals in the expectation that other powers would ensure the rejection of the scheme. If, then, it still seemed likely that the proposals would be adopted, the British delegate could always try to secure modifications in the drafting along the lines put forward by the chiefs of staff and Sir Cecil Hurst.[18] In the event, the latter course was necessary, the Security Committee proceeding to adopt a Model Treaty to Strengthen the Means of Preventing War on 4 July 1928.[19]

In September 1928 the Ninth Assembly combined the three model multilateral conventions into the General Act for the Pacific Settlement of International Disputes, which, like the Geneva Protocol, purported to provide a procedure for settling all international disputes, justiciable and non-justiciable, through arbitration. The first chapter provided for the establishment of conciliation commissions, which were to deal in the first instance with non-justiciable disputes; the second provided for the reference of justiciable disputes to the Permanent Court or an arbitral tribunal; and the third sought to extend the concept of arbitration to non-justiciable disputes which it had not been possible to settle by other means. States would be free to accept either the conciliation procedure alone or the conciliation and judicial chapters conjointly, and they would also be allowed to make reservations with regard to disputes concerning domestic jurisdiction, clearly specified subject matters (such as territorial status) and disputes arising out of facts prior to the accession to the

Act of any of the parties in dispute.[20]

Despite the claims of its authors and adherents, the General Act did not elaborate a system for the settlement of all disputes. Like the Protocol, it failed to provide for the settlement of political disputes, those arising from a demand to change the respective rights of parties as distinct from those arising from a dispute as to what those rights were.[21] Signatories were committed merely to accepting the compulsory jurisdiction of either the Permanent Court or an agreed tribunal in judicial disputes — and even in these cases states retained wide powers of reservation. In effect, therefore, the General Act amounted to little more than a second Optional Clause. Even so, it was anathema to the Conservative government, which, while approving it in principle for nations that wished to adhere to it, steadfastly refused to add Britain's signature.

On 27 August 1928, a month before the Assembly's commendation of the General Act, a further document had been adopted by the powers with a view to increasing international security and creating a climate in which states would be more willing to make concessions in the interests of disarmament — the Kellogg Pact (or, as the British Government tended to term it at the time, the Multilateral Pact).[22] Under this instrument, the fifteen initial signatories — notably Britain, France, Germany, Italy, Japan and the United States — agreed to renounce war as an instrument of national policy and to seek a solution of their disputes by pacific means. The pact was immediately opened to accession by other powers — the first to sign and ratify was the Soviet Union — and progressively it became accepted almost universally. However, as with the General Act, the additional security provided by the Kellogg Pact was negligible, partly because there was no provision for sanctions in cases of breach of obligations (save the releasing of the other signatories from their obligations) and partly because the renunciation of war did not apply to wars of 'self-defence' or cover obligations assumed under the Covenant or other previous treaties. In essence, therefore, the pact did little more than symbolize the revulsion to war apparent in many sections of the community in the post-1919 world, and even in this respect the British government weakened the impact of the agreement by declaring a 'British Monroe Doctrine' before signifying acceptance. As early as 19 May 1928 it was stated that

> ... there are certain regions of the world the welfare and integrity of which constitute a special and vital interest for our peace and safety. His Majesty's Government have been at pains to make it clear in the past that interference with these regions cannot be suffered. Their protection against attack is to the British Empire a measure of self-defence. It must be clearly understood that His Majesty's Government ... accept the new treaty upon the distinct understanding that it does not prejudice their freedom of action in this respect.[23]

'Freedom of action' was, in fact, the key to British security policy. Freedom from general, open-ended commitments had been the cornerstone of the government's approach to the Geneva Protocol in 1924–5, and a similar position had been adopted towards the General Act. Now, with the 'British Monroe Doctrine' reservation to the Kellogg Pact, the very concept was enshrined in an international treaty. The pact was the only general type that the government would really consider, since in essence it committed Britain to nothing. The pact constituted a resounding peace declaration with no provision for action or sanction in case of breach of obligations, and carried a reservation that Britain would act in accordance with her interests whenever and wherever the government desired.

More generally, the only intrinsic difference between the security discussions of December 1927 to September 1928 and those of December 1924 to March 1925 was that international expectations were higher in 1924–5. Of course, there were differences of detail, for example the lack of provision for sanctions in the General Act (as compared with the Geneva Protocol) and the entry into the arena, albeit indirectly through the Kellogg Pact, of the United States; but as regards furthering the possibilities of disarmament nothing substantive was achieved. None of the agreements arrived at initiated a discernible amelioration in international relations, and none, indeed, was destined to come into force officially before the fall of the Conservative government in May 1929. At the same time, there had been no actual breakdown in the security negotiations and time had been gained for the powers to undertake private discussions for a solution to the disarmament problem.

After the temporary lapse in the disarmament discussions in January 1928, the British government began to reconsider its policy regarding the Preparatory Commission once again. Bridgeman, Field and Cushendun held an important meeting at the Admiralty on 6 February, and a number of alternatives were outlined for presentation to the Disarmament Policy Committee as proposed instructions for the British delegate to the commission. Initially, it was agreed, Britain should restate her case for limitation by classes, along the lines of her original proposals at the Geneva Naval Conference. Seven classes were suggested: battleships, carriers; coast defence vessels; cruisers (two types — large and small); flotilla leaders and destroyers; submarines (again two types — large and small); and small vessels exempt from limitation. However, if, as expected, there was opposition to this classification, it was considered that the number of proposed classes might be reduced to six: capital ships; carriers; cruisers of 7–10,000 tons; surface vessels under 7,000 tons; submarines (preferably of two types); and exempt vessels. Excluding capital ships and carriers, the transfer of tonnage between higher and lower categories would be permitted. There would only be a limitation of the proportion of total tonnage that might be utilized for submarines, and states with a total tonnage of lower than 80,000 tons would be exempt from classification. Even this 'Alternative II' was thought likely to prove inadmissible to certain other powers, and so a third alternative was conceived, limitation through agreed programmes of new construction which would not be exceeded during the period of the treaty.[24]

Bridgeman was convinced that 'Alternative III' would eliminate all the controversial points on which it had been impossible to gain agreement in the past. He suggested that the proposal offered many advantages and welcomed it boldly on the grounds that it gave each nation

> ... perfect freedom to construct any type of vessel most suited to its immediate needs excluding, of course, Capital ships and Aircraft Carriers, which [had] already been strictly limited by the Washington Treaty.[25]

It was a most unusual argument for an Admiralty representative, for it was indistinguishable from the French argument in favour of limitation by total tonnage. Indeed, the only real difference between 'Alternative III' and the amended French proposal of April 1927 was that the latter allowed a transfer of tonnage on a year's notification to the Secretary-General of the League.

Before the Disarmament Policy Committee considered the Bridgeman-Field-Cushendun proposals, Chamberlain put Hoare's idea of a tripartite air pact between Britain, France and Italy privately to the French Ambassador. The Foreign Secretary was tentative in his approach, merely enquiring as to the utility of instituting formal conversations, but he evidently realized that however carefully he broached the proposal, it would founder on French objections to parity with Italy. He was not to be confuted — the French response was negative. Fleuriau expressed interest in the suggestion and promised to pass it on to Briand, but he immediately drew Chamberlain's attention to the difficulties imposed by the different organization of the French air force, which was not an independent unit geared for separate operations but an appendage of the military and naval forces. The size of the French air arm grew greater or smaller in relation to the size of the army or navy, and could not be subjected to independent limitation.[26]

The Disarmament Policy Committee held two meetings, on 10 and 13 February 1928, to clarify British policy — but could only agree to temporize, on the grounds that the Preparatory Commission would not meet until 15 March and that inter-governmental conversations would probably take place in the interim. The main debate concerned the Bridgeman-Field-Cushendun proposals, and it was originally agreed that Britain should put 'Alternative II' to France for the French to table at Geneva if they considered the proposals acceptable. But, although 'Alternative II' represented a certain move towards the French position, there was no guarantee that the United States would look on the proposals favourably even if France did, and so on reconsideration the committee decided not to go ahead with its initial recommendation on the question. 'Alternative III' was rejected for similar reasons: it was felt that the Americans would object to the idea of a five-year construction programme and that it would be best not to risk even the possibility of an altercation on the issue. It was finally agreed that the safest course on naval problems was to regret that some of the British proposals at the Geneva Naval Conference did not find favour and to put forward the old suggestions regarding size, age and armament of capital ships only.[27]

The committee discussed a possible revision of policy on one further point — supervision. Chamberlain, who guided the discussions throughout, asked the service representatives if they would reconsider their objections to a more comprehensive system of supervision than anticipated in the British draft convention. He indicated that it would be difficult to enforce control over the armaments of ex-enemy states if a general system of supervision were not established by the disarmament convention, and countered Salisbury's suggestion of relying on the good faith of contracting parties by affirming that arguments which enabled ex-enemy states to claim relief from their existing obligations should not be used at Geneva. But the Foreign Secretary's colleagues were not impressed and after some discussions it was agreed that the matter should be dropped.[28]

In general, the Disarmament Policy Committee concluded that there was no greater assurance than in the previous November that a breakdown of the Preparatory Commission could be avoided and that, if a break occurred, it should take place on military rather than naval questions since the onus of responsibility for the breakdown might fall on powers other than Britain. Two specific courses of action were recommended to secure this end. The British representative at Geneva was to suggest a reversal of the order of debate — air, navy and army instead of army, navy and air — so that military questions would be most in the public eye; and he was to claim that the French were insincere in their support of disarmament because they insisted, on military grounds, on excluding trained reserves from limitation.[29]

Evidently Cushendun was not entirely satisfied with the Disarmament Policy Committee's report and asked the Cabinet for authority to make informal enquiries with the other powers as to the possibility of seeking a solution to the naval problem along the lines discussed in the committee. Rather surprisingly in the light of the contrary report of the committee, the Cabinet went a long way towards meeting the request, and on 17 February the Chancellor of the Duchy of Lancaster was empowered to support any French move towards new conversations. On 3 March Paul-Boncour alluded to the possibility of talks and Cushendun eagerly grasped the opportunity, invoking a Briand-Chamberlain meeting for 9 March.[30]

Chamberlain's major concern on disarmament at this time was to forestall the possibility of Britain voting with Germany and the Soviet Union against France on the question of trained reserves when the second reading of the draft convention was taken. It was a scenario which appeared to be very real, non-too-distant and one which would have shattered his general policy of close co-operation with France. He decided, therefore, to broach with Briand the idea of an Anglo–French agreement trading British concessions on land disarmament for French concessions on naval disarmament. A promising factor was that Paul-Boncour had communicated to Cushendun a personal conviction that the sub-division of cruisers into two categories would not be an insuperable obstacle for the Ministry of Marine.[31]

In his interview with Briand, Chamberlain openly regretted that British and French views were 'diametrically opposed' on 'the two crucial military and naval questions — trained reserves and form of classification respectively — and suggested that French concessions on the latter might be traded for British concessions on the former. He informed the French leader of the modified Admiralty proposals regarding naval classification ('Alternative II' of 6 February), which represented a considerable advance towards the French position, and suggested that if France could accept a formula 'in accordance with' these proposals the British government might withdraw its opposition to French views on reservists. Briand, naturally, was very receptive; he was impressed by Chamberlain's general principles (especially the anti-German and anti-Soviet element) and opined that experience at Geneva showed that if Britain and France stood together, whatever they agreed would be accepted by the other powers. Accordingly, he asked for a personal copy of the revised Admiralty proposals and said he would put them before the French naval authorities and use 'all his influence' to obtain their acceptance. He added, however, that he would need British co-operation in the matter and suggested that if Britain accepted the principle of estimating cruiser strength on the basis of the length of lines of communication to be defended, he might induce his government to accept a sub-division of that class of vessel. Certainly, he argued, it would be to the mutual advantage of the two countries if they jointly pressed the basis for estimating cruiser strength that Britain had put forward at the Geneva Naval Conference; France's position relative to Italy could be regarded in the same way as the British position relative to the United States.[32]

On the evening of 9 March, Chamberlain and Cushendun, in the presence of Kelly and Cadogan, discussed the implications of the new situation and agreed that Briand's proposal was a sufficiently satisfactory basis to recommend for consideration, first by the Admiralty and then the Cabinet. As the Foreign Office record of the meeting stated:

> As far as the near future was concerned, it offered hope of an Anglo-French agreement by the time the two draft Disarmament texts came to be read a second time — possibly in July; in the remoter future — viz. the Disarmament Conference and possible negotiations preliminary to it — it would at any rate ensure that we had French support in a matter vital to us, whereas at present we had none, having alienated at the Three-Power Conference, the Americans, who had been our ally at the Preparatory Commission.[33]

It was further agreed that the initiative with regard to Briand's rider concerning 'lines of communication' in the estimation of cruiser strength should be left with the French. Kelly, apparently, did not agree that a satisfactory basis of negotiation had been achieved.[34]

On 12 March, after Chamberlain had returned to London, the Disarmament Policy Committee reviewed the prospective Anglo-French agreement, and gave it an almost unqualified blessing. The general principle of French support for the Admiralty's 'Alternative II' proposals in return for the withdrawal by Britain of open resistance to French views on trained reserves was accepted without question, and it was agreed that the interval between the fifth and sixth sessions of the Preparatory Commission should be utilized to 'forward the compromise'. Salisbury personally was against 'the cruiser question' being reopened at the time of the American presidential election and, despite a plea by Chamberlain that it was doubtful whether discussion could be postponed until after the election, the majority of the committee adhered to the chairman's line; but, at the same time, the committee did not reject Briand's 'lines of communication' formula. Thus, effectively, the committee reported in favour of delaying consideration of the formula in public and of accepting the Chamberlain-Cushendun agreement that the initiative in the matter be left with the French. The Cabinet assented to the report on 13 March and informed Cushendun in Geneva of the procedure to be adopted.[35]

The fifth session of the Preparatory Commission (15-24 March 1928) was little more than a farce. The delegates knew in advance that there could be no progress towards an international draft convention unless or until an Anglo-French agreement on the outstanding issues was negotiated. If it had not been for the discussion of the Soviet proposals for 'immediate, complete and general disarmament', held over since the fourth session, the fifth session would barely have lasted more than two days. Even this debate had its farcical side. It was clear that the vast majority of delegates from each power favoured a brusque repudiation of the Soviet proposals — with an outward semblance of courtesy — but no one was willing to take the lead in the matter. Cushendun, for example, was against a British lead on the grounds that the lead might not be followed, enabling 'pacifist papers' to stigmatize the British government with frustrating 'the greatest proposal ever made to mankind for getting rid of armaments'. An hour before the debate was due to open, there was still no speaker against the proposals, and it was even insinuated that if no speaker could be found then the proposals would have to be accepted by default. However, at the last minute, in Cushendun's words, the Italian representative, 'a General, elderly, fat and inaudible ... with incredible gallantry' offered his name as a speaker, and in a short but direct speech proposed that the Russian scheme be rejected summarily. The lead was taken and the commission declared that under existing conditions the Soviet proposals were 'incapable of being carried into execution'. Not to be outdone, Maxim Litvinov, the chief Soviet representative, produced an alternative scheme for partial disarmament, discussion of which had to be set aside until the sixth session.[36]

Within the Preparatory Commission, Cushendun subjected the Soviet proposals to biting criticism and for so doing received two specific commendations from the Cabinet — a generosity of spirit that had not been displayed to Cecil. The new Chancellor of the Duchy of Lancaster avoided calling for outright rejection of the proposals, saying that there might be elements that would repay examination, but he stigmatized the scheme as contemptuous of the League and insinuated that its only value was as political propaganda. He even hinted that the Soviet Union saw its draft convention as a convenient means of promoting civil war abroad and for furthering Soviet power at the expense of neighbouring states.[37]

Apart from the debate on the Soviet proposals, there were only two features of the formal proceedings of the fifth session of the Preparatory Commission that were worthy of note. The first was the submission of a German proposal 'concerning the last paragraph of Article 8 of the Covenant', in effect a plea for revising the Armaments Year Book of the League of Nations so as to give further information on the scale of national armaments, military, naval and air programmes and the condition of industries 'adaptable to warlike purposes'. The information would be given in tabular form and a model for discussion was submitted comprising fourteen tables for the solicitation of detailed information.[38] The second was an allusion made by Count Clauzel, substitute delegate for France in the absence of Paul-Boncour (who was electioneering), to the conversations that had been taking place between the technical experts of the powers. On 22 March he suggested that certain governments were 'far advanced' along the path to agreement and that there was 'no occasion to anticipate any very long delay before we arrive at appreciable results'.[39]

Clauzel's remarks came as something of a shock to the other delegates. The Italians in particular complained that whether or not a successful outcome eventuated, they had important reservations to which they would adhere. Moreover, it was not at all clear to which conversations Clauzel had referred, for as late as 21 March he told Cushendun that he knew nothing of the Chamberlain-Briand discussion of 9 March. The Chancellor of the Duchy of Lancaster suspected that Briand had forgotten the meeting on returning to Paris, and on 24 March Chamberlain felt compelled to write to Salisbury:

I do not in the least understand what is happening at Geneva. To what conversations did Clauzel allude? Surely not to mine with Briand, since he told Cushendun that he had heard nothing about it from Briand. Frankly, I am alarmed by the publicity given to the idea that certain powers are on the verge of agreement behind the scenes as well as the continued implication that naval problems alone impede progress.

Que faire?[40]

The Foreign Secretary was evidently worried about the future of his initiative of 9 March, but received reassurance when Crewe reported in a private letter of 28 March that Briand was busy with the Ministry of Marine discussing the projected agreement.[41]

Chamberlain's anxieties seem to have arisen from a series of negotiations held in Paris between French and American naval representatives prior to the opening of the fifth session of the Preparatory Commission. Admiral Kelly held two important conversations with his American counterpart on the commission, Admiral Long, on 13 and 14 March, and on the basis of these conversations and one between Kelly and the French naval representative it seemed that a Franco–American agreement on the naval issue was a distinct possibility. The Americans, apparently, were prepared to accept a compromise based on the French proposal of April 1927, modified to include an exempt class of vessel and a division of surface vessels under 10,000 tons into two categories: ships of 3–10,000 tons and those below 3,000 tons. Transfer of tonnage from capital ships and aircraft carriers to other categories would not be permitted and transfer between other classes limited severely, perhaps to 10 per cent of the total for the approximate category. The French were apparently contemplating extending the period of notice for transfer from one year to eighteen months.[42]

The French at this point seem to have been deliberately obscuring matters to gain the best possible result from their conversations with the British and Americans. On 15 March the French naval representative told Kelly that although a final decision on the British and American proposals had not been taken, it seemed likely that the former would prove unacceptable but that the latter seemed likely to lead to an agreement. On 21 March, after further conversations, the British naval representative reported to Salisbury his 'firm impression' that if the French accepted the British proposals 'as conveyed through M. Briand' it would only be under the certain conviction that the United States would refuse them. Thus the French might offer no opposition to the British proposals at second reading, but after the United States had rejected the scheme they would put forward or accept the American proposal to show how accommodating they were on naval matters.[43]

Courted by both the British and Americans, the French maintained a discreet silence on the disarmament issue in the following weeks, and put British policymakers in a quandary. As Cushendun pointed out in an important memorandum of 1 May, Britain's chief endeavour had been to avoid bringing about a breakdown of the Preparatory Commission on the question of naval armaments alone, thus forestalling attempts by 'hostile critics' to represent the British government as the sole obstacle to an international disarmament agreement; and the chances of this policy succeeding had grown slimmer in the light of the American proposals for the renunciation of war and the projected Franco–American naval compromise. Britain stood in danger of being isolated at the September meeting of the commission and of incurring the wrath of the advocates of disarmament at home.[44]

In the same memorandum, Cushendun examined the possibility of reaching an agreement with France and questioned the utility of such a venture in the absence of American concurrence. He thought it improbable that the French would show any disposition to meet British views on the classification of ships in the light of the Franco–American compromise, and he also recorded that Briand was apparently much more favourable to British views than the Ministry of Marine. The Chancellor of the Duchy of Lancaster further suggested that the chief difference between the Admiralty's 'Alternative II' and the French proposal of April 1927 was Britain's desire for a division of cruisers into two classes, a division that had not formed part of the British draft convention of March 1927. Almost inevitably, he was drawn into asking whether the Admiralty's position was really essential to the national interest, and, indirectly, whether new concessions might be made. The alternative to new concessions was laid out tersely:

> If the Admiralty's present position is essential in the national interest, there is nothing more to be said; but the Government should clearly realise that in that case a breakdown of the whole movement for disarmament by international agreement is inevitable, and that the responsibility for that breakdown will be laid upon us. There is no use disguising the fact that there is a large body of opinion in this country which will severely blame H.M. Government for such a failure.

> If the failure . . . is really unavoidable, I think it would be best to advise the Secretariat of the League at once that H.M. Government see no prospect of being in a position to agree to any convention for the limitation of armaments.[45]

In a separate memorandum of 1 May Cadogan criticized the policy of the Admiralty and suggested that the major obstacle to an agreement within the Preparatory Commission was the British desire for a division of cruisers into two classes. While admitting that the French proposal of April 1927 allowed too much latitude in the transfer of tonnage, he intimated that the recent French concessions — no transfer of capital ship and carrier tonnage, limited transfer between other classes of vessel and eighteen months' notice of transfer — would in reality give Britain sufficient security to justify acceptance of the scheme. After all, even if the Admiralty's 'Alternative II' was endorsed by the commission, the Americans were likely to claim a total tonnage in 7–10,000-ton cruisers that would not meet with the Admiralty's approval — in which case there were no advantages to be gained from adhering to 'Alternative II'. Although there would be no limit to the proportion of cruisers allocated by the Americans to the 7–10,000-ton category rather than the (unlimited) class of under 7,000 tons, in practice under the notification rule Britain would have sufficient warning of American intentions to prepare for any eventuality. Certainly, as Cadogan concluded, an agreement on the basis of the Franco–American scheme seemed to stand a reasonable chance of gaining general acceptance. There was every indication that the Japanese would comply, and although the Italians insinuated that they could not agree to such far-reaching measures it would be difficult for them to stand alone.[46]

Within the Admiralty, there was a slight difference of opinion as to the procedure to be adopted in forthcoming negotiations. Kelly favoured acceptance of the American modifications to the French proposals of April 1927 so far as a general convention was concerned, but advocated a closer classification along the lines of 'Alternative II' for the signatories of the Washington Treaty. Majority opinion favoured an amended, more concise version of 'Alternative II' even for a general agreement. Madden and Bridgeman, however, resigned themselves to the possibility that the Cabinet would concede the eight-inch gun on the secondary class of cruisers and it was agreed that, in the last resort, Britain would accept a classification which differed in only minor respects from that accepted by the Americans at the Geneva Naval Conference: capital ships; aircraft-carriers; 10,000-ton eight-inch-gun cruisers; 8,000-ton eight-inch-gun cruisers, flotilla leaders up to 1,850 tons; destroyers up to 1,500 tons; submarines up to 1,800 tons; and exempt vessels. Madden laid out the details in a note to Bridgeman of 2 May.[47]

On 7 May the Disarmament Policy Committee met to review the situation, and the Admiralty came under extreme pressure to revise its attitude. Cushendun pointed out that there was little prospect of reaching agreement with France and the United States on the basis of 'Alternative II' and that, unless the Admiralty were willing to accept a classification that was agreeable to France, the best course would be to inform the Secretary-General of the League that there was no chance of Britain being able to accept the draft convention. Hoare enquired whether it would be possible to agree to a classification acceptable to the other powers whilst realizing that the real crux of the problem would come when allocating quantities. Hailsham and Chamberlain said they would defer to the French on the classification of cruisers rather than break up the Preparatory Commission. Bridgeman could only reply that the question was one of policy and not one for the Admiralty. On only two points was there general agreement: that conversations with other powers should not be opened until the result of the negotiations for the Multilateral Pact was known; and, rather contradictorily, that Chamberlain should write to Crewe asking him to enquire from Briand whether progress had been made with the Ministry of Marine along the lines of the Briand–Chamberlain conversation of 9 March.[48]

Crewe actually saw the head of the Quai d'Orsay, Phillippe Berthelot, rather than Briand, in order to elicit the required information. Berthelot knew about the conversations at Geneva two months previously and apparently used the interview to gauge the tenacity of Chamberlain's proposals. He stressed the great importance of Britain and France being united on the disarmament question before the Preparatory Commission met again and seemed almost apologetic that his government had been slow to take up the British initiative. He would use the visit of the British Ambassador to activate the Ministries of Marine and War.[49]

On 11 May, in a memorandum for consideration by the Disarmament Policy Committee and Cabinet, Bridgeman suggested a complete change in British strategy — abandoning the quest for international disarmament. He submitted that the Admiralty's 'Alternative II' and the Madden proposals of 2 May should be considered only as *pis-allers* in the event of the Cabinet deciding that an agreement had to be reached, even if it meant surrendering the points that had been insisted on at the time of the Geneva Naval Conference; and he asserted that neither proposal was economical, advantageous or free from serious risk. The adoption of any of the mooted alternatives to the British proposal at the 'Coolidge Conference' would add heavily to the cost of maintaining the Royal Navy unless the number of vessels required for security was abandoned, and to say that Britain could agree to a skeleton form of categories at that moment and 'fight it out' when the time came for fixing numbers would merely delay a breakdown of negotiations. Further, if the government adopted a policy of always admitting that it was Britain's fault if a settlement was not reached, there might be no limit to the lengths to which Britain might be pushed. He continued:

> For these reasons it would surely be better policy to abandon, at any rate for the time [sic], the attempt to draw up careful and detailed formulae, which have hitherto proved impossible to reconcile with the varying needs of the different Nations.

> Mr. Kellogg's invitation to make a Multilateral Treaty offers the opportunity of convincing public opinion that we are as much opposed to war as any other Nation, if we give a ready and generous response to it.

> Is this not the moment to desist from attempts to devise mathematical tables, to avoid the risk of returning to the state of friction which minor differences provoke, and having made a public declaration of the will of all the great Nations for peace to leave it to each Nation to make such reductions as their circumstances demand and their need for self-defence will admit?[50]

Although Bridgeman may have argued powerfully and sincerely, recording feelings that had long been pent up, his case was hardly judicious. The Admiralty had already assented to Chamberlain submitting 'Alternative II' in writing to Briand, and abandoning the quest for disarmament would have cast doubt on Britain's sincerity in accepting the Kellogg Treaty. It was unreasonable to scoff at the idea of dividing cruisers into 10,000-ton eight-inch gun and 8,000-ton eight-inch gun classes, since Britain's existing construction programme was based on vessels of this size, and in any case an 8,000-ton eight-inch gun vessel cost a mere £445,000 extra to build and

£29,000 annually to maintain than a 6,000-ton six-inch gun vessel. Further, the problems foreseen in the Franco–American compromise were likely to be more theoretical than real, especially in a convention of short duration; indeed, the same problems appeared in more extreme form in the absence of a convention. The insinuation that the government already based its policy on constantly admitting British culpability for not reaching a general settlement was groundless.[51]

On 3 June, notwithstanding the appearance of the Bridgeman memorandum, or maybe because of it, Chamberlain followed up the Crewe–Berthelot conversation in an interview with Briand in Paris. It was a meeting that was to have momentous consequences. The French Foreign Secretary vigorously espoused the cause of Anglo–French co-operation on the disarmament question, recording that the Council of Ministers was unanimously of the opinion that an agreement between the two powers must be reached; and he again suggested that the basis of agreement should be a formula which would determine relative cruiser strength 'according to the length of lines of communication'. Chamberlain agreed to take up the formula and he telegraphed the Foreign Office stating that he intended to discuss the matter with Paul-Boncour in order to 'try to get an agreement on these lines'. The Foreign Secretary asked specifically for the observations of Salisbury, Cushendun and the Admiralty on the problem at the earliest possible moment, and it seemed that the path towards a concrete Anglo–French agreement was at last to be opened.[52]

Cushendun, the minister responsible for synchronizing disarmament policy in London, was unable to consult immediately with Bridgeman and Salisbury. He did, however, contact Madden, and found the First Sea Lord strongly disapproved of Briand's cruiser requirement proposal and Chamberlain's proposed course of action. Apart from the British proposal at the Geneva Naval Conference, already rejected by the Americans, Madden thought there were only two methods of calculating 'length of lines of communication' — lines between a country and its overseas possessions; and lines of the whole of the overseas trade of a country — and both had inherent disadvantages. The former would place the five great naval powers in the order Britain, France, America, Italy and Japan as far as cruiser tonnage was concerned — an inconceivable situation — and the latter would allow the powers to claim roughly the same tonnage, an idea rejected consistently by Britain and the Unites States at the Preparatory Commission. In the circumstances, Cushendun had little option but to forward the issue for consideration by the Cabinet at its next meeting, on 6 June, and he informed Chamberlain of the fact.[53]

Madden, who was invited to the Cabinet to put the Admiralty case, decided to utilize the occasion to bring forward Bridgeman's memorandum of 11 May advocating the abandonment of the quest for general disarmament. Very skillfully, he used the politico-technical arguments against the 'lines of communication' proposal to suggest that it was impossible to devise formulae that could be applied universally, either to cruisers or to other categories of vessel; and in the absence of the Foreign Secretary he received considerable support. Amery thought the French proposal should be turned down at once and that Bridgeman's conclusions should be adopted by the Cabinet; Guinness suggested accepting the French proposal in the full knowledge that it would lead to the breakdown of the Preparatory Commission; and Churchill expressed a similar view, opposing any agreement, at least on smaller cruisers, as dangerous for Britain and likely to lead to increased building. The Chancellor of the Exchequer added that if Britain adopted 'a reasonable line' towards the French army, the French in return 'would more and more come round to the position that England depends on the sea and must not be interfered with vexatiously'. His intervention carried great weight and, according to Hankey, represented the instinctive feelings of the Cabinet. It was considered that it would be a real advantage if Britain could 'keep her hands free' regarding small cruisers while showing a 'real desire' to support France 'on the military side', but it was obvious that no one had any clear idea as to how this could be accomplished. The Cabinet therefore adhered to Baldwin, Birkenhead and Percy's line of seeking further information from the French on the 'lines of communication' formula before continuing with the discussions.[54]

Chamberlain, on being informed of the proceedings in London, was indignant; and rightly so since his conduct both during and after his conversation with Briand on 3 June was in complete conformity with the decisions reached at the Disarmament Policy Committee on 12 March and the Cabinet on 13 March. There were no recorded objections to Briand's cruiser requirement formula at these meetings, despite the fact that Bridgeman attended, and indeed it was explicitly agreed that negotiations for an Anglo-French compromise should be pursued forthwith, even if the initiative regarding the 'lines of communication' proposal was to be left with the French. The question at issue seemed to be one of procedure rather than policy.[55]

Chamberlain has been accused, implicitly if not explicitly, of intending to use his forthcoming conversation with Paul-Boncour to commit himself so deeply to Briand's 'lines of communication' proposal that the Cabinet would be faced with accepting a *fait accompli* or forcing his resignation.[56] But the evidence adduced to support the accusation is confined to an intimation that the Foreign Secretary, in asking for the observations of only Salisbury, Cushendun and the Admiralty on the question, was trying to go behind the Cabinet's back, and was prevented from doing so only by the vigilance of Cushendun. In fact, Cushendun himself concurred that the Cabinet had already accepted the principle of the proposed formula of agreement and was as perplexed as the Foreign Secretary regarding the Admiralty's attitude.[57] The hitch in negotiations was caused by Madden and the Admiralty, not by Chamberlain or Cushendun.

In many ways the Cabinet decision of 6 June 1928 was reminiscent of that of 6 July 1927, when a group led by Churchill, Birkenhead and Beatty had successfully engineered a reversal of policy on the question of cruiser parity with the United States. It was also analogous to the informal Cabinet of 11 March 1925, when Churchill and his adherents tried to dilute Chamberlain's policy regarding the proposed quadrilateral pact while the Foreign Secretary was in Paris. This latter revolt had led Chamberlain to threaten resignation, and it might have seemed that a similar threat was in order, so that the latest resistance movement could be put down. The Foreign Secretary apparently did not consider this course, perhaps because he felt that the militants within the Cabinet would take over policy completely if his offer of resignation was accepted. Certainly he felt that the attempt to find a basis of agreement with France would now break down and that Britain would be unsupported on the naval question when the Preparatory Commission met again — with all its consequences. Accordingly, he expressed his frustrations in a strongly worded telegram from Geneva, complaining that although he had asked the Admiralty to study Briand's 'lines of communication' suggestion immediately it was made in March, he could not remember objections being made to the proposal at any time. He openly regretted that his Cabinet colleagues had merely repeated the negative criticisms made by the Admiralty.[58]

Implicitly, the Foreign Secretary was accusing the Admiralty of a breach of faith, manipulating the known propensities of some of his Cabinet colleagues to procure a reversal of British policy on the 'lines of communication' formula. Perhaps, if he had been in London with all the relevant papers before him, he would have made the accusation explicit, since there can be little doubt that the Admiralty's intention was to scupper Briand's proposal by whatever means possible. The Admiralty later claimed that the Cabinet had not asked for objections to the proposal, but this was simply an evasion of the issue as the formula was specifically referred to the Admiralty by Chamberlain and the fact noted by the Cabinet on 21 March. Moreover, Bridgeman, who was fully cognizant of the French proposals, raised no objection when they were discussed by the Disarmament Policy Committee on 7 May.[59]

The Foreign Secretary was not merely disconcerted by the Cabinet's attitude on the naval problem, he was afraid that his general policy of co-operation with France on the disarmament problem was in jeopardy and that the negotiations at Geneva might break down. His fears were heightened on 8 June when he received important communications from Carl von Schubert, acting German Foreign Minister (Stresemann being ill) and Paul-Boncour. The latter suggested that if Anglo–French differences remained unreconciled there could be no practical result in a further meeting of the Preparatory Commission, and that a meeting with no result would be worse than no meeting at all. He added, according to Chamberlain:

It would then be in fact impossible to maintain the disarmament provisions of the Treaties of Peace. He did not conceal from himself in that case that whatever might be the treaty obligations there would be a state of public opinion which would make their enforcement impossible. Agreement between us was therefore a matter of the highest ulterior consequence.[60]

Chamberlain fully agreed, and indeed gave Paul-Boncour his own opinion that 'whatever might be the theoretical obligations of disarmament already imposed upon certain nations, it would, *in fact* be impossible to maintain them in such circumstances.[61]

Schubert put the German case more strongly. As Chamberlain reported to the Cabinet:

> Herr von Schubert . . . wished to draw my serious attention to the fact that unless *some* practical result was shortly realised it would be impossible longer to restrain German opinion. He particularly disclaimed any idea of using language in the nature of a threat, but failure to make some advance . . . would make it impossible for the German Government to resist the conviction . . . that the whole pretence of disarmament was a sham, and that the opening words of the clause in the Treaty of Versailles which imposes disarmament on Germany mean nothing and that the basis of the restrictions imposed upon Germany was gone . . ..[62]

The effect of the statement on Chamberlain was extraordinary; he lectured the Cabinet on the importance of disarmament in terms very reminiscent of Cecil:

> Unless we make some progress in the question of disarmament we shall be faced inevitably by Germany's repudiation of the disarmament provisions of the Treaty of Versailles, with what consequences for the immediate or future peace of the world I cannot at this moment pretend to predict. Germany accepted these provisions under duress, and she has more or less respected them in the hope that they were but the first step to a general limitation of armaments. The moment that this expectation is definitely falsified she will feel herself under no moral obligation to observe the restrictive clauses of the Treaty of Versailles, and no League investigation, nothing, indeed, short of actual violence, will prevent them from becoming practically a dead letter.

> If I am right in thinking that this aspect of the question was not before my colleagues in their recent discussions, I am sure that they will appreciate its gravity now that their attention is called to it. In the light of it, even so important a question as naval strength becomes but one part of a much more complicated and far-reaching problem . . ... If the failure of the conference is not merely laid at our door but, if as a consequence of it, Germany re-arms, the situation will indeed be serious.[63]

The battle lines had been drawn up for a new clash between the opponents and proponents of disarmament.

If, numerically, the effective opponents of disarmament were in a majority within the Cabinet, a decision in favour of Bridgeman's memorandum could hardly be taken in the absence of the Foreign Secretary, at least without compelling either Chamberlain's resignation or his complete subordination to the majority view. So, on 13 June the Cabinet adjourned its consideration of the Bridgeman memorandum until the Foreign Secretary had returned from Geneva. The omens for Chamberlain and his policy, however, did not seem good.[64]

Unknown to the Cabinet, the Admiralty was already in the process of approving a new set of disarmament proposals, ostensibly with a view to resolving Anglo–French differences but more with the aim of securing Britain's position *vis-à-vis* the United States and the Admiralty's position within the government in the event of Bridgeman's memorandum of 11 May not being accepted by the Cabinet. The proposals actually emanated from Captain Deleuze, who, in a private conversation with Kelly on 5 June, envisaged an extension of the Washington Treaty through the limitation of all ships below 10,000 tons mounting guns over six-inch calibre, in which category Britain would accept parity with the United States and France with Italy. Submarines would be limited separately, but surface vessels armed with guns of six-inch calibre or below would be limited only by 'the necessities of the respective states'. The scheme was a purely personal one on the part of the French representative, but it was eagerly adopted by the Admiralty since it offered French support on the gun calibre question against the United States and could be put before the Cabinet as a 'genuine' attempt to facilitate disarmament in the full knowledge that it was likely to be rejected by the United States. An added advantage of the proposals as far as the Admiralty was concerned was that they might be utilized to frustrate an attempt within the Cabinet to engineer a concession to the United States on the cruiser gun issue, a course of action put forward by Cushendun.[65]

At the Cabinet meeting of 22 June, faced with opposition from the ministers most intimately connected with the disarmament problem — Chamberlain, Cushendun and Salisbury — Bridgeman dropped his scheme for abandoning the quest for disarmament. He managed, however, to gain control of proceedings when Chamberlain failed to secure approval for a policy of reopening discussions with the United States; and he did so by springing the Deleuze proposals on his unsuspecting colleagues. The result must have surpassed even his wildest dreams. Very precipitately and incautiously, the Cabinet decided to by-pass analysis of the scheme within the Foreign Office and instructed Chamberlain to inform the French government that if France put forward the proposal officially at Geneva, Britain would support it. In these circumstances, it was added, Britain would not oppose French views on land disarmament even on the question of trained reserves.[66]

On 26 June a despatch was sent to Crewe informing him of the decision to accept the Deleuze proposals. On the following morning, however, the French representative told Kelly that his government could not accept the 'compromise'. The Ministry of Marine had no objection, but certain politicians were said to be demurring on the grounds that French opinion could not be brought to understand a system of limitation which exempted such a large class of surface vessels. Deleuze further suggested — to the obvious confusion of Kelly — that the French and American governments were close to an agreement based on the French proposals to the Preparatory Commission of April 1927 but that there still appeared 'a reasonable prospect of agreement' on the basis of the British proposal ('Alternative II') of March 1928, providing the maximum tonnage of the second class of cruiser could be raised to about 8,000 tons and the transfer of tonnage between categories limited upwards or downwards in line with the Franco–American agreement. In the circumstances, the official British note indicating a willingness to accept the Deleuze proposals was not presented until 28 June.[67]

Deleuze's remarks seem to have caused a degree of consternation within the Admiralty, and it was agreed that Kelly should visit Paris on his return from Geneva for unofficial talks at the Ministry of Marine. Accordingly, on 11 July the British representative discussed the situation with the chief of the French naval staff, Admiral Violette, and on 13 July the French admiral handed Kelly a copy of proposals approved by the Council of National Defence earlier that morning. The terms were rather different to those envisaged by Deleuze and the note was still to be considered unofficial; but the Ministry of Marine was anxious to know if the proposals were acceptable to the Admiralty before an official note was sent to the British government. There were still to be four classes of warship — capital ships (defined as ships over 10,000 tons or armed with guns over eight-inch calibre); aircraft-carriers over 10,000 tons; surface vessels of or below 10,000 tons mounting guns of over six-inch and up to eight-inch calibre; and 'ocean-going' submarines of over 600 tons — and limitation in the first two categories was to continue to be regulated by the Washington Treaty. In categories three and four all powers were to accept the same theoretical maximum total tonnage (Article 3) while indicating at the final Disarmament Conference the tonnage they proposed to reach and promised not to exceed during the period covered by the disarmament convention.[68]

Articles 3 and 4 of the French note embodied principles that the French had first put forward in March 1927 and which implicitly, if not explicitly, had hitherto been rejected by both the Admiralty and the government. However, as Kelly pointed out, Britain could always refuse to sign an eventual convention if the tonnages proposed for the various powers were unsatisfactory, and, as the other aspects of the note were very much to the Admiralty's liking, Admirals Fisher (the new Deputy Chief of the Naval Staff) and Madden agreed that the note should be accepted with minor reservations. Bridgeman concurred.[69]

On 17 July Bridgeman discussed the unofficial note with Chamberlain, and the Foreign Secretary insisted that paragraphs 3 and 4 involved 'such a novel principle' that they must be considered by the Cabinet. This was, in fact, in line with the Admiralty's own proposals for procedure and, accordingly, the Admiralty's reply to the Ministry of Marine was strictly non-commital, although encouraging in general tone. The matter was then broached at the normal weekly meeting of the Cabinet on the following day, and here it was agreed that the Disarmament Policy Committee should report fully on the question on 25 July. On 20 July in a communication to the British Embassy in Paris, the French put their proposals in official form, including the concession that Britain would make on the question of trained reserves. Two minor modifications in the proposals were an explicit division of submarines into two classes (over and under 600 tons, only the former to be limited) and a restriction of the theoretical parity concept to the great naval powers.[70]

The government's acceptance of the French proposals was scarcely in doubt. The first two of the proposed four categories of warship to be limited coincided with the classification continually advocated by Britain; the third (surface vessels mounting guns over six-inch calibre) was equivalent in effect to the cruiser classification anticipated by the Admiralty's 'Alternative II'; and the fourth (submarines *over* 600 tons) had also been envisaged by the Admiralty in drawing up 'Alternative II'. Although an additional restriction covering submarines *under* 600 tons was considered preferable, since this would have limited the security risk from submarines more drastically, the extra risk involved in accepting the French proposals was so small that even the Admiralty was prepared to concede the point in order to come to an agreement. The non-limitation of six-inch gun cruisers was also in accordance with the Admiralty's views, being a logical extension of the British proposals at the Geneva Naval Conference.

In the circumstances, the Disarmament Policy Committee's appraisal of the acceptability of the French proposals was little more than a rationalization of existing policy and the French 'parity' proposal.[71] On the latter issue, for example, it was suggested that as the 'champions' of parity the Americans would find it difficult to reject the concept of theoretical (as distinct from actual) parity for all powers. Even if the Americans did swallow their pride and accept the French concept of parity they were always likely to resist the proposal for coupling the limitation of eight-inch gun cruisers with the non-limitation of six-inch gun cruisers. The United States had refused to accept a milder version of this proposal at the Geneva Naval Conference, where Britain had at least suggested a total tonnage limit for six-inch gun cruisers in return for the United States agreeing to a strict limitation of eight-inch gun cruisers, and there had been no indication since that time that the Americans would modify their policy on the gun calibre question — quite the reverse in fact, as Bridgeman admitted in his memorandum of 11 May.[72] It was inconceivable, therefore, that the Americans would suddenly stand their policy on its head by accepting a limitation of eight-inch gun cruisers while leaving lighter cruisers unlimited.

Almost incredibly, in recommending acceptance of the French proposals the Disarmament Policy Committee paid little attention to the gun calibre question, treating it as a purely technical matter.

The Cabinet had no apparent qualms on the matter and on 25 July accepted the committee's recommendations with the sole proviso (realistically suggested by Cushendun) that the United States and Japan be informed of the compromise before the President of the Preparatory Commission. Chamberlain was charged with handling the diplomatic arrangements for furthering the compromise and on 28 July the official British note of acceptance was passed to Briand. On 30 July identical telegrams were sent to the British representatives in the United States, Japan and Italy outlining the naval aspects of the agreement and asking for the observations of the three powers.[73]

If the government considered the Anglo–French compromise a serious contribution to the quest for disarmament, the question arises as to why the scheme was thought to be acceptable to the United States. Perhaps it was not considered acceptable. Certainly Kelly, in his important memorandum on his conversations with Violette, stated emphatically that 'we' (meaning either the Admiralty or the government) knew the proposals would be rejected by the United States, and Bridgeman, on earlier occasions, had contended that an Anglo–French agreement without American concurrence would be invaluable, if only to put the blame for breaking up the Preparatory Commission on American shoulders. The latter view had also been expressed by Guinness and was not incompatible with Churchill's position and what Hankey described as the 'instinctive feeling' of the Cabinet on 6 June. It seems likely, therefore, that the majority of the Cabinet supported the compromise with France in an attempt to force the United States into an agreement on British terms or into accepting responsibility for a breakdown of the Preparatory Commission.[74]

Other members of the Cabinet, including Chamberlain, Cushendun and Salisbury, seem to have supported the compromise for fear of British isolation at Geneva, more particularly since the Preparatory Commission appeared to be on the verge of collapse. It had long been accepted that it would be better to gain one friend among the naval powers that Britain had alienated (the United States, France and Italy) than to remain aloof and bear the odium for the breakdown of negotiations. The French proposals not only freed Britain from the threat of isolation but represented a continuation, even extension, of the Cabinet's existing naval disarmament policy. The concession on trained reserves was a small price to pay for French support on the naval issue, especially considering that the exclusion of reserves from limitation was a *sine qua non* of a disarmament convention to the great majority of conscriptionist countries. A further, more specific, fear was that if Britain did not reach an understanding with France, the French and Americans would conclude an agreement inimical to British interests. In this eventuality, Britain would have been isolated at Geneva even more effectively than before.[75]

More fundamentally, the Anglo–French compromise represented possibly the only line of advance in disarmament policy which would preserve Cabinet unity. The split between the opponents and proponents of disarmament had barely been patched by the precipitate decision of 22 June in favour of the Deleuze proposals, and non-acceptance of the Violette proposals (which had been derived from the Deleuze scheme) might well have reopened the split and ultimately led to resignations from the government. Certainly at that time there was little or no hope of uniting the Cabinet on any other general programme for disarmament as the fate of Chamberlain's suggestion for reopening discussions with the United States showed.

Any small hopes the government may have entertained that the Anglo–French compromise would improve relations with other powers were soon dispelled. On 30 July, before the proposals had been communicated to the United States, Japan and Italy, and apparently with little or no consultation with his Cabinet colleagues or the Admiralty, Chamberlain announced to the House of Commons that negotiations between Britain and France on the naval disarmament question had produced a formula acceptable to both powers. He could not reveal the terms — it would have been improper to do so — and thereupon unleashed a process of international speculation which had disastrous results for Britain's already tarnished reputation on disarmament.[76]

One of the chief causes of speculation arose from Chamberlain's statement that the Anglo–French compromise was a purely naval affair. The French press began to attribute far-reaching importance to the agreement, and the other powers could scarcely believe that the French had secured no concessions on land disarmament in return for acceding to a naval formula acceptable to Britain. Accordingly, on 4 August the American *chargé d'affaires* in London, Ray Atherton, raised the issue with Sir Ronald Lindsay at the Foreign Office, and the British Ambassador at Berlin, Sir Horace Rumbold, asked for instructions as to how to relieve German fears on the question. The answers given were very different and showed an appalling lack of diplomatic preparation. Atherton was given to understand (by Lindsay, possibly without authorization from the Foreign Secretary) that Britain had agreed to withdraw her objections to the French view on trained reserves only under heavy pressure at a late stage of the negotiations, while Rumbold was informed (correctly, by Chamberlain) that Britain had made the concession at an early stage to induce the French into accepting the British line on the naval question. The issue was further confused when Chamberlain admitted to Rumbold that the compromise was in the nature of a 'bargain', while Cushendun, who became acting Foreign Secretary on 9 August (Chamberlain retiring temporarily due to illness) specifically rejected the usage of the term with the Americans, preferring to view the compromise and the individual elements within it as no more than a 'basis for discussion'. Cushendun even managed to lead Atherton to believe that no agreement had been reached on reservists whilst informing Kellogg that Britain had decided, reluctantly, not to resist the French on the question since it would be impossible to move

France and the majority of other European powers from their entrenched positions; a concession on the issue, suggested the acting Foreign Secretary, would enable the French government to accede to Anglo–American views on naval classification. The latter version of events became Britain's official position on 11 August, or rather Britain's official position *vis-à-vis* the Americans.[77]

Notwithstanding the fact that the Anglo–French compromise represented an attempt to secure Cabinet unity rather than a solution of the disarmament problem, Chamberlain's original suppression of the British concession on trained reserves is difficult to understand, more especially since he admitted to Rumbold that the full terms of the compromise would become known sooner or later and Britain would have to fulfil her obligations when the question of reservists was brought up at Geneva. Even more difficult to understand are Cushendun's tergiversations on the compromise as a whole, since he merely increased suspicions among the powers concerning Anglo–French motives. The Italian attitude towards the compromise changed from equanimity to almost hysterical antipathy from early September onwards, the Fascist government becoming convinced that Britain had 'recognised and consecrated the existing French military hegemony in Europe';[78] and in the United States there was an outcry in the press against the compromise which reflected, indeed surpassed, the hostility to the scheme already apparent in diplomatic circles. On 25 August the *New York World* alleged that Chamberlain had sent a secret letter to Briand (dated 23 July) with a view to pooling the British and French navies and mutual co-operation in the Atlantic and Pacific, and on 5 September, despite strenuous denials by Cushendun and the Foreign Office in the preceding ten days, the American Ambassador, Houghton, asked Lindsay specifically whether moves were afoot to resuscitate Anglo–French co-operation on pre-1914 lines.[79]

American and Italian suspicions might have been dispelled by the publication or private transmission of official documentation concerning the compromise; but Cushendun continually refused to countenance either of these measures until his hand was forced by the publication in the *New York American* on 21 September of a circular letter compiled by the Quai d'Orsay giving a résumé of the negotiations leading to the compromise. How the document came into the hands of the *New York American*, an organ of the anti-British Hearst press, is unknown, but its publication caused a renewed outburst of public feeling against the British and French governments and their compromise, not only in the United States but in Germany and Italy. In Britain, too, the government received a very bad press, being accused of 'selling the pass' to the French on the question of reservists. Cushendun, however, still refused to publish any detailed information regarding the origins of the compromise and British motivations and only very reluctantly consented to a confidential submission to the American, Italian and Japanese governments of the texts of the British notes of 28 June and 28 July and the French note of 20 July. The texts were finally handed to the Americans on 26 September, a mere two days before the American note officially rejecting the compromise was communicated in London by Houghton.[80]

The reason why Cushendun sought to delay, if not prevent, the publication of the Anglo-French negotiations is clear. As he admitted to Lindsay, he 'could not deal satisfactorily' with two of the major points in the compromise: army reserves and 10,000-ton cruisers.[81] On the former, his untruthful and misleading statements to the Americans had left him little room for manoeuvre regarding publication; on the latter, he was aware that the Cabinet had accepted the compromise in the certain knowledge that the cruiser proposals would be rejected by the United States. He lamented:

> Those who complain that we have 'sold the Pass to the French' would have growled still louder if we had broken up the disarmament Conference by sticking out against the French. It is all a matter of argument that cannot be elaborated in a White Paper . . . .[82]

In any publication, he explained to the Cabinet, the compromise proposals 'would require careful editing to explain the circumstances in which the present position had arisen'.[83]

The American note of 28 September, which roundly — and quite legitimately — accused Britain of attempting to forward her national interests at the expense of the United States, effectively killed the compromise. Although the Japanese government expressed its 'concurrence to the purport' of the agreement, there was no realistic way forward without the United States. On 6 October the Italians put paid to any lingering hopes that a basis of discussions had been found, declaring in a *note verbale* that they could not agree to a separate discussion of the naval problem and that, in any case, they still adhered to the principle that naval limitation should be by means of a global limitation on tonnage.[84]

The disapprobation heaped on the British government for its role in the compromise was thoroughly deserved. The idea of utilizing Anglo-French discussions to overcome the obstacle facing the Preparatory Commission was sound and commendable; but it is clear that factors other than the provision of a realistic basis of discussion at Geneva were uppermost in ministers' minds during the negotiations of 1928. These were fear of British isolation on the commission; fear of Britain incurring responsibility for a breakdown of the commission; aversion to siding with Germany and the Soviet Union against France; fear of a Franco-American agreement; a wish to throw responsibility for a breakdown at Geneva onto the United States; temperamental antipathy to disarmament; and the need to preserve Cabinet unity. At best, the government's vision of the putative objective of the compromise was blurred; at worst, it was non-existent.

If Chamberlain and Cushendun, the ministers most intimately connected with the disarmament problem, assessed the general possibilities for progress towards limitation more realistically than their colleagues in the Cabinet, they possessed neither the will-power nor political weight to ensure that their views prevailed. In June 1928 both favoured re-opening discussions with the United States while continuing the dialogue with France, and Cushendun pointed out the particular danger that the United States might not accept an Anglo–French agreement.[85] Yet both meekly accepted the Deleuze proposals, sprung on the Cabinet by Bridgeman on 22 June in the clear knowledge that they would be unacceptable to the United States, without even demanding further investigations by the Foreign Office. The Foreign Secretary and Chancellor of the Duchy of Lancaster also displayed a singular lack of understanding of the susceptibilities of other nations and of the difficulties inherent in bringing multilateral disarmament negotiations to a successful conclusion. The premature announcement of the compromise by Chamberlain in the Commons and the deceptive statements made by Cushendun to the Americans in August were both unwise and counter-productive, and epitomized the ineptitude of British diplomacy.

The deficiencies of Chamberlain and Cushendun during the compromise negotiations may have been considerable, but it would be unfair to lay responsibility for the failure to secure an internationally acceptable agreement solely on their shoulders. Churchill was also culpable in that he pressed, with considerable success, for a renewal in more extreme form of the disastrous policy adopted at the Geneva Naval Conference whereby a stringent limitation would be applied to 'Washington standard' cruisers, which the Americans found best suited their needs, but no limitation to the lighter cruisers which the Admiralty wanted to multiply. But the greatest responsibility for the failure rests with Bridgeman and the Admiralty who, having failed to halt British participation in the disarmament negotiations at Geneva, railroaded through the Cabinet a scheme of limitation — the Deleuze proposal — which they were fully aware stood no chance of success, and followed this by supporting the similarly unsatisfactory Violette proposal. By September 1928 they had led the government to the brink of a scenario envisaged by Cushendun in early June — France accepting the proffered support on trained reserves whilst throwing the onus of a breakdown of the Preparatory Commission over cruisers on Britain.[86]

12 Final discussions
September 1928–May 1929

The government's immediate objective after the rejection of the Anglo–French compromise by the United States was to dampen speculation in the press, both at home and abroad, regarding the real motives behind the compromise. Paradoxically, however, the Cabinet continued to reject the idea of publishing the more important documents concerning the negotiation of the scheme, at least until the American presidential election, which was scheduled to take place on 6 November 1928. The upshot was predictable — press conjecture and revelations (notably in the *Echo de Paris* of 5 October) increased to such an extent that the government soon found itself with little option but to publish a White Paper on the subject, and one was duly issued on 22 October in conjunction with the French. The contents were doctored to omit compromising material, notably the anti-German character of Chamberlain's approach to Briand on 9 March.[1]

Even with the publication of the relevant documents, it took some time to calm the powers most concerned at the implications of the compromise, the United States and Germany. Cushendun, in fact, caused further offence to both powers, though particularly Germany, by proclaiming that there was 'no new entente with France, for the old one had never been dissolved'.[2] Relations with the United States remained so cool that the government delayed its intended reply to the American note of 28 September indefinitely for fear of exacerbating matters at a time when Congress was discussing a considerable increase in naval armaments - the so-called 'Fifteen Cruiser Bill'. The Bill was finally approved in February 1929.

The coalescence of the problems of Anglo–American relations and international disarmament presented the government with additional difficulties in framing a coherent programme for presentation at Geneva. It was clearly necessary to review existing policy, and the options open to the government had narrowed considerably, at least if previous policy was to be appear credible. Lord Eustace Percy, however, evolved a possible way out of the difficulties in an important memorandum of 12 October 1928. His idea was to disengage Britain from 'a confused debate in which we have really little interest but in which we are dangerously involved'; and to this end he suggested that the government take a 'more independent' attitude at the Preparatory Commission, making no more proposals and allowing other powers to take the initiative. Britain could then, he argued, react to proposals on the basis of merit. The ultimate aim was to terminate the proceedings of the commission, which he regarded as 'a positive menace to the peace of the world in general and to the peace of the British Empire in particular'.[3]

In many respects, Percy's memorandum of 12 October was reminiscent of Bridgeman's paper of 11 May, a point the First Lord of the Admiralty was quick to make in the Disarmament Policy Committee on 2 November. Whilst still maintaining his intrinsic opposition to formal disarmament commitments and contempt for the Preparatory Commission, Bridgeman had reluctantly come to the conclusion that the signing of the Kellogg Pact and the rejection of the Anglo–French compromise made it impolitic to abandon the quest for disarmament, whether generally though the League or bilaterally with the United States. He might rile against disarmament (and even Cushendun) in his diary entries; he might make public speeches questioning the idea of pursuing arms limitation through 'elaborate tables and formulae'; but in the Disarmament Policy Committee he suggested that given Britain's existing situation the best policy was to play for time, making no concessions but awaiting the intervention of a third power, outside the Anglo–American quarrel.[4]

Bridgeman's reaction to Percy's memorandum was not atypical. With a general election due within a year, ministers were conscious of the possible repercussions if they openly abandoned the quest for limitation. As Salisbury put it, 'It would certainly be unfortunate if ours is to be the hand that slays the Disarmament Conference.' Unlike Percy, he saw advantages in the policy of 'wait and see'. There might still be a chance of a compromise with the United States especially if, after the presidential elections, the 'Peace Party' gained ascendency over the 'Big Navyites'. Even if this did not materialize, a further 'dilatory expedient' might enable Britain to look successfully for a means of avoiding responsibility for a breakdown at Geneva. Cushendun and the Foreign Office adopted a similar attitude, as did Hailsham and Worthington-Evans. The only real difference within the Policy Committee concerned procedure. Hailsham, supported by Worthington-Evans, made a specific proposal amplifying Bridgeman's suggested strategy, while Cushendun argued that the policy of not taking the lead in discussions might cause France, possibly joined by Italy, to revert to her reported agreements with the Americans — leaving Britain isolated and in much the same position as in March 1928, before the Anglo–French conversations which resulted in the compromise. As a result, the Admiralty was asked to report on the extent to which Britain might accept an agreement on the Franco–American basis.[5]

Not surprisingly, the Admiralty maintained its hardline attitude and opposed any agreement along the lines of the reputed Franco–American agreement, maintaining that Britain would be unable to obtain the number of cruisers required for security. An agreement would only become possible when the United States modified its attitude on the question of gun calibre. Accordingly, on 9 November the Disarmament Policy Committee agreed that the British representative, without taking any undue initiative, should content himself with dissuading the Preparatory Commission from bringing its labours to an untimely end.[6]

Chamberlain, on his return to office on 27 November, evidently believed that the policy adopted in his absence was not strong enough. So, on 7 December 1928 he informed the Cabinet that at the forthcoming meeting of the League Council at Lugano he intended to impress on Briand the importance of not delaying any longer the attempt to reach a settlement on the subject of land armaments, 'owing to the vital bearing of this question on the German attitude towards the Disarmament Clauses of the Treaty of Versailles'.[7] The Cabinet did not disagree, although Churchill asserted that 'All our present troubles are admittedly due to Geneva' and Amery that the Preparatory Commission was 'a step in the wrong direction'.[8]

On 10 December the Foreign Secretary ventilated his ideas to his French counterpart, more especially his fear that lack of progress on disarmament would enable the Germans to proclaim that they no longer felt bound by Part V of the Treaty of Versailles. Briand, however, merely said that he would 'study' the question, and the only real decision taken by the Lugano Council on disarmament was that the Preparatory Commission be asked to reconvene in April 1929. Earlier discussions, it was agreed, were out of the question because of the prospective change of administration in the United States consequent on the choice of Herbert Hoover as President-elect on 6 November. The installation of the new President was not scheduled to take place until 4 March 1929.[9]

The December Council meeting initiated a quiescent period in the government's discussion of the disarmament problem, although privately ministers engaged in a round of insult-throwing on the question. Most entertainingly, in a letter to the Prime Minister, Bridgeman said of Cushendun, a staunch Ulster Unionist:

... old Ronald McNeill has caught the Geneva microbe which gives all English people who get it the idea that they are always in the wrong .... I wish he could be persuaded that the Pope at Rome was at the back of the nations with whom he has to discuss disarmament: it would put new life into him![10]

More seriously, Chamberlain complained that he could not prevail against the combined views of Churchill and Worthington-Evans in securing a reduction of military expenditure in Egypt.[11] The indirect comment on his lack of power to secure greater reductions through disarmament could hardly be missed!

Worthington-Evans' lack of enthusiasm for disarmament was also evident to members of his own department. On 9 January 1929, with the approval of his immediate superior, General Charles (but notably of neither the Minister of War nor the Chief of the Imperial General Staff), Temperley, who had become Deputy Director of Military Operations and Intelligence, sent a lengthy memorandum to Cushendun advocating a radical change in procedure at the sixth session of the Preparatory Commission. With the 'notorious' weakness of Loudon as a chairman, the British military representative at Geneva believed the commission had become bogged down in 'a vicious circle of highly complicated technical discussions which few people outside the Commission really understand', and that if discussions continued along existing lines there was a real chance that a complete breakdown could occur. The commission was far too large for its purpose, and he thus suggested that at the forthcoming session, after dealing with the two items already on the agenda (the German proposal for greater publicity of armaments and the Soviet draft convention), it should appoint a sub-committee of the great powers, including the Soviet Union, to discuss informally and in private the whole field of disarmament. The objective would be to reach agreement unhampered by previous commitments or publicity.[12]

Temperley's counterpart, MacNeece Foster (formerly MacNeece), also desired a change in procedure, though of a very different nature. Against 'the endless friction of mathematical formulae at Disarmament Conferences' he proposed that nations should reaffirm the Kellogg Pact triennially. Such reaffirmation, he believed, would produce a real, gradual and spontaneous improvement in international relations.[13]

Neither Temperley's nor MacNeece Foster's ideas were taken up at the time, although the former's conception of a directing sub-committee of great powers was, in a sense, implemented in the form of the Bureau at the Conference for the Reduction and Limitation of Armaments of 1932-4. Cushendun's view of Temperley's memorandum was, 'There is nothing in this, I think', while Hoare stigmatized MacNeece Foster's concept of reaffirming the Kellogg Pact triennially as the suggestion of a guilty conscience.[14] Ministers were to take more notice of two proposals which emanated from the United States at the end of 1928, one by Allen W. Dulles, a member of the American delegation at the Preparatory Commission in 1926 and at the Geneva Naval Conference of 1927, the other by Walter Lippmann, editor of the influential *New York World*. Dulles, in essence, suggested that an equation be established between six-inch gun and eight-inch gun cruisers by discounting some 10 per cent of the former for limitation purposes; Lippmann submitted that Britain and the United States should respect the status quo in eight-inch gun cruisers on completion of existing programmes, with the understanding that American superiority in eight-inch gun cruisers (twenty-three to twenty) would be compensated by British superiority in six-inch gun cruisers. Both proposals were made privately, but it was understood that Dulles had consulted the State Department before setting out his plan and that Lippmann's plan had originated with Senator Borah, chairman of the Senate Foreign Relations Committee. On 16 January 1929 Chamberlain asked for Bridgeman's ideas and opinions on the schemes.[15]

Bridgeman's reaction to the American 'proposals' was hostile. In transmitting a naval staff memorandum to the Foreign Secretary on 31 January, he made it clear that neither scheme could seriously be entertained. He scorned the Dulles proposal on the grounds that the power of a six-inch gun cruiser could not be compared with that of an eight-inch gun cruiser, arguing that even if the ratio of light to heavy cruisers was three to one Britain would still be at a disadvantage; and he postulated that the Lippmann plan could not be considered if it gave the United States the right to replace obsolescent cruisers by modern eight-inch gun cruisers. Only if the latter scheme predicated an American fleet of twenty-three eight-inch gun cruisers and ten six-inch gun vessels, compared with the British fleet of twenty eight-inch gun vessels, four seven-and-a-half-inch gun vessels and forty six-inch gun vessels — a position that clearly was not contemplated — did Bridgeman think an agreement might be possible.[16]

Evidently stung by the First Lord of the Admiralty's negative attitude, the Foreign Secretary endeavoured to point out the inadequacies of the Admiralty's case. He accused Bridgeman of seeking the unobtainable, asserting that as the government had already agreed to numerical equality in eight-inch gun cruisers, the Admiralty's concept of non-equivalence between six-inch and eight-inch gun cruisers meant in practice that no possible fleet of six-inch gun cruisers could give Britain the security that had been taken as the basis of discussions. He then referred to a speech by Baldwin at the Albert Hall on 28 October 1928 and one by Bridgeman himself at the Constitutional Club on 31 January 1929 in which the intention to compete with the United States in a naval arms race was positively disclaimed. In the light of the disclaimer, he suggested, it was hypocritical to allow the size of the American fleet to dominate discussions. Bridgeman's response was ineffective, accepting that Britain had undertaken 'some risk' in agreeing to equality with the United States whilst arguing that, given time, the Americans would tire of building cruisers and reduce their demands.[17]

On 27 February 1929 the Disarmament Policy Committee reconvened to consider the instructions to be given to the British representative at the sixth session of the Preparatory Commission, scheduled to start on 15 April. Cushendun, aided by Cadogan, enumerated the issues requiring some kind of decision and agreement was quickly reached on three main points — naval armaments, supervision and military effectives. On navies, it was agreed that discussions should be adjourned, although a reported proposal by Stresemann that outstanding questions should be referred to a sub-committee of the five great naval powers might be accepted if tabled formally. On supervision, it was agreed that there should be no change of policy; on effectives, it was decided that the government could not openly renege on the promise given at the time of the Anglo–French compromise that Britain would no longer insist on a limitation of trained reserves. There was, however, considerable disagreement within the committee concerning the limitation of land *matériel*. Cushendun pointed out that Britain had no real policy on the subject, even though there were two proposals on the table at Geneva — direct limitation by categories and indirect limitation by expenditure — and, much to the chagrin of Worthington-Evans, he advocated a more accommodating attitude than previously adopted. Accepting the War Office's opposition to direct limitation, the Chancellor of the Duchy of Lancaster suggested that the possibility of indirect limitation might be reconsidered on the grounds that it had 'pretty general' support at Geneva and that the objections to it — that it might interfere with the policy of mechanization — had no great validity. Certainly the objections should not prevent the government indicating a willingness to accept such budgetary limitation if other countries saw advantage in it. Worthington-Evans was unmoved, merely signifying his continued adherence to the proposal for a combined limitation of expenditure on effectives and *matériel*, outlined in his memorandum of 24 October 1927.[18]

Behind the scenes, the War Office had been preparing its case for some months, and at an early stage it had become clear that the department was unwilling to reconsider its attitude. This was partly due to the inflexibility and obtuseness of Milne, who seems not to have appreciated the intricacies and importance of the whole disarmament problem. For example, when Temperley suggested that if the British representative at Geneva was forced to express an opinion regarding the limitation of *matériel*, he should be empowered to accept, as a principle, limitation by expenditure, the Chief of the Imperial General Staff took this to mean that Britain should be a party to a reduction of *matériel*![19] By 1 March 1929, however, Milne had prepared a reasoned answer to his critics, submitting that Britain should not be stampeded into accepting indirect limitation since only one great power, France, had backed the concept at Geneva. His main concern was to protect the army's mechanization policy, and he claimed that if budgetary limitation applied to *matériel* alone, rather than to *matériel* and personnel combined, any attempt by Britain to increase expenditure on *matériel* during a second five-year convention would lead to accusations of militarism and aggressive tendencies. He also suggested that infinite possibilities for camouflage existed under the model budget approved by the Preparatory Commission and that specifications for *matériel* would soon be evaded. Maliciously, he concluded that 'the only states likely to be penalised, limited, or to suffer in any way by a limitation of armaments are those states which are trying to save the lives of their people by developing their material to the highest degree'.[20]

The *non possumus* attitude of Milne and Worthington-Evans antagonized Cushendun to such an extent that he expressed his feelings in language that would have been heartily approved by his predecessor, Viscount Cecil. It was becoming clear, he declared, that unless the Cabinet was prepared to override the views of the service department no advance was possible at the Preparatory Commission:

> I should be the last to advocate, or to favour, any policy which can be shown to jeopardise the safety of the Country. But military experts are not infallible, especially where political as well as military considerations have to be taken into account, and I respectfully submit that the Memoranda by the Secretary of State for War ... and the Chief of the Imperial General Staff ... fail to give any indication that actual danger would be caused to the British Empire by pursuing a more conciliatory policy in regard to the limitation of warlike material.

> It appears to me indeed that the War Office fail to grasp the essential conditions of the disarmament question. It is obvious that disarmament of any sort must be unwelcome to military administrators, and must involve inconvenience and even some degree of hypothetical risk; it must create difficulties which have to be faced and readjusted; it must interfere with War Office discretion at many points, and impose restrictions which doubtless are galling. But unless you are prepared to accept such disadvantages and to make the best of them, it is idle to talk about disarmament at all.[21]

Cushendun poured further scorn on the War Office's refusal to accept the tables in the German proposal for publicity of armaments which required information concerning reserve stocks of *matériel*:

> I fully appreciate the military reluctance to give this information, but here again that reluctance appears to arise from a dislike of the whole disarmament movement rather than from any serious danger to be apprehended from giving the information.[22]

Giving the information, he submitted, would do Britain less harm than most other powers; and as most other powers, including the normally reluctant United States, were willing to give the information, Britain should not add to the number of 'small refusals' which were giving the impression that Britain was obstructing disarmament.[23]

One of Cushendun's major concerns was the effect of existing government policy on the Conservative Party's chances of winning the forthcoming general election; Parliament had almost run its full five-year course. It was this consideration which was uppermost in the minds of ministers when the Disarmament Policy Committee met on 19 March for a final reappraisal of strategy before the sixth session of the Preparatory Commission. Chamberlain was concerned that if disarmament became an electoral issue, the incoming government might be pledged to adopt measures that were 'fraught with risk from the national point of view'. He urged, therefore, that the British representative be authorized to suggest 'that an end should be put to academic discussions, and that actual proposals for disarmament should be tackled forthwith'. Cushendun, however, while not opposing the proposal, pointed out that it would be contrary to the procedure already adopted at Geneva and that Britain might be accused of scrapping the draft convention and indeed all the work that had been done to date. Hailsham then made the most important contribution to the debate, suggesting that insofar as land and air armaments were concerned, to avoid being placed in the position of objecting party, the British representative should be empowered to announce that: '. . . we felt confident that we could see our way to accept any proposals which met with unanimous agreement on the part of the others'.[24]

Hailsham's main objective in putting forward this proposal was to ensure that at the time of an election, Britain's enemies at home and abroad would not be given the opportunity of blaming the lack of progress towards disarmament on the intransigence of the government. Support for disarmament barely entered into the Lord Chancellor's calculations. Although convinced that Britain could endorse an agreement accepted unanimously by the other powers, he thought it extremely unlikely that the other powers would be able to agree among themselves. In this case Britain would be absolved from responsibility for the breakdown and could put forward an idea approved at the previous meeting of the committee, 'limitation' by means of a publication of building programmes over an agreed period.[25]

Hailsham's remarkable intervention in the Disarmament Policy Committee brought the conflict between Worthington-Evans and Cushendun to an abrupt end. Both agreed to the strategy suggested by the Lord Chancellor, although the former did so simply because he was convinced that unanimity could not be achieved at Geneva. Chamberlain, Salisbury, Hoare and, rather grudgingly, Bridgeman also assented, in a show of unity rarely seen within the committee, primarily because of electoral considerations. On 26 March, the Cabinet accepted the committee's recommendations and agreed the terms of a substantive statement to be made by the British representative at Geneva.[26]

If the government had found what appeared to be a neat way of avoiding its difficulties regarding the prospective discussion of land and air armaments, the same could not be said of naval armaments. The Disarmament Policy Committee had counselled delay, but the problem remained as to what might happen if the land and air discussions reached deadlock at Geneva and the government put forward the plan for agreed programmes over a number of years. The Cabinet of 26 March was aware that this idea might be opposed by the United States, at least in the naval sphere, and so it was necessary to plan future strategy exceedingly carefully. Accordingly, a further Cabinet discussion of the matter was arranged for 11 April; the intervening period to be used for sounding the American government.

The Americans were not entirely happy with the British programme proposal since it envisaged a material modification in the functions of the Preparatory Commission, which was not authorized to deal with quantitative proposals. They further claimed that the proposal would not really constitute an advance towards disarmament, at least in its naval aspect, because the building programmes of the naval powers were generally published already. However, with the changeover of administrations in the United States, the American attitude was not wholly clear and so the Cabinet agreed to give Cushendun full discretion as to whether and, if so, in what form, he should put forward the programme proposal.[27]

As the powers reconvened for the resumption of the Preparatory Commission on 15 April, American intentions remained something of a mystery, the British government receiving conflicting information from different sources. On 10 April Reuters reported that Gibson was returning to Geneva 'with possibly some new plan for determining the specific categories of fighting craft which Mr. Hoover considers to be the hub of the problem'. However, Kellogg assured Howard that Gibson had no such instructions and was to adopt the same attitude as before, following proceedings and initiating nothing but considering with sympathy proposals made by others. At the same time, in Geneva, the American delegation seemed unable to agree on a consistent line in private conversations. On 15 April, Admiral Hilary Jones, admittedly prompted by Kelly, hinted that an Anglo-American agreement might be achieved on the basis of twenty-three heavy cruisers for the United States and twenty for Britain, with compensating advantages for Britain in the number of light cruisers; but the American naval representative also stated that his delegation was quite prepared to accept the French proposal of April 1927, modified to specify surface vessels of 10,000 tons to 1,850 tons (instead of 10,000 tons to 3,000 tons) and a 10 per cent transfer of tonnage allowance. Meanwhile, Gibson and Hugh Wilson, the chief political members of the American delegation, disclaimed the idea of making definite proposals and adhered to the line followed by Kellogg in Washington. At least the political members of the British and American delegations were agreed on one important point — that their respective naval 'experts' should be kept in the background as far as possible.[28]

On 17 April, still anxious at the prospect of exacerbating Anglo-American relations, the Cabinet met to discuss the emergent situation. The tenor of the discussions could hardly have been anticipated; for, on being informed of the hints dropped by Admiral Jones, ministers rallied to the idea of coming to a naval agreement with the United States not substantially different from those resisted in the past. Even Bridgeman admitted that, at first sight, the Jones 'proposals' appeared hopeful, although they did require 'further examination in detail'. Perhaps electoral considerations had again affected the judgement of individual ministers. It was agreed that the First Lord of the Admiralty should concert with Chamberlain to work out the basis of an acceptable policy.[29]

On 19 April, before the Preparatory Commission had started its second reading of the draft convention, Cushendun was able to make the general statement of British policy agreed at the Cabinet on 26 March. Whilst not abandoning Britain's theoretical position on any one point and reserving the right to examine the commission's labours as a whole, he declared that as regards land armaments the government would 'endeavour to accept, and feel confident that they will be able to accept, any scheme which meets with the approval of the rest of the Commission'. He continued by making a similar declaration regarding air armaments. Noting that there was already substantial agreement on the principles of air limitation, he stated that the government would expect 'to be able to agree to any further principles . . . that may secure the unanimous approval of other countries'. On naval armaments he counselled delay.[30]

Except for a brief word of praise from Gibson, Cushendun's statement provoked no reaction from his fellow delegates, almost as if they suspected that Britain was merely trying to avoid responsibility for a breakdown of the commission. In complete contrast, a similar, though slightly more specific statement by Gibson was received enthusiastically. Speaking on 22 April the chief American representative declared that as regards land armaments, the United States would defer to the countries primarily interested in the question 'with such measure of concession' as would materially facilitate an agreement — in other words, would not press for the limitation of trained reserves. More important, however, at least as far as the British government was concerned, he put forward a new set of principles for resolving the naval problem. Accepting the French thesis of April 1927 as the basis of discussion, he stated that as a supplementary method of limitation, his government would be prepared to consider 'a method of estimating equivalent naval values which takes account of other factors than displacement tonnage alone'.[31]

Gibson's speech was to usher in an era of improved Anglo-American relations. Cushendun publicly welcomed the new statement of American policy and the United States' delegate responded in private by suggesting that when the British government was in a position to move ahead, the best plan would be for a Cabinet minister to discuss the matter personally with President Hoover. The suggestion was eagerly taken up in London, where the Cabinet, meeting on 24 April, viewed the developing situation with considerable satisfaction. As a result of the meeting, Cushendun was authorized to tell Gibson that although no final decision had been taken, once the general election was over the government thought it desirable to send a Cabinet member to Washington to discuss the whole question of naval disarmament. In the meantime, the idea of putting forward the 'programmes' proposal at Geneva was dropped.[32]

At this point, the government announced that Parliament would be dissolved on 10 May and that a general election would take place on 30 May. In effect, all the negotiations for disarmament, both at Geneva and bilaterally with the Americans, were put on ice. The Cabinet did discuss the question once more on 1 May, but this was merely to approve a draft telegram to Howard concerned mainly with ensuring the secrecy of developments until after the election.[33]

Fortunately for the government, the secrecy of the Anglo–American conversations held, and the British delegation at Geneva was not faced with angry protestations from other delegations that the two major naval powers were negotiating behind their backs. In consequence, the sixth session of the Preparatory Commission was able to resume its labours in a conciliatory atmosphere. After summarily rejecting the Soviet proposals for proportional disarmament and agreeing to take the second reading of the draft convention, delegates almost tumbled over themselves in an effort to announce concessions that would make agreement possible or, as with Britain, to attempt to avoid responsibility for a breakdown of negotiations. In particular, the French announced that they would no longer insist on budgetary limitation or on-the-spot investigation by international commission. In lieu, they put forward a more general scheme for verification and accepted an American proposal for the publicity of defence expenditure. Real progress was at last being made in the formulation of the draft convention − or so it seemed.[34]

The chief difficulty remained the position of Germany. Intrinsically, the concessions announced by the various powers at the sixth session of the Preparatory Commission had weakened the provisions of the draft convention whilst, implicitly, leaving Germany under the stringent controls of Part V of the Treaty of Versailles. Thus, whereas under the Treaty of Versailles Germany's effectives, trained reserves, *matériel* and reserves of *matériel* were severely limited, under the draft convention only the effectives of other powers would be limited. This was unacceptable to the Germans and on 4 May, two days before the adjournment of the sixth session, Count Bernstorff addressed his fellow delegates in solemn terms:

The Commission has ... lost sight of its task, at any rate so far as the disarmament of land forces is concerned.

For years past I have been co-operating with all my strength in the Commission's work and I have shared in all its responsibilities. But my Government has never left it for one moment in doubt ... that it could not accept, even as a first stage, a solution which did not include *all* forms of armaments, and which would not bring about an appreciable reduction in the excessive armaments of the present day. Such a solution would not correspond with the principles either of the Treaties or of the Covenant. I therefore find myself obliged to dissociate myself definitely from the programme which the majority of the Commission has just drawn up ...[35]

The prevention of such a breach at Geneva had been a prime consideration of Chamberlain and Cushendun. Since the demise of the Anglo-French compromise, in their separate ways they had advocated that Britain take a more active role in the quest for international disarmament. But they did not represent the majority view within the Cabinet, nor even the Disarmament Policy Committee. Their colleagues, many of whom were dubious of the desirability of disarmament, let alone its feasibility, were disposed merely to seek ways of ensuring that the government would not be held responsible for a breakdown of negotiations at Geneva. The more conciliatory posture adopted by Britain at the sixth session of the Preparatory Commission had its roots securely in the putative needs of election policy.

Part VI Conclusion

13 Conclusion

The extent to which the government's disarmament policy contributed to the resounding defeat of the Conservative Party in the general election of May 1929 is debatable. Usually, foreign affairs are held to have little effect on the voting patterns of the general public, and one would imagine that a specialized aspect of foreign affairs such as disarmament would have a negligible impact on voters. Probably this was so in 1929. But it is possible that the votes of a not inconsiderable number of people were influenced by the disastrous handling of the disarmament problem in the previous four-and-a-half years. With the exception of the National government of 1931-5, it is difficult to find a more incompetent handling of disarmament policy by a British government in the twentieth century.[1]

Basically, the failure of governmental policy stemmed from an inability to comprehend the nature or importance of the disarmament problem. The government perceived disarmament as a peripheral issue, outside the mainstream of British foreign policy, and allocated the problem very little time in relation to its importance on the international scene. The question did not appear regularly on the agenda of Cabinet meetings, and when it did appear was mostly treated cursorily. In four-and-a-half years of office, the government was unable, or unwilling, to lay down clear objectives that might be pursued through disarmament. During this time it barely examined the fundamental question of why, if at all, Britain needed a disarmament policy, or whether a resolution of the disarmament problem might help towards a solution of the German problem. Collectively, ministers preferred to adopt an *ad hoc* policy, reacting to discussions and proposals at international level on the unspoken assumption that other countries were attempting to steal a march on Britain. To the Cabinet, disarmament was not so much the problem of power management in international relations as the problem of other nations being reluctant to follow Britain's putative 'disarmament by example'.[2]

It is apparent that many ministers were confused as to the very meaning of the term 'disarmament', not that some made much of an attempt to understand it. Certainly the indiscriminate use of the term tended to blur the distinction between two separate issues in British government policy: the disarmament problem in external policy and the armaments question in internal policy.[3] It is important to maintain a distinction because the Baldwin administration's approach to the two problems was disparate. The government was sceptical of general disarmament and neither accepted its merits nor pursued its success wholeheartedly when negotiations proved unavoidable; but it was willing to base its armaments policy on the concept of minimum perceived requirements, which contributed to the (erroneous) impression that arms reductions were pursued as a goal in themselves. British arms reductions in the years following the Treaty of Versailles were not intended to be an example for other powers to follow: they were practical measures taken only after careful examination of the circumstances of the time and with due regard to national needs.

Similarly, at a time when reductions in public expenditure were thought to be a panacea for economic ills, governments throughout the world were not desirous of over-investing in military insurance, and the great majority formulated their armaments programmes along the same lines as the British. It is sometimes argued that in the 1920s Britain carried her arms reductions to a far greater extent than any other power, with the exception of the defeated states of 1919; although this may be true in a quantitative sense, in relation to plausible security threats it is extremely questionable. With considerable justification, each individual power could claim that it had reduced its armaments to the lowest level consistent with national safety. The government's allegation — supported by a number of historians — that Britain disarmed while other powers did not, is far from the truth.[4]

By no stretch of the imagination can the second Baldwin administration be accused of undertaking a policy of unilateral disarmament. Even its commitment to multilateral disarmament can be questioned. After the negotiation of the Locarno treaties in October 1925 and the relaxation of international tension which that settlement secured, the time seemed ripe for disarmament. The other major powers began to seek a general agreement through the League of Nations, and as far as the British government was concerned there were only a modicum of imperial diversions, notably the longstanding Egyptian question and the Shanghai crisis of 1927. All that was necessary, it seemed, was for the Conservative Cabinet to understand the theoretical and practical questions involved in disarmament and to commit itself to achieving a multilateral convention. In practice, neither the understanding nor the commitment was there.

Directly or indirectly, the great majority of ministers indicated that they were sceptical of, it not outrightly opposed to, the very idea of disarmament. The Prime Minister displayed little interest in the problem, except when it threatened Cabinet unity; and his few interventions in discussions tended to be negative in character. The Foreign Secretary, while not unsympathetic to arms limitation, was slow to realize its importance, and to the end he remained unconvinced of the practicability of a general world conference. He was a novice in foreign affairs, and in his formative months at the Foreign Office was strongly influenced against disarmament by Sir Eyre Crowe. By the summer of 1927 the course of events at Geneva had begun to convince him that disarmament was a serious problem which required an international solution, but he always attached far more importance to other factors in preserving world peace. It is significant in this respect that the question of general disarmament was brought before the Cabinet on only four occasions during the first eighteen months of the government's existence.

Over the years, Chamberlain did gain a solid grasp of the basic elements of the disarmament problem, but he did not give it the priority in terms of overall policy and personal commitment that it deserved. Even if he had done so, however, it is doubtful whether, in the final analysis, he carried the political weight to overcome the united opposition of the more ardent critics of disarmament within the Cabinet. Churchill, Birkenhead and Amery formed a triumvirate which regarded the quest for general disarmament as an exercise in futility — and a potentially dangerous exercise at that. They could, moreover, count on the general backing of Joynson-Hicks, Curzon, Cave and Guinness, who adopted a similar hardline stance. Bridgeman might also be included in this group, while the other service ministers, Worthington-Evans and Hoare, concerned themselves with improving the position of their respective departments rather than with giving a lead to effective disarmament negotiations.

The one member of the Cabinet to regard general disarmament as the most important issue in foreign policy was Viscount Cecil, Chancellor of the Duchy of Lancaster. To him, a general reduction and limitation of armaments was essential to the peace of the world, if not the existence of the British Empire. While not in favour of agreement at any price, he recognized that a solution of the disarmament problem would require concessions by Britain and thought that the signing of a general convention would have greater value than any other political objective. The chief energies of the government should be directed towards an arms agreement at Geneva.

Cecil's inclusion in the Cabinet was due more to Baldwin's perception of the needs of party unity and the wish to symbolize continued theoretical adhesion to the ideals of the League of Nations than to endorsement of his attitude towards disarmament. He had long been distrusted by more orthodox Conservatives and had been criticized by Curzon, Foreign Secretary in Baldwin's first administration, on the grounds that he did not always adhere to instructions when representing his government.[5] Accordingly, one of the Prime Minister's first acts when forming his second administration was to support Chamberlain in his refusal to give Cecil a room at the Foreign Office or immediate access to Foreign Office papers. It was made abundantly clear that the Chancellor of the Duchy of Lancaster would not become a kind of alternative Foreign Secretary with special responsibility for League affairs;[6] he would be required to toe the line in foreign policy from the outset of the government. It was not until March 1926, when the Foreign Secretary was sure that Cecil was 'safe' on the disarmament question, that Chamberlain delegated day-by-day responsibility for general disarmament to the Chancellor of the Duchy of Lancaster.

Cecil's successor as Chancellor of the Duchy, Baron Cushendun, was an 'orthodox sceptic' on the disarmament issue and bore the reputation of an Ulster Unionist hardliner. Nevertheless, as events unfurled at Geneva and the inadequacies of British policy became clear, he was to become one of the few discerning members of the Cabinet on arms control questions, pressing in his own way for a more conciliatory policy.

Most other members of the Cabinet treated the disarmament problem as rather unreal and took little part in internal discussions. There were, however, exceptions, notably Lord Salisbury, who adopted a benevolently neutral attitude, and the more agnostic Neville Chamberlain, Sir Eustace Percy and Sir Douglas Hogg (later Lord Hailsham). The latter, another 'orthodox sceptic', displayed an above-average perception of political realities. Lord Balfour, the elder statesman of the Conservative Party, occupied an enigmatic position, his protestations in favour of disarmament not being entirely consistent with his actions.

Outside the Cabinet but within the foreign policy-making élite there was no real interest in or movement for disarmament. Indeed, there were major obstacles, both personal and institutional. The Foreign Secretary's departmental advisers mirrored the Cabinet in their scepticism of disarmament and the League, and Sir Eyre Crowe, as Permanent Under-Secretary, remained resolutely opposed to the very idea of a general arms limitation agreement. Similarly, Sir Maurice Hankey used his position as Secretary to the Cabinet and Committee of Imperial Defence to propagate the anti-disarmament case whenever and wherever he could — and did so very effectively. The service departments were also antipathetic towards an international agreement, more especially the Admiralty, which for the greater part of the period adopted the futile policy of attempting to use disarmament negotiations to improve British naval strength relative to the other naval powers. Admittedly, Britain's armed forces faced severe problems of re-adjustment in the post-1919 world, but service leaders, with the conspicuous exception of A.C. Temperley, failed to appreciate that the pains of re-adjustment might be eased by international disarmament rather than exacerbated by it. The chiefs of staff were particularly intolerant in this respect. Milne, for one, seems to have found the whole subject of disarmament incomprehensible, while Beatty, as well as being inimical to general disarmament, was instrumental in securing the reversal of British policy which led to the breakdown of the Geneva Naval Conference of 1927.

Internal pressures on the government to treat the disarmament problem more seriously were therefore minimal. The handful of individuals within the foreign policy-making élite who possessed a genuine belief in disarmament raised the issue whenever and wherever they could, for example in the correspondence columns of the 'quality' newspapers, in contemporary journals and periodicals and at meetings of the League of Nations Union; but they carried little weight in political terms, and while they made a lot of noise they were unable to translate noise into influence on policy. Even the extensive campaign in favour of international disarmament run by the League of Nations Union from the autumn of 1927 to the spring of 1929 was to be fruitless in this respect.

Similarly, the Opposition within Parliament had only a marginal effect on disarmament policy. Indeed, both the Labour and Liberal parties were remarkably quiescent on the issue until the break-down of the 1927 naval conference. Disarmament had been a minor question at the 1924 election, despite the unresolved problem of the Geneva Protocol, and debates and questions on the subject in the House were few and far between until the naval conference became enmeshed in difficulties. A small number of individuals, notably Commander J.M. Kenworthy, Liberal (from 1926 Labour) MP for Central Hull, were apt to raise the issue at question time, but their contributions tended to be ineffectual and easily evaded. The government only really became concerned about parliamentary opposition in November 1927, when the Labour party tabled a censure motion covering most aspects of disarmament policy. From this time onward, and especially in the aftermath of the ill-fated Anglo–French compromise of 1928, there was a nagging suspicion among some ministers that successive policy failures would have adverse electoral consequences. Yet policy remained intrinsically the same.

There is little doubt that the government would have avoided discussion of general disarmament if it had been possible. It did not do so for three main reasons. First, through the Geneva Protocol, the disarmament problem was already on the international agenda. Second, Britain was committed to taking part in international discussions through Article 8 of the Covenant, the preamble to Part V of the Treaty of Versailles and the 'Clemenceau Letter'. (This was Chamberlain's main consideration.) And third, the presence of Cecil in the Cabinet made direct avoidance of the issue impolitic.

It was not until July 1925, a full eight months after taking office, that the Cabinet began to consider its policy towards the disarmament obligations of the League Covenant, and then only after a threat of resignation by Cecil. Moreover, the circumstances under which machinery was established for the continuing discussion of the disarmament problem merely emphasized the government's lack of commitment on the issue. The person charged with drawing up the terms of reference was the arch-critic, Hankey, and it was on his recommendation that the political evaluation of disarmament was subordinated to the military which was rather like delegating a programme for the advancement of vegetarianism to the Meat Traders' Association. Only in this case the meat was human. The Cabinet at this point might have established a powerful ministerial committee charged with investigating the problems, prospects and opportunities presented by disarmament, with a view to preparing an overall plan covering both foreign and military policy; instead, discussion of disarmament was shunted into a sub-committee of the CID.

The decision to subordinate the political side of disarmament to the military manifested itself in practical terms in the composition of the Disarmament Committee. Not only did military representatives outnumber the political in the ratio of 5:1, the sole Foreign Office representative was a bureaucrat of first secretary level (Alexander Cadogan). Initially, too, the Cabinet was represented only by Cecil. Salisbury was added at a later date, but in ministerial terms the two brothers were hardly the most influential personages. Besides, before any proposal could be approved as official government policy, it had to be screened by the CID and Cabinet, and in both these bodies the detractors of disarmament if anything exceeded supporters to an even greater degree than in the Disarmament Committee. The appointment of Cecil as chairman of the committee might give the impression that disarmament was being treated seriously; in reality the Chancellor of the Duchy of Lancaster was assured of responsibility without power — a dissentient almost within his own committee.

The inadequacy of the machinery for policy formulation was reflected in the unrealism of the government's proposals of April 1926. The programme that was adopted at that time constituted little more than a series of disjointed suggestions which, both individually and collectively, showed more concern for the interests of the service departments and for Britain's immediate security requirements than for the evolution of a rational set of objectives aimed at heightening Britain's medium- and long-term security through general disarmament. A number of proposals were diluted or omitted because of the stance of the service representatives within the Disarmament Committee; and the Disarmament Committee's own proposals, hardly radical in themselves, were emasculated by a CID and Cabinet which displayed little understanding of the problems or possibilities of general disarmament. At all levels, decisions were taken on each limitation proposal separately, with little or no consideration of the implications for other individual proposals or for the broad effect on the overall problem.

General disarmament necessitated a comprehensive settlement, not the piecemeal attack on isolated problems suggested by the Baldwin government. Adoption of the piecemeal approach might not have been disastrous for Britain in the short term, since British security was not immediately at risk; but in the longer term the continuing unacceptability of this approach to the other powers was likely to be injurious to British interests. The potential vulnerability of Britain's position in the world if threats were to arise simultaneously in more than one theatre, Imperial or European, meant that it was in Britain's interests for international power relationships to be stabilized through an effective and verifiable disarmament convention. A free-for-all in armaments was likely to leave Britain at a considerable disadvantage, as events of the 1930s were to show.

The central problem was that of Germany; and the essential and continuing predicament was that if the former Allies did not limit their armaments by international convention in accordance with their commitments under Article 8 of the Covenant and the preamble to Part V of the Treaty of Versailles — whatever the precise nature of those commitments — sooner or later Germany would consider herself free to re-arm unilaterally. The consequences of such action by Germany would be a weakening of Britain's security position, an international arms race and a renewed danger of European war. To forestall such eventualities two broad options presented themselves: preventive coercion or the negotiation of a general disarmament agreement. The policy of coercion having failed (at the strategic rather than the tactical level) during the occupation of the Ruhr in 1923, both prudence and *Realpolitik* suggested the better alternative was the pursuit of general disarmament. The task was not an easy one, since negotiations were concerned with that most important yet least negotiable facet of inter-state relations, national power; but the potential benefits of success were immense.

In practical terms, the abandonment of the policy of coercion, together with Germany's continued unwillingness to remain a second-class power, meant that the other powers were faced with the inevitability of a redistribution of European power in Germany's favour. Consequently, it was in the interests of the powers to control the extent and speed of this redistribution, and this process might have been facilitated by the negotiation of a multilateral disarmament convention. France, however, needed to ensure that any increase in German power was offset by increased assurances of support from Britain, and thus progress towards a convention was possible only if Britain made concessions to French security requirements on top of the assurances given at Locarno. Such concessions, which might have been made on either side of the disarmament–security equation, were more relevant to Britain's long-term security than, for example, the non-limitation of overseas aircraft and naval effectives in a disarmament convention. But the

British government believed that French security was already protected adequately and was opposed to undertaking new commitments on the European continent or moving meaningfully towards the French position in the disarmament negotiations at Geneva.

British ministers understood that states had to adjust to changes within international society; they failed to realize that British power was integral to the process of change in Europe implied by a disarmament convention acceptable to both France and Germany. Consciously or unconsciously, the government adhered firmly to a policy based on the putative existence of an underlying harmony of interests between nations; ministers sought, and expected, a degree of influence on the European continent out of all proportion to British involvement in the European security system. The government's disarmament policy was based upon a narrow conception of Britain's interests, with little or no foresight as to the effect of this policy on the other powers and on the problem of Germany within international society.

It is not that the government failed to recognize the problem posed by potential German rearmament; rather they refused to admit that failure to negotiate a general disarmament agreement would bring the danger appreciably nearer. To the majority of the cabinet, the disarmament question was neither immediate nor important and might, with luck, be evaded. Alternatively, it was a problem which might, if sufficiently ignored, resolve itself. But it would not, as the ministers who had to deal with the problem at first hand, Cecil, Chamberlain and Cushendun, were to realize.

The failure of the government to appreciate the importance of the disarmament problem at the conceptual and general levels was reflected in a similar failure at the practical. This was not, however, surprising, considering the imperfections of the machinery established for policy formulation.

In general, as the British disarmament proposals of April 1926 displayed, the government was more concerned with possible difficulties and inconveniences than with positive suggestions. Regarding land disarmament, they were opposed to a limitation of *matériel*, direct or indirect, on the grounds that it would hinder the policy of mechanization; and they put forward the idea of a limitation of annual contingents (a backdoor method of abolishing conscription) in the knowledge that, in the past, it had been rejected consistently by France, Italy, Japan and most continental powers. On air disarmament, they opposed all methods of limitation except restriction of first-line, home-based units: partly on the grounds that Britain would be prevented from following a policy of substituting air for ground forces in outlying districts of the Empire; partly because they involved an 'irksome degree' of international control and supervision; and partly because they were opposed in principle to restrictions on civil aviation. The naval proposals — quantitative restrictions within a large number of defined categories of vessel — showed every consideration for the interests of the Admiralty and the Admiralty's perception of British interests, but no consideration for the needs of lesser naval powers. The proposals for supervision, verification and publicity were weak in the extreme, reflecting the lack of faith of the policy-making élite in the League of Nations as a competent arbiter.

The proposals outlined by the Cabinet in April 1926 — and re-affirmed in essentials in the draft convention of March 1927 — repre-sented a misconstruction of long-term interests for short-term advantages. It was hardly in the British interest to suggest that the French abandon conscription, more especially since it was acknow-ledged that Britain's military frontier was now the river Rhine. It was hypocritical to suggest that land effectives be limited but that air and naval effectives remain unrestricted. It was disingenuous, as an imperial power with a significant overseas air force, to insist on metropolitan forces being limited but not overseas or carrier-based forces. And it was fraudulent to oppose stringent control measures on the (private) grounds that other powers would subvert them whereas Britain would not. It would, indeed, have been in the British interest for effective control and publicity measures to have been agreed for all states. As a statement of Britain's maximum position, or even as a bargaining counter in the negotiations at Geneva, the British proposals might have had their uses; but they were not conceived as such, even if Cecil unilaterally began to treat them in that way at the Preparatory Commission in March and April 1927.

The presentation of the British and French draft conventions at the Preparatory Commission in March 1927 represented the real start of substantive negotiations for a general convention. The task was never likely to be easy; however, the inflexible attitude of a British government drawn into negotiations by the impetus of events rather than conscious decision made progress far more difficult than it might have been. On some issues, perhaps, a degree of inflexibility was excusable, but in cases such as air and naval effectives, when British security could hardly be said to be at risk, the reverse was the case. The result was that when the commission adjourned its proceedings on 26 April, progress towards a convention was not as substantial as it might have been. Moreover, unless the British government changed its stance on verification, the limitation of trained reserves and naval disarmament by numbers within nine categories, the possibility of further major progress was negligible.

If Cecil had been given the freedom he desired in negotiating a convention, it is conceivable that a formula for limitation might have been constructed, France moving closer to the British position on the naval problem in return for British acquiescence in the non-limitation of trained reserves and more effective measures for control. Certainly the possibility existed for a *quid pro quo* in April 1927. At the same time, any such formula would have been stiffly resisted by the Admiralty and its supporters in the British Cabinet, nominally on the grounds that acceptance would jeopardize British security. Here was the rub. In practical terms, negotiation of an arms limitation convention demanded an attitude of mind on the part of

the British government that only Cecil possessed. The remainder of
the Cabinet viewed the price demanded by the other powers for an
agreement as far too high. Some, including Chamberlain, were willing to make a modicum of concessions to the French; others were not
nearly so generous. Collectively, they gave every impression of
insisting on 'British terms — or nothing', with little or no consideration of the long-term consequences.

It was clear that at some point a crisis would arise between Cecil
on the one hand and the opponents and detractors of general disarmament on the other. Realistically, there was no way in which the
two views could co-exist within the same government in the longer
term save through the submission of one view to the other. On lesser
issues, for example air and naval effectives, Chamberlain might
mediate an agreement; on the larger issues, notably supervision and
naval limitation, the parties were too far apart for even Chamberlain
to bring them together. Eventually, the crisis would arise over naval
limitation — at the Geneva Naval Conference of 1927 rather than at
the Preparatory Commission.

The failure of the majority of the Cabinet to understand the
problem of disarmament at the level of individual proposals was
shown more clearly at the three-power naval conference than at the
League negotiations. The Admiralty's proposals, approved by the
CID and Cabinet, were drawn up with the idea of improving
Britain's strategic situation at the expense of other powers, notably
Japan, by formalizing a position of British superiority in cruiser
strength. These objectives were inconsistent with the aims of disarmament and in any case were beyond Britain's capabilities and
needs. At least the unrealism of the proposals was appreciated at an
early date by Britain's delegates in Geneva, Bridgeman and Cecil,
who began to work for an agreement that could be endorsed by all
parties represented at the conference. Such an agreement entailed
acceptance by Britain of American parity in all classes of warship
and eight-inch guns in a secondary class of cruiser, and on these two
points the Cabinet baulked. The symbol was the concept of parity. On
30 June the Cabinet acquiesced in the concept but between 1 July
and 6 July Beatty and Churchill used their powerful positions to
secure a reversal of British policy on the issue, causing such mistrust
and discontent between the delegations at Geneva that the task of
negotiating a mutually acceptable convention was made almost
impossible.

The later stages of the Geneva Naval Conference underlined the
predominance of the Admiralty and its supporters on the disarmament issue. At only one stage of the proceedings did an agreement
seem possible, on the basis of the so-called Anglo–Japanese proposals
of 16 July, modified to provide for eight-inch guns in the smaller
class of cruiser. Again Beatty and Churchill carried the Cabinet,
despite the fact that the agreement suggested could hardly have
jeopardized British security. At the crucial Cabinet meeting of 26
July, they secured a majority of ten to six on what was effectively an

anti-agreement position. So far as records are available, it seems that Birkenhead, Joynson-Hicks, ·Worthington-Evans, Hoare, Guinness, Cunliffe-Lister, Hogg, Peel and Gilmour supported the Chancellor of the Exchequer. The fact that Chamberlain, who chaired the meeting in Baldwin's absence in Canada, supported the minority was seen to be irrelevant. At a second, similar meeting on 3 August, during which Chamberlain was faced with four threats of resignation, the result was the same. In effect, the balance of power within the Cabinet was against an agreement; the opponents of disarmament, notably Churchill and Birkenhead, had rallied the sceptics to their cause on the grounds that the price asked by the United States was too high. Yet the terms available were more generous than those accepted by the second Labour government in the London Naval Treaty of 1930.

If Baldwin had been available to chair the critical meetings of the Cabinet on 26 July and 3 August it is conceivable that a compromise settlement of the naval question might have resulted. But it is highly unlikely. Not only was the Prime Minister less sympathetic to disarmament than Chamberlain, his government was essentially one of party unity at almost all costs; while he could afford to lose Cecil on the one hand, he could hardly afford to lose a number of more senior ministers on the other.

The government's debates regarding policy at the Geneva Naval Conference also showed the lengths to which the Admiralty and some members of the Cabinet were willing to twist and turn in order to bring about a settlement of disarmament questions on their own unrealistic terms. The Admiralty's initial proposals, approved by the CID on 20 May 1927 and by the Cabinet on 25 May, differed substantially from those presented at the Preparatory Commission as recently as 21 March (and which were still on the table at the adjournment of the commission on 26 April). The division of the cruiser class was proposed solely to secure advantages for Britain. Later, during the conference itself, Beatty and Churchill reversed their positions on the questions of the eight-inch gun and length of agreement respectively, for similar reasons. More important, from the point of view of policy at the Preparatory Commission, the Admiralty's proposals at the Limitation of Naval Armaments Committee on 25 July were no different in essentials from the French 'amended naval proposals' of April 1927, previously rejected on the grounds of incompatibility with British security requirements.

The one beneficial result of the three-power naval conference was that it made the British government take the disarmament problem more seriously. On 12 October 1927, on Chamberlain's instigation, the Disarmament Policy Committee was established to examine the whole question of disarmament in the light of the failure of the conference and Cecil's resignation. The Foreign Secretary formally acknowledged that, hitherto, the government had ignored the political and conceptual aspects of the problem and placed too much emphasis on the technical. In practical terms the establishment of the committee mattered little. The philosophical consensus for a change in direction in favour of general disarmament did not exist; all that could be expected was a change of strategy by which the underlying policy was pursued.

The composition of the new committee reflected the continuing unimportance of disarmament in the government's thinking. Intellectually, Chamberlain might grasp the need for a more considered approach to the problem, but he did not feel committed enough to disarmament to become a member of the new committee although he attended most of its meetings. The Foreign Secretary was happy to see the chairmanship devolve on Salisbury; and Salisbury was hardly the personality to institute the radical change in direction that was needed. Neither, for that matter, was an effective lead likely to be forthcoming from the service ministers on the committee, nor Hogg, a known sceptic of disarmament. The remaining member, Cushendun, had barely been in post long enough to assess his new responsibilities.

The inpropitious circumstances under which the Disarmament Policy Committee held its inaugural meetings were largely of the government's own making. The Cabinet's inability to understand the disarmament problem as a whole had been compounded by its exaggerated respect for the service point of view which had produced proposals at the Preparatory Commission and three-power naval conference which were unacceptable to the other powers. Not that this was surprising, considering how closely the British proposals had been tied to Britain's immediate security requirements. Yet there was no easy way forward; in fact the breakdown of the 'Coolidge Conference' predicated a hardening of the British position. Having maintained an inflexible attitude on the eight-inch gun, asserted a need for a secondary class of cruiser and demanded a minimum of seventy cruisers in total, it was difficult for the government to climb down and admit that its policy had been unreasonable. Equally, the professions of the government on the principles of the Protocol and collective security over the years made it difficult for a change in direction to evolve on the security side of the disarmament equation.

In practice, the Disarmament Policy Committee was to tackle the symptoms of the government's failings rather than the cause. This first showed itself in British policy at the Preparatory Commission's Arbitration and Security Committee, where the rigidity of the government's position was the greatest single obstacle to progress. The policy of placing responsibility for increasing security on other powers, without involving Britain, was self-defeating; moreover, it was hypocritical to accept the Finnish proposal for financial assistance primarily as a means of evading British commitments under Article 16 of the Covenant. This *non possumus* attitude towards security merely ensured that the 1928 discussions were little more than a repetition of the abortive negotiations on the Protocol, with lower initial expectations.

The government's continuing failure to understand the realities of disarmament can be seen in the 'Anglo–French compromise' negotiations of 1928. The concept of Anglo–French discussions to break the deadlock at Geneva was admirable, the actuality disastrous. Britain's breach with the United States on the naval issue was widened; the Germans were angered at the intimacy of Anglo–French co-operation; and reaction to the compromise within Britain was generally hostile. The outcome is not altogether surprising, however, considering the less than altruistic motivations of the British government. Even at the time, it was clear that the compromise, as negotiated, would be unacceptable to the Americans, yet many members of the Cabinet, perhaps a majority, thought in terms of using the agreement to force the Americans into either accepting the British line or assuming responsibility for the break-up of the Preparatory Commission. Others, including the ministers nearest to the negotiations at Geneva (Cushendun, Chamberlain and Salisbury), wished to use the compromise to stave off the possibility of British isolation on the Preparatory Commission; while a third group, temperamentally averse to disarmament, may have thought it an excellent contrivance for precipitating a breach of the League commission. Certainly, if the government had an agreed objective in mind — which is doubtful — it was not primarily the conclusion of a disarmament convention. Most probably, the compromise represented the only means of synchronizing the conflicting motivations of individual ministers — in other words, of preserving Cabinet unity.

The ignominious end to the compromise negotiations finally convinced the government that its disarmament strategy over the previous four years had been unrealistic, although not that its policy had been mistaken. With a general election scheduled to take place during 1929 many ministers became concerned that an alternative strategy be formulated. Accordingly, there was a strong movement, led by Percy, for complete disengagement from the Geneva discussions. It was, at least, an honest approach. Given the philosophical propensities of the Cabinet, the quest for agreement at Geneva was inherently futile. The proposal was discounted on the grounds that disengagement would be too embarrassing politically in an election year.

In the circumstances, it is not surprising that British disarmament policy took a final, deceitful turn in March 1929. Hailsham provided the basis of the new approach. It was generally agreed that the other powers would not be able to agree among themselves at the Preparatory Commission, so the Lord Chancellor suggested that, as regards land and air disarmament, the government should announce that it felt confident of accepting any proposals agreed unanimously by the other powers. With regard to naval armaments, the chief stumbling block to an agreement, he counselled delay. Advanced with the specific intention of absolving Britain from responsibility for the predicted breakdown at Geneva, Hailsham's suggestion constituted an effective admission that Britain had indeed been responsible, in great part, for the deadlock that had been reached. Cadogan's phrase of May 1927 was apt: British policy was one of procrastination verging on duplicity.

Of course, responsibility for the lack of progress towards disarmament cannot be laid on the shoulders of the British government alone. Other governments must share the blame, in particular the French and American. But, given the circumstances of the time, the policies of the latter powers are easily comprehensible. British policy is not. The government adopted proposals that offered little or no chance of securing general agreement, and concessions that might have eased the path towards a settlement were often made belatedly and very reluctantly, even in cases where there was no real risk to British security.

In the final analysis, however, it is not so much the government's approach to individual questions of disarmament policy that must be criticized, nor even the Foreign Secretary's lethargy in tackling the issue; rather it is the Cabinet's inability to understand the disarmament problem, appreciate its international importance and act accordingly. The government's proposals on individual points merely reflected an attitude of mind which, fundamentally, was sceptical of, antipathetic or even opposed to general disarmament. The one member of the Cabinet to grasp the importance of the problem and understand its major implications was Cecil. Most importantly, he recognized the intrinsic link between security and disarmament and appreciated that if France was to co-operate in the disarmament process, it would be necessary for Britain to give her former ally security compensations for any resultant loss of power relative to Germany. Chamberlain and Cushendun also understood this point but, being less committed to achieving general disarmament than Cecil, were unwilling to make concessions to the same extent, more especially when they involved increased commitments in the European security system. It was not that Cecil was willing to buy agreement at any price; rather, in his opinion, greater British involvement in the European power system was preferable to the international anarchy of the arms race.[7] Temperamental, impulsive and sensitive to criticism, Cecil was not the easiest of colleagues to work with, nor possibly the best advocate of his own case; but he understood the workings of international society in relation to disarmament better than his fellow ministers. He was neither a unilateralist nor a pacifist; he was a realist who believed in multilateral disarmament with guarantees.[8]

If the second Baldwin government was less than wholehearted in its commitment to resolve the disarmament problem, British historians have been equally reluctant to research it. In fact, it is probably the greatest untouched question in twentieth-century international history. It is some fifty years since the disarmament problem in the 1920s was the subject of a full-length published study; and an identical period has elapsed since British disarmament policy received similar treatment.[9] Even academic articles on the subject are few and far between. A re-evaluation is long overdue in the light of public documents released under the Thirty-Year Rule and the private papers now available for research. The task is prodigious; not only is the field of multilateral disarmament in the 1930s almost virgin territory, there are enormous gaps in the literature relating to the 1920s. Even within the context of the present study, a number of questions have barely been touched upon, for example the arms trade; chemical warfare policy, including the Geneva (Gas) Protocol of 1925; and the role of public opinion. Whatever new conclusions are drawn in the light of future research, the judgement of an unidentified Cabinet minister on the disarmament policy of the Conservative government of 1924–9 is likely to remain central. The British government's policy was one of 'rattling an olive branch'.[10] It was a policy which was developed and refined under predominantly the same ministers and policy-making élite in the National government of 1932–4 and was to be a primary factor in the breakdown of the Geneva Disarmament Conference of 1932–4. The failure of the disarmament negotiations at that conference was to mark a turning point in international relations. The post-war world became a pre-war world.

Explanation of Notes

1 For full bibliographical information, see the Bibliography.
2 The following abbreviations are used:
  (a) Material in the Public Records

CID	Committee of Imperial Defence
FO Papers	Foreign Office Papers
GP	Geneva Protocol Committee
LNA	Further Limitation of Naval Armaments Committee
NPC	Naval Programme Committee
PRA	Disarmament Policy Committee
RLA	Disarmament Committee (Reduction and Limitation of Armaments Committee)
WO Papers	War Office Papers

  (b) Other material

BM Add MSS	British Museum Additional Manuscripts
Cmd	Command Papers
DPC	League of Nations, *Documents of the Preparatory Commission for the Disarmament Conference*
FRUS	United States, Department of State, *Foreign Relations of the United States, Diplomatic Papers*
RCLNA	Conference for the Limitation of Naval Armament, *Records of the Conference for the Limitation of Naval Armament*
RSCA	League of Nations, *Preparatory Commission for the Disarmament Conference: Report of Sub-Commission A*

3 The papers of Austen Chamberlain are referred to throughout as *Chamberlain Papers*, those of Neville Chamberlain as *Neville Chamberlain Papers*. All references to the former are from the collection in the University of Birmingham Library, except for the documents referred to in Chapter 3, note 1, and Chapter 8, note 9, which are in the Public Record Office collection.
4 With regard to the papers of Sir Maurice Hankey, 'Cab' references refer to the papers deposited in the Public Record Office, 'HNKY' references to those in the Archives Centre, Churchill College, Cambridge.

Notes

Chapter 1

1 Viscount Grey of Fallodon, *Twenty-Five Years*, pp. 160-2.
2 Throughout the present work, unless otherwise qualified, 'disarmament' is defined as 'arms limitation and/or control by international agreement'. Support for the cause transcended party lines in Britain, though there were always more adherents on the political Left. See, e.g., Viscount Cecil of Chelwood (Conservative), *A Great Experiment*, pp. 183-4, 236-8; Cecil, *All The Way* pp. 168-70, 183-4; Memorandum by Lloyd George (Liberal), 25 March 1919: Some Considerations for the Peace Conference, *Parliamentary Papers*, Cmd 1614 of 1922; Viscount Samuel (Liberal), *Memoirs*, p. 223; P.J. Noel-Baker (Labour), *The First World Disarmament Conference 1932-33*; Baron Parmoor (Labour) *A Retrospect*, pp. 159-60, 188-9, 191-2; Speech by Field-Marshal Sir W. Robertson, 11 July 1931, cited in Noel-Baker, *The Private Manufacture of Armaments*, p. 20.
3 See, e.g., Grey, *loc. cit*; Noel-Baker, *The Arms Race*, pp. 73-84.
4 See, e.g., Noel-Baker, *The Private Manufacture of Armaments*, especially Part III.
5 See, e.g., Noel-Baker, *Disarmament*; S. de Madariaga, *Disarmament*.
6 See, e.g., Memorandum by [Sir Maurice Hankey] (Secretary to the Cabinet, 1919-38, and Committee of Imperial Defence, 1912-38), undated: 'Disarmament. A Plea for Fundamental Research', *Hankey Papers*, HNKY 8/28; Notes by Sir Eyre Crowe (Foreign Office), 12 October 1916, *Committee of Imperial Defence* (hereafter cited as CID) *Memoranda*, P-19, Cab 29/1.
7 See especially, ibid. Of course, many opponents of disarmament did not bother arguing their case, merely contending that disarmament was 'impossible'. See, e.g., Sir R. Vansittart, *Lessons of my Life*, p. 79; A.D. Cooper, *Old Men Forget*, p. 165.
8 For Shearer's activities, see, e.g., Noel-Baker, *The Private Manufacture of Armaments*, pp. 357-64. The term 'creature' was applied by the British Delegation at the Geneva Naval Conference, see London (Geneva) to Foreign Office, 2 July 1927, *Foreign Office Papers* (hereafter cited as FO Papers), FO 371/12670.
9 See, e.g., A.C. Temperley, *The Whispering Gallery of Europe*, p. 53.
10 For analysis and critique of the concept of collective security, see I.L. Claude, *Swords into Plowshares*, ch. 12; I.L. Claude, *Power and International Relations*, chs. 4-5.

11 The Treaty of Peace between the Allied and Associated Powers and Germany, 28 June 1919, *Parliamentary Papers*, Cmd 153 of 1919.
12 D.H. Miller, *My Diary at the Conference of Paris, 1918-1919*, vol. 19, p. 207; G.R. Crosby, *Disarmament and Peace in British Politics 1914-1919*, pp. 126-7.
13 Reply of the Allied and Associated Powers to the Observations of the German Delegation on the Conditions of Peace [16 June 1919], *Papers Relating to the Foreign Relations of the United States, Diplomatic Papers* (hereafter cited as FRUS), Paris Peace Conference, 1919, vol. 6, pp. 954-6.
14 League of Nations, *Documents of the Preparatory Commission for the Disarmament Conference* (hereafter cited as DPC), Series IV, p. 206.
15 See, e.g., Great Britain, Foreign Office, *Documents on British Foreign Policy 1919-1939*, Series 2, vol. 4, no. 92.
16 The Treaty of Peace, 28 June 1919, *Parliamentary Papers*, Cmd 153 of 1919.

Chapter 2

1 J.R. MacDonald, *Protocol or Pact*, pp. 2, 5.
2 League of Nations, *Records of the Third Assembly: Plenary Meetings*, p. 291.
3 For the naval terms of the Washington Treaty, see Treaty for the Limitation of Naval Armament, undated, *Cabinet Papers*, CP 3738, Cab 24/133.
4 On the British side, the main negotiator was Viscount Cecil of Chelwood. For his appreciation, see Cecil, *A Great Experiment*, pp. 151-3.
5 The official objections of the British government to the draft Treaty were conveyed in a letter from the Prime Minister to the Secretary-General of the League, Sir Eric Drummond, on 5 July 1924: MacDonald to Drummond, 5 July 1924, *FO Papers*, W 4724/134/98, FO 371/10568. See also, Naval Staff Memorandum, 3 July 1923, ibid., W 7127/30/98, FO 371/9420.
6 See R. Higham, *Armed Forces in Peacetime*, pp. 325-7; Memorandum by M. Jakobsen (Secretary of the Committee of Experts on Budgetary Questions at the Preparatory Commission for the Disarmament Conference), 26 March 1927, *Cecil Papers*, BM Add MSS 51099; W.P. Coates, *U.S.S.R. and Disarmament*, p. 82. In 1913, faced with the German threat, Britain had spent some 3.6 per cent of national income on defence. Figures for other powers in the mid-1920s were: Belgium 2.8 per cent, France 3.7 per cent, Germany 1.4 per cent, Italy 4.1 per cent, Japan 4.4 per cent and the United States 1.3 per cent. On the basis of expenditure per head of population, Britain spent considerably more on her forces than any other power, some 1¾ times that of France, over twice that of the United States, 2½ times that of Italy, 3½ times that of Japan, five times that of Germany and six times that of the Soviet Union. Cf, Jacobsen, 'Armaments Expenditure of the World', *The Economist*, 19 October 1929.
7 Review of Imperial Defence, 1926, by the Chiefs of Staff Committee, 22 June 1926, *Cabinet Papers*, CP 296(26), Enclosure, Cab 24/180.
8 For the terms of the Protocol, see League of Nations, *Protocol for the Pacific Settlement of International Disputes*.
9 Parmoor, *op. cit.*, p. 253.

Chapter 3

1 Memorandum by Chelmsford, 27 September 1924, *Cabinet Papers*, CP 456(24), Cab 24/168; Memorandum by Chelmsford, 27 October 1924, ibid., CP 478(24); E.H.J.N. Dalton, *Call Back Yesterday*, p. 175; [R. Bassett], 'Notes on Disarmament', pp. 13–14, *Templewood Papers*, XX: 10; Austen Chamberlain to MacDonald, 1 December 1927, *Chamberlain Papers*, FO 800/261.
2 Austen Chamberlain quotes MacDonald as stating that he would never have signed the Protocol in the form in which it emanated from Geneva. See Chamberlain to Viscount Cecil of Chelwood, 19 June 1925, *Cecil Papers*, BM Add MSS 51078. MacDonald himself, in his contemporary pamphlet *Protocol or Pact*, also gives the impression that he was not averse to changes in the Protocol. However, Philip Noel-Baker, who worked with MacDonald at the Fifth Assembly, is convinced that the Labour Prime Minister was earnest about the Protocol and would have attempted to carry it through (interview with Baron Noel-Baker, 18 February 1980) while MacDonald again, writing ten years after the event, suggested that linked with a disarmament convention, the Protocol was a feasible proposal and that 'a grave responsibility' rested on the authors of its rejection. See Macdonald to Cecil, 5 March 1934, *Cecil Papers*, BM Add MSS 51081.
3 I. Kirkpatrick, *The Inner Circle*, pp. 38–9.
4 Cecil to Baldwin, 10 March 1927, *Baldwin Papers*, vol. 130; G.M. Young, *Stanley Baldwin*, p. 173.
5 Ibid; Cecil, *All the Way*, p. 166; Cecil, *A Great Experiment*, p. 141.
6 Cecil to Baron Irwin (Viceroy of India), 29 September 1927, *Cecil Papers*, BM Add MSS 51084.
7 See Chamberlain to Ivy Chamberlain (Wife), 10 October 1924, *Chamberlain Papers*, AC 6/1/563; Chamberlain to Ida Chamberlain (Sister), 14 September 1924, ibid., AC 5/1/330. In the latter, he asks Ida to explain 'on half a sheet of notepaper' what is happening in China since 'I cannot understand anything where names are so strange or unintelligible'.
8 Speech by Chamberlain, 14 July 1924, *Parliamentary Debates, Commons*, Fifth Series, vol. 176, cols. 109–10.
9 Chamberlain to Cecil, 14 August 1927, *Cecil Papers*, BM Add MSS 51079; Note by Chamberlain, [3 April 1929], *Baldwin Papers*, vol. 113.
10 Chamberlain to Cecil, 11 November 1924, *Cecil Papers*, BM Add MSS 51078.
11 See Cecil, *A Great Experiment*, p. 163.
12 Sir Samuel Hoare, 'Typescript Memoirs of the 1920s: Draft Chapter on First and Second Baldwin Governments', p. 15, *Templewood Papers*, XX(A):5. Hoare was created Viscount Templewood in 1944.
13 Irwin to Cecil, 20 January 1927, *Cecil Papers*, BM Add MSS 51084; Baron Chatfield, *The Navy and Defence: It might happen again*, p. 10.
14 W.C. Bridgeman, 'Political Notes', pp. 167, 201, *Bridgeman Papers*.
15 Ibid., p. 191; Interview with H.T. Russell (United Press of America) published in the *North China Star* of 18 October 1928, *Worthington-Evans Papers*, Box 1.
16 Ibid; Worthington-Evans to Cecil, 11 August 1922, *War Office Papers* (hereafter cited as WO Papers), WO 32/5941.
17 Chamberlain to Ivy Chamberlain, 13 October 1924, *Chamberlain Papers*, AC 6/1/566.

18 Bridgeman, 'Political Notes', p. 195, *Bridgeman Papers*.
19 Lecture by Hoare to the Union Belgo-Brittanique, 16 February 1951, *Templewood Papers*, XVII:2; Templewood, *Nine Troubled Years*, p. 117.
20 See, e.g., Memorandum by Hoare, October 1925, *Cabinet Papers*, CP 421(25), Cab 24/175.
21 *CID Minutes*, 190th meeting, 4 December 1924, Cab 2/4; Churchill to Cecil, 20 January 1925, *Cecil Papers*, BM Add MSS 51097.
22 See, e.g., *Naval Programme Committee* (hereafter cited as NPC) *Minutes*, 1st meeting, 10 November 1927, Cab 27/355.
23 See *Further Limitation of Naval Armaments Committee* (hereafter cited as LNA) *Minutes*, 3rd meeting, 19 July 1927, Cab 27/350.
24 Churchill to Donald Fergusson (Private Secretary), 9 September 1928, cited in M. Gilbert, *Winston S. Churchill*, Companion vol. 5:1, p. 1335; Churchill to Sir Warren Fisher (Permanent Secretary to the Treasury) *et. al.*, 14 September 1928, cited in ibid., p. 1337.
25 Speech at Epping, 25 October 1928, cited in ibid., vol. 5, p. 305.
26 Baldwin to Churchill, 27 October 1928, cited in ibid., p. 306.
27 Sir Samuel Hoare, 'Typescript Memoirs', p. 18, *Templewood Papers*, XX(A):5.
28 Glasgow University Rectorial Address, November 1923, cited in W. Camp, *The Glittering Prizes*, p. 216.
29 See L.C.M.S. Amery, *The Forward View*, pp. 52-72; L.C.M.S. Amery, *The Leo Amery Diaries*, J. Barnes and D. Nicholson (eds), vol. 1, pp. 324, 516 (Diary entries for 11 April and 13 July 1927).
30 See Cecil to Sir W. Wiseman, 19 August 1918, cited in Cecil, *All the Way*, pp. 142-4.
31 See, e.g., Cecil, *A Great Experiment*, pp. 138-9.
32 See ibid., pp. 122-3, 183; Memorandum by Cecil, 7 March 1927, *Cabinet Papers*, CP 79(27), Cab 24/185.
33 Cecil, *All the Way*, p. 184; T. Jones, *Whitehall Diary*, vol. 1, p. 302. Considering that the Prime Minister's chief aim during his five years in office was the maintenance of the unity of his recently reunited party, it would seem that the idea behind the appointment of Cecil was to secure the allegiance of the (admittedly small) internationalist section of the Conservative Party and to divert any charges that his government was not really interested in the League or disarmament. He definitely thought that Cecil would handicap the Foreign Secretary. See ibid., p. 304.
34 Chamberlain to Baldwin, 9 November 1924, *Baldwin Papers*, vol. 42; [Chamberlain] to Lloyd George, 19 November 1924, *Chamberlain Papers*, AC 24/6/35.
35 Cecil, *A Great Experiment*, p. 163; Cecil, *All the Way*, p. 185.
36 Bridgeman, 'Political Notes', p. 199, *Bridgeman Papers*.
37 Madariaga, *Morning without Noon: Memoirs*, p. 92. Amery, *The Leo Amery Diaries*, vol. 1, pp. 565, 567 (Diary entries for 1 and 15 October 1928).
38 See Notes by Crowe, 12 October 1916, *CID Memoranda*, P-19, Cab 29/1.
39 See Memorandum by [Hankey], 9 February 1925, *Hankey Papers*, MO(25)01, Cab 63/37; Memorandum by Hankey, 4 August 1925, ibid., MO(25)5; Hankey to Cecil, 18 August 1925, ibid., MO(25)6; Memorandum by [Hankey], undated, ibid., HNKY 8/28. The first three papers are located in the Public Record Office (Cab references), the fourth at the Archives Centre, Churchill College, Cambridge (HNKY reference).
40 W.S. Chalmers, *The Life and Letters of David, Earl Beatty*, p. 410.

41 Edinburgh University Rectorial Address, 28 October 1920, cited in ibid., p. 465.
42 Temperley, op. cit., pp. 26–7, 347–8.
43 Aubrey Smith to [Admiral Field], 14 April 1927, *Admiralty Papers*, M 01169/27, Adm 116/2598; Kelly, 'Draft Memoirs', p. 37, *Kelly Papers*, KEL/6.
44 Cecil to Bridgeman, 22 November 1927, *Cecil Papers*, BM Add MSS 51099.
45 MacNeece to J.M. Steel (Deputy Chief of Air Staff), 24 March 1924, *Air Ministry Papers*, Air 5/360; Memorandum by MacNeece, 24 March 1924, ibid.
46 See, e.g., C. Barnett, *The Collapse of British Power*, Ch. 5.
47 The nature of the British foreign-policy-making élite and the influences on it are discussed in detail in D.C. Watt, *Personalities and Policies*, essay 1.

Chapter 4

1 Draft Report on the Protocol, 20 February 1925, *Registered Files*, Cab 21/289.
2 Joint Memorandum by the Chiefs of Staff, [29 October 1924], *CID Memoranda*, 527-B, Cab 4/11; Memorandum by Chelmsford, 27 October 1924, ibid., 541-B, Cab 4/12; Memorandum by R.H. Campbell (Foreign Office), 20 November 1924, ibid., 540-B.
3 Memorandum by Chelmsford, 27 September 1924, *Cabinet Papers*, CP 456(24), Cab 24/168; Joint Memorandum by the Chiefs of Staff, [29 October 1924], *CID Memoranda*, 527-B, Cab 4/11; Memorandum by Lloyd-Greame (President of the Board of Trade), 24 November 1924, ibid., 536-B, Cab 4/12; Memorandum by Llewellyn Smith (Board of Trade), November 1924, ibid., enclosure; Memorandum by the Treasury, 26 November 1924, ibid., 537-B.
4 Joint Memorandum by the Chiefs of Staff, [29 October 1924], ibid., 527-B Cab 4/11.
5 Minute by Crowe, 17 November 1924, ibid., 538-B, Cab 4/12. See also Memorandum by Campbell, 20 November 1924, ibid., 540-B.
6 Minute by Crowe, 17 November 1924, ibid., 538-B.
7 Note by Cecil, undated, *Chamberlain Papers*, AC 51/44; Cecil to Gilbert Murray (Chairman, League of Nations Union), 25 September 1924, *Cecil Papers*, BM Add MSS 51132; Cecil to Colonel Réquin, 19 October 1924, ibid., BM Add MSS 51097.
8 Chamberlain to Cecil, 19 November 1924, ibid., BM Add MSS 51078; Minute by Chamberlain, 23 November 1924, *FO Papers*, W 9974/134/98, FO 371/10571; Minute by Chamberlain, undated, ibid., W9788/134/98; Chamberlain to Howard, 22 December 1924, *Chamberlain Papers*, AC 51/149.
9 *CID Minutes*, 190th and 192nd meetings, 4 and 16 December 1924, Cab 2/4.
10 Amery to Governors-General of Canada, Australia, New Zealand and South Africa and Governor of Newfoundland, 19 December 1924, *FO Papers*, W 5873/9/98, FO 371/11066.
11 Ibid.
12 General Report submitted to the Fifth Assembly on behalf of the First and Third Committees, *League of Nations Official Journal*, Special

Supplement 24, p. 125.

13 Memorandum by Hurst, 18 June 1924, *CID Memoranda*, 538-B, enclosure 5, Cab 4/12.

14 General Report submitted to the Fifth Assembly on behalf of the First and Third Committees, *League of Nations Official Journal*, Special Supplement 24, p. 131; Report of the British Delegates relating to the Protocol, November 1924, *CID Memoranda*, 538-B, enclosure 2, Cab 4/12.

15 Ibid.

16 General Report submitted to the Fifth Assembly on behalf of the First and Third Committees, *League of Nations Official Journal*, Special Supplement 24, p. 136.

17 Crowe and the Foreign Office apparently accepted at face value the claim that the Protocol provided for the pacific settlement of *all* disputes, and drew the conclusion that provision had been made for the settlement of political disputes by arbitration. See Minute by Crowe, 17 November 1924, *CID Memoranda*, 538-B, Cab 4/12; Memorandum by Campbell, 20 November 1924, ibid., 540-B. The Foreign Office considered that the 'Assembly Report' interpretation was incorrect as it amounted to an 'emasculation' of the Protocol. See *FO Papers*, W 10677/134/98, FO 371/10572. Crowe was strongly opposed to a political or ministerial committee discussing the Protocol (see Hankey to Curzon, 12 December 1924, *Registered Files*, Cab 21/289) and in the CID sub-committee that was eventually appointed he was careful to ensure that the Foreign Office interpretation of the Protocol, implicitly accepted by the CID, was not questioned. See *Geneva Protocol Committee* (hereafter cited as GP) *Records*, Cab 16/56.

18 *GP Minutes*, 1st meeting, 18 December 1924, Cab 16/56.

19 Minute by Crowe, 17 October 1924, *FO Papers*, W 9654/134/98, FO 371/10571.

20 *GP Report*, 23 January 1925, Cab 16/56.

21 Ibid.

22 Ibid.

23 Ibid.

24 [Cecil] to Balfour, 5 December 1924, *Cecil Papers*, BM Add MSS 51071; Hankey to Cecil, 9 December 1924, *Registered Files*, Cab 21/289; Hankey to Hurst, 22 January 1925, ibid; *GP Minutes*, 3rd and 6th meetings, 19 and 30 December 1924, Cab 16/56; Crowe to Hankey, 2 January 1925, *GP Memoranda*, GP(24)8, Cab 16/56.

25 Cf. Hankey's memoranda of 21 November and 23 December 1924, *CID Memoranda*, 539-B and 558-B, Cab 4/13 and the *GP Report*, 23 January 1925, Cab 16/56.

26 The best indication was his speech in the Commons on 14 July 1924, already cited in Chapter 3.

27 Minute by Chamberlain, 4 January 1925, *FO Papers*, W 362/9/98, FO 371/11064.

28 Ibid; [Chamberlain] to F.D. Lugard (British Member, Permanent Mandates Commission, League of Nations), 1 December 1924, *Chamberlain Papers*, AC 51/185.

29 The conclusions of the conference of 22 January 1925 were set out in a Foreign Office memorandum of 23 January 1925 which was drawn up by Harold Nicolson and R.H. Campbell under the supervision of Sir Eyre Crowe, *FO Papers*, W 2035/9/98, FO 371/11065. This memorandum formed the basis of *Cabinet Paper* CP 106(25) of 20 February 1925, Cab 24/172,

which outlined and explained Chamberlain's recommendations for resolving the security problem.

30 German memorandum on security, forwarded on 20 January 1925, *FO Papers*, C 980/459/18, FO 371/10726.

31 Minute by Crowe, 22 January 1925, ibid; Minute by Lampson (Foreign Office), 30 January 1925, ibid., C 1372/459/18, FO 371/10727; Chamberlain to D'Abernon, 30 January 1925, ibid., C 1454/459/18.

32 Note by the General Staff regarding French security, undated, *Cabinet Papers*, CP 116(25), Cab 24/172; Foreign Office Memorandum, 15 January 1925, *CID Memoranda*, 567-B, Cab 4/12; Memorandum by the Naval Staff, 8 December 1924, ibid., 545-B; Memorandum by the Air Staff, 17 December 1924, ibid., 560-B.

33 Ibid; Memorandum by the Naval Staff, 8 December 1924, ibid., 545-B: Foreign Office Memorandum, 15 January 1925, ibid., 567-B; Note by the General Staff regarding French security, undated, *Cabinet Papers*, CP 116(25), Cab 24/172.

34 Chamberlain to Crewe (Ambassador, Paris), 5 May 1925, ibid., CP 233(25), Cab 24/173; Draft Report on the Protocol, 20 February 1925, *Registered Files*, Cab 21/289; *CID Minutes*, 195th meeting, 13 February 1925, Cab 2/4.

35 Ibid; Amery, *My Political Life*, vol. 2, p. 301. See also, Chamberlain to Crewe, 16 February 1925, *Crewe Papers*, Box C/8.

36 Memorandum by Hoare on security, 5 February 1925, *CID Memoranda*, 575-B Cab 4/12; *CID Minutes*, 195th meeting, 13 February 1925, Cab 2/4.

37 Ibid., 196th meeting, 19 February 1925.

38 Memorandum by Cecil regarding the Geneva Protocol, 23 February 1925, *Cabinet Papers*, CP 112(25), Cab 24/172; *Cabinet Conclusions*, 12(25)1 of 2 March 1925, Cab 23/49.

39 Ibid; Bridgeman, 'Political Notes', p. 109, *Bridgeman Papers*; *CID Minutes*, 195th and 196th meetings, 13 and 19 February 1925, Cab 2/4; Memorandum by [Churchill, 23 February 1925], *Chamberlain Papers*, AC 52/156; Note by Cecil on the Geneva Protocol, undated, ibid., AC 51/44; Percy to Chamberlain, 5 March 1925, ibid., AC 52/663; Crowe to Chamberlain, 12 March 1925, ibid., AC 52/240; Memorandum by Churchill, 24 February 1925, *Cabinet Papers*, CP 118(25), Cab 24/172; Memorandum by Hoare, 27 February 1925, ibid., CP 121(25); Joynson-Hicks to Baldwin, 2 March 1925, *Baldwin Papers*, vol. 115; Amery, *The Leo Amery Diaries*, vol. 1, p. 399 (Diary entry for 4 March 1925).

40 *Cabinet Conclusions*, 12(25)1 of 2 March 1925, Cab 23/49.

41 Ibid.

42 Ibid., 13(25)2 and 14(25)1 of 4 March 1925. See also Cecil to Chamberlain, 2 March 1925, *Chamberlain Papers*, AC 52/120; Cecil, *A Great Experiment*, p. 166.

43 Chamberlain to Crowe, 7 March 1925, *FO Papers*, C 3367/459/18, FO 371/10728; Chamberlain to Crowe, 7 March 1925, *ibid.*, C 3368/4591 18; Chamberlain to Crowe, 8 March 1925, *Chamberlain Papers*, AC 52/238; Memorandum by Chamberlain, 16 March 1925, *Cabinet Papers*, CP 168(25), Cab 24/172.

44 Crowe to Chamberlain, 12 March 1925, *Chamberlain Papers*, AC 52/240; Baldwin to Chamberlain, 12 March 1925, ibid., AC 52/80; Crowe to Baldwin, 14 March 1925, *Baldwin Papers*, vol. 115. Cf. Bridgeman, 'Political Notes', p. 109, *Bridgeman Papers*.

45 Chamberlain to Crowe, undated, *Chamberlain Papers*, AC 52/141; Crowe

to Chamberlain, 15 March 1925, ibid., AC 52/244; *Cabinet Conclusions*, 17(25)2 of 20 March 1925, Cab 23/49.

46 Note by [Chamberlain], 19 March 1925, *Baldwin Papers*, vol. 115.

47 Final Protocol of the Locarno Conference, 1925, *Parliamentary Papers*, Cmd 2525 of 1925.

48 See *Committee on Foreign Policy — Security* (hereafter cited as CFP-S) *Minutes*, 2nd meeting, 28 May 1925, Cab 27/275.

49 See *Cabinet Papers*, CP 245(25), CP 268(25) and CP 272(25), Cab 24/173; *Cabinet Conclusions*, 26(25)2 of 20 May 1925 and 27(25)3 of 28 May 1925, Cab 23/50; *CFP-S Minutes*, 1st and 2nd meetings, 26 and 28 May 1925, Cab 27/275.

50 See, e.g., D'Abernon to Drummond, 8 March 1925, *Cecil Papers*, BM Add MSS 51110; D'Abernon to Chamberlain, 2 June 1925, *Chamberlain Papers*, AC 52/275; Drummond to Cecil, 16 April 1925, ibid; Final Protocol of the Locarno Conference, 1925, *loc. cit.*

51 For analyses of international relations in the years 1925-9, see J. Jacobson, *Locarno Diplomacy* and S. Marks, *The Illusion of Peace: International Relations in Europe 1918-1933*.

Chapter 5

1 Cecil to Baldwin, 30 June 1925, *Baldwin Papers*, vol. 115; *Cabinet Conclusions*, 32(25)1 of 1 July 1925, Cab 23/50.

2 Note by Cecil, 6 July 1925, *Cabinet Papers*, CP 329(25), Cab 24/174.

3 See *FO Papers*, W 6497/9/98, FO 371/11066.

4 Memorandum by Chamberlain, 16 July 1925, *Cabinet Papers*, CP 357(25), Cab 24/174.

5 [Cecil] to Churchill, 24 July 1925, *Cecil Papers*, BM Add MSS 51097. For Churchill's fight on the cruiser question, see Chapter 8.

6 *Cabinet Conclusions*, 39(25)6 of 22 July 1925 and 41(25)8 of 29 July 1925, Cab 23/50; Note by Hankey, 27 July 1925, *Cabinet Papers*, CP 365(25), Cab 24/174.

7 Chamberlain to Cecil, 14 August 1927, *Cecil Papers*, BM Add MSS 51079; Churchill to Cecil, 20 January 1925, ibid., BM Add MSS 51097; Cecil to Churchill, 24 July 1925, ibid; Cecil to Gilbert Murray, 12 November 1925, ibid., BM Add MSS 51132.

8 Note by Butler, August 1925, *FO Papers*, W 7679/9/98, FO 371/11066.

9 Minute by Chamberlain, 17 September 1925, ibid., W 8824/9/98; Minute by Chamberlain, 22 September 1925, ibid., W 8942/9/98.

10 Chamberlain to Cecil, 18 September 1925, ibid., W 8909/9/98; Minute by Chamberlain, 2 October 1925, ibid., W 9183/9/98.

11 Note by Cecil, undated, *Cabinet Papers*, CP 419(25), Cab 24/175.

12 Minute by Chamberlain, 2 October 1925, *FO Papers*, W 9183/9/98, FO 371/11066; Note by Chamberlain, 31 October 1925, *Cabinet Papers*, CP 454(25), Cab 24/175.

13 *Cabinet Conclusions*, 52(25)1 of 11 November 1925, Cab 23/51; *CID Minutes*, 205th meeting, 17 November 1925, Cab 2/4.

14 Memorandum by the Treasury, 23 November 1925, *Reduction and Limitation of Armaments Committee* (hereafter cited as RLA) *Memoranda*, RLA(25)6, Cab 16/61; Memorandum by the General Staff, [5 November 1925], *CID Memoranda*, 641-B, Cab 4/13.

15 Ibid.

16 Ibid.
17 Memorandum by the Air Staff, 23 October 1925, ibid., 644-B.
18 Ibid.
19 Ibid.
20 Memorandum by Hankey, 4 August 1925, *Cecil Papers*, BM Add MSS 51088; Hankey to Cecil, 6 August 1925, ibid; Summary by Hankey of the Material in the Archives of the CID concerning Disarmament, [24 September 1925], *CID Memoranda*, 628-B, Cab 4/13.
21 Memorandum by Hankey, 4 August 1925, *Cecil Papers*, BM Add MSS 51088. See also, Hankey to Cecil, 18 August 1925, *Hankey Papers*, MO(25)6, Cab 63/37.
22 Hankey to Chamberlain, 21 August 1925, *Chamberlain Papers*, AC 24/7/16.
23 [Cecil] to H. Wilson Harris, 20 November 1925, *Cecil Papers*, BM Add MSS 51164.
24 Cecil to Hankey, 24 August 1925, ibid., BM Add MSS 51088.
25 *RLA Minutes*, 1st, 2nd and 3rd meetings, 19, 23 and 25 November 1925, Cab 16/61.
26 *Cabinet Conclusions*, 57(25)6 of 3 December 1925, Cab 23/51; *CID Minutes*, 206th meeting, 30 November 1925, Cab 2/4; *RLA Report*, November 1925, Cab 16/61.
27 *DPC*, Series I, pp. 17–40.
28 *RLA Reports and Minutes*, Cab 16/71.
29 Cecil to Baldwin, 6 January 1926, *Baldwin Papers*, vol. 129.
30 Cecil to Baldwin, 5 December 1925, ibid.
31 Cecil to Baldwin, 6 January 1926, ibid; *RLA Minutes*, 1st meeting, 6 January 1926, Cab 16/71.
32 Ibid., 2nd meeting, 12 February 1926.
33 Memorandum by the General Staff, 20 January 1926, *RLA Memoranda*, RLA(26)9, Cab 16/73; Memorandum of the General Staff, 22 March 1926, ibid., RLA(26)32; *RLA Minutes*, 2nd meeting, 12 February 1926, Cab 16/71.
34 Ibid; Memorandum by the General Staff, 17 February 1926, *RLA Memoranda*, RLA(26)19, Cab 16/73.
35 *RLA Minutes*, 2nd meeting, 12 February 1926, Cab 16/71.
36 Ibid., 3rd meeting, 19 February 1926. See also, *RLA Memoranda*, RLA(26)14, Cab 16/73.
37 Joint Memorandum by the Treasury and Board of Trade, 1 March 1926, ibid., RLA(26)23.
38 *RLA Minutes*, 4th meeting, 3 March 1926, Cab 16/71.
39 Ibid., 1st, 3rd and 4th meetings, 6 January, 19 February and 3 March 1926; Memorandum by the General Staff, 20 January 1926, *RLA Memoranda*, RLA(26)9, Cab 16/73; Memorandum by the Admiralty, 28 January 1926, ibid., RLA(26)8, Appendix A; Note by the Air Staff, 26 January 1926, ibid., RLA(26)11.
40 Memorandum by the Treasury, 23 November 1925, ibid., RLA(25)6, Cab 16/61; Treasury Memorandum on the Limitation of Expenditure on Armaments, undated, ibid., RLA(26)25, Cab 16/73.
41 *CID Minutes*, 212th meeting, 19 April 1926, Cab 2/4; *RLA Minutes*, 8th meeting, 26 April 1926, Cab 16/71; *Cabinet Conclusions*, 19(26)7 of 28 April 1926, Cab 23/52; Revised *RLA Report*, 28 April 1928, Cab 16/71.

Chapter 6

1 Cecil to Gilbert Murray, 24 January 1926, *Murray Papers*, Box 16C; Cecil to Gilbert Murray, 25 March 1926, ibid.

2 Minute by Chamberlain, 20 February 1926, *FO Papers*, W 1075/78/98, FO 371/11878; Minute by Chamberlain, 20 February 1926, ibid., W 1507/78/98; FO 371/11879.

3 Minute by Chamberlain, 20 February 1926, ibid., W 1075/78/98, FO 371/11878; Minute by Chamberlain, 25 February 1926, ibid.

4 Ibid; Minute by Chamberlain, 20 February 1926, ibid; Minute by Cecil, 23 February 1926, ibid; Minute by Cecil, 5 March 1926, ibid; Memorandum by Cecil, 5 March 1926, ibid.

5 Note handed to Chamberlain by Fleuriau (French Ambassador, London) on 10 February 1926, undated, ibid.

6 Madariaga, *Disarmament*, p. 135.

7 In practice, Sub-Commission 'A' differed very little from the Permanent Advisory Commission, except for the addition of American representatives, and was served by the same secretariat. Sub-Commission 'B' was little more than a face-saving device for the American delegation; it assigned the majority of its work to the Joint Commission.

8 J. Paul-Boncour, *Entre deux guerres*, vol. 2, p. 187; Proposal by Paul-Boncour, 22 May 1926, *DPC*, Series II, pp. 110-1.

9 Memorandum by Paul-Boncour, undated, ibid., pp. 111-2.

10 London (Geneva) to Foreign Office, 22 May 1926, *FO Papers*, W 4466/78/98, FO 371/11880; Memorandum by Cecil, 24 May 1926, ibid., W 4737/78/98, FO 371/11882; *CID Minutes*, 213th meeting, 1 June 1926, Cab 2/4.

11 Minute by Chamberlain, 24 May 1926, *FO Papers* W 4466/78/98, FO 371/11880.

12 Villiers (Foreign Office) to London, 25 May 1926, ibid.

13 Memorandum by Cecil, 24 May 1926, ibid., W 4737/78/98, FO 371/11882.

14 *DPC*, Series II, pp. 83-6, 108-9.

15 *Cabinet Conclusions*, 35(26)11 of 2 June 1926 and 37(26)16 of 9 June 1926, Cab 23/53. As events turned out, Sub-Commission 'A' adjourned before Onslow could be despatched.

16 Madariaga, *Disarmament*, pp. 200-1.

17 Temperley, op. cit., pp. 50-1.

18 London to Foreign Office, 26 June 1926, *FO Papers*, W 4931/78/98, FO 371/11882; Proceedings of Sub-Committee 'A' on 11 June 1926: Summary by the service representatives, 14 June 1926, ibid., W 5550/78/98, FO 371/11883.

19 Minute by Kirkpatrick (Foreign Office), 19 June 1926, ibid; Minute by Villiers, 19 June 1926, ibid.

20 Minute by Cecil, undated, ibid; Minute by Chamberlain, 28 June 1926, ibid.

21 League of Nations, *Preparatory Commission for the Disarmament Conference: Report of Sub-Commission 'A'* (hereafter cited as RSCA), pp. 11, 19-23.

22 Ibid., pp. 29-36; Proceedings of Sub-Committee 'A' on 14 June 1926: Summary by the service representatives, 14 June 1926, *FO Papers*, W 5550/78/98, FO 371/11883; Proceedings of Sub-Committee 'A' on 16 June 1926: Summary by the service representatives, 16 June 1926, ibid., W 5652/78/98.

23 *RSCA*, pp. 24-7.
24 *RLA Minutes*, 11th meeting, 13 July 1926, Cab 16/71; Note by Roberts (Foreign Office), 19 June 1926, *FO Papers*, W 5746/78/98, FO 371/11883.
25 Discussion in Military, Naval and Air Sub-Committee on 10 June 1926: Summary [by the service representatives], 19 June 1926, *ibid*; Minute by Chamberlain, 20 February 1926, *ibid.*, W 1075/78/98, FO 371/11878.
26 *RSCA*, pp. 30, 35-6, 76, 123.
27 Ibid., pp. 74-5, 126; Temperley to Charles (Director of Military Operations and Intelligence), 3 September 1926, *FO Papers*, W 8951/78/98, FO 371/11888.
28 Proceedings of the Military Sub-Committee of Sub-Commission 'A' on 25 June 1926: Summary [by the service representative], 25 June 1926, ibid., W 5929/78/98, FO 371/11884; *RSCA*, pp. 39-41, 71-2.
29 Ibid.
30 Ibid., pp. 51, 123-4.
31 Ibid., pp. 123-4, 137-40.
32 Ibid., pp. 111-12, 133-5, 148-50.
33 Summary by Roberts, 6 August 1926, *FO Papers*, W 7319/78/98, FO 371/11885; Note by the French delegation on the personnel employed in civil aviation, 5 August 1926, ibid., W 7487/78/98; Proceedings of the Air Sub-Committee of Sub-Commission 'A' on 10 August 1926: Summary [by the service representative], 10 August 1926, ibid., W 7729/78/98, FO 371/11886; Proceedings of the Air Sub-Committee of Sub-Commission 'A' on 17 August 1926: Summary [by the service representative], 17 August 1926, ibid., W 7883/78/98.
34 Summary of a meeting with general Dusmesnil on 24 June 1926: [MacNeece to Air Ministry], 28 June 1926, *Cecil Papers*, BM Add MSS 51113; American amendment to British metropolitan formula: [MacNeece to Air Ministry], 28 June 1926, ibid; The position of question VI in the questionnaire: [MacNeece to Air Ministry], 28 June 1926, ibid; Hoare to Trenchard, 1 December 1926, ibid; BM Add MSS 51083; *RSCA*, p. 150; *RLA Minutes*, 11th meeting, 13 July 1926, Cab 16/71.
35 Hoare to Cecil, 24 March 1926, *Cecil Papers*, BM Add MSS 51083; Bullock (private secretary to Hoare) to Newall (Deputy Chief of Air Staff), 1 December 1926, ibid., Hoare to Cecil, 23 December 1926, ibid.
36 *RSCA*, pp. 133, 135-6.
37 Ibid., pp. 46-7, 112; Report of the Air Committee, 26 June 1926, *FO Papers* W 6227/78/98, FO 371/11884.
38 London to Foreign Office, 24 June 1926, ibid., W 5869/78/98, FO 371/11883; *RSCA*, p. 135; Summary of a meeting with General Dusmesnil on 24 June 1926: [MacNeece to Air Ministry], 28 June 1926, *Cecil Papers*, BM Add MSS 51113.
39 American amendment to British metropolitan formula: [MacNeece to Air Ministry], 28 June 1926, ibid; *RSCA*, p. 116.
40 Ibid., pp. 117-18.
41 Ibid., p. 113; Proceedings of the Air Sub-Committee of Sub-Commission 'A' on 22 June 1926: Summary by th Air representative, 24 June 1926, *FO Papers*, W 5934/78/98, FO 371/11884; Proceedings of the Air Sub-Committee of Sub-Commission 'A' on 3 September 1926: Summary [by the service representative], 7 September 1926, ibid., W 8751/78/98, FO 371/11888; Note by the French delegation on the personnel employed in civil aviation, 5 August 1926, ibid., W 7487/78/98, FO 371/11885.
42 Temperley, op. cit., p. 59.

43 Memorandum by [Milne], undated, *CID Memoranda*, 926-B, Cab 4/18.
44 Chamberlain to D'Abernon, 2 February 1927, *D'Abernon Papers*, BM Add MSS 48926B; Chamberlain to Briand, 29 July 1926, *Chamberlain Papers*, AC 53/81; Chamberlain to Tyrrell, 3 December 1926, ibid., AC 53/565; Chamberlain to Tyrrell, 6 December 1926, ibid., AC 53/568. See also J. Jacobson, *Locarno Diplomacy*, pp. 91-8 and H.W. Gatzke, *Stresemann and the Rearmament of Germany*, pp. 53-71.
45 [Crewe] to Selby, 14 February 1926, *Crewe Papers*, Box C/8.
46 London to Foreign Office, 19 August 1926, *FO Papers*, W 7791/78/98, FO 371/11886.
47 Proposal by the French delegation: Questions connected with the supervision of armaments, 9 August 1926, ibid., W 7487/78/98, FO 371/11885; *RSCA*, pp. 163-4, 166-7.
48 Ibid., pp. 162-9, 171; Questions regarding the supervision of armaments: Views of the Italian delegation, 9 August 1926, *FO Papers*, W 7487/78/98, FO 371/11885; Proceedings of Sub-Commission 'A' on 9 August 1926: Summary by the service representatives, 9 August 1926, ibid., W 7582/78/98; Declaration by the British, Chilean, American, Italian, Japanese and Swedish delegations, 19 August 1926, ibid., W 7853/78/98, FO 371/11886.
49 *RSCA*, pp. 66-8, 70, 141-2, 172-4.
50 League of Nations, *Preparatory Commission for the Disarmament Conference: Reports of Sub-Commission 'B'*, No. 1, p. 5.
51 Ibid., pp. 5, 22.
52 Ibid., No. 3, pp. 16-18.
53 Ibid., pp. 37-9.
54 Ibid., No. 2, pp. 2-4.
55 Temperley, op. cit., p. 53.
56 Chamberlain to Cecil, 8 August 1926, *FO Papers*, W 7347/78/98, FO 371/11885.
57 Madariaga, *Disarmament*, p. 199.
58 Did the Council really require to know that one of the special characteristics of land armaments was their 'particular suitability for the effective occupation of territories?' *RSCA*, p. 15.
59 Memorandum by Roberts, 6 August 1926, *FO Papers*, W 7319/78/98, FO 371/11885.
60 Madariaga, *Morning Without Noon: Memoirs*, p. 81.
61 Temperley, loc. cit; London to Foreign Office, 24 June 1926, *FO Papers*, W 5869/78/98, FO 371/11883.
62 London to Foreign Office, 4 June 1926, ibid., W 5028/78/98; London to Foreign Office, 24 October 1926, ibid., W 9999/78/98, FO 371/11889.
63 See Flint (Admiralty) to Tyrrell, 12 August 1926, ibid., W 7466/78/98, FO 371/11885.
64 Madariaga, *Disarmament*, p. 202; Temperley, op. cit., pp. 49-50; *RLA Minutes*, 11th meeting, 13 July 1926, Cab 16/71. The fact that arguments were held in good faith should not, however, be held to imply that delegates actually *desired* disarmament.
65 Report by Aubrey Smith, 23 November 1926, *Admiralty Papers*, M 02785/26, Adm 116/2272.
66 Temperley, op. cit., p. 50.

Chapter 7

1 Cecil to Tyrrell, 27 September 1926, *FO Papers*, W 9365/78/98, FO

371/11889.
2 Memorandum by Cecil, 3 November 1926, *CID Memoranda*, 733-B, Cab 4/15.
3 *CID Minutes*, 217th meeting, 11 November 1926, Cab 2/4.
4 See, e.g., a speech by Parmoor (head of British delegation, Fifth Assembly, 1924), 17 November 1926, *Parliamentary Debates, Lords*, Fifth Series, vol. 65, cols. 644-51, esp. cols. 645-6.
5 Cecil to Chamberlain, 29 November 1926, *Chamberlain Papers*, AC 53/118; Memorandum by Cecil, 5 December 1926, *FO Papers*, W 11398/78/98, FO 371/11890; Minute by Kirkpatrick, 9 December 1926, ibid.
6 Cecil to Chamberlain, 1 January 1927, ibid., W 61/61/98, FO 371/12660; Minute by Chamberlain, undated, ibid; Minute by Hurst, 11 January 1927, ibid.
7 Trenchard to Cecil, 13 January 1927, *Cecil Papers*, BM Add MSS 51098; Draft Sketch of Disarmament Treaty, undated, ibid; Noel-Baker to Cecil, 31 January 1927, ibid., BM Add MSS 51106: E.C. Henty (private secretary to Cecil) to Hankey, 2 February 1927, *Registered Files*, Cab 21/305.
8 Minute by Cadogan (Foreign Office), 7 February 1927, *FO Papers*, W 942/61/98, FO 371/12660; Minute by Campbell, 8 February 1927, ibid; Minute by Gregory (Foreign Office), 8 February 1927, ibid.
9 Minute by Cadogan, 7 February 1927, ibid.
10 Draft Treaty for the Limitation of Military, Naval and Aerial Armaments, undated, *RLA Memoranda*, RLA(26)57, Cab 16/74.
11 Memorandum by the Admiralty, 13 January 1927, ibid. RLA 26(56) Enclosure; Memorandum by the General Staff, 9 February 1927, ibid. RLA (26)58: *RLA Minutes*, 15th and 16th meetings, 11 and 21 February 1927, Cab 16/72.
12 Hankey to Cecil, 8 February 1927, *Registered Files*, Cab 21/305.
13 Revised Draft Treaty for the Limitation of Military, Naval and Aerial Armaments, [25 February 1927], *RLA Memoranda*, RLA(26)63, Cab 16/74; *RLA Minutes*, 17th meeting, 1 March 1927, Cab 16/72.
14 *CID Minutes*, 228th meeting, 4 March 1927, Cab 2/5; Chamberlain to Cecil, 4 March 1927, *Cecil Papers*, BM Add MSS 51079; Cecil to Chamberlain, 4 March 1927, *Chamberlain Papers*, AC 54/61; Amery, *The Leo Amery Diaries*, vol. 1, p. 499 (Diary entry for 4 March 1927).
15 *CID Minutes*, 228th meeting, 4 March 1927, Cab 2/5; *RLA Minutes*, 17th meeting, 1 March 1927, Cab 16/72.
16 Memorandum by Cecil, 7 March 1927, *Cabinet Papers*, CP 79(27), Cab 24/185. Despite Cecil's regrets about the lack of provision for a limitation of air and naval effectives, he did not include any provision in his original sketch of a treaty. He preferred the lead to come from other powers and for Britain then to make a concession. [Cecil] to Noel-Baker, 1 February 1927, *Cecil Papers*, BM Add MSS 51106.
17 Cecil, *A Great Experiment*, p. 183.
18 Memorandum by Cecil, 7 March 1927, *Cabinet Papers*, CP 79(27), Cab 24/185.
19 *Cabinet Conclusions*, 15(27)3 of 9 March 1927, Cab 23/54.
20 See Cecil to Baldwin, 10 March 1927, *Baldwin Papers*, vol. 130.
21 Bridgeman to Cecil, 8 February 1927, *Cecil Papers*, BM Add MSS 51098. For a discussion of the proposals in question, see Chapter 9.
22 Memorandum by Drummond, 23 November 1926, *FO Papers*, W 11114/78/98, FO 371/11889.
23 Cecil to Chamberlain, 13 March 1927, *Chamberlain Papers*, AC54/63;

Cecil to Chamberlain, 15 March 1927, ibid., AC 54/66.

24 Graham (Ambassador, Rome) to Chamberlain, 17 February 1927, *FO Papers*, W 1386/61/98, FO 371/12660; [Memorandum by the naval, military, air and press attachés in Rome], undated, ibid; Minute by Campbell, 22 February 1927, ibid; Minute by Cecil, 27 February 1927, ibid. Perhaps the best comment on the military virtues of the Italians was that of the former French Prime Minister, Georges Clemenceau. Shortly *after* the First World War, at a meeting between himself, the British prime minister, David Lloyd George, and President Woodrow Wilson of the United States, the decision was taken to instruct an Italian ship to leave Taranto harbour. Thereupon, in Clemenceau's words, 'an Italian admiral who was present rose and said that never while he lived would he give consent to the vessel going out of port. He said it was a very dangerous thing for ships to go to sea in that way, and they might easily get injured or destroyed'. Memorandum by Cecil, May 1929, *Cecil Papers*, BM Add MSS 51099.

25 Cecil to Chamberlain, 13 March 1927, *Chamberlain Papers*, AC 54/63; Cecil to Paul-Boncour, 21 March 1927, *Cecil Papers*, BM Add MSS 51099; Paul-Boncour to Cecil, 21 March 1927, ibid; London to Foreign Office, 21 March 1927, *FO Papers*, W 2499/61/98, FO 371/12662; *DPC*, Series IV, pp. 8-12; Temperley, op. cit., pp. 58-9. the form of the British draft differed slightly from that accepted by the Cabinet on 9 March, the only adjustment of importance being that effectives were defined as troops that could be available for despatch to the fighting line within an agreed number of weeks of an outbreak of hostilities. The provision regarding service within the previous seven years was dropped. See Draft Convention submitted by Cecil, undated, *DPC*, Series IV, pp. 358-60.

26 Preliminary Draft Convention submitted by the French Delegation, ibid., pp. 361-9.

27 Ibid., pp. 8-38.

28 Cecil to Chamberlain, 23 March 1927, *FO Papers*, W 2666/61/98, FO 371/12663.

29 London to Foreign Office, 28 March 1927, ibid., W 2760/61/98; Temperley to Cecil, 23 March 1927, *Cecil Papers*, BM Add MSS 51099; Temperley to Cecil, 27 March 1927, ibid; Temperley to Cecil, 29 March 1927, ibid; *DPC*, Series IV, pp. 45-69.

30 Minute by Campbell, 29 March 1927, *FO Papers*, W 2760/61/98, FO 371/12663.

31 *DPC*, Series IV, pp. 60-2.

32 Temperley to Cecil, 27 March 1927, *Cecil Papers*, BM Add MSS 51099.

33 See *DPC*, Series IV, pp. 69-108 for the full discussion of these questions and ibid., pp. 383-5 for the agreed text of the draft convention.

34 Cecil to Onslow, 5 April 1927, *Cecil Papers*, BM Add MSS 51099; Cecil to Chamberlain, 6 April 1927, *Chamberlain Papers*, AC 54/72.

35 Cecil to Chamberlain, 27 March 1927, *FO Papers*, W 2766/61/98, FO 371/12663; London to Foreign Office, 30 March 1927, ibid., W 2860/61/98; Foreign Office to London, 31 March 1927, ibid., W 2883/61/98.

36 *RLA Minutes*, 19th meeting, 1 April 1927, Cab 16/72.

37 *DPC*, Series IV, pp. 109-10.

38 London to Foreign Office, 1 April 1927, *FO Papers*, W 2926/61/98, FO 371/12663.

39 London to Foreign Office, 1 April 1927, ibid., W 2927/61/98.

40 Foreign Office to London, 13 April 1927, ibid., W 2950/61/98; *RLA*

Minutes, 19th meeting, 1 April 1927, Cab 16/72; Salisbury to Cecil, 2 April 1927, *Cecil Papers*, BM Add MSS 51086.

41 *DPC*, Series IV, pp. 121-35.
42 MacNeece to Cecil, 23 March 1927, *FO Papers*, W 2766/61/98, FO 371/12663; Foreign Office to London, 31 March 1927, ibid., W 2803/61/98.
43 Ibid; Foreign Office to London, 31 March 1927, ibid., W 2877/61/98; London to Foreign Office, 1 April 1927, ibid., W 2927/61/98. The proponents of a limitation of overseas aircraft were themselves divided as to the precise method of restriction. The French favoured a straight division between home and overseas forces; the Italians preferred a tripartite division between home forces, forces in colonies near the homeland and forces in distant colonies. See *DPC*, Series IV, pp. 133-5.
44 London to Foreign Office, 1 April 1927, *FO Papers*, W 2927/61/98, FO 371/12663.
45 London to Foreign Office, 2 April 1927, ibid., W 2941/61/98.
46 *CID Minutes*, 224th meeting, 4 April 1927, Cab 2/5; Salisbury to Cecil, 5 April 1927, *Cecil Papers*, BM Add MSS 51086.
47 *CID Minutes*, 224th meeting, 4 April 1927, Cab 2/5.
48 Ibid.
49 *DPC*, Series IV, pp. 136-41.
50 Ibid., pp. 178, 193-211, 223-5.
51 Ibid., pp. 212-22.
52 Ibid., pp. 302-7.
53 Cecil to Chamberlain, 13 March 1927, *Chamberlain Papers*, AC 54/63; Cecil to Chamberlain, 24 March 1927, ibid., AC 54/67; Service representatives to Cecil, 28 March 1927, *Cecil Papers*, BM Add MSS 51099; Cecil to Salisbury, 14 April 1927, ibid., BM Add MSS 51086; Salisbury to Cecil, 18 April 1927, ibid. For the naval issue, see Chapter 8.
54 *DPC*, Series IV, pp. 273-87.
55 Ibid., p. 308.
56 Ibid., pp. 308-10.
57 Memorandum by Cadogan, 17 May 1927, *FO Papers*, W 4575/61/98, FO 371/12667.
58 Ibid.
59 Minute by Cecil, 20 May 1927, ibid.
60 Ibid.
61 Minute by Gregory, 26 May 1927, ibid; Cadogan to Cecil, 23 May 1927, *Cecil Papers*, BM Add MSS 51089.
62 Minute by Chamberlain, 27 May 1927, *FO Papers*, W 4575/61/98, FO 371/12667.
63 Chamberlain to Cecil, 11 April 1927, *Cecil Papers*, BM Add MSS 51079.
64 Cecil to Irwin, 7 June 1927, *Cecil Papers*, BM Add MSS 51084.
65 Chamberlain to Cecil, 28 March 1927, ibid., BM Add MSS 51079; Chamberlain to Cecil, 11 April 1927, ibid; Chamberlain to Cecil, 14 August 1927, ibid; Salisbury to Cecil, 5 April 1927, ibid., BM Add MSS 51086; Chamberlain to Crewe, 8 April 1927, *Crewe Papers*, Box C/8; Chamberlain to Salisbury, 14 April 1927, *Chamberlain Papers*, AC 54/438.
66 Cecil to Irwin, 7 June 1927, *Cecil Papers*, BM Add MSS 51084.
67 *CID Minutes*, 222nd and 224th meetings, 4 March and 4 April 1927, Cab 2/5; Hoare to Cecil, 11 April 1927, *Cecil Papers*, BM Add MSS 51083; Cecil to Chamberlain, 16 August 1927, *Chamberlain Papers*, AC 54/95.
68 Cecil to Chamberlain, 6 April 1927, ibid., AC 54/72; Salisbury to Cecil,

5 April 1927, *Cecil Papers*, BM Add MSS 51086.

69 Cecil to Chamberlain, 4 March 1927, *Chamberlain Papers*, AC 54/61; Cecil to Chamberlain, 24 March 1927, ibid., AC 54/67; Chamberlain to Cecil, 28 March 1927, ibid., AC 54/68; Salisbury to Cecil, 9 April 1927, ibid., BM Add MSS 51086; London to Foreign Office, 4 April 1927, *FO Papers* W 3080/61/98, FO 371/12664; Minute by Cecil, 20 May 1927, ibid., W 4575/61/98, FO 371/12667.

70 Foreign Office to London, 5 April 1927, ibid., W 3042/61/98, FO 371/12664; [London] to Foreign Office, 6 April 1927, *Cecil Papers*, BM Add MSS 51104; *DPC*, Series IV, pp. 123-4; London to Foreign Office, 6 April 1927, *FO Papers*, W 3148/61/98, FO 371/12665.

71 *DPC*, Series IV, p. 354.

Chapter 8

1 Howard to Chamberlain, 18 December 1924, *Cabinet Papers*, CP 87(25), Cab 24/171; Howard to Chamberlain, 22 December 1924, ibid; *Cabinet Conclusions*, 7(25)20 of 11 February 1925, Cab 23/49.

2 Ibid., 8(25)1 of 12 February 1925.

3 Plans Division Memorandum, 13 February 1925, *Admiralty Papers*, PD 02164/25, Adm 1/8653/131. For British cruiser policy at the Washington conference, see S.W. Roskill, *Naval Policy between the Wars*, vol. 1, pp. 325-6.

4 Memorandum by Beatty, undated, *Chamberlain Papers*, FO 800/257; Draft Despatch, Chamberlain to Howard, *Cabinet Papers*, CP 96(25), Cab 24/171; *Cabinet Conclusions*, 9(25)3 of 18 February 1925, Cab 23/49.

5 Ibid., 19(25)1 of 1 April 1925; Memorandum by Bridgeman, 30 April 1925, *Cabinet Papers*, CP 221(25), Cab 24/173.

6 *CID Minutes*, 199th meeting, 2 April 1925, Cab 2/4.

7 Memorandum by the Admiralty, 4 February 1925, *Cabinet Papers*, CP 67(25), Appendix, Cab 24/171; Churchill to Baldwin, 15 December 1924, *Baldwin Papers*, vol. 2; *Cabinet Conclusions*, 8(25)1 of 12 February 1925, Cab 23/49.

8 Memorandum by Bridgeman, 18 June 1925, *NPC Memoranda*, NPC(25)26, Cab 27/273; Programme of New Construction, 30 June 1925, ibid., NPC(25)26A.

9 *NPC Minutes*, 8th and 9th meetings, 30 June and 2 July 1925, Cab 27/273; *Cabinet Conclusions*, 39(25)3 of 22 July 1925, Cab 23/50.

10 Plans Division Draft Memorandum, August 1925, *Admiralty Papers*, PD 02296/25, Adm 1/8653/131; Naval Staff Memorandum, 9 October 1925, *RLA Memoranda*, RLA(25)2, Appendix D, Cab 16/61.

11 Plans Division Draft Memorandum, August 1925, *Admiralty Papers*, PD 02296/25, Adm 1/8653/131; Minute by Beatty, undated, ibid; Naval Staff Draft Memorandum, 9 October 1925, ibid., M 01943/25; Naval Staff Memorandum, 9 October 1925, *RLA Memoranda*, RLA(25)2, Appendix D, Cab 16/61.

12 Plans Division Draft Memorandum, August 1925, *Admiralty Papers*, PD 02296/25, Adm 1/8653/131; Naval Staff Memorandum, 9 October 1925, *RLA Memoranda*, RLA(25)2, Appendix D, Cab 16/61.

13 *RLA Minutes*, 1st meeting, 19 November 1925, Cab 16/61; *RLA Report*, November 1925, Cab 16/61; *CID Minutes*, 206th meeting, 30 November 1925, Cab 2/4; *Cabinet Conclusions*, 57(25)6 of 3 December 1925, Cab

23/51. The CID had wanted to go further, suggesting that Britain should be ready at the proper moment to make a positive proposal for the limitation of cruisers and other auxiliary naval craft, but the Cabinet rejected the idea.

14 Admiralty Memorandum, 28 January 1926, *RLA Memoranda*, RLA(26)8, Cab 16/73.

15 *RLA Report*, 28 April 1926, Cab 16/71.

16 Ibid; Draft Instructions to Cecil, undated, *Cabinet Papers*, CP 177(26), Cab 24/179. Cf. *Cabinet Conclusions*, 9(25)3 of 18 February 1925, Cab 23/49.

17 *RSCA*, pp. 81-2.

18 Ibid., pp. 89-90, 98, 104-5.

19 Ibid., pp 90-2, 99-100, 105.

20 Ibid., pp. 92-8, 100-4, 106-8.

21 London to Foreign Office, 24 June 1926, *FO Papers*, W 5878/78/98, FO 371/11883; London to Foreign Office, 1 July 1926, ibid., W 6123/78/98, FO 371/11884; Summary of the Proceedings of the Naval Committee, 30 June 1926, ibid., Minute by Cecil, 18 July 1926, ibid., W 6887/78/98.

22 London to Foreign Office, 23 June 1926, ibid., W 5819/78/98, FO 371/11883; Aubrey Smith to Sir Oswyn Murray (Admiralty), 23 November 1926, *Admiralty Papers*, M 02785/26, Adm 116/2272.

23 Temperley hints at this. See his *Whispering Gallery of Europe*, pp. 59-60.

24 Summary of the Proceedings of the Naval Committee, 30 June 1926, *FO Papers*, W 6123/78/98, FO 371/11884; Minute by Cecil, 18 July 1926, ibid., W 6887/78/98; Aubrey Smith to Sir Oswyn Murray, 23 November 1926, *Admiralty Papers*, M 02785/26,. Adm 116/2272.

25 Minute by Chamberlain, 22 July 1926, *FO Papers*, W 6887/78/98, FO 371/1884.

26 Summary of the Proceedings of the Naval Sub-Committee, 11 September 1926, ibid., W 8706/78/98, FO 371/11888.

27 *RSCA*, pp. 43-4, 46, 110.

28 Aubrey Smith to Sir Oswyn Murray, 23 November 1926, *Admiralty Papers*, M 02785/26, Adm 116/2272.

29 Draft Treaty for the Limitation of Military, Naval and Aerial Armaments, undated, *RLA Memoranda*, RLA(26)57, Cab 16/74.

30 See *RLA Minutes*, 15th, 16th and 17th meetings, 11 and 21 February and 1 March 1927, Cab 16/72; *CID Minutes*, 222nd meeting, 4 March 1927, Cab 2/5; *Cabinet Conclusions*, 15(27)3 of 9 March 1927, Cab 23/54; Draft Convention, undated, *Cabinet Papers*, CP 78(27), Enclosure 2.

31 For the Admiralty's plans for a new conference, see Chapter 9.

32 Memorandum by Cecil, 5 December 1926, *FO Papers*, W 11398/78/98, FO 371/11890.

33 French Preliminary Draft Convention, undated, *DPC*, Series IV, pp. 361-9.

34 Cecil to Noel-Baker, 1 February 1927, *Cecil Papers*, BM Add MSS 51106; Cecil to Chamberlain, 23 March 1927, *FO Papers*, W 2666/61/98, FO 371/12663; Flint (Admiralty) to Tyrrell, 25 March 1927, ibid., W 2685/61/98; Cecil to Chamberlain, 27 March 1927, ibid., W 2766/61/98; Foreign Office to London, 3 April 1927, ibid., W 2950/61/98; London to Foreign Office, 3 April 1927, ibid., W 2995/61/98, FO 371/12664; Minute by Egerton (Admiralty), 30 March 1927, *Admiralty Papers*, M 0938/27, Adm 116/3609; *RLA Minutes*, 19th meeting, 1 April 1927, Cab 16/72; *CID Minutes*, 224th meeting, 4 April 1927, Cab 2/5; *DPC*, Series IV, p. 248.

The only remaining difference between the powers on this question was that the French government desired to restrict the percentage of officers whereas the British government did not, despite having pressed for a similar limitation regarding army offices. See ibid., p. 400; London to Foreign Office, 6 April 1927, *FO Papers*, W 3148/61/98, FO 371/12664.

35 *DPC*, Series IV, pp. 246–8; Flint to Tyrrell, 26 April 1927, *FO Papers*, W 3812/61/98, FO 371/12666; Note by Cecil, 12 May 1927, ibid.

36 *DPC*, Series IV, pp. 199, 407.

37 London to Foreign Office, 4 April 1927, *FO Papers*, W 3080/61/98, FO 371/12664.

38 Ibid.

39 Paul-Boncour to Cecil, 6 April 1927, *Cecil Papers*, BM Add MSS 51099; London to Foreign Office, 6 April 1927, *FO Papers*, W 3092/61/98, FO 371/12664.

40 Cecil to Paul-Boncour, 6 April 1927, ibid., W 3297/61/98, FO 371/12665.

41 London to Foreign Office, 6 April 1927, ibid., W 3092/61/98, FO 371/12664; London to Foreign Office, 6 April 1927, ibid., W 3122/61/98, FO 371/12665.

42 Foreign Office to London, 7 April 1927, ibid., W 3203/61/98; London to Foreign Office, 8 April 1927, ibid., W 3204/61/98.

43 London to Foreign Office, 8 April 1927, ibid., W 3235/61/98.

44 Ibid.

45 Foreign Office to London, 11 April 1927, ibid.

46 Aubrey Smith to Field, 8 April 1927, *Admiralty Papers*, M 01108/27, Adm 116/2578; Aubrey Smith to [Field], 9 April 1927, ibid; Redraft of British Draft Convention, chapter III, undated, ibid., It would appear that Cecil put forward his proposed modifications to the naval chapter of the British draft convention in a private letter to Salisbury of 9 April. Unfortunately, it has not been possible to trace this letter. The only copy of his 'draft modifications' seems to be that in the Admiralty Papers.

47 Foreign Office to London, 11 April 1927, *FO Papers*, W 3235/61/98, FO 371/12665; Salisbury to Cecil, 16 April 1927, *Cecil Papers*, BM Add MSS 51086. Aubrey Smith at one point devised a redraft of Cecil's redraft and forwarded it to the Admiralty for consideration. See [Aubrey Smith Redraft], 9 April 1927, *Admiralty Papers*, M 01108/27, Adm 116/2578.

48 Cecil to Chamberlain, 12 April 1927, *Chamberlain Papers*, AC 54/78.

49 Chamberlain to Salisbury, 14 April 1927, ibid., AC 54/439.

50 [Cecil] to Salisbury, 14 April 1927, *Cecil Papers*, BM Add MSS 51086; *DPC*, Series IV, pp. 230–3. The Italians, in fact, far from accepting the Paul-Boncour 'compromise' of 6 April, would only concede that nations should notify the League Secretariat of the characteristics of new vessels at least six months before laying down new keels. See ibid., pp. 229–30.

51 Memorandum by Salisbury, 11 April 1927, *Cecil Papers*, BM Add MSS 51086.

52 See Cecil to Salisbury, 8 April 1927, ibid; Graham to Foreign Office, 17 February 1927, *FO Papers*, W 1269/61/98, FO 371/12660; Graham to Foreign Office, 21 February 1927, ibid., W 1432/61/98, FO 371/12661; Memorandum communicated by the Italian Under-Secretary for Foreign Affairs to the United States' Ambassador, 21 February 1927, ibid., W 1657/61/98, Enclosure.

53 See Phipps (Paris) to Chamberlain, 12 April 1927, *ibid.*, W 3359/61/98, FO 371/12665; Crewe to Chamberlain, 12 April 1927, *Chamberlain Papers*, AC 54/126; Cecil to Salisbury, April 8 1927, *Cecil Papers*, BM

Add MSS 51086.

54 Ibid.

55 Memorandum by Chamberlain, 21 May 1927, *FO Papers*, W 4903/61/98, FO 371/12667.

56 See especially Cecil to Chamberlain, 6 April 1927, *Chamberlain Papers*, AC 54/72; Cecil to Chamberlain, 12 April 1927, ibid., AC 54/78; Cecil to Salisbury, 8 April 1927, *Cecil Papers*, BM Add MSS 51086.

57 Salisbury to Chamberlain, 15 April 1927, *Chamberlain Papers*, AC 54/440.

58 Salisbury to Cecil, 16 April 1927, *Cecil Papers*, BM Add MSS 51086.

59 *DPC*, Series IV, pp. 173, 233-5; Cecil to Chamberlain, 12 April 1927, *Chamberlain Papers*, AC 54/78; Cecil to Salisbury, 14 April 1927, *Cecil Papers*, BM Add MSS 51086.

60 London to Foreign Office, 8 April 1927, *FO Papers*, W 3204/61/98, FO 371/12665; London to Foreign Office, 8 April 1927, ibid., W 3235/61/98.

Chapter 9

1 Foreword to a Memorandum by the Sea Lords, [January 1927], *Admiralty Papers*, Adm 167/76; Admiralty Board Minute 2286, 27 January 1927, ibid. Adm 167/75.

2 Memorandum by Field, Chatfield and Dreyer, 21 December 1926, ibid., M 03056/26, Adm 1/8699/118; Memorandum by Haggard (Admiralty), [23 July 1926], ibid., M 02902/26; Memorandum by Sulivan (Admiralty), July 1926, ibid.

3 Memorandum by the Sea Lords, [January 1927], ibid., Adm 167/76.

4 Ibid; Admiralty Board Minute 2286, 27 January 1927, ibid., Adm 167/75.

5 Memorandum by the Sea Lords, [January 1927], ibid., Adm 167/76; Plans Division Memorandum, 12 October 1928, ibid., M 03152/28, Adm 116/3629; War Memorandum (Eastern), 29 August 1924, ibid., M 00370/24, Adm 116/3125; [Admiralty Memorandum], 6 March 1925, *NPC Memoranda*, NP(25)7, Cab 27/273. During the discussions of the Naval Programme Committee of 1927, the First Sea Lord, Sir Charles Madden, admitted directly that the Admiralty demand for seventy cruisers devolved from the war plan against Japan. See *NPC Minutes*, 2nd and 3rd meetings, 18 and 22 November 1927, Cab 27/355.

6 Memorandum by the Sea Lords, [January 1927], ibid., Adm 167/76.

7 Ibid.

8 Memorandum communicated by the United States Embassy, 10 February 1927, *FO Papers*, W 1052/61/98, FO 371/12660.

9 Minute by Chamberlain, 14 February 1927, ibid., W 1052/61/98.

10 French Reply to the Coolidge Proposals, 15 February 1927, ibid., W 1283/61/98; Graham to Chamberlain, 25 February 1927, ibid., W 1657/61/98, FO 371/12661.

11 *Cabinet Conclusions*, 48(26)2 of 28 July 1926, Cab 23/53; Lord E. Percy, *Some Memories*, p. 142.

12 Foreign Office Memorandum, 25 February 1927, *FO Papers*, W 1581/61/98, FO 371/12661; Chamberlain to Howard, 25 February 1927, ibid.

13 Memorandum by Egerton, 17 February 1927, *Admiralty Papers*, PD 02773/27, Adm 116/3371; Plans Divisions Memorandum, 17 March 1927, ibid., PD 02807/27; Naval Staff Memorandum, 14 April 1927, *CID Memoranda*, 808-B, Cab 4/16.

14 Minute by Beatty, 13 April 1927, *Admiralty Papers*, M 01052/27, Adm 1/8715/188; Minute by Bridgeman, 26 April 1927, ibid; Note by Hankey,

23 May 1927, *Cabinet Papers*, CP 159(27), Cab 24/187; *CID Minutes*, 227th meeting, 20 May 1927, Cab 2/5.

15 Ibid; *Cabinet Conclusions*, 34(27)3 of 25 May 1927, Cab 23/55.

16 Memorandum by Cecil, 24 September 1926, *FO Papers*, W 9494/78/98, FO 371/11889.

17 Howard to Foreign Office, 6 July 1927, ibid., W 6349/61/98, FO 371/12670.

18 Conference for the Limitation of Naval Armament, *Records of the Conference for the Limitation of Naval Armament* (hereafter cited as RCLNA), pp. 19-21, 132-3.

19 Ibid., pp. 23-4.

20 Ibid., pp. 21-3.

21 Gibson to Kellogg, 23 June 1927, *FRUS*, 1927 vol. 1, p. 52.

22 Howard to Foreign Office, 22 June 1927, *FO Papers*, W 5793/61/98, FO 371/12669.

23 Howard to Foreign Office, 28 June 1927, ibid., W 6026/61/98; Gibson to Kellogg, 22 June 1927, *FRUS*, 1927, vol. 1, pp. 52-3.

24 *Cabinet Conclusions*, 37(27)10 of 29 June 1927, Cab 23/55.

25 Foreign Office to London, 29 June 1927, *FO Papers*, W 6026/61/98, FO 371/12669. The text differed slightly from the draft formulated by Balfour, viz:

> For diplomatic reasons we think it most desirable to say publicly and at once what we believe to be the line on which you are working namely, that while we mean to build cruisers up to our needs we lay down no conditions limiting America's cruisers to a smaller number.
>
> Do you see any objection.

26 Gibson to Kellogg, 30 June 1927, *FRUS*, 1927 vol. 1, p. 65. Cf. Minutes of Fifth Conference of British Delegations, held on 1 July 1927, *LNA Records*, Cab 27/350. During this latter meeting, Bridgeman was quoted as saying that Britain had 'no desire whatever to question the American claim to parity in all respects'.

27 London to Foreign Office, 30 June 1927, *FO Papers*, W 6110/61/98, FO 371/12670.

28 Foreign Office to Howard, 1 July 1927, ibid.

29 Minute by Baldwin, 1 July 1927, ibid.

30 *Cabinet Conclusions*, 38(27)5 of 4 July 1927, Cab 23/55; Note by Tyrrell, 2 July 1927, *FO Papers*, W 6110/61/98, FO 371/12670; Minute by Kirkpatrick, 2 July 1927, ibid; Chamberlain to Cecil, 5 July 1927, *Cecil Papers*, BM Add MSS 51079.

31 *Cabinet Conclusions*, 38(27)5 of 4 July 1927, Cab 23/55.

32 *NPC Minutes*, 3rd meeting, 22 November 1927, Cab 27/355; Memorandum by Bridgeman, 9 November 1927, *NPC Memoranda*, NP(27)3, Cab 27/355; Memorandum by Bridgeman, 15 November 1927, ibid., NP(27)5; Plans Division Memorandum, 12 October 1928, *Admiralty Papers*, M 03152/28, Adm 116/3629. See also, War Memorandum (Eastern), 29 August 1924, ibid., M 00370/24, Adm 116/3125; Richmond (Admiralty) to Sir Oswyn Murray, 13 April 1925, ibid., M 00382/25.

33 Memorandum by Churchill, 29 June 1927, *Cabinet Papers*, CP 189(27), Cab 24/187; Amery, *The Leo Amery Diaries*, vol. 1, pp. 14-5. (Diary entry for 4 July 1927.)

34 *Cabinet Conclusions*, 38(27)5 of 4 July 1927, Cab 23/55; Foreign Office to Howard, 4 July 1927, *FO Papers*, W 6229/61/98, FO 371/12670. The latter version has an 'of' between 'conditions' and 'limiting'.

35 Memorandum by the Sea Lords, [January 1927], *Admiralty Papers*, Adm 167/76.

36 Kellogg to Coolidge, 28 June 1927, *FRUS*, 1927 vol. 1, p. 63; Kellogg to Gibson, 6 July 1927, ibid., p. 74; *RCLNA*, pp. 54-5.

37 Ibid., pp. 140-2. The discussions in the Technical Committee which led to these agreements can be followed in ibid., pp. 89-109.

38 Ibid., pp. 140-2. The American reservation was redrafted when it was decided to release the Technical Committee's report to the press, see ibid., pp. 57-9, 142-4.

39 Ibid., p. 92.

40 Ibid., pp. 82-3

41 Ibid., pp. 109-10

42 United States Archives, General Board No. 438, Serial 1347-7(c) of 25 April 1927, Naval Record Group 80, cited in R.G. O'Connor, *Perilous Equilibrium*, p. 16

43 Final Minutes of Third Conference of British Empire Delegations held on 24 June 1927, *LNA Records*, Cab 27/350; *RCLNA*, p. 84; Kellogg to Houghton, 12 July 1927, *FRUS*, 1927 vol. 1, pp. 101-2; Minute by Binney (Admiralty), 29 July 1927, *Admiralty Papers*, PD 02896/27, Adm 116/3371.

44 Memorandum by the Sea Lords, [January 1927], ibid., Adm 167/76; Memorandum by the Naval Staff, 14 April 1927, *CID Memoranda*, 808-B, Cab 4/16; *RCLNA*, pp. 28, 82; *CID Minutes*, 228th meeting, 7 July 1927, Cab 2/5; Minutes of Eighth Conference of British Delegations, held on 11 July 1927, *LNA Records*, Cab 27/350; Steel-Maitland (Minister of Labour) to Cecil, 29 July 1927, *Cecil Papers*, BM Add MSS 51099; Neville Chamberlain Diary, 30 July 1927, *Neville Chamberlain Papers*, NC 2/22.

45 Memorandum by the Sea Lords, [January 1927], *Admiralty Papers*, Adm 167/76; Plans Division Memorandum, 12 October 1928, ibid., M 03152/28, Adm 116/3629; War Memorandum (Eastern), 29 August 1924, ibid., M 00370/24, Adm 116/3125; Memorandum by the Naval Staff, 14 April 1927, *CID Memoranda*, 808-B, Cab 4/16; *Cabinet Conclusions*, 38(27)5 of 4 July 1927, Cab 23/55; *RCLNA*, pp. 28-9. According to Gibson, Captain W. Egerton, a junior member of the British delegation, claimed an 'irreducible minimum' of *seventy-five* cruisers, see Gibson to Kellogg, 2 July 1927, *FRUS*, 1927 vol. 1, p. 66.

46 *RCLNA*, p. 34; London to Foreign Office, 14 July 1927, *FO Papers*, W 6660/61/98, FO 371/12672.

47 London to Foreign Office, 16 July 1927, ibid., W 6722/61/98.

48 Memorandum by Churchill, 29 June 1927, *Cabinet Papers*, CP 189(27), Cab 24/187; *Cabinet Conclusions*, 39(27)8 of 6 July 1927, Cab 23/55; London to Foreign Office, 5 July 1927, ibid., W 6269/61/98, FO 371/12670; London to Foreign Office, 5 July 1927, ibid., W 6270/61/98; Foreign Office to London, 7 July 1927, ibid., W 6352/61/98, FO 371/12671.

49 *CID Minutes*, 228th meeting, 7 July 1927, Cab 2/5; Code Telegram to British Delegation at Geneva, No. 102 of 7 July 1927, *CID Memoranda*, 816-B Revise, Cab 4/16; Memorandum by Beatty, 7 July 1927, ibid., 818-B.

50 Foreign Office to London, 7 July 1927, *FO Papers*, W 6352/61/98, FO 371/12671.

51 Ibid.
52 *CID Minutes*, 229th meeting, 14 July 1927, Cab 2/5.
53 Ibid; Foreign Office to London, 14 July 1927, *FO Papers*, W 6647/61/98, FO 371/12672.
54 London to Foreign Office, 14 July 1927, ibid., W 6656/61/98; Foreign Office to London, 15 July 1927, ibid.
55 Foreign Office to London, 15 July 1927, ibid., W 6705/61/98.
56 *LNA Minutes*, 1st meeting, 15 July 1927, Cab 27/350; Chamberlain to Cecil, 5 July 1927, *Cecil Papers*, BM Add MSS 51079; Minute by Chamberlain, 7 July 1927, *Balfour Papers*, BM Add MSS 49749; Hankey to Chamberlain, 15 July 1927, *FO Papers*, W 6705/61/98, FO 371/12672.
57 London to Foreign Office, 15 July 1927, ibid., W 6719/61/98.
58 Cecil to Chamberlain, 17 July 1927, *Chamberlain Papers*, AC 54/89.
59 Ibid.
60 London to Foreign Office, 16 July 1927, *FO Papers*, W 6721/98, FO 371/12672.
61 *LNA Minutes*, 2nd meeting, 18 July 1927, Cab 27/350; Foreign Office to London, 18 July 1927, *FO Papers*, W 6722/61/98, FO 371/12672.
62 *LNA Minutes*, 3rd meeting, 19 July 1927, Cab 27/350.
63 *Cabinet Conclusions*, 43(27)1 of 22 July 1927, Cab 23/55.
64 Memorandum by Bridgeman and Cecil, 23 July 1927, *LNA Memoranda*, LNA(27)2, Cab 27/350.
65 Draft Statement by Balfour, 22 July 1927, *Cabinet Conclusions*, 43(27) Appendix, Cab 23/55.
66 Cecil to Chamberlain, 24 July 1927, *Chamberlain Papers*, AC 54/90.
67 Conclusions of the Cabinet Committee, 26 July 1927, *Cabinet Papers*, CP 212(27), Cab 24/188; Final Modified Anglo–Japanese Scheme, undated, *Cabinet Conclusions*, 44(27) Appendix 2, Cab 23/55.
68 Ibid., 44(27)1 of 26 July 1927; Hankey to Baldwin, 28 July 1927, *Baldwin Papers*, vol. 130. Hankey asserts that Bridgeman, Cecil, Balfour and Salisbury were included in the minority; but the Cabinet records show that Salisbury was not present at the crucial meeting of 26 July. The three other members of the Cabinet associated with the minority view were therefore probably Chamberlain, who is known to have favoured the policy pursued by the Geneva delegates on most questions and intimated to the Prime Minister that he favoured an agreement based on the Anglo–Japanese proposals (see Chamberlain to Baldwin, 22 July 1926, ibid.), and, less certainly, Neville Chamberlain (see Neville Chamberlain Diary, 30 July 1927, *Neville Chamberlain Papers*, NC 2/22) and Lord Eustace Percy, who were instrumental in suggesting a new compromise, based on the eight-inch gun, on the final day of the conference. Churchill, Birkenhead and Sir William Joynson-Hicks are known to have opposed Cecil's line (see ibid., also Joynson-Hicks to Cecil, 7 September 1927, *Cecil Papers*, BM Add MSS 51165; also Cecil to Chamberlain, 16 August 1927, *Chamberlain Papers*, AC 54/95), while Cecil severely criticized the attitude of Worthington-Evans and Walter Guinness towards disarmament as a whole (see ibid.). Presumably these two members of the Cabinet were in the majority faction on 26 July. If these deductions are correct, the five other Cabinet members in attendance (Hoare, Cunliffe-Lister, Sir Douglas Hogg, Viscount Peel and Sir John Gilmour) must have opposed the concessions urged by Bridgeman and Cecil.
69 See, e.g., *LNA Minutes*, 1st and 5th meetings, 15 and 25 July 1927, Cab 27/350.

70 Cecil to Salisbury, 31 July 1927, *Cecil Papers*, BM Add MSS 51086. Cecil puts the date of the crucial Cabinet meeting at 25 July 1927, but this is either a misprint or an error on his part.

71 Ibid; Neville Chamberlain Diary, 30 July 1927, *Neville Chamberlain Papers*, NC 2/22.

72 Third Revise of Draft Statement, 26 July 1927, *Cabinet Conclusions*, 44(27) Appendix 1, Cab 23/55.

73 Bridgeman to Chamberlain, 6 August 1927, *FO Papers*, W 8063/61/98, FO 371/12674.

74 London to Foreign Office, 28 July 1927, ibid., W 7184/61/98, FO 371/12673; *RCLNA*, p. 122.

75 London to Foreign Office, 28 July 1927, *FO Papers*, W 7184/61/98, FO 371/12673; London to Foreign Office, 28 July 1927, ibid., W 7192/61/98; Bridgeman to Cecil, 17 April 1928, *Cecil Papers*, BM Add MSS 51099.

76 *Cabinet Conclusions*, 46(27)1 of 29 July 1927, Cab 23/55; Foreign Office to London, 29 July 1927, *FO Papers*, W 7192/61/98, FO 371/12673. See also, Neville Chamberlain Diary, 30 July 1927, *Neville Chamberlain Papers*, NC 2/22.

77 *RCLNA*, pp. 122, 125; London to Foreign Office, 1 August 1927, *FO Papers*, W 7273/61/98, FO 371/12673; London to Foreign Office, 1 August 1927, ibid., W 7276/61/98; London to Foreign Office, 2 August 1927, ibid., W 7277/61/98; Minutes of Twelfth Conference of British Delegations, held on 1 August 1927, *LNA Records*, Cab 27/350; Alternative Draft Political Clause, Minutes of Twelfth Conference of British Delegations, Appendix 4, ibid., Cab 27/350.

78 *RCLNA*, pp. 126-7; Kellogg to Coolidge, 3 August 1927, *FRUS*, 1927 vol. 1, pp. 148-9; London to Foreign Office, 2 August 1927, *FO Papers*, W 7311/61/98, FO 371/12673; London to Foreign Office, 2 August 1927, ibid., W 7312/61/98.

79 London to Foreign Office, 31 July 1927, ibid., W 7230/61/98; Cecil to Salisbury, 31 July 1927, *Cecil Papers*, BM Add MSS 51086.

80 [Cecil to Salisbury], 1 August 1927, ibid.

81 Salisbury to Cecil, 3 August 1927, ibid; *Cabinet Conclusions*, 47(27) of 3 August 1927, Cab 23/55; Chamberlain to Ida Chamberlain, 7 August 1927, *Chamberlain Papers*, AC 5/1/427. Beatty's appointment had come to an amicable end after successive terms lasting some 7½ years.

82 *Cabinet Conclusions*, 47(27) of 3 August 1927, Cab 23/55; Salisbury to Cecil, 3 August 1927, *Cecil Papers*, BM Add MSS 51086; Foreign Office to London, 3 August 1927, *FO Papers*, W 7312/61/98, FO 371/12673.

83 London to Foreign Office, 4 August 1927, ibid., W 7363/61/98.

84 *RCLNA*, p. 126.

85 Note by Hankey, 6 July 1927, *CID Memoranda*, 815-B, Cab 4/16.

86 *NPC Minutes*, 3rd meeting, 22 November 1927, Cab 27/355.

87 Ibid., 3rd and 4th meetings, 22 November and 1 December 1927.

88 Memorandum by Churchill, 6 November 1927, *NPC Memoranda*, NP(27)2, Cab 27/355.

89 RCLNA, pp. 138, 145, 154.

90 *NPC Minutes*, 3rd and 4th meetings, 22 November and 1 December 1927, Cab 27/355.

91 Chamberlain to Baldwin, 22 July 1927, *Baldwin Papers*, vol. 130.

92 Campbell ˙to Villiers, 16 July 1927, *FO Papers*, W 7297/61/98, FO 371/12673.

93 *Cabinet Conclusions*, 44(27)1 of 26 July 1927, Cab 23/55; Minute [for

Controller], 24 August 1927, *Admiralty Papers*, PD 02909/27, Adm 116/3371; Beatty to Field, 10 July 1927, ibid.

94 See *CID Minutes*, 227th meeting, 20 May 1927, Cab 2/5; Beatty to Field, 10 July 1927, *Admiralty Papers*, PD 02909/27, Adm 116/3371.

95 London to Foreign Office, 28 July 1927, *FO Papers*, W 7184/61/98, FO 371/12673; Cecil to Salisbury, 31 July 1927, *Cecil Papers*, BM Add MSS 51086.

96 Memorandum by Egerton, 18 August 1927, *Admiralty Papers*, PD 02909/27, Adm 116/3371; Gibson to Kellogg, 18 July 1927, *FRUS*, 1927 vol. 1, p. 113; Kellogg to Gibson, 19 July 1927, ibid., p. 116; Kellogg to Coolidge, 22 July 1927, ibid., p. 126. It seems that the Americans would have insisted on building fifteen 'Washington standard' cruisers; see Campbell to Villiers, 10 July 1927, *FO Papers*, W 7351/61/98, FO 371/12673; 'Geneva 1927, Diary of Frank H. Schofield', pp. 84–5, 16 July 1927, in United States Archives, General Board files, cited in O'Connor, p. 18.

97 Cf. Howard to Foreign Office, 14 July 1927, *FO Papers*, W 6683/61/98, FO 371/12672; Gibson to Kellogg, 5 July 1927, *FRUS*, 1927 vol. 1, p. 71.

98 London to Foreign Office, 17 July 1927, *FO Papers*, W 6824/61/98, FO 371/12672.

99 *Cabinet Conclusions*, 38(27)5 of 4 July 1927, Cab 23/55.

Chapter 10

1 Salisbury to Cecil, 3 August 1927, *Cecil Papers*, BM Add MSS 51086; Salisbury to Cecil, 4 August 1927, ibid; Cecil to Chamberlain, 7 August 1927, *Chamberlain Papers*, AC 54/92.

2 Chamberlain to Cecil, 8 August 1927, *Cecil Papers*, BM Add MSS 51079.

3 Cecil to Chamberlain, 10 August 1927, *Chamberlain Papers*, AC 54/93.

4 Chamberlain to Cecil, 14 August 1927, *Cecil Papers*, BM Add MSS 51079.

5 Ibid.

6 Ibid.

7 Cecil to Chamberlain, 16 August 1927, *Chamberlain Papers*, AC 54/95. 'F.E.' was Lord Birkenhead and 'Jix' Sir William Joynson-Hicks.

8 Ibid.

9 Cecil to Gilbert Murray, 17 August 1927, *Murray Papers*, Box 16c; Cecil to Irwin, 29 September 1927, *Cecil Papers*, BM Add MSS 51084; [Cecil] to Bridgeman, 18 November 1927, ibid., BM Add MSS 51099.

10 Cecil to Chamberlain, 16 August 1927, *Chamberlain Papers*, AC 54/95.

11 Cecil to Chamberlain, 21 August 1927, ibid., AC 54/96.

12 Cecil to Baldwin, 9 August 1927, *Registered Files*, Cab 21/297.

13 Ibid.

14 Cecil to Baldwin, 25 August 1927, ibid.

15 [Summary by Hankey of events in regard to Lord Cecil's resignation], 30 August 1927, ibid.

16 Ibid; [Cecil] to Salisbury, 2 September 1927, *Cecil Papers*, BM Add MSS 51086.

17 Ibid; Hankey to Baldwin, 30 August 1927, *Registered Files*, Cab 21/297; [Summary by Hankey of events in regard to Lord Cecil's resignation], 30 August 1927, ibid. This registered file deals exclusively with Cecil's resignation and gives the form of all Cecil's minutes except an unimportant 'fourth version'; it also gives the replies drafted by Hankey

and other relevant documents.

18 Cecil to Baldwin, 25 August 1927, ibid.

19 Hankey to Baldwin, 30 August 1927, ibid; Hankey to Balfour, 30 August 1927, ibid.

20 [Draft Reply by Hankey], undated, ibid.

21 Baldwin to Cecil, 29 August 1927, ibid.

22 Chamberlain to Tyrrell, 19 September 1927, *Chamberlain Papers*, AC 54/482.

23 Bridgeman to Baldwin, 21 August 1927, *Baldwin Papers*, vol. 131.

24 Chamberlain to Baldwin, 12 September 1927, ibid., vol. 129.

25 See, e.g., Chamberlain to Cecil, 5 July 1927, *Cecil Papers*, BM Add MSS 51079.

26 Beatty to Lady Beatty, 17 June 1927, cited in W.S. Chalmers, *Life and Letters of David, Earl Beatty*, p. 414.

27 Crewe to Chamberlain, 12 April 1927, *Chamberlain Papers*, AC 54/126; Cecil to Chamberlain, 17 June 1927; ibid., AC 54/86; Chamberlain to Cecil, 5 July 1927, *Cecil Papers*, BM Add MSS 51079.

28 Memorandum by Cadogan, 17 May 1927, *FO Papers*, W 4575/61/98, FO 371/12667; Minute by Gregory, 26 May 1927, ibid; Lindsay to Chamberlain, 31 August 1927, *Chamberlain Papers*, AC 54/337.

29 Minute by Chamberlain, 27 May 1927, *FO Papers*, W 4575/61/98, FO 371/12667; Minute by Cecil, 20 May 1927, ibid., W 4742/61/98.

30 Baldwin to Chamberlain, 6 September 1927, *Chamberlain Papers*, AC 54/29.

31 Onslow to Tyrrell, 22 September 1927, *FO Papers*, W 9063/61/98, FO 371/12675; Proposal of the French Delegation, 16 September 1927, ibid., W 8860/61/98.

32 Ibid.

33 Cadogan to Villiers, 18 September 1927, ibid., W 8979/61/98.

34 Ibid.

35 Chamberlain to Tyrrell, 18 September 1927, ibid., W 8894/61/98; Onslow to Tyrrell, 22 September 1927, ibid., W 9063/61/98; Chamberlain to Tyrrell, 19 September 1927, *Chamberlain Papers*, AC 54/482.

36 Onslow to Tyrrell, 22 September 1927, *FO Papers*, W 9236/61/98, FO 371/12675; Drummond to Chamberlain, 24 October 1927, ibid., W 10040/61/98, FO 371/12676.

37 Memorandum by Hoare, 6 October 1927, *Cabinet Papers*, CP 234(27), Cab 24/188.

38 Ibid.

39 *Cabinet Conclusions*, 50(27)9 of 12 October 1927, Cab 23/55.

40 Disarmament Policy Committee (hereafter cited as PRA) Report, 23 November 1927, *Cabinet Papers*, CP 293(27) Revise, Cab 24/189.

41 Ibid; Memorandum by Worthington-Evans, 24 October 1927, *PRA Memoranda*, PRA(27)3, Cab 27/362; Admiralty Memorandum, 18 November 1927, ibid., PRA(27)12; *PRA Minutes*, 3rd meeting, 21 November 1927, Cab 27/361.

42 Admiralty Memorandum, 18 November 1927, *PRA Memoranda*, PRA(27)12, Cab 27/362.

43 PRA Report, 23 November 1927, *Cabinet Papers*, CP 293(27) Revise, Cab 24/189.

44 Ibid; Memorandum by Hoare, 6 October 1927, ibid., CP 234(27), Cab 24/188.

45 Hankey to Tyrrell, 18 October 1927, *FO Papers*, W 9868/61/98, FO

371/12676. [Memorandum by Hankey]: Disarmament: A Suggestion for increasing Security, 18 October 1927, ibid; Clinton to Hankey, 19 October 1927, *CID Memoranda*, 846-B, Annexure 2, Cab 4/17; Note by Clinton, 20 October 1927, ibid.

46 Minute by Kirkpatrick, 20 October 1927, *FO Papers*, W 9868/61/98, FO 371/12676; Minute by Chamberlain, 21 October 1927, ibid. Hankey later laid the scheme before the Committee of Imperial Defence where it died a natural death; see *CID Memoranda*, 846-B and annexures, Cab 4/17; *CID Minutes*, 231st Meeting, 19 December 1927, Cab 2/5.

47 See, e.g., Cadogan to Villiers, 18 September 1927, *FO Papers*, W 8979/61/98, FO 371/12675; Minute by Kirkpatrick, 22 September 1927, ibid; Minute by Villiers, 23 September 1927, ibid.

48 Minute by Hurst, 3 November 1927, ibid., 10403/61/98, FO 371/12676.

49 *Compulsory Arbitration Committee Report*, 25 October 1926, Cab 27/330; Minute by Kirkpatrick, 3 November 1927, *FO Papers*, W 10403/61/98, FO 371/12676; Minute by Chamberlain, 7 November 1927; ibid. One member of the Cabinet committee, Cecil, favoured compulsory jurisdiction of justiciable disputes; see Memorandum by Cecil, 23 October 1926, *Cabinet Papers*, CP 360(26), Cab 24/181.

50 Minute by Hurst, 3 November 1927, *FO Papers*, W 10403/61/98, FO 371/12676; Minute by Chamberlain, 7 November 1927, ibid.

51 Minute by Chamberlain, 27 October 1927, *Cabinet Papers*, CP 256(27), Cab 24/189; Minute by Kirkpatrick, 3 November 1927, *FO Papers*, W 10403/61/98, FO 371/12676; Minute by Chamberlain, 7 November 1927, ibid.

52 Minute by Chamberlain, 27 October 1927, *Cabinet Papers*, CP 256(27), Cab 24/189. For the origin and history of the Finnish proposals, see League of Nations Section Memorandum, January 1927, *FO Papers*, W 1059/61/98, FO 371/12660. For Chamberlain's attitude, see Minute by Chamberlain, 27 October 1927, *Cabinet Papers*, CP 256(27), Cab 24/189. For the Treasury's attitude, see Leith-Ross (Treasury) to Tyrrell, 12 August 1927, ibid., W 7692/61/98, FO 371/12674.

53 PRA Report, 23 November 1927, *Cabinet Papers*, CP 293(27) Revise, Cab 24/189.

54 Ibid; *PRA Minutes*, 1st and 2nd meetings, 8 and 15 November 1927, Cab 27/361.

55 *Cabinet Conclusions*, 57(27)3 of 23 November 1927 and 58(27)3 of 24 November 1927.

56 Ibid., 49(27)5 of 25 August 1927 and 55(27)3 of 11 November 1927; *NPC Minutes*, 1st meeting, 10 November 1927, Cab 27/355. The Admiralty found, much to its chagrin, that the breakdown of the Geneva Naval Conference had led to a reduction in the British construction programme without any corresponding reductions in the American and Japanese programmes.

57 Memorandum by Chamberlain, 26 October 1927, *Cabinet Papers*, CP 258(27), Cab 24/189; Memorandum by Chamberlain, 16 October 1927, ibid., CP 258(27), Appendix 2; McNeill (Cushendun) to Chamberlain, 4 November 1927, *Chamberlain Papers*, AC 54/387; Chamberlain to McNeill, 7 November 1927, ibid., AC 54/151; *Cabinet Conclusions*, 57(27)7 of 23 November 1927, Cab 23/55.

58 See, e.g., Minute by Cecil, 18 August 1926, *FO Papers*, W 7802/78/98, FO 371/11886; Cecil to Chamberlain, 4 March 1927, *Chamberlain Papers*, AC 54/61; Cecil to Chamberlain, 24 March 1927, ibid., AC 54/67; Salisbury to Cecil, 9 April 1927, *Cecil Papers*, BM Add MSS 51086.

59 Chamberlain to Cecil, 28 March 1927, ibid., BM Add MSS 51079; Chamberlain to Crewe, 8 April 1927, *Crewe Papers*, Box C/8; [Berthelot (head of Quai d'Orsay) to Fleuriau], 11 April 1927, ibid.
60 Cushendun to Chamberlain, 14 November 1927, *Chamberlain Papers*, AC 54/152.
61 *DPC*, Series V, pp. 9-12, 23-6.
62 Ibid., pp. 13-7, 24-9.
63 *NPC Minutes*, 2nd meeting, 18 November 1927, Cab 27/355.
64 Minute by Chamberlain, 27 October 1927, *Cabinet Papers*, CP 256(27), Cab 24/189.
65 Memorandum by Worthington-Evans, 24 October 1927, ibid., CP 254(27); PRA Report, 23 November 1927, ibid, CP 293(27) Revise.

Chapter 11

1 Kelly to Sir Oswyn Murray, 29 November 1927, *Admiralty Papers*, M 03426/27, Adm 116/2578.
2 See ibid.
3 Kelly to Field, 3 December 1927, ibid., M 03486/27.
4 Kelly to Field, 7 December 1927, ibid., M 03426/27.
5 Minute by Egerton, 8 December 1927, ibid., Plans Division Memorandum, 15 December 1927, ibid; Egerton to Field, 16 December 1927, ibid; Admiralty Memorandum, December 1927, *PRA Memoranda*, PRA(27)20, Cab 27/362.
6 Temperley to Cushendun, 7 December 1927, ibid; PRA(27)19.
7 Cushendun to Chamberlain, 9 December 1927, *FO Papers*, W 11629/61/98, FO 371/12677.
8 Ibid; Chamberlain to Cushendun, 12 December 1927, ibid; Memorandum by Cushendun, 20 January 1928, *Cabinet Papers*, CP 16(28), Cab 24/192.
9 Observations of His Majesty's Government, undated, *DPC*, Series VI, pp. 166-76. The version in the PRA archives is dated 8 February 1928; see *PRA Memoranda*, PRA(27)22, Cab 27/362.
10 For an extended discussion of the concept of 'harmony of interests' see E.H. Carr, *The Twenty Years' Crisis 1919-1939*, pp. 41-62.
11 *PRA Minutes*, 4th meeting, 10 February 1928, Cab 27/361.
12 Ibid.
13 Ibid., 4th and 5th meetings, 10 and 13 February 1928; PRA Report, 14 February 1928, *Cabinet Papers*, CP 44(28), Cab 24/192; *Cabinet Conclusions*, 8(28)3 of 17 February 1928, Cab 23/57. Cf. Chamberlain's comment to Gilbert Murray: 'The present Government have consistently supported the League and based their whole foreign policy upon the League.' Chamberlain to Gilbert Murray, 11 January 1928, *Chamberlain Papers*, AC 55/38.
14 *DPC*, Series VI, p. 181.
15 See ibid., pp. 15-18, 225, for the submission of the German proposals.
16 Suggestions of the German Delegation, undated, ibid., p. 225; Cushendun to Chamberlain, 29 February 1928, *FO Papers*, W 1977/28/98, FO 371/13373.
17 Ibid; *PRA Minutes*, 7th, 8th and 9th meetings, 7 May, 21 and 22 June 1928, Cab 27/361; *Chiefs of Staff Committee Minutes*, 70th, 71st and 72nd meetings, 30 May, 18 June and 21 June 1928, Cab 53/2; PRA Report, 23 June 1928, *Cabinet Papers*, CP 203(28), Cab 24/196; Reports by the

Chiefs of Staff Sub-Committee, 4, 18 and 21 June 1928, ibid., CP 203(28), Enclosures 1, 3 and 4; Note by Hurst, undated, ibid., CP 203(28), Enclosure 2; Memorandum by Jacquemyns, 25 May 1928, ibid., CP 203(28), Enclosure 2, Appendix.

18 PRA Report, 23 June 1928, ibid., CP 203(28).
19 For the text, see *DPC*, Series VII, pp. 123-4.
20 For the text of the General Act, see *League of Nations, Official Journal*, Special Supplement 64, pp. 492-7.
21 See ibid., article 28, also Carr, *op. cit.*, pp. 202-3.
22 The pact has also been termed, *inter alia*, the Briand-Kellogg Pact (since it originated in a suggestion made by the French Foreign Minister in a personal message to the American People on 6 April 1927, the anniversary of American entry into the First World War, that France and the United States might sign a mutual undertaking to outlaw war between the two countries), the Kellogg-Briand Pact, the Pact of Paris, the Peace Pact and the Peace Pact of Paris. Officially, the pact was termed the General Treaty for the Renunciation of War.
23 Chamberlain to Houghton, 19 May 1928, *Cabinet Papers*, CP 212(28), Appendix 1, Cab 24/196.
24 Memorandum by Bridgeman, 11 February 1928, *PRA Memoranda*, PRA(27)23 Revise, Cab 27/362.
25 Ibid.
26 Chamberlain to Crewe, 9 February 1928, *Chamberlain Papers*, AC 55/89; Fleuriau to Chamberlain, 9 February 1928, ibid., AC 55/156; Chamberlain to Fleuriau, 11 February 1928, ibid., AC 55/157; Crewe to Chamberlain, 12 February 1928, ibid., AC 55/90; *PRA Minutes*, 4th and 5th meetings, 10 and 13 February 1928, Cab 27/361. For some reason (scepticism? forgetfulness?) Chamberlain omitted to mention that the proposed tripartite agreement would cover only metropolitan-based air forces and not overseas forces, but when he filled in the details with Briand the following month the reaction to the proposal was equally negative. See Foreign Office Record, 10 March 1928, *Cabinet Papers*, CP 82(28), Cab 24/193.
27 *PRA Minutes*, 4th and 5th meetings, 10 and 13 February 1928, Cab 27/361; PRA Report, 14 February 1928, *Cabinet Papers*, CP 44(28), Cab 24/192.
28 *PRA Minutes*, 5th meeting, 13 February 1928, Cab 27/361.
29 PRA Report, 14 February 1928, *Cabinet Papers*, CP 44(28), Cab 24/192.
30 *Cabinet Conclusions*, 8(28)3 of 17 February 1928, Cab 23/57; Memorandum by Cushendun, 4 March 1928, *FO Papers*, W 2173/28/98, FO 371/13374. Briand and Chamberlain were in Geneva for the March session of the League Council.
31 Ibid.
32 Foreign Office Record, 10 March 1928, *Cabinet Papers*, CP 81(28), Cab 24/193; Memorandum by Kelly, 10 March 1928, *Admiralty Papers*, M 0796/28, Adm 116/2578. The British compromise proposal was handed to the French by means of a Chamberlain-Briand letter of 10 March. See [Chamberlain] to Briand, 10 March 1928, *FO Papers*, W 2473/28/98, FO 371/13374.
33 Foreign Office Record, 10 March 1928, *Cabinet Papers*, CP 81(28), Cab 24/193.
34 Ibid; Minute by Flint, 13 March 1928, *Admiralty Papers*, M 0796/28, Adm 116/2578; Kelly to 'Admiral', undated, ibid., M 01691/28. There are no

objections by Kelly in the Foreign Office Record.

35 *PRA Minutes*, 6th meeting, 12 March 1928, Cab 27/361; Draft telegram to Cushendun, undated, *Cabinet Papers*, CP 79(28), Cab 24/193; *Cabinet Conclusions*, 14(28)3 of 13 March 1928, Cab 23/57.

36 Cushendun to Salisbury, 21 March 1928, *Cabinet Papers*, CP 101(28), Cab 24/194; Cushendun to Chamberlain, 2 April 1928, *FO Papers*, W 3343/28/98, FO 371/13376; *DPC*, Series V, pp. 239-77, 279-85, 307-13; Draft Convention for Immediate, Complete and General Disarmament, undated, ibid., pp. 324-37; [Soviet] Memorandum explaining the Draft Convention for Immediate, Complete and General Disarmament, undated, ibid., pp. 337-9; Soviet Draft Convention [for partial disarmament], undated, ibid., pp. 347-55.

37 *Cabinet Conclusions*, 15(28)4 of 21 March 1928 and 16(28)6 of 28 March 1928, Cab 23/57; *DPC*, Series V, pp. 245-51.

38 Proposal by Count Bernstorff, undated, ibid., pp. 315-23.

39 Ibid., p. 277.

40 Chamberlain to Salisbury, 24 March 1928, *Chamberlain Papers*, AC 55/452.

41 Crewe to Chamberlain, 28 March 1928, ibid., AC 55/102; Chamberlain to Crewe, 29 March 1928; *Crewe Papers*, Box C/8. For Italian reservations on the negotiations referred to by Clauzel, see Cushendun to Chamberlain, 2 April 1928, *FO Papers*, W 3343/28/98, FO 371/13376, also *DPC*, Series V, pp. 294, 304.

42 London to Foreign Office, 14 March 1928, *FO Papers*, W 2536/28/98, FO 371/13374; Memorandum by Cushendun, 1 May 1928, *PRA Memoranda*, PRA(27)45, Cab 27/362; Memorandum by Cadogan, 1 May 1928, *FO Papers*, W 4230/28/98, FO 371/13376.

43 Ibid; Kelly to Cushendun, 21 March 1928, *Cushendun Papers*, FO 800/228; Kelly to Field, 21 March 1928, *Admiralty Papers*, M 0945/28, Adm 1/8724/56.

44 Memorandum by Cushendun, 1 May 1928, *PRA Memoranda*, PRA(27)45, Cab 27/362.

45 Ibid.

46 Memorandum by Cadogan, 1 May 1928, *FO Papers*, W 4230/28/98, FO 371/13376.

47 Minute by Bellairs (Admiralty), 26 April 1928, *Admiralty Papers*, M 01188/28, Adm 116/2598; Minute by Kelly, 28 April 1928, ibid; Minute by Fisher (newly-appointed DCNS), 30 April 1928, ibid; Madden to Bridgeman, 2 May 1928, ibid; Minute by Bridgeman, 2 May 1928, ibid.

48 *PRA Minutes*, 7th meeting, 7 May 1928, Cab 27/361.

49 Chamberlain to Crewe, 8 May 1928, *Crewe Papers*, Box C/8; Crewe to Chamberlain, 9 May 1928, *Chamberlain Papers*, AC 55/109.

50 Memorandum by Bridgeman, 11 May 1928, *Cabinet Papers*, CP 190(28), Cab 24/195.

51 Cost of building and maintaining a Cruiser force of sixty vessels under twenty years of age: [Admiralty Memorandum], undated, ibid., CP 190(28), Appendix. See also, Memorandum by Cushendun, 16 May 1928, ibid., CP 191(28) and Memorandum by Cadogan, 1 May 1928, *FO Papers*, W 4230/28/98, FO 371/13376.

52 *Cabinet Conclusions*, 31(28)1 of 6 June 1928, Cab 23/58.

53 Ibid.

54 *Cabinet Conclusions*, 31(28)1 of 6 June 1928, Cab 23/58; Hankey to Chamberlain, 7 June 1928, *Chamberlain Papers*, AC 55/235.

55 See Cazalet (Geneva) to Foreign Office, 7 June 1928, *FO Papers*, W
5461/28/98, FO 371/13377; *PRA Minutes*, 6th meeting, 12 March 1928,
Cab 27/361; *Cabinet Conclusions*, 14(28)3 of 13 March 1928, Cab 23/57.
56 D. Carlton, 'The Anglo-French Compromise on Arms Limitation, 1928',
Journal of British Studies, 8(1969), p. 146.
57 Foreign Office to Cazalet, 8 June 1928, *FO Papers*, W 5461/28/98, FO
371/13377. The Foreign Secretary had long accepted the general principle
that the full Cabinet was not the best place for discussing questions
bristling with technical points. See Chamberlain to Cecil, 14 August
1927, *Cecil Papers*, BM Add MSS 51079.
58 Cazalet to Foreign Office, 7 June 1928, *FO Papers*, W 5461/28/98, FO
371/13377.
59 Foreign Office Record, 10 March 1928, *Cabinet Papers*, CP 81(28), Cab
24/193; *Cabinet Conclusions*, 15(28)4 of 21 March 1928, Cab 23/57; *PRA
Minutes*, 7th meeting, 7 May 1928, Cab 27/361. Cf. [Fisher?] to Kelly, 11
June 1928, *Admiralty Papers*, M 01980/28, Adm 116/2578. Within the
Admiralty, two objections to the 'lines of communication' formula were
recorded in the period 10 March to 3 June: Minute by Bellairs, 16 March
1928, ibid., M 0796/28; Minute by Bellairs, 17 May 1928, ibid., M
01462/28.
60 Memorandum by Chamberlain, 9 June 1928, *Cabinet Papers*, CP 184(28),
Cab 24/195.
61 Ibid. Italics original.
62 Memorandum by Chamberlain, 9 June 1928, ibid., CP 183(28). Italics
original.
63 Ibid.
64 *Cabinet Conclusions*, 32(28)2 of 13 June 1928, Cab 23/58.
65 For the origin and text of Deleuze's proposals, see Kelly to Fisher, 5 June
1928, *Admiralty Papers*, M 01980/28, Adm 116/2578; also Plans Division
Memorandum, 22 June 1928, ibid., M 01981/28. For the Admiralty's
acceptance of the proposals and realization of the likely American
attitude towards them, see ibid; Minute by Bellairs, 8 June 1928, ibid.,
M 01980/28; Minute by Fisher, 8 June 1928, ibid; Minute by Madden, 9
June 1928, ibid; [Fisher?] to Kelly, 11 June 1928, ibid; Madden to
Bridgeman, 21 June 1928, ibid., M 01981/28; Minute by Fisher, 2 July
1928, ibid., M 01994/28. For Cushendun's views, see Memorandum by
Cushendun, 16 June 1928, *Cabinet Papers*, CP 189(28), Cab 24/195.
66 Memoranda by Chamberlain, 9 June 1928, ibid., CP 183(28) and CP
184(28); Memorandum by Cushendun, 16 June 1928, ibid., CP 189(28);
Memorandum by Salisbury, 18 June 1928, ibid., CP 193(28); *Cabinet
Conclusions*, 34(28)4 of 22 June 1928, Cab 23/58; Amery, *The Leo Amery
Diaries*, vol. 1, p. 546 (Diary entry for 22 June 1928). As tabled by
Bridgeman, the Deleuze proposals referred to the limitation of *all
cruisers of 10,000 tons and below* armed with guns above six-inch calibre,
not merely the cruisers *below 10,000 tons* armed with guns over six-inch
calibre referred to in Kelly's letter to Fisher of 5 June 1928. See ibid.
There is no foundation to Carlton's accusation that Chamberlain
impetuously took the lead in promoting the proposals (see Carlton, op.
cit., p. 150). The initiative was solely the Admiralty's and the prospective
move was considered fully by the Cabinet. Even Kelly admits to initial
Admiralty responsibility. See Kelly, 'Draft Memoirs', p. 43, *Kelly Papers*,
KEL/6.
67 Cushendun to Crewe, 26 June 1928, *FO Papers*, W 6039/28/98, FO

371/13377; London to Foreign Office, 27 June 1928, ibid., W 6087/28/98; Crewe to French Ministry for Foreign Affairs, 28 June 1928, ibid., W 6245/28/98; Memoranda by Kelly, 27 June 1928, *Admiralty Papers*, M 01994/28, Adm 116/2578.

68 Memorandum by Kelly, undated, *PRA Memoranda*, PRA(27)63, Cab 27/362; Kellogg to Sir Oswyn Murray, 16 July 1928, ibid; Violette to Kelly, 16 July 1928, ibid; Literal Translation of the French Note on Disarmament: Naval Armaments, undated, *Cabinet Papers*, CP 253(28), Appendix 1, Cab 24/197; Violette to Kelly, 19 July 1928, *Admiralty Papers*, M 02226/28, Adm 116/2579.

69 Memorandum by Bellairs, 16 July 1928, ibid., M 02130/28, Adm 116/2578; Minute by Fisher, 17 July 1928, ibid; Minute by Madden, 17 July 1928, ibid; Minute by Bridgeman, 17 July 1928, ibid.

70 See references in note 52; also *Cabinet Conclusions*, 39(28)19 of 18 July 1928, Cab 23/58 and [French] Ministry of Foreign Affairs to British Embassy [Paris], 20 July 1928, *FO Papers*, W 6987/28/98, FO 371/13379.

71 See PRA Report, 24 July 1928, *Cabinet Papers*, CP 253(28), Cab 24/197.

72 Memorandum by Bridgeman, 11 May 1928, ibid., CP 190(28), Cab 24/195.

73 PRA Report, 24 July 1928, ibid., CP 253(28), Cab 24/197; *Cabinet Conclusions*, 41(28)7 of 25 July 1928, Cab 23/58; Chamberlain to Henderson (Paris), 27 July 1928, *FO Papers*, W 6987/28/98, FO 371/13379; Foreign Office to Chilton (Washington), Dormer (Tokyo) and Graham, 30 July 1928, ibid. Chilton forwarded the agreement to Kellogg on 31 July. See Chilton to Kellogg, 31 July 1928, ibid., W 7873/28/98, FO 371/13380.

74 Kelly to 'Admiral', undated, *Admiralty Papers*, M 01980/28, Adm 116/2578; Memorandum by Cushendun, 1 May 1928, *PRA Memoranda*, PRA(27)45, Cab 27/362; Memorandum by Bridgeman, 11 May 1928, *Cabinet Papers*, CP 190(28), Cab 24/195; Hankey to Chamberlain, 7 June 1928, *Chamberlain Papers*, AC 55/235; Minute by Fisher, 21 June 1928, *Admiralty Papers*, M 01981/28, Adm 116/2578; Memorandum by Kelly, undated, *PRA Memoranda*, PRA(27)63, Cab 27/362. Cf. the British naval representative's statement in his draft memoirs, where he claims that the Americans might have accepted the agreement if the diplomatic arrangements had been handled correctly. See Kelly, 'Draft Memoirs', pp. 44-5, 47, *Kelly Papers*, KEL/6.

75 For fears of British isolation and the breakdown of the Preparatory Commission, see, e.g., Memorandum by Cushendun, 1 May 1928, *PRA Memoranda*, PRA(27)45, Cab 27/362; Cazalet to Foreign Office, 7 June 1928, *FO Papers*, W 5461/28/98, FO 371/13377; Memorandum by Chamberlain, 9 June 1928, *Cabinet Papers*, CP 183(28), Cab 24/195; Memorandum by Chamberlain, 9 June 1928, ibid., CP 184(28); Memorandum by Cushendun, 16 June 1928, ibid., CP 189(28); Memorandum by Salisbury, 18 June 1928, ibid., CP 193(28). For fears of a Franco-American accord, see, e.g., ibid; Memorandum by Cushendun, 1 May 1928, loc. cit; Memorandum by Cadogan, 1 May 1928, *PRA Memoranda*, PRA(27)46, Cab 27/362; Memorandum by Kelly, undated, ibid., PRA(27)63 (it is clear from the context that this memorandum was written on either 11 or 12 July 1928); Memorandum by Cushendun, 16 June 1928, loc. cit; Memorandum by Salisbury, 18 June 1928, loc. cit; Madden to Bridgeman, 21 June 1928, *Admiralty Papers*, M 01981/28, Adm 116/2578; Memorandum by Kelly, 27 June 1928, ibid., M 01994/28; Memorandum by Kelly, 28 June 1928, ibid., M 01998/28.

76 Speech by Chamberlain, 30 July 1928, *Parliamentary Debates, Commons*, 5th Series, vol. 220, cols. 1837-8; Hankey to Balfour, 25 October 1928, *Balfour Papers*, BM Add MSS 49705; Kelly, 'Draft Memoirs', p. 45, *Kelly Papers*, KEL/6.

77 Rumbold to Foreign Office, 4 August 1928, *FO Papers*, W 7409/28/98, FO 371/13379; Foreign Office to Rumbold, 5 August 1928, ibid; Cushendun to Chilton, 10 August 1928, ibid, W 7564/28/98 and W 7771/28/98; Cushendun to HM Reps in Washington, Paris, Rome and Tokyo, 11 August 1928, ibid., P 1223/2/150, FO 395/424; Atherton to Kellogg, 4 August 1928, *FRUS*, 1928 vol. 12, pp. 272-3; Atherton to Kellogg, 10 August 1928, ibid., pp. 273-5.

78 Wingfield (Rome) to Cushendun, 20 August 1928, *FO Papers*, W 8095/28/98, FO 371/13380; Graham to Cushendun, 19 October 1928, ibid., W 10074/28/98, FO 371/13381. On 4 September 1928, the Chief of the Italian Naval Staff, Admiral Burzagli, told the British naval attaché at Rome, Captain, R.H.L. Bevan, that the Italian government found nothing to object to in the compromise and had framed a favourable reply. See Bevan to Wingfield, 5 September 1928, ibid., W 8583/28/98, FO 371/13380.

79 Chilton to Foreign Office, 25 August 1928, ibid., W 8179/28/98; Statement by Cushendun, 30 August 1928, ibid., W 8352/28/98; Memorandum by Lindsay, 5 September 1928, ibid., W 8815/28/98. A copy of the forgery is preserved in the Foreign Office archives, ibid., W 8169/28/98.

80 See Foreign Office to Chilton, 21 September 1928, ibid., W 9042/28/98; Tyrrell to Foreign Office, 22 September 1928, ibid., W 9103/28/98; Campbell (Washington) to Foreign Office, 23 September 1928, ibid., W 9130/28/98; Foreign Office to Campbell (Washington), 26 September 1928, ibid; Campbell (Washington) to Foreign Office, 26 September 1928, ibid., W 9262/28/98; Houghton to Cushendun, 28 September 1928, ibid., W 9332/28/98.

81 Cushendun to Lindsay, 4 September 1928, *Cushendun Papers*, FO 800/228.

82 Ibid. Ronald Campbell (Foreign Office) put the matter more directly — '... we cannot publish the text of the "agreement" without revealing in its nakedness the ugly fact that it gives us what we failed to secure at Geneva, viz. liberty to build as many small cruisers as we like ....' Minute by Campbell, 3 September 1928, *FO Papers*, W 8272/28/98, FO 371/13380.

83 *Cabinet Conclusions*, 44(28)4 of 24 September 1928, Cab 23/58.

84 Dormer to Foreign Office, 13 September 1928, *FO Papers*, W 8733/28/98, FO 371/13380; Dormer to Foreign Office, 29 September 1928, ibid., W 9358/28/98, FO 371/13381; *Note verbale*, 6 October 1928, ibid., W 9685/28/98. In the event of a favourable American reply to the British note of 30 July, the Italians would have accepted the compromise. See Wingfield to Cushendun, 7 October 1928, ibid.

85 *Cabinet Conclusions*, 34(28)4 of 22 June 1928, Cab 23/58; Hankey to Chamberlain, 7 June 1928, *Chamberlain Papers*, AC 55/235; Memorandum by Cushendun, 16 June 1928, *Cabinet Papers*, CP 189(28), Cab 24/195. See also *PRA Minutes*, 7th meeting, 7 May 1928, Cab 27/361; Memorandum by Cushendun, 1 May 1928, *PRA Memoranda*, PRA(27)45, Cab 27/362.

86 Hankey to Chamberlain, 7 June 1928, *Chamberlain Papers*, AC 55/235.

Chapter 12

1 *Cabinet Conclusions*, 45(28)2 of 1 October 1928 and 46(28)2 of 10 October 1928. Cf. the original record of Chamberlain's conversation with Briand on 9 March 1928, Foreign Office Record, 10 March 1928, *Cabinet Papers*, CP 81(28), Cab 24/193 and the version published in the White Paper, Cmd 3211 of 1928. See also Amery, *The Leo Amery Diaries*, vol. 1, p. 566 (Diary entry for 10 October 1928).
2 Speech of 25 October 1928, *The Times*, 26 October 1928.
3 Memorandum by Percy, 12 October 1928, *Cabinet Papers*, CP 301(28), Cab 24/198. See also, Memorandum by Percy, 12 November 1928, *PRA Memoranda*, PRA(27)87, Cab 27/363.
4 *PRA Minutes*, 12th meeting, 2 November 1928, Cab 27/361; Bridgeman, 'Political Notes', pp. 161, 163, 165, 167, *Bridgeman Papers*; Speech by Bridgeman, 13 November 1928, *Parliamentary Debates, Commons*, Fifth Series, vol. 222, col. 834.
5 *PRA Minutes*, 12th meeting, 2 November 1928, Cab 27/361; Hoare to Baldwin, 15 October [1928], *Baldwin Papers*, vol. 129; Memorandum by Salisbury, 31 October 1928, *PRA Memoranda*, PRA(27)77, Cab 27/363; Memorandum by Campbell, 29 October 1928, ibid., PRA(27)79.
6 Admiralty Memorandum, 8 November 1928, ibid., PRA(27)84; *PRA Minutes*; 13th meeting, 9 November 1928, Cab 27/361.
7 *Cabinet Conclusions*, 55(28)2 of 7 December 1928, Cab 23/59.
8 Ibid; Memorandum by Churchill, 19 November 1928, *Cabinet Papers*, CP 358(28), Cab 24/199; Memorandum by Amery, 26 November 1928, ibid., CP 367(28).
9 *Cabinet Conclusions*, 55(28)2 of 7 December 1928 and 57(28)6 of 19 December 1928, Cab 23/59; Memorandum by Chamberlain, 13 December 1928, *FO Papers* W 11929/28/98, FO 371/13383.
10 Bridgeman to Baldwin, 23 December 1928, *Baldwin Papers*, vol. 163.
11 Chamberlain to Worthington-Evans, 14 January 1929, *Chamberlain Papers*, AC 55/515.
12 Memorandum by Temperley, 8 January 1928, *Cushendun Papers*, FO 800/228; Temperley to Butler (Cushendun's private secretary), 9 January 1929, ibid.
13 Memorandum by MacNeece Foster, 1 February 1929, *Cecil Papers*, BM Add MSS 51113; MacNeece Foster to Trenchard, 7 February 1929, ibid.
14 Minute by Hoare, 7 February 1929, ibid; Undated minute by Cushendun on Temperley to Butler, 9 January 1929, *Cushendun Papers*; FO 800/228.
15 Howard to Chamberlain, 7 December 1928, *FO Papers*, W 11585/28/98, FO 371/13382; Howard to Chamberlain, 19 December 1928, ibid., W 12298/28/98, FO 371/13383; Chamberlain to Bridgeman, 16 January 1929, *Chamberlain Papers*, AC 55/47.
16 Bridgeman to Chamberlain, 31 January 1929, ibid., AC 55/48; Naval Staff Memorandum, 31 January 1929, ibid., AC 55/49.
17 Chamberlain to Bridgeman, 1 February 1929, ibid., AC 55/50; Bridgeman to Chamberlain, 9 February 1929, ibid., AC 55/51.
18 Memorandum by Cadogan, 15 February 1929, *PRA Memoranda*, PRA(27)94, Cab 27/363; Memorandum by Cushendun, 20 February 1929, ibid., PRA(27)95; *PRA Minutes*, 14th meeting, 27 February 1929, Cab 27/361.
19 Minute by Temperley, 22 October 1928, *WO Papers*, WO 32/4102; Minute by Charles, 23 October 1928, ibid; Minute by Milne, 25 October 1928,

ibid; Minute by Charles, 29 October 1928, ibid; Minute by Milne, 12 November 1928, ibid.

20 Memorandum by Milne, 1 March 1929, *PRA Memoranda*, PRA(27)98, Cab 27/363. It should be noted that Milne implies that other powers would attempt to evade their obligations but not Britain!

21 Memorandum by Cushendun, 13 March 1929, ibid., PRA(27)100.

22 Ibid.

23 Ibid.

24 *PRA Minutes*, 15th meeting, 19 March 1929, Cab 27/361.

25 Ibid.

26 Ibid., 15th and 16th meetings, 19 and 22 March 1929; Draft Report by Salisbury, 20 March 1929, *PRA Memoranda*, PRA(27)103, Cab 27/363; Draft Outline of Declaration, undated, ibid., PRA(27)103, Annex; PRA Report, 22 March 1929, *Cabinet Papers*, CP 91(29) Revise, Cab 24/202; Outline of Declaration, undated, ibid., CP 91(29) Revise, Annex; *Cabinet Conclusions*, 13(29)4 of 26 March 1929, Cab 23/60.

27 Chamberlain to Howard, 26 March 1929, *FO Papers*, W 2796/50/98, FO 371/14103; Howard to Chamberlain, 4 April 1929, ibid., W 3137/50/98; Chamberlain to Howard, 8 April 1929, ibid; *Cabinet Conclusions*, 16(29)1 of 11 April 1929, Cab 23/60.

28 Chamberlain to Howard, 11 April 1929, *FO Papers*, W 3137/50/98, FO 371/14103; Howard to Chamberlain, 13 April 1929, ibid., W 3407/50/98; Patteson (Geneva) to Foreign Office, 16 April 1929, ibid., W 3614/50/98; Patteson to Foreign Office, 19 April 1929, ibid., W 3697/50/98; Cushendun to Chamberlain, 20 April 1929, ibid., W 3750/50/98; Record by Kelly, 15 April 1929, ibid., W 3750/50/98, Enclosure; Cushendun to Chamberlain, 20 April 1929, *Chamberlain Papers*, AC 55/128.

29 *Cabinet Conclusions*, 17(29)3 of 17 April 1929, Cab 23/60.

30 *DPC*, Series VIII, pp. 42-3.

31 Ibid., Series VIII, pp. 56-8.

32 Ibid., Series VIII, pp. 58-9; Patteson to Foreign Office, 23 April 1929, *FO Papers*, W 3848/50/98, FO 371/14103; Foreign Office to Patteson, 24 April 1929, ibid., W 3930/50/98; *Cabinet Conclusions*, 18(29)4 of 24 April 1929, Cab 23/60.

33 Ibid., 19(29)1 of 1 May 1929; Chamberlain to Howard, 1 May 1929, *FO Papers*, W 4263/50/98, FO 371/14103.

34 For the progress of the sixth session of the Preparatory Commission, see *DPC*, Series VIII.

35 Ibid., Series VIII, p. 182.

Chapter 13

1 There has, as yet, been no full-scale published study of the National government's disarmament policy. Recourse, however, can be made to P.J. Noel-Baker, *The First World Disarmament Conference, 1932-33*, A.C. Temperley, *The Whispering Gallery of Europe*, M. Vaïsse, *Sécurité d'abord* and an unpublished Ph.D. dissertation, J.J. Underwood, *The Roots and Reality of British Disarmament Policy 1932-34*. That the National government's handling of the disarmament problem was as incompetent as that of the second Baldwin government is hardly surprising since the composition of both the Cabinet and the foreign policy-making élite was essentially the same. See also an unpublished M.A.

dissertation, R.C. Richardson, *The Problem of Disarmament in British Diplomacy 1932-1934*, and Dick Richardson, 'Process and Progress in Disarmament: some Lessons of History', forthcoming in *TAPRI Yearbook 1989*.

2 See, e.g., Note by Butler, August 1925, *FO Papers*, W 7679/9/98, FO 371/11066.

3 See, e.g., Templewood, *Nine Troubled Years*, pp. 111-19.

4 See, e.g., R. Higham, *Armed Forces in Peacetime*, p. 285; R.R. James, *Churchill: A Study in Failure*, pp. 214-17; F.S. Northedge, *The Troubled Giant*, p. 330; Sir C. Petrie, *Twenty Years' Armistice — and after*, p. 71.

5 See, e.g., Chamberlain to Baldwin, 9 November 1924, *Baldwin Papers*, vol. 42.

6 See, e.g., Cecil, *A Great Experiment*, p. 163.

7 Memorandum by Cecil, 7 March 1927, *Cabinet Papers*, CP 79(27), Cab 23/54.

8 It is interesting to note that while Cecil's policy was criticized by more orthodox Conservatives at the time for being too weak, the essentials of his policy have constituted the new orthodoxy of Conservative disarmament policy in the post-1945 era — and have been criticized as being too militaristic. See D. Carlton, 'Disarmament with Guarantees: Lord Cecil 1922-1927', *Disarmament and Arms Control*, 3, 2, Autumn 1965, pp. 153-64.

9 J.W. Wheeler-Bennett, *Disarmament and Security since Locarno, 1925-1931* and *Information on the Reduction of Armaments*; R.A. Chaput, *Disarmament in British Foreign Policy*.

10 T. Jones, *Whitehall Diary*, vol. 2: 1926-1930, p. 115.

Bibliography

1 British government archives, Public Record Office

Admiralty Papers (Adm 1, Adm 116 and Adm 167)
Air Ministry Papers (Air 5, Air 8 and Air 9)
Cabinet Conclusions (Cab 23)
Cabinet Papers (Cab 24)
Chiefs of Staff Committee (Cab 53)
Committee of Imperial Defence Memoranda (Cab 2 and Cab 29)
Committee of Imperial Defence Minutes (Cab 4)
Foreign Office Papers (FO 371 and FO 395)
Arms Traffic Convention Committee (Cab 16/59 and Cab 27/274)
Compulsory Arbitration Committee (Cab 27/330)
Disarmament Policy Committee (Cab 27/361-3)
Foreign Policy — Security Committee (Cab 27/275)
Further Limitation of Naval Armaments Committee (Cab 27/350)
Geneva Protocol Committee (Cab 16/56)
Naval Programme Committee (Cab 27/273 and Cab 27/355)
Reduction and Limitation of Armaments Committee (Cab 16/61 and Cab 16/71-4)
Supply of Arms to Foreign Countries Committee (Cab 16/69)
Various private papers (FO 800 and Cab 63) (See Section 2 of Bibliography)
Registered Files (Cab 21)

2 Unpublished private papers

Stanley Baldwin	Cambridge University Library
Earl of Balfour	British Museum
William Bridgeman	Salop County Record Office
Viscount Cecil of Chelwood	British Museum
Austen Chamberlain	Birmingham University Library and Public Record Office
Neville Chamberlain	Birmingham University Library
Marquess of Crewe	Cambridge University Library
Baron Cushendun	Public Record Office
Viscount D'Abernon	British Museum
Sir Maurice Hankey	Archives Centre, Churchill College, Cambridge and Public Record Office

Sir Samuel Hoare   Cambridge University Library
Admiral Howard Kelly   National Maritime Museum
Gilbert Murray   Bodleian Library, Oxford
Admiral Sir Herbert Richmond   National Maritime Museum
Sir William Tyrrell   Public Record Office
Sir Laming Worthington-Evans   Bodleian Library, Oxford

3 Published documents and official sources

Belgium

Ministère des Affaires Etrangères, *Documents diplomatiques belges 1920–1940*, Ch. de Visscher and F. Vanlangenove (eds), Brussels, Palais des Academies, 1964–6 (4 vols).

France

Chambre des Deputés, *Débats parlementaires*, Paris, Imprimerie des Journaux Officiels, 1881 *et seq.*
Sénat, *Débats parlementaires*, Paris, Imprimerie des Journaux Officiels, 1881 *et seq.*
———, *Documents parlementaires*, Paris, Imprimerie des Journaux Officiels, 1881 *et seq.*

Germany

Auswärtiges Amt, *Akten zur deutschen auswärtigen Politik 1918–1945*, Series B, Göttingen, Vandenhoeck and Ruprecht, 1966 *et seq.*

Great Britain

Foreign Office, *Documents on British Foreign Policy 1919–1939*, Series IA, W.N. Medlicott, D. Dakin and M.E. Lambert (eds), London, HMSO, 1966 *et seq.*
House of Commons, *Parliamentary Debates*, Fifth Series, London, HMSO, 1909 *et seq.*
House of Lords, *Parliamentary Debates*, Fifth Series, London, HMSO, 1901 *et seq.*
Parliamentary Papers.

League of Nations

Disarmament Section, *Armaments Yearbook*, Annual, Geneva, League of Nations, 1924–1939/40.
——— *Conference for the Control of the International Trade in Arms, Munitions and Implements of War: historical survey*, Geneva, League of Nations, 1925.
——— *Convention for the Supervision of the International Trade in Arms and*

Ammunition and in Implements of War, Geneva, League of Nations, 1925.
—— *Documents of the Preparatory Commission for the Disarmament Conference*, Geneva, League of Nations, 1926-31 (11 series).
—— *Preparatory Commission for the Disarmament Conference: Corrections to the draft Disarmament Convention submitted by the Delegation of the Union of Socialist Soviet Republics*, Geneva, League of Nations, 1928.
—— *Preparatory Commission for the Disarmament Conference: Draft Disarmament Convention submitted by the Delegation of the Union of Soviet Socialist Republics*, Geneva, League of Nations, 1928.
—— *Preparatory Commission for the Disarmament Conference: Report of Sub-Commission A (military, naval and air)*, Geneva, League of Nations, 1926.
—— *Preparatory Commission for the Disarmament Conference: Sub-Commission B: Report no. 1.*, Geneva, League of Nations, 1926.
—— *Preparatory Commission for the Disarmament Conference: Sub-Commission B: Report no. 2.*, Geneva, League of Nations, 1927.
—— *Preparatory Commission for the Disarmament Conference: Sub-Commission B: Report no. 3.*, Geneva, League of Nations, 1927.
—— *Proceedings of the Conference for the Supervision of the International Trade in Arms and Ammunition and in Implements of War*, Geneva, League of Nations, 1925.
—— *Protocol for the Pacific Settlement of International Disputes*, Geneva, League of Nations, 1924.
—— *Report of the Temporary Mixed Commission on Armaments*, Geneva, League of Nations, 1921-4 (5 parts).
—— *Statistical Year-book of the Trade in Arms and Ammunition*, Annual, Geneva, League of Nations, 1924-38.
League of Nations Official Journal, Geneva, League of Nations, 1920-40.
Records of the Meetings of the Assembly Committees, Geneva, League of Nations, 1920-40.
Records of the Plenary Meetings of the Assembly, Geneva, League of Nations, 1920-40.

Union of Soviet Socialist Republics

Degras, J. (ed.) *Soviet Documents on Foreign Policy, 1917-1941*, London, Oxford University Press, 1951-3 (3 vols).
Lenin, V.I., *et. al. The Soviet Union and the Path to Peace*, London, Lawrence and Wishart, 1936.

United States of America

Department of State, *Papers relating to the Foreign Relations of the United States, Diplomatic Papers*, Washington, Government Printing Office, 1870 *et seq.*
Senate Sub-Committee on Disarmament, *Disarmament and Security: a Collection of Documents, 1919-1955*, Washington, Government Printing Office, 1956.

Miscellaneous

Berber, F.J. (ed.) *Locarno, a Collection of Documents*, London, Hodge, 1936.
Conference for the Limitation of Naval Armament, *Records of the Conference for the Limitation of Naval Armament*, Geneva, Imprimerie Atar, 1927.
Dupuy, T.N. and Hammerman, G.M. (eds) *A Documentary History of Arms Control and Disarmament*, Dunn Loring, Dupuy Associates, 1973.
Royal Institute of International Affairs, *Documents on International Affairs*, Annual, London, Oxford University Press, 1928 *et seq*.

4 Memoirs, autobiographies, speeches, etc.

Amery, L.C.M.S. *The Forward View*, London, Bles, 1935.
—— *The Leo Amery Diaries*, (vol. 1: 1896-1929), J. Barnes and D. Nicholson (eds), London, Hutchinson, 1980.
—— *My Political Life*, London, Hutchinson, 1953-5 (3 vols).
Angell, Sir N. *After All*, London, Hamish Hamilton, 1951.
Avon, Earl of *The Eden Memoirs: Facing the Dictators*, London, Cassell, 1962.
Baldwin, S. *On England: And other Essays*, London, Philip Allan, 1926.
Beck, Col. J. *Dernier rapport*, Neuchâtel, Editions de la Bacconière, 1951.
Cadogan, Sir A. *The Diaries of Sir Alexander Cadogan 1938-1945*, D. Dilks (ed.), London, Cassell, 1971.
Cecil of Chelwood, Viscount *All the Way*, London, Hodder and Stoughton, 1949.
—— *A Great Experiment*, London, Cape, 1941.
—— *The Way of Peace*, London, Philip Allan, 1928.
Chamberlain, Sir J.A. *Down the Years*, London, Cassell, 1935.
—— *Peace in Our Time*, London, Philip Allan, 1928.
Chatfield, Baron *The Navy and Defence: It Might Happen Again*, London, Heinemann, 1947.
Cooper, A.D. *Old Men Forget*, London, Hart-Davis, 1953.
D'Abernon, Viscount *An Ambassador of Peace*, London, Hodder and Stoughton, 1929-30 (3 vols).
—— *Portraits and Appreciations*, London, Hodder and Stoughton, 1931.
Dalton, E.H.J.N. *Call Back Yesterday*, London, Muller, 1953.
—— *Toward the Peace of Nations*, London, Routledge, 1928.
Davidson, J.C.C. *Memoirs of a Conservative*, R.R. James (ed.), London, Weidenfeld and Nicolson, 1969.
Dawes, C.G. *Journal as Ambassador to Great Britain*, New York, Macmillan, 1939.
Flandin, P. *Politique française 1919-1940*, Paris, Nouvelles, 1947.
Gregory, J.D. *On the Edge of Diplomacy*, London, Hutchinson, 1928.
Grey of Fallodon, Viscount *Twenty-five Years*, London, Hodder and Stoughton, 1928 (3 vols).
Hamilton, M.A. *Remembering my Good Friends*, London, Cape, 1944.
Harris, H.W. *Life So Far*, London, Cape, 1954.
Herriot, E. *Jadis*, Paris, Flammarion, 1948-52 (2 vols).
Hoover, H.C. *The Memoirs of Herbert Hoover*, New York, Macmillan, 1952 (3 vols).
Howard, Sir E.W. *Theatre of Life*, London, Hodder and Stoughton, 1935-6 (2 vols).

Hymans, P. *Mémoires*, Brussels, Institut de Sociologie Solvay, 1958 (2 vols).
Jones, T. *Whitehall Diary*, R.K. Middlemas (ed.), London, Oxford University Press, 1969 (3 vols).
Kenworthy, J.M. *Sailors, Statesmen — and Others*, London, Rich and Cowan, 1933.
Kirkpatrick, Sir I.A. *The Inner Circle*, London, Macmillan, 1959.
Laroche, J. *Au Quai d'Orsay avec Briand et Poincaré 1913-1926*, Paris, Hachette, 1957.
—— *La Pologne de Pilsudski*, Paris, Flammarion, 1953.
Liddell Hart, B.H. *Memoirs*, London, Cassell, 1965 (2 vols).
Macmillan, H. *Winds of Change*, London, Macmillan, 1966.
Madariaga, S. de *Morning without Noon: Memoirs*, Farnborough, Saxon House, 1974.
Miller, D.H. *My Diary at the Conference of Paris, 1918-1919*, New York, Miller, 1924-6 (21 vols).
Parmoor, Baron *A Retrospect*, London, Heinemann, 1936.
Paul-Boncour, J. *Entre deux guerres*, Paris, Plon, 1945-6 (3 vols).
Percy, Lord E. *Some Memories*, London, Eyre and Spottiswoode, 1958.
Samuel, Viscount *Memoirs*, London, Cresset, 1945.
Snowden, Viscount *An Autobiography*, London, Nicolson and Watson, 1934 (2 vols).
Stresemann, G. *Essays and Speeches on various Subjects*, C.R. Turner (tr.), London, Thornton Butterworth, 1930.
—— *Gustav Stresemann: His Diaries, Letters and Papers*, E. Sutton (ed.), London, Macmillan, 1935-40 (3 vols).
Swinton, Earl *I remember*, London, Hutchinson, 1949.
Temperley, A.C. *The Whispering Gallery of Europe*, London, Collins, 1938.
Templewood, Viscount *Empire of the Air*, London, Collins, 1957.
—— *Nine Troubled Years*, London, Collins, 1954.
Vansittart, Sir R.G. *Lessons of My Life*, London, Hutchinson, 1943.
—— *The Mist Procession*, London, Hutchinson, 1958.
Weygand, M. *Mémoires*, Paris, Flammarion, 1950-7 (3 vols).

5 Biographies

Baldwin, A.W. *My Father: The True Story*, London, Allen and Unwin, 1955.
Boyle, A. *Montagu Norman: A Biography*, London, Cassell, 1967.
—— *Trenchard*, London, Collins, 1962.
Butler, J.R.M. *Lord Lothian*, London, Macmillan, 1960.
Chalmers, W.S. *The Life and Letters of David, Earl Beatty*, London, Hodder and Stoughton, 1951.
Elletson, D.H. *The Chamberlains*, London, Murray, 1966.
Feiling, Sir K.G. *The Life of Neville Chamberlain*, London, Macmillan, 1947.
Gilbert, M. *Winston S. Churchill*, (vol. 5/companion vol. 5:1), London, Heinemann, 1976/1979.
Hamilton, M.A. *Arthur Henderson*, London, Heinemann. 1938.
—— *Ramsay MacDonald*, London, Cape, 1929.
Hyde, H.M. *Baldwin*, London, Hart-Davis, MacGibbon, 1973.
Jenkins, E.A. *From Foundry to Foreign Office*, London, Grayson and Grayson, 1933.
Kiernan, R.H. *Wavell*, London, Harrap, 1945.
Kirkpatrick, Sir I.A. *Mussolini*, London, Odhams, 1964.

McCoy, D.R. *Calvin Coolidge: The quiet President*, New York, Macmillan, 1967.

Marder, A.J. *Portrait of an Admiral: The Life and Papers of Sir Herbert Richmond*, London, Cape, 1952.

Marquand, D. *Ramsay MacDonald*, London, Cape, 1977.

Middlemas, R.K. and Barnes, A.J.L. *Baldwin: A Biography*, London, Weidenfeld and Nicolson, 1969.

Nicolson, Sir H. *King George the Fifth*, London, Constable, 1952.

Petrie, Sir C.A. *The Life and Letters of the Rt. Hon. Sir Austen Chamberlain*, London, Cassell, 1939–40 (2 vols).

Roskill, S.W. *Admiral of the Fleet Earl Beatty*, London, Collins, 1980.

—— *Hankey: Man of Secrets*, London, Collins, 1970–4 (3 vols).

Soulié, M. *La Vie politique d'Edouard Herriot*, Paris, Armand Colin, 1962.

Steed, H.W. *The Real Stanley Baldwin*, London, Nisbet, 1930.

Suarez, G. *Briand: Sa vie, son oeuvre*, Paris, Plon, 1938–52 (6 vols).

Vallentin, A. *Stresemann*, E. Sutton (tr.), London, Constable, 1931.

Wrench, Sir J.E.L. *Geoffrey Dawson and our Times*, London, Hutchinson, 1955.

Young, G.M. *Stanley Baldwin*, London, Hart-Davis, 1952.

6 Monographs and other special studies

Albrecht-Carrié, R. *France, Europe and the two World Wars*, Geneva, Droz, 1960.

Angell, N. *The Great Illusion*, London, Heinemann, 1911.

Barnett, C. *The Collapse of British Power*, London, Eyre Methuen, 1972.

Berdahl, C.A. *The Policy of the United States with respect to the League of Nations*, Geneva, Graduate Institute of International Studies, 1932.

Binion, R. *Defeated Leaders*, New York, Columbia University Press, 1960.

Bond, B. *British Military Policy between the Two World Wars*, London, Oxford University Press, 1980.

Bonnet, G.E. *Le Quai d'Orsay sous trois républiques 1870–1961*, Paris, Fayard, 1961.

Brailsford, H.N. *Olives of Endless Age*, New York, Harper and Brothers, 1928.

Bretton, H.L. *Stresemann and the Revision of Versailles*, Stanford, Stanford University Press, 1953.

Buckley, T.H. *The United States and the Washington Conference, 1921–2*, Knoxville, University of Tennessee Press, 1970.

Bull, H. *The Control of the Arms Race*, London, Weidenfeld and Nicolson, 1961.

Carr, E.H. *German-Soviet Relations between the two World Wars, 1919–1939*, New York, Harper and Row, 1966.

—— *International Relations between the two World Wars*, London, Macmillan, 1959.

—— *The Twenty Years' Crisis 1919–1939*, New York, Macmillan, 1966.

Carter, G.M. *The British Commonwealth and International Security*, Toronto, Ryerson Press, 1947.

Ceadel, M. *Pacifism in Britain 1914–1945*, London, Oxford University Press, 1980.

Chaput, R.A. *Disarmament in British Foreign Policy*, London, Allen and Unwin, 1935.

Charvet, J.F. *L'Influence brittanique dans la Société des nations*, Paris, Rodstein, 1938.

Claude, I.L. *Power and International Relations*, New York, Random House, 1962.

—— *Swords into Plowshares*, London, University of London Press, 1965.

Coates, W.P. *U.S.S.R. and Disarmament*, London, Anglo-Russian Parliamentary Committee, 1928.

Connell, J. *The 'Office'*, London, Wingate, 1958.

Craig, G.A. and Gilbert, F. *The Diplomats 1919–1939*, New York, Atheneum, 1963 (2 vols).

Crosby, G.R. *Disarmament and Peace in British Politics 1914–1919*, Cambridge, Harvard University Press, 1957.

Davis, G.T. *A Navy Second to None*, Westport, Greenwood, 1971.

Davis, K.W. *The Soviets at Geneva*, Geneva, Kundig, 1934.

Dingman, R. *Power in the Pacific*, Chicago, University of Chicago Press, 1976.

Djourivitch, D. *Le Protocole de Genève devant l'opinion anglaise*, Paris, Jouve, 1929.

Edwards, W.H. *This Pact Business*, London, Gollancz, 1928.

Ellis, L.E. *Frank B. Kellogg and American Foreign Relations 1925–1929*, New Brunswick, Rutgers University Press, 1961.

Engely, G. *The Politics of Naval Disarmament*, H.V. Rhodes (tr.), London, Williams and Norgate, 1932.

Fagerberg, E.P. *The 'anciens combattants' and French Foreign Policy*, Geneva, Graduate Institute of International Studies, 1966.

Ferrell, R.H. *Peace in their Time: the Origins of the Kellogg-Briand Pact*, New Haven, Yale University Press, 1952.

Fleming, D.F. *The United States and World Organization, 1920–1933*, New York, Columbia University Press, 1938.

François-Poncet, A. *De Versailles à Potsdam*, Paris, Flammarion, 1948.

Gatzke, H.W. *Stresemann and the Rearmament of Germany*, Baltimore, Johns Hopkins Press, 1954.

Glasgow, G. *From Dawes to Locarno*, London, Benn, 1925.

Goldblat, J. *Arms Control Agreements: A Handbook*, London, Taylor and Francis, 1983.

Hall, C. *Britain, America and Arms Control, 1921–37*, London, Macmillan, 1987.

Harris, H.W. *Arms or Arbitration?*, London, Hogarth Press, 1928.

Henig, R.B. *The League of Nations*, Edinburgh, Oliver and Boyd, 1973.

Hiden, J.W. *Germany and Europe 1919–1939*, London, Longmans, 1977.

Higham, R. *Armed Forces in Peacetime: Britain, 1918–1940, a Case Study*, London, Foulis, 1962.

—— *The Military Intellectuals in Britain, 1918–1939*, New Brunswick, Rutgers University Press, 1966.

Hinsley, F.H. *Power and the Pursuit of Peace*, Cambridge, Cambridge University Press, 1963.

Hogg, Q.M. *The Left was Never Right*, London, Faber and Faber, 1945.

Howard, M.E. *The Continental Commitment*, London, Temple Smith, 1972.

—— *Studies in War and Peace*, London, Temple Smith, 1970.

Hughes, J.M. *To the Maginot Line*, Cambridge, Harvard University Press, 1971.

Jacobson, J. *Locarno Diplomacy*, Princeton, Princeton University Press, 1972.

Jaffe, L.S. *The Decision to Disarm Germany*, London, Allen and Unwin, 1985.

James, R.R. *Churchill: A Study in Failure*, London, Weidenfeld and Nicolson, 1970.

Johnson, F.A. *Defence by Committee*, London, Oxford University Press, 1960.

Jordan, W.M. *Great Britain, France and the German Problem, 1918–1939*, London, Oxford University Press, 1943.

Kennedy, M.D. *The Estrangement of Great Britain and Japan 1917–1935*, Manchester, Manchester University Press, 1969.

Kennedy, P.M. *The Realities behind Diplomacy*, London, Allen and Unwin, 1981.

—— *The Rise and Fall of British Naval Mastery*, London, Allen Lane, 1976.

—— *Strategy and Diplomacy*, London, Allen & Unwin, 1983.

Liddell Hart, B.H. *Deterrent or Defence*, London, Stevens, 1960.

Lyon, J. *Les Problèmes du désarmement*, Paris, Boivin, 1931.

McCallum, R.B. *Public Opinion and the Last Peace*, London, Oxford University Press, 1944.

Machray, R. *The Little Entente*, London, Allen and Unwin, 1929.

McKercher, B.J.C. *The Second Baldwin Government and the United States, 1924–1929*, London, Cambridge University Press/London School of Economics, 1984.

Madariaga, S. de *Disarmament*, Port Washington, Kennikat Press, 1967.

Margueritte, V. *The League Fiasco (1920–1936)*, N. Macfarlane (tr.), London, Hodge, 1936.

Marks, S. *The Illusion of Peace: International Relations in Europe, 1918–1933*, London, Macmillan, 1976.

Medlicott, W.N. *British Foreign Policy since Versailles, 1919–1963*, London, Methuen, 1968.

—— *Contemporary England, 1914–1964*, London, Longmans, 1967.

Miller, D.H. *The Geneva Protocol*, New York, Macmillan, 1925.

—— *The Peace Pact of Paris*, New York, Putnam, 1928.

Miller, K. *Socialism and Foreign Policy*, The Hague, Nijhoff, 1967.

Minart, J. *Le Drame du désarmement français*, Paris, La Nef de Paris, 1959.

Mitrany, D. *The Problem of International Sanctions*, London, Oxford University Press, 1925.

Mowat, C.L. *Britain between the Wars, 1918–1940*, London, Methuen, 1955.

Murray, G.G.A. *The Ordeal of this Generation: The War, the League and the Future*, London, Allen and Unwin, 1930.

Newman, W.J. *The Balance of Power in the Inter-War years, 1919–1939*, New York, Random House, 1968.

Noel-Baker, P.J. *The Arms Race*, London, Calder, 1958.

—— *Disarmament*, London, Hogarth Press, 1926.

—— *Disarmament and the Coolidge Conference*, London, Woolf, 1927.

—— *The First World Disarmament Conference 1932–33*, Oxford, Pergamon, 1979.

—— *The Geneva Protocol for the Pacific Settlement of International Disputes*, London, King, 1925.

—— *The Private Manufacture of Armaments*, New York, Dover, 1972.

Nollet, C.M.E. *Une expérience de désarmement: cinq ans de contrôle militaire en allemagne*, Paris, Gallimard, 1932.

Northedge, F.S. *The Troubled Giant*, London, Bell, 1966.

O'Connor, R.G. *Perilous Equilibrium*, Lawrence, University of Kansas Press, 1962.

——— *War, Diplomacy and History*, Lanham, University Press of America, 1979.

O'Neill, R. and Schwartz, D.N. *Hedley Bull on Arms Control*, London, Macmillan, 1987.

Pensa, H. *De Locarno au Pacte Kellogg*, Paris, Roustan, 1929.

Petrie, Sir C.A. *Twenty Years Armistice - and After*, London, Eyre and Spottiswoode, 1940.

Potter, W.C. (ed.) *Verification and Arms Control*, Lexington, Heath, 1985.

Preston, A. (ed.) *General Staffs and Diplomacy before the Second World War*, Totowa, Rowman and Littlefield, 1978.

Ramsden, J. *The Age of Balfour and Baldwin, 1902–1940*, London, Longmans, 1978.

Rappard, W.E. *The Geneva Experiment*, London, Oxford University Press, 1931.

——— *The Quest for Peace since the World War*, Cambridge, Harvard University Press, 1940.

Raymond, J. (ed.) *The Baldwin Age*, London, Eyre and Spottiswoode, 1960.

Renouvin, P. (ed.) *Histoire des relations internationales*, Paris, Hachette, 1953–8 (8 vols).

Reynolds, P. A. *British Foreign Policy in the Inter-War Years*, London, Longmans, 1954.

Rohde, H. *Franco-German Factors of Power*, Berlin, Berliner Börsen-Zeitung, 1932 (2 vols).

Rosenbaum, K. *Community of Fate*, Syracuse, Syracuse University Press, 1965.

Roskill, S.W. *Admiral of the Fleet Earl Beatty*, London, Collins, 1980.

——— *Naval Policy between the Wars: The Period of Anglo–American Antagonism 1919–1929*, London, Collins, 1968.

Rössler, H. (ed.) *Locarno und die Weltpolitik 1924–1932*, Göttingen, Musterschmidt-Verlag, 1969.

Royal Institute of International Affairs *Survey of International Affairs*, Annual, London, Oxford University Press, 1920/3 *et seq.*

Salter, J.A. *Security: Can We Retrieve it?*, London, Macmillan, 1939.

Schwarzschild, L. *World in Trance*, London, Hamish Hamilton, 1943.

Scott, G. *The Rise and Fall of the League of Nations*, London, Hutchinson, 1973.

Shotwell, J.T. *War as an Instrument of National Policy and its Renunciation in the Pact of Paris*, New York, Harcourt, Brace, 1929.

——— and Salvin, M. *Lessons on Security and Disarmament from the History of the League of Nations*, New York, King's Crown Press, 1949.

Sipple, C.E. *British Foreign Policy since the World War*, Iowa City, University of Iowa, 1932.

Somervell, D.C. *The Reign of King George the Fifth*, London, Faber and Faber, 1935.

Stratis, C. *Le pacte générale de renonciation à la guerre*, Paris, Rivière, 1931.

Tate, M. *The United States and Armaments*, New York, Russell and Russell, 1969.

Taylor, A.J.P. *English History 1914–1945*, Oxford, Clarendon Press, 1965.

——— *The Origins of the Second World War*, Harmondsworth, Penguin, 1964.

——— *The Troublemakers*, London, Panther, 1969.

Temperley, H.W.V. (ed.) *A History of the Peace Conference of Paris*, London, Oxford University Press, 1920–4 (6 vols).

Tucker, W.R. *The Attitude of the British Labour Party towards European and Collective Security Problems 1920-1939*, Geneva, Imprimerie de Journal de Genève, 1950.

Tuleja, T.V. *Statesmen and Admirals*, New York, Norton, 1963.

Turner, H.A. *Stresemann and the Politics of the Weimar Republic*, Princeton, Princeton University Press, 1963.

Vaïsse, M. *Sécurité d'abord*, Paris, Pedone, 1981.

Vigor, P.H. *The Soviet View of Disarmament*, London, Macmillan, 1986.

Walters, F.P. *A History of the League of Nations*, London, Oxford University Press, 1952.

Wandycz, P.S. *France and her Eastern Allies 1919-25*, Minneapolis, University of Minneapolis Press, 1962.

Watt, D.C. *Personalities and Policies*, London, Longmans, 1965.

—— *Too Serious a Business*, London, Temple Smith, 1975.

Webster, C.K. and Herbert, S. *The League of Nations in Theory and Practice*, London, Allen and Unwin, 1933.

Wellesley, Sir V. *Diplomacy in Fetters*, London, Hutchinson, 1945.

Wheeler-Bennett, J.W. *Disarmament and Security since Locarno, 1925-1931*, London, Allen and Unwin, 1932.

—— *Information on the Reduction of Armaments*, London, Allen and Unwin, 1925.

—— *Information on the Renunciation of War, 1927-1928*, London, Allen and Unwin, 1928.

—— *The Nemesis of Power*, London, Macmillan, 1953.

—— and Langermann, F.E. *Information on the Problem of Security (1917-1926)*, London, Allen and Unwin, 1927.

Windrich, E. *British Labour's Foreign Policy*, Stanford, Stanford University Press, 1952.

Wolfers, A. *Britain and France between Two Wars*, New York, Harcourt, Brace, 1940.

Zilliacus, K. *The League, the Protocol and the Empire*, London, Allen and Unwin, 1925.

Zimmern, A.E. *The League of Nations and the Rule of Law, 1918-1935*, London, Macmillan, 1936.

Zuylen, Baron P. van *Les mains libres*, Paris, Desclée de Brouwer, 1950.

7 Articles

Angell, N. 'M. Herriot seeks Security and will pay the Price', *New Leader*, 27 June 1924.

Beck, P.J. 'From the Geneva Protocol to the Greco-Bulgarian Dispute: The Development of the Baldwin Government's Policy towards the Peacekeeping Role of the League of Nations, 1924-1925', *British Journal of International Studies*, 6, 1980, pp. 52-68.

Carlton, D. 'The Anglo-French Compromise on Arms Limitation 1928', *Journal of British Studies*, 8, 1969, pp. 141-62.

—— 'Disarmament with Guarantees: Lord Cecil 1922-1927', *Disarmament and Arms Control*, 3, 2, Autumn 1965, pp. 143-64.

—— 'Great Britain and the Coolidge Naval Disarmament Conference of 1927', *Political Science Quarterly*, 83, 4, December 1968, pp. 573-98.

—— 'Great Britain and the League Council Crisis of 1926', *Historical Journal*, 11, 1968, pp. 354-64.

———— 'The Problem of Civil Aviation in British Air Disarmament Policy, 1919-1934', *Journal of the Royal United Service Institution*, 44, November 1966, pp. 307-16.

Clemens, W.C. 'Ideology in Soviet Disarmament Policy', *Journal of Conflict Resolution*, VIII:1, March 1964, pp. 7-22.

Crowe, S.E. 'Sir Eyre Crowe and the Locarno Pact' *English Historical Review*, 342, January 1972, pp. 49-74.

Cushendun, Baron 'Disarmament', *International Affairs*, 7, 2, March 1928, pp. 77-93.

Dubay, R.W. 'The Geneva Naval Conference of 1927: A Study of Battleship Diplomacy', *Southern Quarterly*, 8, January 1970, pp. 177-99.

Edwards, P.G. 'Britain, Mussolini and the "Locarno-Geneva System"', *European Studies Review*, 10, 1980, pp. 1-16.

Ferrell, R.H. 'Disarmament Conferences: Ballets at the Brink', *American Heritage*, 22, February 1971, pp. 5, 7, 96, 98-100.

Fox, J.P. 'Britain and the Inter-Allied Military Commission of Control 1925-26', *Journal of Contemporary History*, 4, 1969, pp. 143-64.

Frase, R.W. 'Disarmament in Perspective', *Current History*, 34, October 1957, pp. 227-32.

Fuller, J.F.C. 'Disarmament and Delusion', *Current History*, 36, September 1932, pp. 649-54.

Grün, G.A. 'Locarno: Idea and Reality', *International Affairs*, 31, 4, October 1955, pp. 477-85.

Jacobsen, P. 'Armaments Expenditure of the World', *The Economist*, 19 October 1929.

Johnson, D. 'Austen Chamberlain and the Locarno Agreements', *University of Birmingham Historical Journal*, 8, 1, 1961, pp. 62-81.

Jones, H.P. 'Reduction and Limitation of Armaments', *Annals of the American Academy of Political and Social Science*, 138, July 1928, pp. 173-8.

Kerr, P. 'Naval Disarmament', *Round Table*, 75, June 1929, pp. 447-64.

Richardson, Dick. 'Process and Progress in Disarmament: some Lessons of History', *TAPRI Yearbook 1989*.

Smith, H.A. 'The Problem of Disarmament in the Light of History', *International Affairs*, 10, 1931, pp. 600-21.

Stambrook, F.G. '"Das Kind" — Lord D'Abernon and the Origins of the Locarno Pact', *Central European History*, 1, 1968, pp. 233-63.

8 Unpublished theses

Brode, M.J. *Anglo-American Relations and the Geneva Naval Conference of 1927*, Ph.D., University of Alberta, 1969.

Cottereau, S.R. *The Search for Security (Autumn 1924 - Spring 1926): A Study in English and French Public Opinion*, B. Litt., University of Oxford, 1953.

Moreton, C.E. *Great Britain and the Locarno Treaties (December 1924 - October 1925)*, M.Phil., University of London, 1969.

Raffo, P.S. *Lord Robert Cecil and the League of Nations, 1916-27*, Ph.D., University of Liverpool, 1967.

Richardson, R.C. *The Disarmament Problem in British Diplomacy, 1932-1934*, M.A., University of British Columbia, 1970.

Underwood, J.J. *The Roots and Reality of British Disarmament Policy 1932-*

34, Ph.D., University of Leeds, 1977.

9 Newspapers and contemporary journals

Daily Herald
International Conciliation
The Round Table
Le Temps
The Times

10 Interview

Baron Noel-Baker, 18 February 1980

11 Pamphlets

Baldwin, S. *The Prime Minister on World Peace and the League of Nations*,
London, National Union of Conservative and Unionist Associations, 1928.
Benes, E. *The Diplomatic Struggle for European Security and the Stabiliza-
tion of Peace*, Prague, Orbis, 1925.
Borden, Sir, R.L. *Canada and the Geneva Protocol*, London, League of
Nations Union, 1925.
Cecil of Chelwood Viscount, *A Letter to an MP on Disarmament*, London,
Hogarth Press, 1931.
Chamberlain, Sir J.A. *The League of Nations*, Glasgow, Jackson Wylie, 1926.
Henderson, A. *The New Peace Plan: Labour's Work at the League of Nations
Assembly*, London, Labour Publications Department, 1924.
Labour Party *Labour and the Nation*, London, Labour Party, 1928.
Labour Party, International Department Advisory Committee on Interna-
tional Questions, *The American Treaty Offer*, London, Labour Party, 1928.
―――― *The British Reply to Mr. Kellogg*, London, Labour Party, 1928.
League of Nations Union, *Armaments: Their Reduction and Limitation*,
London, League of Nations Union, 1926.
―――― *Disarmament*, London, League of Nations Union, 1927.
―――― *The General Act of September 26 1928*, London, League of Nations
Union, 1929.
―――― *Law not War: Arbitration not Armaments*, London, League of Nations
Union, 1927.
―――― *The Optional Clause*, London, League of Nations, 1928.
MacDonald, J.R. *Protocol or Pact*, London, Labour Party, 1925.
National Union of Conservative and Unionist Associations, *What the Conser-
vative Government has done for Peace, 1925-1929*, London, National Union
of Conservative and Unionist Associations 1929.
No More War Movement, *Conservatives and Disarmament: The Facts*,
London, No More War Movement, 1929.
Raffo, P. *The League of Nations*, London, Historical Association, 1974.

Index